THE
TEACHER'S
TREASURE CHEST

Winslow Homer. THE COUNTRY SCHOOL

The
TEACHER'S
TREASURE
CHEST

Edited by

LEO DEUEL

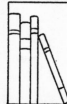

PRENTICE-HALL, INC.

Englewood Cliffs, N. J.

Library of Congress Catalog Card Number 56-9778

The editor gratefully acknowledges the counsel
and assistance of Mr. William Theodore Johnson,
librarian, Indiana State Teachers College,
Terra Haute, Indiana.

TABLE OF CONTENTS

v

INTRODUCTION

by Benjamin Fine

Education Editor, The New York Times

FOR WHATEVER REASON, TEACHERS AND PROFESSORS HAVE ATTAINED an unfortunate reputation of being stodgy, academic, long-haired and rather impossible. You don't associate a sense of humor with an egg-head. Alas, even the sneering term "egg-head" is in itself an indictment of those who would dedicate their lives to the cultural improvement of the human race.

This stereotype is far from true. Not only is it grossly exaggerated, it is libelous. Never before in our history have our teachers been as important as they are today. We are engaged in a desperate struggle—a struggle for our very existence. We are building a mighty arsenal—untold billions will go toward making our democratic traditions safe, our nation strong enough to ward off whatever blows may befall it in the days ahead.

Here is where the teachers come into the picture: Although a strong army, navy and air force are essential, a strong and inspiring devotion to our democratic ideals is even more important. Teachers can help develop that tradition and help strengthen those ideals.

Because our teachers are so important, because our educational system is so valuable, it is good to take time out now and then to see what teachers really think about in off-moments, what they look like, as seen through the eyes of poets and dreamers, what they wear and how they adjust themselves in general. In other words, why is a teacher?

This anthology, The Teacher's Treasure Chest, edited by Leo Deuel gives us a good selection, of both fun and frolic. There have been various anthologies about teachers, about the critical issues facing American education (and Heaven knows there are many!), about the attacks upon teachers, about academic freedom. You won't get much of that here. But you will get a better "feel" of the teaching profession, from the viewpoint of the teacher himself. You will find the selection will make you laugh as you read the Prep School anecdotes. And then again, you will wipe a silent tear away when you finish *The Teacher's Prayer*.

The author has selected wisely and well. Most of the material is of the anecdotal, informal, easy-to-read variety. This is truly a "treasure chest," to read and re-read in off-moments, when the day's chores have ended, when you want to relax in an easy-chair, or when you are propped up on two pillows, content with the world.

Out of the various snatches, poems, interesting tidbits, and more serious excerpts of well-known stories emerges a composite story, a happy picture of the more or less "typical" teacher. We find that the teacher is a human being, with likes and dislikes, foibles and idiosyncrasies, trials and rewards, glad hours and sad hours. Some readers may have wished for more than a titillating taste of some of the excerpts. But then, the reader can always follow through if he wants to read all of *The Thread That Runs So True*, or *And Gladly Teach*.

You will enjoy browsing through this anthology. You will, I am confident, get the same lift that I did in finding out that teachers are not a bad sort at all. Perhaps you will also resolve, as I did, to do whatever you can to make the lot of the teacher a happier one, a more respected one in our community, a more desirable one. We are confronted, as is all too well known, with a critical teacher shortage. For whatever reason, our bright young boys and girls refuse to enter the teaching profession. They feel that a teacher is a different breed.

I daresay that if the youngsters, or their parents, read this anthology they may well change their minds. Not, of course, that this book was intended for that purpose. It was designed,

I would guess, to be good happy fun, to chuckle and amuse, to bring a bit of sunshine to one who may have become enmeshed in too great a struggle with the tensions of the day. The dark mood can quickly change when it is brought smack up against Ogden Nash's *The Mind of Professor Primrose*.

Although probably designed for teachers and others of an academic bent, The Teacher's Treasure Chest can be read with profitable enjoyment and heaps of fun by almost anyone. Indeed, it may be that the non-educator will find this anthology even more to his liking than the teacher. Both the academic and the non-academic fraternity will, I am confident, chuckle over many of the pages, be inspired by many others, and profit from them all.

THE TEACHER'S PRAYER

by Gabriela Mistral
(translated by James H. McLean)

LORD, THOU WHO DIDST TEACH, FORGIVE ME FOR TEACHING,
And for presuming to carry the name of teacher,
A name that thou didst carry while on earth.
Give me a single-hearted love for my school,
So that not even the blazing whirl of beauty could steal from
    me my tenderness
At all times.
Teacher, make my fervor everlasting and my despondency a
    passing phase.
Snatch from me this impure desire for justice that still troubles
    me—
This protest that arises within me when I am grieved.
Grant that when my pupils neglect me, I may not be forlorn
Nor be pained when they misunderstand me.
Make me more of a mother than all the mothers,
In order that I may love and defend, with like devotion,
Those who are not flesh from my flesh.
Grant that I may be successful in moulding one of my pupils
Into my perfect poem,
And in weaving her into my most haunting melody,
Against the day when the song of my lips shall be silent.

Show me how thy Gospel is possible in this day and age,
So that I may never renounce the good fight of faith.
In my democratic school let thy radiance
Rest upon the circle of barefoot boys.
Make me strong even in my position—
That of a poor and despised woman.
Help me to scorn all power that is not pure
And all force that is not in harmony with thy flaming will.
Friend, stand by my side, sustain me.
Many times I shall have no one but thee on my side.
When my doctrine is purer and my truth is glowing,
I shall be alone, but thou shalt press me to thy heart,
Thou who wert lonely and forsaken.
I shall seek approbation only in thy look.
Give me simplicity and give me depth.
Free me from the temptation of being vainglorious
Or commonplace in my teaching.
Permit me to lift my eyes from my wounded breast each morning
As I enter my school.
Grant that I may never carry to my desk my petty cares,
My trifling disappointments.
May my hand be light in punishment and smooth in caresses.
Help me to reprove with pain
That I may be sure that while I am correcting I yet love the child.
Grant that my school may not be built of bricks but of spirit.
May the splendor of my enthusiasm be reflected from the bare
    walls
And fill the classroom.
Let my heart be a sustaining bulwark and my good will be a
    brighter gold
Than all the gold and all the pillars in the halls of the wealthy.
Let this be my supreme lesson, inspired by the pallid beauty of
    Velasquez' "Crucifixion"—
To teach and love with fervor on this earth
Means to enter, finally, with the spear-thrust of Longinus, the
    Roman Centurion,
Into the throbbing, cosmic heart of Love.

MY FIRST EXPERIENCE
IN TEACHING

by Mary Ellen Chase

ALL MY FATHER'S IDEAS WERE FIXED AND STURDY. ONE OF THEM was that each of his daughters should teach a country school either before going to college or as an interruption between the second and third year there. He contended, with truth as I afterwards realized, that teaching not only was the best discipline for the retention and enlargement of one's own meagre knowledge, but that it engendered maturity through the responsibility which it placed squarely upon one's own shoulders. If you had anything in you at all, said my father, three terms in a country school would bring it out. If you had nothing, then the entrance to college or the continuation therein was obviously a waste both of time and money.

Unlike my older sister, who taught her school before she entered college, I taught mine in the spring of my sophomore year and in the year following. I had entered the University of Maine at seventeen to continue happily in Greek and Latin and most unhappily in higher algebra and trigonometry. I think, in fact, that my disgraceful record in college mathematics, together with a somewhat

From *A Goodly Fellowship*. Copyright 1939 by Mary Ellen Chase. Reprinted by permission of the Macmillan Co.

chimerical love affair, decided my father that I needed to get down
to what he termed the brass tacks of life as soon as possible. He,
therefore, scouted about the country in search of the most difficult
rural school he could find which was in need of a teacher for the
spring term. Such a school he unearthed in the village of South
Brooksville, Maine, then familiarly known as Buck's Harbor, and
summarily informed me that the school officials of that place had
graciously, if perhaps unwisely, consented to give me a try and
for my services would pay me ten dollars a week.

Buck's Harbor was a coast village, little more than a hamlet,
some twelve miles from Blue Hill and situated beyond Eggemoggin
Reach in the neighborhood of Penobscot Bay. It has now become
known as a pleasant and quiet summer resort, but in the spring
of 1906, in spite of two small boarding houses, it was a native community of fishermen, small tradespeople, farmers and sailors. Most
of the twenty-odd families were large and interlaced by marriage,
as were most coast families in small settlements thirty years ago.
The nearest academy or high school was our own, and few Buck's
Harbor children in those days went beyond the rural school. There
was one general store, which sheltered the post-office, and one small
church, Methodist, I think, by nature, with no settled pastor. There
are a hundred counterparts of just such a village on a hundred
small harbors along the Maine coast.

The people of such a village were the products of their environment. In 1906 most of them were practically untouched by any
outside influences since, after the manner of the Maine coast native,
they looked upon their few summer visitors only with curiosity
and a faint suspicion. The only persons who had been far afield,
or perhaps better far afloat, were the men and boys who were
deckhands on small steamers or who were engaged in fishing or
in the coastwise schooner trade; and they were mostly around
their own air-tight stoves in the winter. Blue Hill was to Buck's
Harbor what Boston was in pre-motor days to the people of
Bangor. Roads were bad in early spring and in winter often im-
passable. An automobile was almost are rare as an earthquake and
an object of monstrous fear to the possessors of horses. Whatever
distant travelling was done, and it was extremely rare, was accomplished by coastwise steamers, which in those days during the summer months brought and carried freight and passengers to a hundred village wharves now rotting and dismantled.

The school-teacher of such a village was the object of interest, terse comment, and not infrequently, at least at the start, of suspicion, particularly if she had come from "away." Her appearance, manners, morals, friendliness or lack of it, were far more important elements in her success or failure than was any mental equipment which she might or might not possess. Maine coast natives, then even more than now, have a tendency to assume the worst until they have become convinced that their assumption is wrong; and to the people of Buck's Harbor a girl from college had just that much more to live down than she might have had as a product of the Castine Normal School or of no discernible school at all.

It was on a cold, bleak, foggy Monday morning in April, 1906, that my father deposited me, bag and baggage, on the steps of the Buck's Harbor school-house and left me to sink or swim, survive or perish. I have often wondered since, whether, as he drove away, the milk of human pity had any place within his stern frame. If there, it was not in any way apparent. His good-bye was brief, although he did present me with a parting gift with injunctions to use it if necessary. This gift proved to be a stout razor strop; and without its moral as well as physical support I should have given up teaching for good and all one half hour after I had begun it.

My first morning in my first school was dedicated both to the theory and the practice of the survival of the fittest. The spring was a late one, and certain boys of sixteen or older, who otherwise might have been at sea, were at school for a season, ostensibly to learn, actually to discover of what stuff the new teacher was made. Had my father himself been constructed of less inflexible stuff, could I have been sure of receiving understanding and sympathy at home instead of disappointment and contempt, I should then and there have run for cover, leaving the Buck's Harbor school to whatever fate awaited it.

But the fear of returning home in defeat was far more terrible than the fear of staying where I was; and I began my teaching experience with an unseemly display of passions which I had never known I possessed—anger and disgust, scorn and fury. I was a veritable Maenad in frenzy as I stormed up and down my narrow aisles. This pathetic pretense of courage, aided by the mad flourishing of the razor strop, brought forth to

my amazement as though by magic the expression of respectful fear upon the faces of young giants who could have accomplished my terrified exit either by physical strength or by a like
display of temper, and who had come to school with the express
purpose of doing so. But no one moved to further insurrection,
and although, when the reign of terror to which both forces had
contributed had subsided, my quaking knees could hardly support
me at my desk, I had no more trouble from discipline through
eleven long weeks.

I have since wondered how a teacher, trained in modern and
more pacific ways of governing a school, would have made herself mistress of such a situation, one, moreover, whose parents
possessed hearts and doors more readily open that did mine. Perhaps it is as well for the principles and the practice of the new
education that district schools are fast disappearing from the American landscape. Perhaps the race is growing gentler! Surely even
in the smallest of communities today there are other interests than
the advent of a new teacher.

A young teacher told me recently that for other than patriotic
reasons she should always look upon the American flag with respect
and veneration. She said that in her first year of teaching when all
other sources of interest failed and she felt herself becoming en-
gulfed in the imminent dangers of inattention and recalcitrance,
she was given to calling suddenly for a salute to the flag. She
depended, she said, upon this break in affairs either to quell rising
mutiny or at least to relegate it to a fresh and more easily handled
start. We had no American flag at Buck's Harbor, and the now
common words of salute had not yet reached our confines even if,
at that date, they had been composed. But, instead of the flag, I
shall always look with respect and veneration upon a razor strop,
seeing in this ugly object not only the symbol of my emancipation
from terror and disgrace, but as well the initial inspiration and vision
which resulted two years later in my choice of a profession.

The school at Buck's Harbor demanded of me more mental and
physical agility than mere knowledge. I had forty-nine children
of all ages from five to sixteen. When I had once sorted them out
in accordance with age and progress, I found myself with twenty-
nine classes a day to teach. The hours from nine until four, with
fifteen minutes each morning and afternoon for recess, contained

all told in minutes but three hundred and thirty. This resulted even by my poor arithmetic in a maximum of eleven minutes for each class, or to be more accurate, in ten, since the classes must move in order from their seats to the bench before my desk.

Since some combination of classes must be made if any child was to learn anything at all, I conceived the notion of hearing five reading lessons in quick succession while those who were not reading were doing problems in arithmetic at the blackboards. Although the corporeal frame is subject to the boundries of space, I soon learned that the mind can be in two or even three places at one time. One portion of my mind was riveted on the behavior of the children presumably at study in their seats; another portion fearfully scanned the blackboards in the hope that no assistance would be summoned; a third listened to and corrected the reading of those on the bench before me. By this method arithmetic and reading were out of the way by ten-thirty recess, leaving decent room for four classes in geography from ten-forty-five until noon. I ruthlessly combined the afternoon grammer classes, since all alike needed the same fundamentals, and by two o'clock we had a clear straightaway for history, which we all liked best, and for spelling which closed the day for everyone but me.

Needless to say, we had no frills and extras in our school. We even had no music since the good day of outside music teachers, even for the rural schools, had not yet come, and since I myself could not carry a tune. Had I been able to do so, however, we had no song or hymn books and no time. Even the Lord's Prayer and the Bible reading had to be hurried, so impending were arithmetic and reading. When we were once organized, we clicked on like a well-regulated machine from nine until four.

I am sure that such an iron-clad program was bad for my children; no school at any time should be systematized to that extent. But I am equally sure that it was the best thing that could have happened to me. I had always been a dreamy child, given to states of absent-mindedness and particularly irritated by attention to detail. I had seemingly been born with no sense of time, and the rigorous order and discipline of home and school, although I had perforce submitted to it, had not wrought the transformation hoped for by my parents. Two years of relative freedom at college had afforded blissful opportunities for the indulgence of all my worst mental habits; and the school at Buck's Harbor could not have presented itself at a more opportune moment. There was now no time for dreams of either the past or the future. It was dangerous to lose one's head for the fraction of a second. On and on the minutes raced with questions to be quickly put or as quickly answered. There was no time even for self-pity, let alone self-indulgence. For eleven weeks the stark necessity of the Buck's Harbor school held me in a nerve-loosened vise. When they were over, I was a different person.

The school-house was on a high ledge above the harbor. From its door one got a wide and lovely sweep of sea and islands, but I do not remember ever having much time in the superintendence of dunces and in the correction of papers; and when I had once locked the school-house door, I had no extra life within me to be uplifted even by Penobscot Bay.

I boarded for two dollars and a half a week with a certain Mrs. Billings in her house below the school-house hill. She was a silent young woman with a poor complexion and with two talents which were never buried in the earth. She knit numberless baby blankets for a Portland firm, and she cooked as few women I have ever known have cooked.

For two dollars and fifty cents a week Mrs. Billings stuffed me with fat, starch, and sugar. She served my bountiful meals in her dining-room, but, although I assumed she ate her own in the kitchen, I never saw her eat a morsel during my residence with her, nor in her kitchen was there any sign whatever of the means of food consumption. Mrs. Billings made no distinction in her offerings for breakfast, dinner, or supper. The pork chops, fried potatoes, hot bread, doughnuts, cake, apple pie, and cheese which I had for breakfast were repeated at noon and night with an occasional change in kind but never in bulk. School must have been more exhausting than I realized, for I was always hungry and devoured more calories than ever since in my life. I have worried for many years over Mrs. Billings' obvious lack of monetary profit by our arrangement, and have often felt that, if she still cooks in her immaculate kitchen and still knits baby blankets on her front piazza, I ought even now to set things right with her.

She housed me in her front chamber, a curiously depressing room with a huge bedstead and a feather bed and with Biblical scenes in colors, ingeniously framed in shells. I used to add to its depression through weeping at night over bank discount and compound proportion by my rickety stand with its kerosene lamp. Necessity proved, however, not so much the mother of invention in our sense of the word as the means to accomplishment; and before a month had passed I came to be, within limits and for the time being, a fairly apt arithmetician.

As the spring advanced and the roads improved, my father generously allowed me to keep our pony and cart in Mrs. Billings' barn so that I might drive home on Saturday and back again on Sunday. Perhaps he accorded me this favor because he was pleased with me, although if he was, he never divulged the fact. The pony was miraculously fed also on my two dollars and a half and by a mythical Mr. Billings, whom in eleven weeks I never saw or heard, although, since his existence was vouched for by my pupils, I presume he was extant somewhere.

Mrs. Billings and I never became friendly as she was not a talkative woman. She provided and I consumed. And, although I knew and liked the few parents of my forty-nine, I saw little of them. They were quite too busy feeding and clothing their children and getting them to school on time to pay much attention to their teacher. I think they liked me more because I made no objection to housing their pre-school youngsters than for any other reason. On most days in my school there were half a dozen babies of varying ages between two and four. The smallest of these I used to confine in large low barrels or tubs with which the village cooper provided me and from which the babies used to stare in delighted wonder at our furious educational progress.

I grew to love my charges, and I think they liked me. School to most of them was a necessary evil, alleviated only by recess and by the stories I told or read to them for two hours on Friday afternoons as a reward for good behavior. Few of them saw in it any present pleasure or any step toward the future. Like all country children they were fond of animals and flowers, and like all coast children they were shrewd in the ways of wind and weather. They could manage boats under any circumstances, though again, like most coast children, few of them could swim. Swimming, indeed, seemed but an indulgence, a pastime enjoyed by summer visitors, before whom they were always shy and sometimes rude.

I am sure I taught them very little. It was I who was educated in Buck's Harbor. But I like to remember how their sharp faces glowed on Friday afternoons over *Treasure Island* and even over *The Story of a Short Life* and *The Little Lame Prince*. Their homes were relatively bookless, and such stories as these were new fields to them. Occasionally I see certain of them now, here and there as lesser officers on summer yachts or at the county fair as stout mothers with broods of far more sophisticated sons and daughters. Three of them are teachers who, I trust, have never emulated my desperate and stumbling efforts either at discipline or at instruction.

I think I must from the beginning have looked upon teaching as a sport rather than as a respectable way of earning one's living. For on the late June Saturday when I had gathered by belongings, locked my school-house door, and harnessed my pony to drive homeward, I completely forgot to collect my wages from the First Selectman of Buck's Harbor and drove home empty-handed. My father saw in this inexcusable neglect, this disregard of one hundred and ten dollars, a proof that absent-mindedness was still with me. He sent me back that very afternoon, feeling most incompetent, to procure it. But he was somewhat less scornful when I told him upon my return that with his permission and approval I had decided to teach three more terms of school before I went back to college. . .

★ *To know how to suggest is the great art of teaching. To attain it we must be able to guess what will interest; we must learn to reach the childish soul as we might a piece of music. Then, by simply changing the key, we keep up the attraction and vary the song.*

AMIEL

THE OLD BROWN SCHOOLHOUSE

Anonymous

IT STOOD ON A BLEAK COUNTRY CORNER,
  The houses were distant and few,
A meadow lay back in the distance,
  Beyond rose the hills to our view.
The roads crossing there at right angles,
  Untraversed by pomp and array,
Were cropped by the cows in the summer;
  I've watched them there many a day.

In memory's hall hangs the picture,
  And though years of sad care are between,
It hangs with a beautiful gilding,
  And well do I love it, I ween.
It stood on a bleak country corner,
  But boyhood's young heart made it warm.
It gloried in the sunshine of summer;
  'Twas cheerful in winter and storm.

The teacher, oh, well I remember;
  My heart has long kept him a place;

Perhaps by the world he's forgotten,
  His memory no time can efface.
He met us with smiles on the threshold,
  And in that rude temple of art,
He left with the skill of a workman
  His touch on the mind and the heart.

Oh, gay were the sports of the noontide,
  When winter winds frolicked with snow;
We laughed at the freaks of the storm king,
  And shouted him on, all aglow.
We dashed at his beautiful sculptures,
  Regardless of all its array,
We plunged in the feathery snowdrift
  And sported the winter away.

We sat on the old-fashioned benches,
  Beguiled with our pencils and slate;
We thought of the opening future,
  And dreamed of our manhood's estate.
O days of my boyhood! I bless you;
  While looking from life's busy prime,
The treasures are lingering with me
  I gathered in life's early time.

O still to that bleak country corner
  Turns my heart in its weariness yet,
Where leading my gentle young sisters
  With youthful companions I met.
I cast a fond glance o'er the meadow;
  The hills just behind it I see
Away in the charm of the distance,
  Old schoolhouse! a blessing on thee!

FIRST LESSON

by Irwin Edman

Every autumn in normal times I walk, with rather deliberate briskness, into a classroom in which are gathered about forty young men who have voluntarily enrolled themselves in a course entitled "Introduction to Philosophy." They have come to this class not as they came to similar enterprises in physics, chemistry, or history. They come to those subjects expecting to find out more about what they already know something about. They come to this class hoping to find out by the end of the year what it is that they are studying. And, as I am a disciple of Socrates, I do not propose to tell them. I propose, by asking the proper questions, to have them tell me, and to assist them in the discovery that they have in essence always known what philosophy is.

I look around and light on the most likely looking candidate. I find a young man whom I know by sight, Alfred Jeremy, hitherto undebauched by philosophy.

"Mr. Jeremy," I say without preamble, "I suppose you believe you exist?"

From *Philosopher's Quest*, by Irwin Edman. Copyright 1947 by Irwin Edman. Reprinted by permission of The Viking Press, Inc., New York.

Young Jeremy looks at me quizzically. I feel he is wondering if this is what professors of philosophy are paid to do.

"Of course I exist," he says, and I detect the slightest note of impatience in his courteous and somewhat surprised tone.

"What makes you so sure?" I ask.

The large football player in the second row shifts his bulk impatiently in the seat too small for him, as if suddenly wondering what is going on here.

"Well," says Jeremy, "it's me. I mean I. I brought myself in here." The class smiles a little at that.

"How do you know it's you?" I say.

"I can pinch myself," he says. The football player does that very thing. Then he pinches his neighbor. I tap warningly on the table with a piece of chalk.

"I can feel my hands if I press them hard, and I have a pain in the crick of my neck."

"You mean you have sensations," I say. "But how do you know they're yours?"

"Well, whose else would they be?" asks Jeremy in great surprise.

"But who are you?" I insist. "Simply this cluster of sensations at the present moment?"

"Oh, no," says Jeremy. "I'm the guy, excuse me, the fellow, who went through the Horace Mann School, and who entered Columbia College last year as a freshman. I left the dormitory this morning and had breakfast at the Sandwich Shop, no, it was in the Lion's Den, and I had a class in advanced French, and I talked to a couple of guys, I mean fellows, and now I'm here."

"But all that was up to the present moment; it was all in the past, wasn't it?"

"Yes, sir," says Jeremy.

"It was pure memory," I say. "Might it not be false memory, pure fiction? You know how difficult it is to get a reliable witness of what has happened in the past. You can't be sure, can you, that it *was* you, can you now?"

"Who else could it be?" asks Jeremy.

"It might be a dream that you in the present are having of what you call the immediate past, mighn't it?"

During this colloquy some members of the class are sitting in absorbed attention. There is a bright-looking, very young man who can scarcely wait until I ask him a question. His hand is already up. The football player is not exactly absorbed, but he looks a little as if he would really like very much now to know what is going on here. The nice-looking boy in the third row seems vaguely troubled. Several look as if they think I am trying to play some trick on them.

The very young-looking boy can wait no longer.

"Well?" I say. (I recognize him, too. He had come to interview me yesterday for the college paper.) "Mr. Gottesman, what do *you* think?"

"Well, I not only remember, but I expect," he says. "I know for pretty certain that I'm going to be around tomorrow, having breakfast and lunch and coming to classes."

"But that," I say, "is mere expectation, is it not? It's an act of faith. You can't really believe you exist on the ground that somebody to whom unhappened things have not yet happened is going to be there to have them happen to him. And is that the ground for your believing that you now exist—because somebody not in existence is going to exist? That future 'you' does not yet exist, does he?"

"No", says young Gottesman ruefully, "I suppose he doesn't." There is a hand raised in the back now. I look at the pleasant blue-eyed Irish face behind it.

"Your name, please."

"Farrell, John."

"Well, Mr. Farrell, what do you think? Why do *you* think you exist?"

"Because I can't think of myself not existing while I'm sitting here talking—or thinking," he adds after a moment's thought. "Who else is doing it?"

"Have you ever read Descartes?" I ask.

"Never heard of him," he says, almost in a tone of disclaiming unsavory acquaintance.

"Well, he is a famous French philosopher of three centuries ago. He would be inclined to agree with you."

"He would?" asks Farrell.

"Well, let's see where we are," I say. "The past is an illusion, the future a gamble. We have only ourselves of the moment— feeling, thinking, sensing—to be sure of. But surely, Mr. Farrell, you wouldn't call that enough to call 'Mr. Farrell,' would you? The John Farrell your parents know has a past and a future, hasn't he?"

"I sure hope so," says Mr. Farrell. "So do my parents, especially about the future."

"Well," I say, "let's take a vote for a moment. How many are willing to assume they exist?"

The class is unanimous in favor of their own existence.

"But it's only an assumption, mind," I say. "We haven't proved it yet. Now how about other people?"

John Farrell looks appraisingly at his neighbor to the left and then to the right. Many members of the class do the same. The football player looks appraisingly at me.

"How do we know other people exist?"

"How do we know other people exist?" Farrell repeats.

Jeremy raises his hand. I nod.

"Well, I hear them, I see them. Seeing is believing, as they say."

"Yes, but gentlemen, we are obviously often deceived. There are mirages in the desert; we think we see things that turn out to be not there, or to be something else. The man you see is not the one you thought you saw, but his brother. The stick looks broken in water, but it is the shadow, not the stick, that you see. Perhaps it is a devil who has masked as your friend and classmate. Perhaps it is a dream, or a nightmare."

The bright youngster in the front row looks at me as if he wondered if I were more than half joking.

"And how about *things*, this blackboard, this desk?" I ask, turning to Farrell, whose blue eyes seem to be speculating curiously on this panorama of illusion I have opened before him.

"Me?" he says, his attention recalled. "Well, the same thing as other people. I see it, I can touch it. The blackboard has a sort of odor, too."

I take the class on a little imaginary tour through the history of thought. I remind them how uneasy Plato was about the senses; how Berkeley whisked the world away into a semblance constituted by our ideas; how Schopenhauer emphasizes the dreamlike quality of existence, despite the regularity and order of the dream.

"But things," persists the bright young boy, "are there in space, and that blackboard will be there tomorrow when we come back. Or," he added, "if we don't."

I had been rather waiting for this opening.

"What," I say, turning to Smith, having found his name next to his seat number, "what, Mr. Smith, is *space*?"

Mr. Smith considers a moment. He waves his hand comprehensively in the air. "Space is what everything else is in," he says.

The football player leans forward. "Yeah, like a box," he bursts out.

"But what," I say, "is space in?" Some of the boys look faintly disgusted, some perplexed.

"Yes, sir," says the football player slowly and ruefully, "what *is* it in?"

For the next fifteen minutes or so, without knowing the words, the young men, aided and abetted by myself, explore, in elementary form, some of the mysteries and paradoxes that Immanuel Kant turned up. We come out at about the same place he did. Perhaps space is just a way our mind has of arranging our sensations. Experience, we determine tentatively, is impossible without space, and yet it is impossible to find space in experience.

"Is it the same about time?" says a rather blasé youth in the third row who has not up to that point taken any part in the discussion.

"Well, surely the present is here," says Mr. Gottesman.

"And the past *has* been here," says the football player.

"And the future is surely going to be here," says Mr. Jeremy.

"You are going too fast for me, gentlemen," I interrupt. "Why are you so sure, Mr. Jeremy, that the past *was* here? Is it not, like yourself of yesterday, a memory? You cannot see the past clearly, can you? Or hear it? It's gone forever.

"And as for the future, you can bet, if you care to, that it is going to take place, but surely at the present moment it does not exist. If it did, it would be the present, wouldn't it? There's just this moment, isn't there? All the rest is memory or imagination."

"It doesn't leave us very much," says Mr. Smith.

There are several students who have not entered into the discussion at all. But I suspect I know what is going on in their heads. Some of them look bored, and I am not sure they will not change their registration after all. Some of them are pleasantly bewildered, some embarrassed by their bewilderment. The football player finally says, "But that's all very well, maybe, for philosophers. But for plain ordinary people, time and space and other people and themselves do exist, don't they now, professor? Right here now, aren't we in this actual room, talking to each other, today, Monday?"

For the next ten minutes we have quite a heated controversy. There are those who side with the football player, who take the side of common-sense men in all ages, who will have no traffic with such nonsense. In a class every sort of temperament in the history of mankind is likely to reveal itself. Young Gottesman is a kind of poet, and I can see already that he is impressed by the poetry and suasion of the idea that all that we see and hear is a dream.

I intend myself before the term is over to try to show these young men that it would be silly to pretend that they need seriously doubt their own existence, that of the world, of time and space and other people and things. My purpose this morning has been to get them to look at these things with a difference. If only one can get them to be critical of their most usual preconceptions, one is on the road. A little later we'll see what we can do about good and evil, right and wrong, justice and injustice. These students are very young, but they are already full of age-old prejudices. At least an Introduction to Philosophy may start them on the quest for more rational standards of life, of knowledge, of action, of society.

The bell is ringing, announcing the end of the hour. Young Farrell leans forward. "But *do* we exist?" he says.

"Here endeth the first lesson," I say.

★ *Given a mastered subject and a person committed heart and soul to teaching it, a class accustomed to think, attend, and be led; the result will be, under God, as near to the discourse of men and angels as it is fit to go.*

JACQUES BARZUN

PASSING THE BUCK

by Glenn Seeley

THE COLLEGE PROFESSOR SAYS:
"Such rawness in a student is a shame,
But high school preparation is to blame."

The high school teacher remarks:
"From such youth I should be spared;
They send them up so unprepared."

The elementary school teacher observes:
"A cover for the dunce's stool,
Why was he ever sent to school?"

The kindergarten teacher whispers:
"Never such lack of training did I see!
What kind of person must the mother be?"

The mother replies:
"Poor child, but he is not to blame;
His father's folks were all the same."

From *High Points*, Feb. 1953. Reprinted by permission.

DEFINITIONS

by John Erskine

Nothing in education needs explaining more than this, that a teacher may be neither a professor nor an educator, that a professor may mature to the age of retirement without teaching or educating, and that an educator, without loss of reputation, may profess nothing, and never face a class.

A teacher is one who shows his fellow man how to do something, who imparts an active skill, and who kindles the desire to acquire this skill and to use it. In all creatures there is a natural ambition to live, which necessarily includes an ambition to learn, but even a natural ambition will need encouragement. The cow teaches the newborn calf to walk, the mother bird teaches her young to fly, though neither cow nor bird, so far as we know, has a teacher's diploma, or the equivalent, from a normal school. If the calf is reluctant to stand up, the cow gets behind and under, and gives a dramatic boost. If the fledgling recoils from the unsolid air, the mother bird pushes it overboard. This is teaching, of no mean sort.

A professor is a person who knows all about a subject, or professes to know all about it, or at least a good deal about it, or about a part of it. If the part he knows is a very small part, the professor is called a specialist. When a sufficient number of specialists are assembled on a college faculty, the subject of which each knows only a small part is said to be covered, and the academic department to which they all belong is regarded as fully manned. In ancient Ireland, if legend may be trusted, there was a tower so high that it took two persons to see to the top of it. One would begin at the bottom and look up as far as sight could reach, the other would begin where the first left off, and see the rest of the way.

I would not imply that no professor is a good teacher, but I do say plainly that professors are not necessarily teachers; they are not trained to be, colleges and universities do not engage them as such. A professor wears his Ph.D. to show not that he can teach, but that as a reservoir of knowledge he is reasonably full.

Scholarship is not judged by its usefulness; it is supposed to imply other and superior qualities. A scholar is honored for his industry, for his thoroughness, and for the correctness of his methods. Whether his fellow men wish to acquire or share any of the knowledge stored up in him, is an irrelevant question. In fact, whenever scholarship is applied with success to the amelioration of life, it risks the reputation of being tarnished; it is no longer "pure."

If a university can afford to maintain not only a staff of professors, those who know, but also a staff of junior instructors who can teach, the inarticulate elders are more highly honored and receive the big salaries. A professor does no harm to his reputation, he may even improve it, by saying and writing nothing. The patina of silence is admired by connoisseurs. It is not to Oxford dons exclusively that George Santayana's mordant remark applies: "The thoughts of these men are like the sibylline leaves, profound but lost."

Educators are those who plan the work of teachers, or make possible a scholarly career. College presidents are educators, so are college trustees, so was Andrew Carnegie, so was Cecil Rhodes. Just as a scholar may still be a scholar, even though his knowledge is unused or unusable, so an educator retains the reputation of an educator even though the program he invents is lopsided or prejudiced.

James Russell Lowell, speaking in 1886 at the two hundred and fiftieth anniversary of the founding of Harvard University, quoted from a letter by John Winthrop, Jr. in 1663 to an English friend: "I make bold to send here inclosed a kind of rarity . . . It is two papers of Latin composed by two Indians now scollars in the Colledge in this country, and the writing is with their own hands . . . Possibly as a novelty of that kind it may be acceptable, being a reall fruit of that hopeful worke yt is begun amongst them . . . testifying thus much that I received them of those Indians out of their own hands, and had ready answers from them to many questions I propounded to them in yt language, and heard them both express several sentences in Greeke also."

From this passage, it may be concluded that in primitive Harvard the art of teaching was further advanced than the philsophy of education. One of these Indians was graduated and received his diploma. The other, having learned to write Latin, went back to the woods. It is not recorded that the one who took his degree ever appeared at a class reunion. Perhaps his feelings were hurt. Perhaps he expected his clever Latin teachers to reciprocate by mastering his American tongue, but they seem to have been indifferent, even as to the correct pronounciation of his name.

. . . For most of my life my temperament and my occupation was that of a teacher, but now and then I have been quite scholarly, and at moments I have played the part of an educator, more often than not on a large stage. But I liked teaching best. The teacher deals directly with youth, and I love youth. The teacher, through his pupils, may influence the future, which is perhaps the part of time which most deserves our attention.

★ *A teacher should, above all things, first induce a desire in the pupil for the acquisition he wishes to impart.*

HORACE MANN

★ *The true teacher defends his pupils against his own personal influence. He inspires self-distrust. He guides their eyes from himself to the spirit that quickens him. He will have no disciple.*

AMOS BRONSON ALCOTT

"We might try putting him in Mrs. Maynard's class for a while. She's planning to leave us anyway."

THE PROFESSOR'S PUNCH

by Stephen Víncent Benét

I WAS TEACHING IN SUMMER SESSION AT STATE AND MY GIRL lived in New Hamburg. That's seventy-four and six tenths away on the speedometer, but I had it down to a system and, one Friday night, I made it in 1.31.

I'd get coffee, about halfway, at an all-night stand, and, when I got to Ella's house, there'd be sandwiches and cold milk in the refrigerator. She wouldn't get up, usually. What was the point? We had it down to a system. I'd get in between one and two, and eat the sandwiches and drink the milk, and know I'd see her in the morning. So that was all right.

Ella's people were awfully decent to us, and Mrs. Veitch certainly tried hard to feed me up, Saturdays and Sundays. All the same, I lost twelve pounds that summer, and I've never been fat. Summer session's no joke in the first place—especially when you've been taking three extra divisions through the regular year and reading most of your chief of department's bluebooks for him too.

But I had my programme mapped out, and it was exciting, working it—it was like playing a game. If it worked out, I'd be in line for an assistant professorship—and Ella and I could get married in the fall. If it didn't work out—well, I didn't think about that.

I didn't think about it, because I couldn't afford to. I like teaching, and I don't expect to get rich at it. And, heaven knows, I was used to the life you lead—student-waiter and student-laundry and peanut-butter sandwiches in the graduate school and try to pay off your debts on an assistant instructor's salary. But if you like the work, you like the work.

So far, I'd only had one real setback—and that was missing out on the Francis Grier Fellowship last year.

But every now and then, all the same, I'd feel as if I were pedaling a bicycle up a steep hill. About halfway up the hill, there was a point if I could reach it. That point meant being married to Ella and having enough money for us both to live on.

Once you got there, you could stop and breathe, and then it would be easy to go up the rest of the hill. But, meanwhile, you had to pedal and pedal, and the nearer you got, the more your front wheel wobbled.

I didn't think so much about that at the start of summer session— I'd had ten days off, in between, and a lot of sleep. But it wasn't quite enough, because even toward the end of the first month, I started to worry about going stale. And I couldn't afford to go stale. So I worked harder and drank more coffee and sometimes I knew I was teaching better than I ever had and sometimes I thought I was terrible. But there was always the drive to New Hamburg— and that little quiet time in the kitchen, with the sandwiches and milk in front of me and knowing Ella was asleep upstairs.

There was that, and Saturday.

Saturday was our best day, of course. Saturday night, we'd go down to the *Brauhaus*, under the bridge, and drink beer and listen to the music and watch the river go by. New Hamburg's still a pretty German town, and they've got a remarkable choral society —Ella's always sung on the women's side. Well, you sit at tables outdoors and whole families come and stay for hours. Then the men will get together and sing—or the women—or sometimes both —really sing, you know—Bach and Mozart and old *lieder* their families brought over. It's like being abroad, almost.

Sometimes we'd sit with Ella's family and sometimes we'd sit by ourselves. When I first met Ella's family—well, I was a little surprised. I mean—I wouldn't have cared if they'd run the county poor farm—it couldn't change Ella. But Ella was president of her class at State and, when I first met her, she struck me as pretty sophisticated. While Mr. Veitch likes to eat dinner in his shirt sleeves, when it's warm, and Mrs. Veitch calls him "the *Vater*." And there aren't any better people.

So that was the good part—oh, all the time up till after Sunday dinner was the good part. But I'd know the going-away part had begun and she'd know. I'd try to leave early because that was the sensible thing to do, and she'd try to make me because she knew it was sensible—but, of course, I'd always stay as late as I could.

Then, during the week, I'd be up to my ears and so would she. She was working part time in the bank and giving music lessons on the side. We had money in a savings account—we felt we had to have some things in the apartment.

July's always hot in our section, and, about the middle of July, I started having dreams. For one thing, Professor Stout was down two weeks with flu and I had to take over "The Age of Pope." That meant three extra full-dress lectures a week—and it wasn't my specialty. I drank more coffee those two weeks than I ever had in my life and only wrote Ella twice. I could have done the "Appreciation and Criticism" course on my head, but Gwinnet took that. I'd never been particularly intimate with Gwinnett, but I didn't hate him till then.

I hated him because he had money and was married to a nice girl and was teaching in summer session for "experience"—not bread and butter. I hated him because he'd been to Harvard and Europe and wore a hand-made dinner coat when he went to the president's and yet didn't put on any side. Most of all I hated him because he was a good teacher—you couldn't deny it. We were about the same age, but he'd had all the breaks. I hated him for that.

And that was ridiculous. But that didn't help when I'd wake in the night with a jump, dreaming I'd pulled some terrible boner in front of a class. I could hear myself saying solemnly that Oliver Goldsmith had written "The Sun Also Rises"—and then I'd wonder if I had. And then I used to dream I was driving to New Hamburg —driving and driving through the night but never getting there.

Stout came back, the first week in August, and he was very nice to Gwinnett and myself about the way we'd filled in. He had us both to dinner—the president was there, with Mrs. Jerome and "our distinguished visitor," Rutgers Walling, who was giving the Hartswick Lectures. It could have been a fine evening. But it wasn't.

I was next Mrs. Gwinnett at dinner, and I've always liked her—
she's one of the people I'd like to have Ella know. But tonight
I couldn't like her because I'd started hating her husband. She tried
hard to be pleasant to me, but I didn't give her any help—so, naturally, she turned to "our distinguished visitor," on her other side.
And I sat there crumbling bread—it was Mrs. Church, on my other
side, and, of course, she was all wrapped up in the president. Now
and then I'd look across the table and see how well Gwinnett was
getting on with Mrs. Jerome. And that was a help, indeed.

The Stout—and he meant it kindly—started drawing out Gwinnett and myself in front of "our distinguished visitor" and the
president. And Gwinnet drew out beautifully. He was easy, he
was amusing, he talked about his own subject but not too much,
he talked about Walling's and knew a lot. I knew Gwinnett hadn't
done a tenth of the research I had, but he asked just the right
questions and made just the right answers. You could see old
Walling expand.

Then we went into the other room, and that was worse. Because
Gwinnett had warmed Walling up on his subject, and Walling
simply wouldn't stop. It was fascinating—it was stuff I'd give my
eye teeth for, any other time. But I'd only had one small cup of
coffee after dinner instead of my usual three big ones—and I hadn't
been in that other room two minutes, before I knew, if I didn't
look out, I'd fall asleep.

I took the hardest-looking chair I could find. I pinched myself
when no one was looking, I sat bolt upright, I dug my nails in my
palms. Now and then I'd catch the president's eye, and it looked
to me as cold as marble. I could feel my tie creep up and my
eyes blur—I could feel my chin start to drop and jerk it up again.
It was a nightmare. And Walling went on. And then, suddenly,
there was a silence, and Professor Stout's voice. He was talking
to me.

"Oh, Carroll," he said, "Professor Walling was asking—"

"It's just on the tip of my tongue," said Walling, in his deep
baritone, "but of course you'll know, Mr. Carroll—Professor
Stout has told me about your work. 'The Day of Doom' was
written by—"

"Oh, yes—Oliver Goldsmith," I said.

It wasn't, needless to say, the right answer. In fact, it was just
about as wrong as it could be. And the minute it was out of my
mouth, I knew I'd sounded like an undergraduate, bluffing.

Stout did his best to cover me up, for he's decent. "Michael Wigglesworth—exactly—thank you very much for telling us, Carroll," he said in loud tones. But I'd seen Walling's eyes flicker, and I knew it didn't fool him. And, after a moment, Mrs. Walling rose.

"I think we'd better be going, Rutgers," she said playfully. "You know how Rutgers is when he gets on his subject—he's apt to send people to sleep—"

She looked at me as she said it, and I got up, too, and stepped on her handbag. I didn't intend to step on it, but she dropped it just as I got up. She said it didn't matter at all, but I heard something crack inside it. I imagined it was a mirror and, if it was, I imagined I knew who was due for the seven years' bad luck.

Then I drove down to New Hamburg and got there at 2 a.m. They'd left the milk and the sandwiches, but I wasn't feeling hungry.

And all that week-end it was hot—too hot to picnic, too hot to canoe on the river. It was hot, even sitting on the back porch and holding each other's hands. We hadn't seen each other for three weeks, and we'd written how fine it would be when we were together again. But we were just tired, instead.

And all that week, I kept noticing things I'd never noticed before —how Mr. Veitch drank his coffee through his mustache, and Mrs. Veitch's German accent. They were just as kind as they'd always been. But I kept wondering if Ella would be as big and slow-moving as her mother when she was her age. And yet I'd never minded Mrs. Veitch's being big before. We drank beer and heard the music, Saturday night—but it wasn't the same.

And, going back, on the road, it was just a jam of cars. I drove the way you do, automatically. And, as I drove, I kept thinking —we had it all mapped out, but what then? I'd worried about losing the game before. But now I worried about winning it, and that was bad.

I got to State about one a.m. and left the car in front of the boarding house. But then I was still thinking, and wide awake. So I decided to walk down to the diner and get some coffee—I knew I couldn't feel any worse, no matter what I did. Well, the only other person in the diner was a big, rather prosperous-looking fellow who was, obviously, sobering up. I could see him take a dislike to me the minute I came in, the way some drunks will, but I wasn't paying any attention. I passed a couple of words with Mike, the counterman, and drank my coffee slowly and got up to go.

But, to get out of the diner, I had to pass the drunk. I'd noticed he was staring at me, the way they do, and let it pass. But, as I brushed him, he goggled up at me and said: "Hey, Sour-eyes, what's the price of violets today?"

Well, I don't get into fights with drunks—I'm not the type. But suddenly, and for once, it got right under my skin. I was that sort of guy—the sort of guy that even a drunk can laugh at. That was where my programme and my thinking and my working it all out got me— and that was all I was worth.

"What's that you said?" I said to him.

"Violets, violets, violets," he said, with a big laugh. "What's the price of violets, Percy?"

And, with that, I leaned over and slapped him square in the face.

He let out a roar, and the next second we were out of the diner and fighting in the middle of the street. It was one of the fastest two minutes I ever lived. Because he wasn't nearly as drunk as he looked, and he landed one on my cheekbone that made me see stars. But I finally connected with his jaw—just right—the kind of thing you dream of, and he went down like a ton of bricks.

Mike said, "Judas, Prof!" in a voice, and started to feel him all over. Then he straightened up and said, "It's okay. He didn't bump his head—he's just out. But beat it while there's open country."

"Okay, Mike," I said. "Sorry it happened."

"Oh, he was asking for it," said Mike. "He gets that way. Now he'll sober up. Judas, Prof.—I didn't know you could do it!"

Then I saw the big fellow's eyelids start twitching, and I went away. I didn't want to be there when he waked up. It was bad enough as it was. I could see the papers already—"INSTRUCTOR IN FIST FIGHT AT DINER."

Or one of those funny ones—"The punch is mightier than the pen, as George Carroll, instructor in English at State, discovered yesterday—"

But it didn't much matter how they played it. There are lots of things you can't do, if you're teaching in a university, and this was one of them. And yet, do you know, I didn't feel badly at all.

I was thinking of all the years I'd worked and the people I'd been polite to—the stuffed shirts like President Jerome and the nice but dead old dodos like Professor Stout—I was thinking I was tired of that. I was thinking they ought to know when a man's half dead with overwork and no sleep and not ask him freshman questions.

And just then I found myself passing the president's house. There wasn't another soul in the streets, and everything was dim with the early light. It's a big, impressive house, and I stood and looked at it. And, all of a sudden, it made me feel pretty sore. Because I bet that President Nelson Jerome couldn't teach one of my courses—and yet, there he was in a big house with lots of sleep.

So, before I knew what I was doing, I picked a half-brick from the ornamental border and heaved it straight at his window. I heard the glass crash, and then I was running away down the street and laughing as I ran, for I could see him waking up in his stuffed shirt and looking surprised.

I haven't laughed like that since I was a kid. And the funny thing is, it must have been good for me, for, after I got into bed, the next thing I knew was my landlady shaking me—and it was four in the afternoon.

Well, I was sure of what had happened, the minute she said the president's office had telephoned. But when I went over, I was still laughing, though it didn't show outside. And there he was, in the big office, every inch a president.

He's got two nicknames—"Old Humanity" and "Blood and Iron"—and I thought I knew which one was on top.

"Good-afternoon, Mr. Carroll," he said, "I tried to get you before, but with no success."

"Yes, sir," I said—and I was surprised to hear how normal my voice sounded—I'd always found it hard to talk to him before— "I must have been asleep. I suppose I missed my classes—still, they'll rather enjoy that." And I gave him a pleasant smile.

He didn't act as if he'd heard me at all.

"Yes, indeed," he said. "Well, Mr. Carroll—something has come up which made me anxious to talk with you at the earliest opportunity."

I wondered which it was—the fight in the diner, or his window, or going to sleep at the Stouts'—but he wasn't saying.

"It lies within my power—and the board's—to nominate a candidate for the Francis P. Grier Traveling Fellowship," he said.

"You know of the fellowship, naturally—in fact, your name was considered for it last year. But we did not feel we could spare you from State—" and he gave me a crocodile smile. "This year, however," he said, "an odd circumstance has arisen. Naturally, we like to consider the Grier family's wishes when we can—the elder Mr. Grier was a generous friend of the university's—and—well, I wonder if you'd mind sitting there just a moment, Mr. Carroll—"

He pressed a buzzer, and the door opened and in walked my big drunk of the night before.

"Is this—ahem!" said President Nelson Jerome. The drunk took one look at me. He was sober now, and his face was different. But I could see the little lump on his jaw.

"Yeah," said my noble antagonist, "that's the man." He walked over and stuck his hand at me. "I'm Frank Grier," he said. "Glad to see you. No hard feelings, I hope."

"Nope," I said. "It was a good scrap." Though I knew I was sunk, right there.

"I've had worse," he said. "But it's the only thing to do to me when I am potted. I've got a glass jaw—always had," he said, with some pride. "One tap on the button and I'm out. And then I'll go home and be a good boy for a while. But, man, try and get me home before! No, I want to go on scattering roses. I was trying as hard as I could to get Mike to take a poke at me before you came in—but he knows me too well. Scared." He bit off the end of a cigar.

"Jerome, here, has been trying to get me to take an interest in this university for ten years," he said. "Keep up Father's tradition and all that. Well, I always hated the place—and I never got on with Father. He made me go here for a year, and I showed everybody I hated it—but no one of them would dare to fire me, because I was Francis Grier's son. Maybe you'd have had the guts, Jerome —but that was before your time. Then I quit and went out and made more money than Father ever thought of." He laughed. "And that didn't raise my respect for either universities or professors," he said."

"Mr. Grier does himself an injustice," said President Jerome smoothly. "He—"

"Oh, I've given the town money—and the college, too," said Grier. "But the place gets on my nerves—every time I come back

to it. I'd been on the wagon for a year till I came back here yesterday." He stared at me. "Jerome's been telling me they had a
new breed of professors and college men," he said. "But I thought
he was haywire. In fact, I bet him that there wasn't a professor in
his whole blame college with a punch! But I guess I was wrong
about that." And he rubbed his jaw. Well, when I'm wrong, I
admit it. I was going to take away the Francis Grier Fellowship—
it isn't a trust, you know. But now I'll let it stick—on the understanding that it's given to you. I've talked it over with Jerome, and
he says that's all right."

He looked at me as if he expected me to say something, but I
didn't say anything.

"Say, how do you stand the life anyway?" he said. "How does
any real man?"

"I like it." I said.

"A fellow with a punch ought to be in business," he said. "Even
with business the way it's been. Suppose you had an opening—
would you take it?"

"Nope," I said. Then I took a long breath. "And I wouldn't take
your fellowship, if it was for life," I said.

He looked at me curiously. "Sore?" he asked.

"Yes," I said, "I'm sore. I can teach and I know it. You can ask
the kids who listen to me. I've been doing three men's work since
the first of January and doing it all right. Though it's got me so
I'd trade my right eye for a flock of sleep. But the thing I'm to get
promoted for—is socking a rich man on the jaw and sobering him
up. No, thanks. You can take your fellowship and your whole
university and—"

Then I stopped, for the other two were looking at each other
and nodding. And Grier said with a big laugh, "You win, Jerome,"
and Jerome said, "I told you you were wrong, Grier," and looked
as pleased as a pussycat.

Then Jerome turned to me—and it was the first time I'd ever
seen him smile like a human being, though I'd often heard he
could.

"Sorry, Mr. Carroll," he said. "It's all very irregular, I know.
But, you see, I have had quite an argument with Mr. Grier for some
years. Not only as to whether professors had—er—punch—but
whether they had genuine independence and would stick by their

principles. Mr. Grier has rather old-fashioned ideas about absent-minded professors and so forth."

"You owed me that," said Grier—and when he really smiled, he was different, too.

"As a matter of fact," said Jerome, "Mr. Grier is not quite as—er—raucous as he sometimes likes to pretend he is. He has already given us extremely intelligent and not merely financial help. I'm not running a rich man's college—and I think Mr. Grier knows it. But he's sometimes been rather dubious, when I spoke of the independence of the intellect that we try, at least, to foster. So I was glad to show him one practical demonstration—"

"With me for the guinea pig?" I said, for it made me madder than ever to think of having been drawn into a grandstand play by those two old birds. "Well, Mr. President, if that's what you think of—"

But the president just smiled again—not like a stuffed shirt.

And you could see, somehow, why people, like Winterblick, the physicist, were willing to work at State.

"It sounds like it, doesn't it?" he said. "But don't you think I owe you a little something, Mr. Carroll?"

And he opened the drawer of his desk and took something out of it. It was a half-brick and I looked at it. And he looked at it and then at me.

"I don't sleep as well as I used to," he said, reflectively; "otherwise, it might have startled me. Though it wouldn't have surprised me—no. I wanted to do it myself—my last year in graduate school. I was taking a Ph.D. and working nights as a telephone operator. Only I thought I'd use an alarm clock because I never got any sleep. I was going to heave it through the dean's front window—it was quite a big one. But I didn't have the nerve." And he sighed, rather wistfully.

I didn't say anything; there wasn't anything to say.

But I started to laugh, and I laughed for quite a while.

When Jerome had got me a glass of water and I'd sobered up—Grier had left by then—he looked at me over his spectacles.

"Perhaps you'd like to see this," he said. "The committee on appointments had a special meeting last Saturday before—er—before you had encountered Mr. Grier. You were unanimously recommended for an assistant professorship with the option of taking the Grier Fellowship either this year or the next. So there's no shenanigan about it."

He touched me on the shoulder.

"And now get some sleep," he said. "We've been working you hard—I do that. But you have to work a man to see what he's like—I don't know any other way. Stout can take your classes for two days—I'll tell him you're ill. Go off somewhere and rest for forty-eight hours. I'm afraid we can't spare you any longer. But we're getting to the end of the summer session, anyway—I'm always glad when it ends." He looked at his desk a moment, and there were lines in his face. "And yet, when they come here from fourteen states—I think it was fourteen, this year—one can't turn them away. Well, I'll get a week's fishing before the legislature meets and we have to fight about the budget. Now I've got to see your friend, Gwinnett, and reassure him about his work—he's the kind of brilliant fellow that always thinks he's doing badly and won't rest till he cracks. Then, his wife is going to have a baby— and the first child is a nervous affair. I wish all you had to do as a college president was look impressive at convocation. Did you ever try fishing, Mr. Carroll? It's a remarkable sedative—even if some of the fishes' faces remind you of our friends in the legislature. But you get over that."

Well, I left him and went back to the boarding house and fell into bed. But I set the alarm clock for 10:30 p.m. not a.m.—and drove down to New Hamburg.

I hadn't telephoned Ella, but I knew where the key of the back door was. And when I went into the kitchen, I half expected to find the milk and sandwiches in the refrigerator, but they weren't there, of course. I half expected to find them because I was still pretty tired, but it was a pleasant kind of tiredness. It made me feel a little light-headed, but it was swell.

I drank a glass of water and started to go up to the room they kept for me, automatically. But on my way I passed Ella's door. It was half open—the day had been a scorcher—and I could see her, asleep. She was sleeping with her back turned toward me and her yellow hair over the pillow. And, the way you do, she'd kicked one foot out from under the sheet. She's got pretty feet, and she's still a lot of a kid in spite of being serious. Well, I said I felt a little light-headed. So I held my breath and tiptoed into the room. Then I reached for her ankle suddenly and yanked.

She says if I ever wake her up like that again, she'll shoot me. Well, she did give one long yell—enough to wake the Veitches— but I tell her it was pretty musical, at that.

When Mrs. Veitch came down, we were both of us laughing. Then we all went down to the kitchen—and Ella made me the sandwiches herself.

★ *The biology professor peered at his class and said, "The time has come for us to dissect a frog. I have one in my pocket for the experiment." He took a crumpled paper bag out of his pocket and extracted from it a very tired-looking cheese sandwich. The professor trembled visibly, and ejaculated, "Goodness me, I distinctly remember eating my lunch."*

BENNETT CERF
'Laughter Incorporated'
(Garden City Publishing Co., 1950)

THE THREAD
THAT RUNS SO TRUE

by Jesse Stuart

Helen Kirsten was our only faculty member not from Kentucky. She was from New York City. She was born, educated, and had lived all her life, in New York City; and when she came to the small town of Landsburgh in faraway Kentucky she had many adjustments to make. We didn't know this. Not one of us had ever been in New York City. Teachers and pupils in Landsburgh High School were more interested in Miss Kirsten's dialect. And she was very much interested in our dialect and in our idioms of speech. She was interested in everything. Especially in work. We didn't have a faculty member that worked harder than this tall, slender, black-haired, blue-eyed young teacher from New York City.

After our first faculty meeting she never complained about the work given her. When she learned the number of pupils we had in school and the too-few teachers to do the work, she didn't complain about her load. She was hired for the position of part-time librarian and part-time teacher, but after we had our first teachers' meeting, Miss Kirsten was made almost a full-time teacher. She assumed also responsibility for the library.

"I think I can work this situation out, Mr. Stuart," she said. "Don't you worry too much about it. Don't expect too much for about two weeks."

In two weeks Miss Kirsten had selected girls from the high school and had trained them in simple library rules. She selected two girls to stay in the library for each period during the day, and at intermission between class bells Miss Kirsten would hurry to the library to see if any problem had arisen the girls couldn't handle. She had one free period in the afternoon, when she could remain in the library. But she worked out a library system with the help of our pupils and her supervision, which operated smoothly. We didn't lose a single book during the year. A few were mislaid, but Miss Kirsten found and returned them.

At first, we regarded Miss Kirsten as very different from us. Her speech was different. Her training was different. She had different ideas about teaching school. She was an exacting person. She didn't give, and she didn't take. If a pupil lacked 1 per cent of making a passing grade, that pupil failed in Miss Kirsten's Freshman English. She was the first teacher at school each morning, and she was the last to leave in the afternoon. At faculty meetings she was very quiet unless she was asked for an opinion. And she was never without opinions on school problems. She had her own ideas how to solve them. Her ideas were very different from ours.

Soon we faculty members learned to know and to understand Miss Kirsten. She learned to know and to understand us. Once she came to me and said: "Mr. Stuart, now I am teaching English and composition for you, I want you to tell me exactly how you want me to teach. I want to do it your way, so you will be perfectly satisfied."

"Miss Kirsten, when I have a teacher with your originality," I said, "I would like to put the responsibility of teaching English directly into your own hands. Original English teachers are hard to find. You are one of the few. All I ask you to do is to teach English your way. I'll give you all the freedom you want."

This pleased Helen Kirsten more than anything I ever said to her. One day she came to me with a smile.

"Here, Mr. Stuart," she said, giving me a sheaf of theme papers. "I know you are interested in creative writing and I want you to see these themes from my classes."

When I read these themes, I got a great surprise. In them was the beauty of simple English language where many common nouns, simple verbs, and few adjectives were used. There was something in these Freshmen high-school themes that was akin to early English and Irish poetry. There was something in the mood of them that left in me a feeling such as I had had when I first read *Riders to the Sea* and *Playboy of the Western World*. I had regarded these plays as poetry. And I regarded these themes as poetry. They sang themselves. They were as natural in their singing as little streams of melted snow water, pouring over the rocks on a steep Kentucky hill in March. They were as natural in their choice of simple common nouns, verbs used as nouns, and nouns used as verbs, as red sails of redbud blossoms and white sails of dogwood blossoms are to the bright April winds in Kentucky.

I try to write, why don't I write like this? I thought, as I returned these themes to Helen Kirsten.

"How did you get work like this from pupils who have never written themes before?" I inquired. "I know many of your pupils have never been required to write a theme. I think this is excellent work. I've never read better creative work from high-school pupils. These themes are poetry."

"Yes, Mr. Stuart," Miss Kirsten smiled, "poetry is in these people from your hills. Your hills, rivers, trees, log shacks, crying waters, wild flowers, and little fields of grain—green in spring, ripening in summer, and harvested in autumn—have put this poetry in them. But the language," she sighed, "ah, the language! I've never heard anything like it. It's not too soft. It's not harsh. For the first time in my life, I've heard people talk with rhythm. It's poetry. You never pronounce *g* at the end of a word. And you supplement the prefix *a*. I've noticed that in all my pupils. Their language is poetry. Poetry is in them. Why don't they write it? They are crying for creative expression."

"Tell me more of your observation of the people here, Miss Kirsten," I said. "I've never thought of these things before."

"No, you live in them," she said. "You grew up here. You are a part of all this. That is why you don't see it. You live poetry instead of writing it. All of you do. Your pupils do."

"But tell me, how do you get your pupils to express themselves like this?" I asked.

"I let them write their own thoughts any way they see fit," she said. "I give them all the freedom they want to express themselves, and on any subject they choose to write. I let them put it in any form they choose. After they have written their themes," she explained, "we read them in class. Anybody has the right to offer any suggestion he may have on his classmate's theme. We don't always correct all the mistakes. You've noticed that."

"Yes, I have."

"We don't correct a mistake when it gives color and originality to a theme," she said.

Though Helen Kirsten had come to Kentucky a stranger, she was not a stranger very long. Soon the pupils and teachers began to know her better. The pupils from the Greenwood County hills were especially fond of her. They invited her to their homes over the week end. Often on Friday afternoons, I saw her climb onto one of the crowded school busses with a suitcase in her hand. She went into the valleys and hollows, to the land of log shacks and lonesome waters. She went to shacks where there had never been an electric light, a bathroom, or a telephone. And surely, Miss Kirsten, from New York City, had been used to these conveniences all her life.

Helen Kirsten had never seen men cut corn, dig potatoes, make sorghum at a cane mill in a bright gold-leafed autumn. She had never seen men chop down trees and draw the logs on the ground with cattle and mules to a woodyard, and saw these logs into sticks with a crosscut saw, and burn the sticks on the big open fireplaces. She had never seen cellars and smokehouses filled with provisions for winter and the way the Greenwood County people, who were often isolated during the winter, had provided for the hard winters ahead. And she had not been among people who had to make their own entertainment, such as dances, games, and old-time music. It was these pupils, who played the old-time music without knowing a note of music, who had written the good themes for her.

Our having Helen Kirsten, with an entirely different background, added to our school. It gave me the idea: That there should be an exchange of teachers in the schools of America. That teachers from different parts of America gave pupils a broader outlook on life, gave them better background and preparation for the future. That each school needed a variety of faculty members. That to select all teachers from the home town would eventually mean intellectual inbreeding and that soon the results would begin to show in the community. That the whole of America was greater than any of its parts, and, therefore, we should have a cross section of thought and stimulation from different parts of America to give us originality, to make us vigorous and strong. Each of America's regions complemented the other materially and made the wealthy whole! Then why wouldn't each of America's parts complement the other intellectually in our school systems, to give us greater understanding of each other and to give wisdom to the whole? I knew that Helen Kirsten was one teacher who would be on my faculty as long as she wanted to stay.

★ *A courage which looks easy and yet is rare; the courage of a teacher repeating day after day the same lesson—the least rewarded of all forms of courage.*

BALZAC

★ *Let our teaching be full of ideas. Hitherto it has been stuffed only with facts. . . . The whole art of teaching is only the art of awakening the natural curiosity of young minds for the purpose of satisfying it afterwards.*

ANATOLE FRANCE

OLD-MAID SCHOOLMA'AMS HAD THEIR PLEASANT SIDE

by Richard Attridge

THIS MAY BE THE PSYCHOLOGICAL MOMENT TO PAY A LONG-DELAYED tribute to the nation's "old-maid schoolteachers." We've made jokes about them, overworked and underpaid them, depreciated and depended on them for generations. Except for an occasional local retirement honor to one of these "old maids" for her long-time devotion to other people's children, we've seldom bothered to come right out and admit that they have carried out their difficult tasks with amazing dedication, understanding and efficiency. The plain fact is that if the rest of us—including most parents in dealing with their own children—had succeeded in doing our job with the same constancy and competence, our country and everybody in it might be a lot better off.

This salutary thought comes to mind with the report in The New York Times of April twelfth, [1953] that "the married teacher finally has broken the spinster's hold on the nation's elementary classrooms. Fewer than 50 per cent of the nation's teachers are now unmarried, according to a study at Southern Illinois University. Colleges of education, the study observes, will adjust the curriculum for the married teachers."

It would certainly be stupid and silly to object to the present trend in many states to permit married women to continue their teaching jobs or to question that they have a great deal to bring to the classroom. There's obviously no objection, either, to the statement by Dr. Sina Motta, professor of education at the university which conducted the study, that "the modern teacher is a vital part of her community as a teacher, wife and mother," or to her recommendation that "the woman who is to lead a dual life of homemaker and teacher should be taught careful budgeting of time, how to co-ordinate activities, how to make the daily transition from home to school and how to serve her community." These qualities would be of value generally to all of us, and most "spinster" teachers have had to learn them in their time.

But when Professor Motta comes out with the flat opinion that instead of being "an old maid's last resort, teaching is a stronghold for the intelligent, well-adjusted married women of the nation," it seems evident that her just praise of married teachers works, at least by implication, some injustice to their unmarried-schoolma'am colleagues. There have certainly been plenty of good "spinster" schoolteachers, and probably some poor married ones.

On the whole, it's a pretty safe bet that all wives and mothers, in the home or in the classroom, can still learn a lot from "old-maid teachers" about what makes any child tick.

★ *The day of a big snowstorm, the country school teacher felt called upon to warn her charges against playing too long in the snow. She said, "Now, children, you must be careful about colds and over-exposure. I had a darling little brother only seven years old. One day he went out in the snow with his new sled and caught cold. Pneumonia set in and three days later he died."*

The room was silent and then a youngster in the back row raised his hand and asked, "Where's his sled?"

EDMUND FULLER
from 'Thesaurus of Anecdotes'
(Crown Publishing Co., 1942)

SHOPPING TRIP

by James Reid Parker

Anxious to annoy Dr. Overton as much as possible, Mr. Bradley deferred writing his letter of resignation until the latter part of July, when the summer vacation was well under way. Since the mathematics chairman had irritated Mr. Bradley for three years, driving him at times into that frenzy of desperation that only an active monologist has the power to evoke, the instructor had shrewdly chosen the very best revenge at his disposal. Nothing stimulated Dr. Overton so much as interviewing candidates for his staff, but he liked to have plenty of time in which to do it. An entire semester, if possible. A sociable exchange of letters with department heads all over the country, expeditions to Harvard and Columbia, and lengthy meetings with applicants were part of the ritual which invariably began as soon as a member of the staff announced his intention of resigning.

With only a month or so in which to purchase an acceptable slave, Dr. Overton was even more irritated than Mr. Bradley had foreseen. The little shopping trips, which normally would have taken place during weekends when the college was in session, would have to be replaced by a single journey—probably to Harvard, where a good bargain could always be obtained. After all, one hated to interrupt one's holiday more than was necessary, even for the delightful task of conducting interviews. As soon as Dr. Overton had read the Bradley valedictory, he wrote a letter to the Harvard Placement Service, telling exactly when he would arrive at Cambridge and expressing a hope that it would be possible for them to round up some promising candidates for inspection, despite the fact that it was already mid-summer. The professor was depressed by a fear that the Service might not be able to submit many specimens of the genuine Harvard article, and might be obliged, instead, to let him see the alumni of less glorious institutions, who were studying in the summer session of the Graduate School. ("Bradley should be horsewhipped!" he informed Mrs. Overton.)

A week later, having received a batch of credentials from the Placement Service, he went to Cambridge and engaged for two days one of the least expensive rooms in the Hotel Commander. This same hotel had provided the background for much of his previous talent-scouting. It had been at the Commander, in fact, that he had decided that Mr. Bradley ("—and are you fond of Russian Bank, Mr. Bradley?") would fit his purposes admirably.

It was Dr. Overton's policy not to inspect candidates in the Placement Service office in University Hall, but to have them sent over to the hotel. Establishing himself in a chair in the lobby, he liked to see how a man behaved on learning that the visiting chairman, who had presumably forgotten about the appointment, failed to answer the telephone operator's signal. Any young man who dispatched a bellboy to page Dr. Overton made an excellent first impression. Dr. Overton adored being paged. The moment he heard his name spoken in a gratifyingly loud tone, he was likely to rouse himself with a start, looking not only bewildered but actually alarmed, and hurry toward the bellboy in great agitation. There were many other little tests that a candidate was required to pass, but these were generally conducted during the subsequent cross-examination upstairs in Dr. Overton's room.

On this trip most of the applicants proved disappointing. Oberlin graduates getting their M.A.'s at Harvard did not excite Dr. Overton in the least. He spent a day and a half interviewing a series of uninteresting specimens, all of whom talked much too freely, lacking what Dr. Overton later described to his wife as "a sense of the necessary give-and-take." On the afternoon of the second day, a young man named Ekins arrived.

Mr. Ekins had the professor paged. It was an auspicious beginning. Dr. Overton suggested that they would be subject to fewer distractions if they retired to his quarters for a chat.

"I was gratified to learn from the data sent me by the Placement Service that you pursued your undergraduate work here at Harvard, in addition to your graduate studies," said Dr. Overton, as they went up in the elevator. He added handsomely, "I might say that while I am not a Harvard man myself, I am always inclined to give a shade of preference *to* Harvard men. After all, a Princetonian or a Pennsylvanian is not quite the same thing as a Cantabrigian, is it, Mr. Ekins?"

Mr. Ekins said that it wasn't.

"Here we are," said Dr. Overton when they reached his room. "The only accommodations that the tavern was able to offer me; hence the proximity to the first floor." They went in. "The Placement Service mailed your credentials to my summer home. We have a little cottage in the mountains—a retreat that is ample for our needs, however. Mrs. Overton and I always welcome the thought of going to a rather small house in the summer, in view of the fact that we spend the winter in one of the larger houses on the campus. A veritable barn. It has seven bedrooms, which needless to say we seldom attempt to keep filled with guests. Most of my colleagues' houses have only four or five bedrooms. Forgive me, Mr. Ekins. Do sit down." Mr. Ekins sat down. "Your credentials seemed excellent, by the way. I noted that they included letters of recommendation from some very able members of your faculty. Really, you must be quite a phenomenal young man."

Since there was nothing Mr. Ekins could say in reply to this, he merely glanced at the professor with an expression that suggested the birth of mild dislike.

"Is your love for mathematics a casual love or the love that passeth all understanding? My young men must teach their subjects *con amore.*"

Mr. Ekins observed with evident sincerity that he liked mathematics better than anything else.

"On the other hand," said Dr. Overton, "I require the members of my department to be more than mathematicians. I insist that they be well-bred gentlemen, with a lively interest in the realm of literature and current affairs and so on. A polished, civilized man has generally formed tastes of his own by the time he has entered graduate school. What are some of *your* tastes, for example, Mr. Ekins?"

"My tastes?" asked Mr. Ekins, a little puzzled.

"As regards the academic life, let us say. Do you prefer a small rural college or a large urban university?"

Mr. Ekins said that he knew very little about the life in small rural colleges although he had often driven through college towns and had once gone out of his way to visit the library at Wesleyan. Dr. Overton frowned. "I trust you have no prejudice against a small college," he said sharply.

"No, indeed," said Mr. Ekins. "I meant that my experience had been limited."

"We have a very different type of student from the young men you have met at Harvard. Ours are not quite so capable intellectually perhaps, but we feel they deserve, and should be given, the very best instruction that scholarship affords. I believe we are considered the third best institution of our size in the country. Of course, we have no Einsteins on our staff, although perhaps that is not so serious a drawback as some persons might imagine."

"I once met Professor Einstein," said Mr. Ekins. "He told me he got quite a kick out of our newsreel theaters."

"Really? Do you speak German?"

"Yes."

"Mmmm. I suppose you do a great deal of general reading from time to time. Do you keep up with most of our modern novelists?"

"I'm afraid not."

"I once had the pleasure of meeting Willa Cather in Nantucket. I inadvertently happened to pat her dog, and it was not until after I had patted the dog that I learned who its owner was. Are you an admirer of good music, may I ask, Mr. Ekins?"

"Why, yes. I belong to a quartet."

"I wasn't referring to the close harmony type of singing, as I believe it's called. I was referring to classical music."

"Ours is a string quartet. I play second fiddle."

"Second fiddle? Oh, I see what you mean. Second *fiddle*. I'm a devotees of symphonies, myself. Tell me, Mr. Ekins, do you get along well with young people?"

"Fairly well, I think."

"I gather from your credentals that you've never taught before."

"No."

"The young teacher must learn to put himself in the student's place if he is to succeed. By any chance, do you feel that you have a talent for the work?"

"I am very fond of college life, so I'm more or less predisposed to like teaching."

"I see. Are you fond of bridge?"

"I'm afraid not."

Dr. Overton seemed pleased. "Neither am I. It's such an appalling waste of time. People who play bridge nowadays are so interested in the game that they seldom like to talk while they play. On the other hand, one can always carry on a conversation during Russian Bank, can't one? Are you fond of Russian Bank, Mr. Ekins?"

"I've never played it," said Mr. Ekins. "But I play a good deal of poker."

"Ah, yes, poker," said Dr. Overton doubtfully. "You seem to have the interests of the average young man, I take it, aside from your enthusiasm for the—er—the violin. I suppose you are fond of dancing and its concomitant pleasures?"

"Yes, I like to dance."

"Indeed. But I trust you are equally fond of informed conversation."

"Yes."

"When one enters a new environment, one must adapt himself to that environment. The members of my staff must be, if I may use the word 'malleable.' I like my men to be individuals and at the same time capable of making themselves agreeable to others. Once a week Mrs. Overton and I make a point of inviting one of the young members of my staff to dinner. We feel that it keeps us in touch with the younger men. Also, it permits the instructors to have a little more social life than would otherwise be the case."

Mr. Ekins nodded thoughtfully.

"You are the only applicant who has taken his undergraduate and graduate work at Harvard. As I have already suggested, this greatly advances your suit. You will be interested to know that we pay our beginners a salary of fourteen hundred a year. Unless an unlooked-for development should take place during the remainder of my stay in Cambridge, I think I can say that you may depend on hearing from me shortly. You understand, of course, that I am unable to say anything *now*. When I am faced with the necessity of adding a new man to my staff, I am obliged to submit my choice to the Administration. I might add, however"—here he bent forward confidentially—"that my recommendations are always accepted."

Mr. Ekins rose. "I know your appointment schedule must be pretty well filled, and I don't want to take up too much of your time," he said. "It was very good of you to see me."

"Not at all," said Dr. Overton. He gave a significant little smile, which indicated that they had not seen the last of each other but that, pending the Administration's approval, nothing could be settled at the moment. "You can be reached at the address of your credentials, I presume?"

Mr. Ekins hesitated. "I feel sure you could find someone else who would prove more suitable, Dr. Overton."

"You mean you are not interested in securing a position?" asked Dr. Overton, completely stunned.

"Oh, yes, I am very much interested in getting a job," said Mr. Ekins politely, "but I have an idea that you'd find me disappointing, and I *know* there are others who would be just exactly right." He held out his hand. "Thank you again."

Still dazed, the Professor shook hands with Mr. Ekins and accompanied him to the door. "If you should change your mind—" he said, floundering in an effort to achieve the nonchalance that the occasion seemed to demand.

"No, I'm *sure* you could make a more satisfactory choice," said Mr. Ekins, who had begun to look rather cheerful. "Thank you very much. Good-by."

"Good-by," said Dr. Overton. He closed the door and stood there bewildered. What in the world had been Mr. Ekin's objection? It was remotely possible, of course, that the young man was considering an offer from another college. Now that Mr. Ekins was no longer available, Dr. Overton became even more convinced that this was the instructor he wanted—far and away the most desirable applicant. Yes, someone *must* have made him a better offer. For the hundredth time the Professor asked himself why, in the name of all that was reasonable, Bradley had resigned in July.

"Of all months!" Dr. Overton muttered hopelessly, as he sat down on the edge of the bed.

He thumbed over the data from the Placement Service to see who was scheduled to arrive next, and whether there would be time for him to have a little drink by himself in the bar.

PREFACE TO A SCHOOLMASTER'S BIOGRAPHY

by George W. Martin

THERE IS A CHALLENGING MYSTERY ABOUT THE CAREER OF Endicott Peabody. For more than fifty years he was Head Master of Groton, and during this period it became a matter of great and increasing interest how he did it. Intelligent and expert persons repaired to the School and examined the process and made reports. Mr. Peabody himself wrote a piece, which was duly published, explaining the system: with the result that everyone agreed that he himself did not understand his own technique. As for the experts, they exhausted all the stock phrases about "orientation, integration, motivation," etc., and then it became apparent that they were like the three blind men describing the elephant—there was no agreement on anything. They differed not only in their conclusions but in the factual reports of what they found going on.

Eduction is one of those subjects, like divorce or constitutional law, on which everyone has an opinion. Some think it is involved with vocational instruction; some think it is to "discipline the mind"; some hold it to be the acquirement of media of self-expression; and some think it is just a formal process to which the young should be exposed for a certain length of time.

The Rector never sold out to any one school of thought in this connection. Sometimes he was sure education ought to be connected with discipline; sometimes he thought well of science, but more often not; and as the world changed he changed too.

This capacity to change was referred to by his admirers as "growing." His detractors noted the changes but considered them the irrational results of outside stimuli, the unconscious response of intellectual inertia to current pressures. The conclusions of any particular person in this respect are observed to be heavily influenced by his own investment of time and effort in any particular department of education. When one has labored long years at Latin and Greek one is scornful of the educational value of engineering. And anyone who has put years of work on the study of chemistry is apt to prescribe that subject positively as the way to the good life—although chemists make a rather comic noise in the ears of "educated persons."

When the Rector supported the thesis of the advocates of science they considered him intelligent; when he opposed the emphasis on science the scientists thought him a mossback. As an actual fact, he was not profound; but he was alert and intelligent and completely devoid of any shame about changing his mind when he thought he was wrong. This was disconcerting. Indeed, it is hardly fair. He never spent any time or effort proving he was right yesterday; he simply went on to the next thing. He never tried to get even with anybody or bore any grudge. Thus he saved so much time that life appeared leisurely.

II

The Rector had a great talent for firing incompetents. He did not fire boys often; he worked over them. But he was entirely aware of the strong and weak points of the masters; and those who did not measure up to the requirements he eliminated. This kept the School from becoming a Home for Indigent Incompetents.

He did this himself. He hired the masters. He sat in their classes. He listened to their suggestions. When they returned from a trip to Boston he sat up and cross-examined them. He may have had great faith in human nature, but it was a kind of general, impersonal faith. He knew what he was working for, and there was nothing vague or half-hearted in his contact and control. He was just but not particularly sympathetic.

It was sometimes felt that a clergyman should have cultivated a more trustful nature which could be imposed on. Well—he didn't.

He was not trustful, but he was completely reliable. When he was on duty he was always the same—always. He always first appeared before the School at Chapel in the morning, when he wore the usual priest's robes.

After Chapel the boys went at once to the schoolroom at the School House—all the boys. Every desk was occupied. A master stood at the desk and surveyed the assemblage. He rang the bell and there was silence.

And then the Rector would come in. He never hurried. He never sauntered. He always looked the School right in the eye as though he were looking for trouble. The quick cadence of his step was always exactly the same. His black shoes were polished. His blue suit, starched collar, white bow-tie, also starched, were always exactly and precisely as expected.

He mounted the steps to the dais. He took the framed schedule of events from the master. He turned slightly to the right. "First Form—History. . . . Second Form—Latin. . . ." Under his eye the School filed out to the first recitation of the day.

Four hours later he dismissed the School from the same platform. He did it— no one else. He read the detention, sent out the mail, and made what announcements were in order.

At dinner the School stood at their places while he asked a blessing. The blessing never varied. It was short and impersonal.

His next official appearance was at supper. No matter what he had been doing during the afternoon, at supper he was back in the blue suit, white starched tie, and black shoes. He asked the blessing. The boys went from the dining room to the schoolroom, and he conducted evening prayers. He stood at the desk and read from the New Testament—always. Then he knelt down on the floor and read some familiar prayers. When prayers were concluded he went out in the hall; and Brooks House filed by and said "Good-night, sir"; and to each he said, "Good-night, my boy," and shook his hand.

That was the system. So far as a casual observer could see, that was all there was to it. The experts came and talked about Freud and Jung and looked for hidden significances, and neurotic parents moaned and chattered; but nothing was ever done to change it.

Long, long afterward, boys could recall the tones of his voice as he read the prayers: "Watch over our School as its years increase . . . until we come to thine everlasting kingdom."

He taught the First Form Latin. The boys learned no Latin to speak of and picked up no interesting information on the side. He was not unkind, but the children were ill at ease. The class never seemed to get going. There were no interludes, no nonsense—not even explosions. Whenever the Latin suspended for an instant there was a kind of Peter Parley talk which bored the boys.

The contrast between this and the Greek classes conducted by Amory Gardner was stupefying. Mr. Gardner did not actually juggle balls and Indian clubs, but only because it did not occur to him or any of the boys. He did not actually cut himself with clamshells, because he had no clams handy; but he would leap up in the air, and beat his breast, and tear his hair, and faint with fervor. And, withal, a lot of boys learned a lot of Greek; while the gossip they picked up about Sanskrit, Egypt, the zoetrope or wheel-of-life, Max Müller, Grimm's Law, and the private lives of the denizens of Mt. Olympus was wholly incredible.

Amory Gardner was always wanting to address the School, and the Rector was forever thwarting this ambition. The Rector was right.

Besides this Latin class, Mr. Peabody undertook the instruction of the Fifth and Sixth Form in Sacred Studies. The origin of the ensuing difficulties is obscure. From time to time some tough-minded intellectuals turned up among the boys; but the Rector knew what he was talking about—in the beginning at any rate—and no confusion ought to have occurred.

But confusion there was. Somehow the subject would get turned round; and it seemed as if the class were enamored of Mohammed and on the verge of embracing Islam. And this of course was quite all right if only these exuberant explorers were open-minded enough to see, before the end of the hour, that Christianity was best after all. But sometimes it was just touch and go whether they could be brought back into the fold and the gate safely shut before the clock struck. It was nervous work. Buddha was disposed of without difficulty. Apparently Nirvana excited no interest, and Gautama no converts. But when Zoroaster came along there were ten short minutes spent on him; and for the other fifty minutes the faithful St. Bernard dogs were searching the Alps for the yodeling Parsees straying far from the company compound.

Often it seemed as though there were something almost diabolical in the way the wrong side was put on the defense. The spectacle made some boys nervous, and the stupider a boy was the more embarrassed he became. But there were volatile devils who enjoyed it and the range of whose speculations never failed to exceed all reasonable bounds.

III

Chapel came every morning in the form of morning prayers, a hymn, and a psalm. One became familiar with a lot of psalms, and with Cranmer's Prayer Book. On Sunday there were services morning and evening. In the evening the hot tears coursed down the cheeks of the little new boys during the Nunc Dimittis—but the others never noticed it, having been through it themselves. At the morning service the Rector would alternate with Mr. Billings in preaching the sermon. Both of them preached without dramatics in the strict New England tradition.

The importance of sermons is underestimated. At an evening service in the Town Hall at Groton, in May one year, Dr. Rainsford made some remarks about the *Origin of Species* which resulted in at least thirty boys reading that book; and it was a topic of discussion for weeks.

The sermons of Mr. Billings were excellent. The Rector's sermons were stuffy. For some reason the boys did not seem to believe them. Certain phrases recurred continually: "The dyer's hand is subdued to what it is dipped in. . . . Sanctify yourselves for their sakes." . . . The boys wanted to live dangerously and see life. The Rector wanted them to be pure in heart and to keep unspotted from the world. These objectives are not inconsistent; but you cannot capture the imagination of boys by talking of goodness or self-sacrifice or strong silent heroism. What the beggars wanted was to excite the admiration and astonishment of the other monkeys: in short, just what everyone wants to-day, and always has wanted since Cheops built the pyramid.

After St. George killed the dragon he was very popular; and it is obviously up to the proprietor of a large stable of boys to provide dragons right along. Now there was something phony about Mr. Peabody's dragons. Instead of getting into some old clothes, and sneaking up on the dragon, and grabbing him by the neck, and sinking your teeth in his jugular vein, while he roared and writhed and breathed out clouds of smoke—but you hung on: it wasn't like that. . . . In the first place, you had to go in training;

and then when the dragon was brought round it appeared you were to *talk* him to death, or set him a good example, or something: more like St. Georgianna than St. George.

It was a continuous puzzlement what kind of a man the Rector really was. The way he walked was incompatible with the way he talked; and the boys believed their eyes rather than their ears. He was humble with the cortex maximums—by an effort of will—and he was "liberal" the same way. He was determined to be liberal—if it killed him. And so of course he was not really liberal; he was only determined, like the man who is honest because honesty is the best policy: such a man is not honest; he is politic.

It was his true essence which he communicated to the boys. They learned determination, to know cricket from noncricket, to be unafraid; and these attributes carried some to honor and glory, and some to infamy and disgrace. Lord Rosebery is reported to have said as a young man that he had three ambitions: to marry an heiress, to own a Derby winner, and to be Prime Minister. He achieved all three, but he was not generally admired. It was felt that he paid too high a price.

Living is complicated. Exhortation is useless. Boys scorn precepts, but they will imitate heroes.

The selection of heroes to introduce to the attention of boys is an important matter. Socrates, Jesus, Servetus, Bruno, Galileo, Cromwell, John Hampden, George Washington were all lawbreakers. Most of them were tried and executed according to the law of their time.

Prohibition came along. It proved completely unenforceable. Practically all the graduates of the School became criminals. Admittedly the noble experiment operated to breed corruption, to teach girls to drink gin, to flout the law, to create disorder, and to produce a host of ills. When one consulted solemnly with oneself it was evident that, measured by any frame of reference that made sense, the situation demanded resistance as clearly as the imposition of Ship Money Taxes by Charles I. To comply was to co-operate with tyranny.

The graduates, from the first, saw this clearly and saw it whole, and contributed steadily to the breakdown of enforcement. The Rector went through a slow mutation. He first fell under the influence of Mr. Horace Taft, who persuaded him that to be a criminal was the worst thing that could happen to his boys; and so he started out to urge compliance.

Then someone called him the Vicar of Bray and said he had sold out his real convictions for a mess of pottage called "law and order." All the criminal graduates came up to the School, and for the first time in their lives felt morally superior. The biographies of the great, mentioned above, were pointed out to him. The worst of it was everyone was kind and solicitous about it; and the amount of interest taken in the New Testament was prodigious. Even the stockbrokers were reading it.

This was a wonderful and chastening experience. For once a moral question got so complicated that it was not instantly apparent what the proper course was. And though many a graduate had an attack of the dry grins on observing the Rector's predicament, not one had any thought that he was cowardly or taking the easy path. And when the Cromwellians finally won they admired him for sticking it out all by himself: and they knew he never did really think any less of them even if they were criminals.

IV

The Rector complained a good deal about the vacations—especially the short vacations at Christmas and Easter. He said the younger boys came back infected with various contagious maladies, and the older boys lost from five to fifteen pounds in weight, and were returned exceedingly demoralized. Said they spent their time at the theater, and later discussed, not the merits of character portrayal, nor the problems presented, but "the beauty of actresses."

He just had not thought this out. Any boy of seventeen who was more interested in the technique of drama than in feminine pulchritude would have been an object of suspicion to the Rector at the very first contact. But he was right in complaining about the vacations. They were too violent. The boys reacted from the ascetic, cloistered existence at Groton like sailors getting shore liberty; and though the damage was not permanent it was unnecessary and exasperating.

The role of the parents was difficult. If they were rich they took their boys to Jekyll Island, and thus supplied a sterilized playground from which there was no escape. But if they had to live in New York or Boston the boys ran themselves ragged. The Rector exercised a kind of remote control which operated to involve the parents in collusive and clandestine breaches of unenforceable edicts. The problem continued to be a worry for many years; but the attempted control became less, and more responsibility was left to the parents. No satisfactory solution was ever evolved. The young continue to be interested in actresses.

V

When one reads *Tom Brown's School Days* one does not get the impression that Dr. Arnold had any noticeable sense of humor. Perhaps the best people did not have one in those days. *Punch* was started in 1841; and a good deal of Aristophanes is more modern than those early copies.

What went on around the Rector was not funny. Life was real and life was earnest. It was often gay and cheerful and friendly; but not funny.

All the same, some wonderful things happened. First Amory Gardner built the Chapel. Then he built the Pleasure Dome. A visiting fireman, observing Mr. Gardner in a bath wrapper drinking whiskey after a game of squash, approached him curiously. Thereupon Gardner rose and dropped him an eleborate curtsy. The visitor (whose collar buttoned in the back) concluded he was in the presence of extreme depravity—in which delusion he was of course encouraged by a couple of irresponsible graduates—and was going to tell the Rector about it. He had to be personally escorted to Ayer, and sent home to grow up.

The Rector's conception of what was funny was Burnand's *Happy Thoughts*. This book was published in 1871, having previously come out piecemeal in *Punch*. It *is* funny too—if you have plenty of time. He used to read it aloud when he and Mrs. Peabody went on picnics with the Fifth Form in the springtime.

He was born in 1857; and the decade from 1870 to 1880 he spent in England being subjected to formal education. If anyone will look through the bound volumes of *Punch* for those ten years a great light will break on him. For there are all the jokes, the preoccupation with playing fields, the impatience with vulgarity, the social dilemmas of the well-endowed dowagers, the total ignorance of life on any other plane, the complete confidence in the morality of property, the feminine women, the protective and possessive men, the swells and the bounders and the snobs—in short, there is portrayed the benign complacency of a ruling class which had no regrets for the past and no fears for the future. The remarkable thing is not that, brought up in this society, the Rector was inscrutable and different from home-grown grass-root Americans, but that when he finally came back to Boston he was endurable at all. He was not only endurable; he was very popular. He was also indestructible.

He counted himself a clergyman. He had loyal labor-union ties with clergymen. He was always helping worthless ones. But many people were more impressed with his executive ability. Julius A. Atwood, Bishop of Arizona, a lifelong intimate of the Rector's (he used to preach sermons at School; he was bald as a billiard ball, and was known by the boys as "the Mexican Hairless") not only insisted that Mr. Peabody was a great executive, but said he would have made a wonderful banker: that the way he got money for the School was little short of miraculous. Others said he was a great leader, a teacher, a noble character, a guide, philosopher, and friend. They agreed only on one point: he did not remotely resemble a clergyman. He was something like Coke of Norfolk.

VI

Sophisticated persons know that it is not enough to be right. In this world it is necessary to be successful also. This is often resented by closet theorists—especially women—but wise men accept the universe and get on with their knitting. Of all this the Rector was fully aware. He never formulated it because he was essentially inarticulate; and what he knew did not find expression in words. But the boys were indoctrinated with this philosophy; and when they grew up they wasted no time feeling sorry for themselves or weeping over past mistakes.

This attitude is conducive to an urgency which tended to push boys a little farther along the road to success than they would have got under their own steam. Unfortunately it did not induce any increased discrimination in the selection of occupations, and the graduates took to finance as eagerly as to medicine.

The Rector saw this very clearly; but his only weapon of opposition was exhortation. He urged the boys to go into the professions and keep away from Wall Street. He lectured on vocations in Sacred Studies: and they asked him how an Army Officer could possibly send his son to Groton. He had not thought of it. His

whole School project required a large income for its customers.
When he urged the boys to be true to themselves and drop out of
their parents' income class, they simply did not hear him. They
were going to make money enough to be able to send their sons to
Groton. That was the first and great commandment.

This business of money and vocations was fantastic, and the
Rector got no help on it. Everybody from Jacob Riis to Booker
Washington undertook to give talks to the boys and advise them.
In the very early years of the century Gifford Pinchot, who was
then a forester, came up to lecture on forestry. The lecture is long
forgotten; but, at its close, he looked at the boys meaningly, almost
menacingly, and said: "Fortunate is the man so rich he does not
have to work; but twice fortunate is the rich man who works hard
though he does not have to."

He might have saved his breath. When the annual product grew
up, rich and poor alike fell to the task of making money and getting
power with a fury which astounded their classmates in college.

T. R. came up when he was President, and he too made a few
remarks. He urged the boys not to take champagne or butlers with
them on camping trips in the Adirondacks—honestly, that is
what he said. It sounded awfully *pukka* at the time; but long afterward many wondered what it was all about.

While the exhortations were complete duds, the civilizing influences organized by the Rector were at work all the time. If a
boy was oversensitive or spastic or hysterical the School was,
certainly during some periods, a cruel place; for neither wealth
nor prominence availed to buy peace. But for the average youngster
there were interludes which almost seemed a link with the great
world. There was "parlor night" twice a week in Mrs. Peabody's
house, which was always polite and often amusing; and Mrs.
Peabody always remembered a boy's first name—which restored
morale, somehow. Another morale-tonic was the requirement that
shirts be changed for supper and also shoes. And there were
"sing-songs" in the wintertime and debates and the choir and the
play—in short, various arenas where excellence did not depend
on physique or seniority; and these were all to the good.

VII

Why should the cat lying in the sunshine bother its head about
astrophysics? And why should one try to analyze a benign influ-

ence, and label it "Victorian," or "Neo-Anglican," or "Muscular Christianity"? To classify the Rector does not contribute to any better understanding of him. All one can do is to tell what was visible, and let each appraiser put it together as he sees it.

That he was inarticulate was evident. That he probably was quite as sensitive as anybody normally is, was not so evident. He was exceedingly polite, but there is no doubt he got very angry on occasion. In being polite he was not just suave—he was friendly and frank and controlled.

He forgave a lot of mean things that were done to him—even some outrageous ones—and thereby disarmed his enemies. And this was not merely a pose. He really did forgive them. This was one of the secrets of his indestructibility.

He had little conception of the strains men are subjected to in the modern world; and he used to infuriate fathers of sinful sons by summoning them to come to School and confer about their brats. At the conference it usually appeared that the son was white as snow compared with the father at the same age. This unawareness of the world's standards was the principal—perhaps only—clergy-man-attribute which he had. He said, himself, that his greatest regret was his failure to inculcate a livelier moral sense in boys; but he was up against the whole world. After all, morals are customs; but he thought they were absolutes. If he had been attacked by a thug he would have observed the Marquis of Queensberry rules.

His real occupation at the School was the enforcement of civilization. The boys got up early and went to bed tired. There was a first-class library, and there were educated men on the faculty. These were the ingredients; and he kept them in balance. He was just, according to his lights, and he was consistent; and he dealt out rewards and punishments without hesitation or misgivings. On the whole, he was rather more reliable on punishment than on rewards. He never disappointed the School by overlooking infractions of decorum or virtue. He made it quite plain to boys that each must live his own life—that no one else could do this for him —and he was unsympathetic when any of them felt sorry for themselves.

He was the *pater familias*, and the boys instinctively trusted him even when they criticized him. And he just walked back and forth in the cool of the day.

HONOR OUR TEACHERS

by Margery Wilson

WE NEED INSPIRED, DEDICATED TEACHERS. WE NEED TO ENCOURAGE the good ones we have. We need to make the teaching field attractive to fine people with fine talents. The first and most important step is to raise the prestige of the profession. Other advantages would follow more easily.

Though more money and good surroundings are fine assets, they are not the primary, deciding factor in attracting or holding superior teachers. Besides, these points must be left to those in charge of them. *But there is an important job for you and me.*

It has been proved that the deepest yearning of the human heart is for recognition, for honor! And in this we have failed our teachers.

We, you and I, have let the teaching profession slide downward in prestige. A traveling teacher is overjoyed if no one guesses her to be a teacher! The "schoolma'am" of comic-valentine smear is the mental picture impressed in the national mind. *Teaching is at its lowest ebb in our country.* Intentional and unintentional enemies have made it so. You and I can raise it by *honoring our teachers.* Everybody can help.

[60]

About a hundred years ago in Germany, the same sad state existed—and *one* man changed it. He went to his emperor and explained his plan for honoring professors and all teachers of both sexes. In a short time respect had been so built up for *Herr Professor* that his rank was next to royalty! And German education went rapidly forward to top rank.

We must *honor our teachers*—and *quickly*. We do not need to wait for funds, or official approval. There is no red tape involved. We need but to touch an already ripe public opinion . . .

★ *It is a great tribute to an artist to say that he plays Beethoven or Bach, and puts nothing between them and his audience. But in so doing he becomes one with both the composer and the listener. In the listener's memory he anonymously shares the composer's immortality. The teacher, too, is remembered who is thus forgotten. He lives in what has happened in the minds of his students, and in what they remember of things infinitely greater than themselves or than himself.*

IRWIN EDMAN

TEACHER—
ANNE SULLIVAN MACY

by Helen Keller

IT WAS A BRIGHT, CLEAR SPARK FROM TEACHER'S SOUL THAT BEAT back the sooty flames of thwarted desire and temper in little Helen's no-world. That spark was the word "water." Compassion in the old sense does not describe the springs of Teacher's motives. Her disbelief in nature as an unfailing friend of humanity lay back of her efforts to liberate Helen—"Phantom" I prefer to call the little being governed only by animal impulses, and not often those of a docile beast. Teacher's fight against her own blindness began in her childhood, and the partial restoration of her sight while she was in school at Perkins Institution for the Blind in Boston had not ended her struggle to maintain her ascendancy over nature. That struggle lasted as long as her earth-life.

Secretly or openly she always resented what seemed to her the purposeless evils that had marred her sight and laid waste the health, sanity, and happiness of millions throughout the world. How ruthless then was her assault upon the blindness, deafness, and muteness that bound her little pupil in a triple dungeon of thwarted instincts. Boldly she resolved to put herself in the place of nature and topple it from its aimless supremacy over Helen by substituting love and inventive thought for the unconscious cruelty of the child's fate.

This is a period in Teacher's life which distresses me to remember. Naturally I wish that after the intoxicating tide of delight that swept over her when the operations made it possible for her to read with her eyes, she might have found a child responsive to her sympathetic touch. But, alas! Phantom had no sense of "natural" bonds with humanity. All the sweetness of childhood created by friendly voices and the light of smiling faces was dormant in her. She did not understand obedience or appreciate kindness. I remember her as plump, strong, reckless, and unafraid. She refused to be led, and had to be carried by force upstairs when she received her first lesson. Another time her table manners required correction. Phantom was in the habit of picking food out of her own plate and the plates of others with her fingers. Annie Sullivan would not put up with such behavior, and a fight followed during which the family left the room. Phantom acted like a demon, kicking, screaming, pinching her would-be deliverer and almost throwing her out of her chair, but Annie succeeded in compelling her to eat with a spoon and keep her hands out of the plate. The Phantom threw her napkin on the floor, and after an hour's battle Annie made her pick it up and fold it. One morning Phantom would not sit down to learn words which meant nothing to her, and kicked over the table. When Annie put the table back in its place and insisted on continuing the lesson, Phantom's fist flew like lightning and knocked out two of Annie's teeth.

A sorrier situation never confronted a young woman on fire with a noble purpose. Phantom's parents were apt to interfere whenever attempts were made to discipline her. For this reason Annie won their consent to get her away to a quiet place, and, at their suggestion, took the child to a vine-covered annex near the homestead, Ivy Green. The furniture was changed so that Phantom would not recognize it—my smell memory too is different—and it was agreed that the family would come to them every day, without letting Helen know of their visits. From Teacher's later testimony I know that the two were, so to speak, caged in the annex, and I marvel that Annie dared to stay alone with such a menace to her personal safety.

Already I have referred to several fights between Annie and Phantom, not because I have any coherent or detailed remembrance of them, but because they indicate the grueling nature of the work Teacher had undertaken. In *The Story of My Life*, which I wrote with the carelessness of a happy, positive young girl, I

failed to stress sufficiently the obstacles and hardships which confronted Teacher—and there are other defects in the book which
my mature sense of her sacrifice will not permit to go uncorrected.

In my memory of the annex I am conscious of a Phantom lost
in what seemed to her new surroundings. I perceive sudden jerks,
pulls, and blows not dealt by Annie but by Phantom herself trying
to escape restraining arms. How like a wild colt she was, plunging
and kicking! Certainly it was a sturdy Phantom who belabored her
supposed enemy. There comes back to me a scuffle round and
round an object that my touch recollections represent as a bed,
and a firm gesture of Annie to make her lie down or get up and
dress.

Phantom had no sense of time, and it was years before she
learned of the many exhausting hours which Annie spent trying to
bring her under control without breaking her spirit. Even that
was only partly accomplished when the two went home. Then
Phantom grew angry over Annie's repeated attempts to impress
upon her the differences between "water" and "mug." Tactually
I recall quick footsteps in the room, a hand—my mother's—seizing
Phantom and dragging her away for a sound spanking. After that
Phantom began to improve, but still she lacked the normal child's
love of praise. She was not aware that she had been punished
because she did not distinguish between right and wrong. Her
body was growing, but her mind was chained in darkness as the
spirit of fire within the flint. But at last, on April 5, 1880, almost
exactly a month after her arrival in Tuscumbia, Annie reached
Phantom's consciousness with the word "water." This happened
at the well-house. Phantom had a mug in her hand and while she
held it under the spout Annie pumped water into it, and as it
gushed over the hand that held the mug she kept spelling w-a-t-e-r
into the other hand. Suddenly Phantom understood the meaning of
the word, and her mind began to flutter tiny wings of flame.
Caught up in the first joy she had felt since her illness, she reached
out eagerly to Annie's ever-ready hand, begging for new words
to identify whatever objects she touched. Spark after spark of
meaning flew through her mind until her heart was warmed and
affection was born. From the well-house there walked two enraptured beings calling each other "Helen" and "Teacher." Surely
such moments of delight contain a fuller life than an eternity
of darkness . . .

SCULPTURE

Anonymous

I TOOK A PIECE OF PLASTIC CLAY
And idly fashioned it one day.
And as my fingers pressed it, still
It moved and yielded to my will.

I came again when days were past:
The bit of clay was hard at last.
The form I gave it still it bore,
And I could fashion it no more!

I took a piece of living clay,
And gently pressed it day by day,
And moulded with my power and art
A young child's soft and yielding heart.

I came again when years had gone:
It was a man I looked upon.
He still that early impress bore,
And I could fashion it no more!

CHARLES

by Shirley Jackson

THE DAY LAURIE STARTED KINDERGARTEN HE RENOUNCED CORDUROY overalls with bibs and began wearing blue jeans with a belt; I watched him go off the first morning with the older girl next door, seeing clearly that an era of my life was ended, my sweet-voiced nursery-school tot replaced by a long-trousered, swaggering character who forgot to stop at the corner and wave goodbye to me.

He came home the same way, the front door slamming open, his cap on the floor, and the voice suddenly become raucous shouting, "Isn't anybody *here?*"

At lunch he spoke insolently to his father, spilled Jannie's milk and remarked that his teacher said that we were not to take the name of the Lord in vain.

"How *was* school today?" I asked, elaborately casual.

"All right," he said.

"Did you learn anything?" his father asked.

Laurie regarded his father coldly. "I didn't learn nothing," he said.

"Anything," I said. "Didn't learn anything."

"The teacher spanked a boy, though," Laurie said, addressing his bread and butter. "For being fresh," he added with his mouth full.

"What did he do?" I asked. "Who was it?"

Laurie thought. "It was Charles," he said. "He was fresh. The teacher spanked him and made him stand in a corner. He was awfully fresh."

"What did he do?" I asked again, but Laurie slid off his chair, took a cookie, and left, while his father was still saying "See here, young man."

The next day Laurie remarked at lunch, as soon as he sat down, "Well, Charles was bad again today." He grinned enormously and said, "Today Charles hit the teacher."

"Good heavens," I said, mindful of the Lord's name, "I suppose he got spanked again?"

"He sure did," Laurie said. "Look up," he said to his father.

"What?" his father said, looking up.

"Look down," Laurie said. "Look at my thumb. Gee, you're dumb." He began to laugh insanely.

"Why did Charles hit the teacher?" I asked quickly.

"Because she tried to make him color with red crayons," Laurie said. "Charles wanted to color with green crayons so he hit the teacher and she spanked him and said nobody play with Charles but everybody did."

The third day—it was Wednesday of the first week—Charles bounced a seesaw onto the head of a little girl and made her bleed and the teacher made him stay inside all during recess. Thursday Charles had to stand in a corner during storytime because he kept pounding his feet on the floor. Friday Charles was deprived of blackboard privileges because he threw chalk.

On Saturday I remarked to my husband, "Do you think kindergarten is too unsettling for Laurie? All this toughness and bad grammar, and this Charles boy sounds like a bad influence."

"It'll be all right," my husband said reasurringly. "Bound to be people like Charles in the world. Might as well meet them now as later."

On Monday Laurie came home late, full of news. "Charles," he shouted as he came up the hill; I was waiting anxiously on the front steps, "Charles," Laurie yelled all the way up the hill, "Charles was bad again."

"Come right in," I said, as soon as he came close enough. "Lunch is waiting."

"You know what Charles did?" he demanded, following me through the door. "Charles yelled so in school they sent a boy in from first grade to tell the teacher she had to make Charles keep quiet, and so Charles had to stay after school. And so all the children stayed to watch him."

"What did he do?" I asked.

"He just sat there," Laurie said, climbing into his chair at the table. "Hi Pop, y'old dust mop."

"Charles had to stay after school today," I told my husband. "Everyone stayed with him."

"What does this Charles look like?" my husband asked Laurie. "What's his other name?"

"He's bigger than me," Laurie said. "And he doesn't have any rubbers and he doesn't ever wear a jacket."

Monday night was the first Parent-Teachers meeting, and only the fact that Jannie had a cold kept me from going; I wanted passionately to meet Charles' mother. On Tuesday Laurie remarked suddenly, "Our teacher had a friend come see her in school today."

"Charles' mother?" my husband and I asked simultaneously.

"Naaah," Laurie said scornfully. "It was a man who came and made us do exercises. Look." He climbed down from his chair and squatted down and touched his toes. "Like this," he said. He got solemnly back into his chair and said, picking up his fork, "Charles didn't even *do* exercises."

"That's fine," I said heartily. "Didn't Charles want to do exercises?"

"Naaah," Laurie said. "Charles was so fresh to the teacher's friend he wasn't *let* do exercises."

"Fresh again?" I said.

"He kicked the teacher's friend," Laurie said. "The teacher's friend told Charles to touch his toes like I just did and Charles kicked him."

"What are they going to do about Charles, do you suppose?" Laurie's father asked him.

Laurie shrugged elaborately. "Throw him out of school, I guess," he said.

Wednesday and Thursday were routine; Charles yelled during story hour and hit a boy in the stomach and made him cry. On Friday Charles stayed after school again and so did all the other children.

With the third week of kindergarten Charles was an institution in our family; Jannie was being a Charles when she cried all afternoon; Laurie did a Charles when he filled his wagon full of mud and pulled it through the kitchen; even my husband, when he caught his elbow in the telephone cord and pulled telephone, ash tray, and a bowl of flowers off the table, said, after the first minute, "Looks like Charles."

During the third and fourth weeks there seemed to be a reformation in Charles; Laurie reported at lunch on Thursday of the third week, "Charles was so good today the teacher gave him an apple."

"What?" I said, and my husband added warily, "You mean Charles?"

"Charles," Laurie said. "He gave the crayons around and he picked up the books afterward and the teacher said he was her helper."

"What happened?" I asked incredulously.

"He was her helper, that's all," Laurie said, and shrugged.

"Can this be true, about Charles?" I asked my husband that night. "Can something like this happen?"

"Wait and see," my husband said cynically. "When you've got a Charles to deal with, this may mean he's only plotting."

He seemed to be wrong. For over a week Charles was the teacher's helper; each day he handed things out and he picked things up; no one had to stay after school.

"The P.-T.A. meeting's next week again," I told my husband one evening. "I'm going to find Charles' mother there."

"Ask her what happened to Charles," my husband said. "I'd like to know."

"I'd like to know myself," I said.

On Friday of that week things were back to normal. "You know what Charles did today?" Laurie demanded at the lunch table, in a voice slightly awed. "He told a little girl to say a word and she said it and the teacher washed her mouth out with soap and Charles laughed."

"What word?" his father asked unwisely, and Laurie said, "I'll have to whisper it to you, it's so bad." He got down off his chair and went around to his father. His father bent his head down and Laurie whispered joyfully. His father's eyes widened.

"Did Charles tell the little girl to say *that*?" he asked respectfully.

"She said it *twice*," Laurie said. "Charles told her to say it *twice*."

"What happened to Charles?" my husband asked.

"Nothing," Laurie said. "He was handing out the crayons."

Monday morning Charles abandoned the little girl and said the evil word himself three or four times, getting his mouth washed out with soap each time. He also threw chalk.

My husband came to the door with me that evening as I set out for the P.-T.A. meeting. "Invite her over for a cup of tea after the meeting," he said. "I want to get a look at her."

"If only she's there," I said prayerfully.

"She'll be there," my husband said. "I don't see how they could hold a P.-T.A. meeting without Charles' mother."

At the meeting I sat restlessly, scanning each comfortable matronly face, trying to determine which one hid the secret of Charles. None of them looked to me haggard enough. No one stood up in the meeting and apologized for the way her son had been acting. No one mentioned Charles.

After the meeting I identified and sought out Laurie's kindergarten teacher. She had a plate with a cup of tea and a piece of chocolate cake; I had a plate with a cup of tea and a piece of marshmallow cake. We maneuvered up to one another cautiously and smiled.

"I've been anxious to meet you," I said. "I'm Laurie's mother."

"We're all so interested in Laurie," she said.

"Well, he certainly likes kindergarten," I said. "He talks about it all the time."

"We had a little trouble adjusting, the first week or so," she said primly, "but now he's a fine little helper. With lapses, of course."

"Laurie usually adjusts very quickly," I said. "I suppose this time it's Charles' influence."

"Charles?"

"Yes," I said, laughing, "you must have your hands full in that kindergarten, with Charles."

"Charles?" she said. "We don't have any Charles in the kindergarten."

WINDOWS FOR THE CROWN PRINCE

by Elizabeth Gray Vining

IN THE SPRING OF 1946 AN AMERICAN EDUCATION MISSION COMPOSED of twenty-seven distinguished educators headed by Dr. George D. Stoddard visited Japan to survey the educational system and make suggestions for its reform. In the course of a reception at the Imperial Palace, the Emperor suddenly turned to Dr. Stoddard and asked him if he could get an American tutor for his son, the Crown Prince.

It has often been assumed that the American tutor was imposed by the Occupation. Nothing could be further from the fact. The idea proceeded from the Emperor himself; he made the proposal on his own initiative without even consulting the people in charge of the Crown Prince's education, and it was an unprecedented step for him to take. For a long time after my arrival in Japan I did not realize just how extraordinary it was for the Emporer, who traditionally accepted the decisions of the experts about his son without question and even without comment, to make himself a decision of this kind.

From *Windows For The Crown Prince*, copyright 1952 by Elizabeth Gray Vining; published by J. B. Lippincott Company. Reprinted by permission of the publishers.

The next day two or three Japanese gentlemen called on Dr. Stoddard at the Imperial Hotel to discuss the terms and arrangements for the American tutor. It was to be a woman, "a Christian but not a fanatic," and not an "old Japan hand," but one who came fresh to the country, without even a knowledge of the Japanese language, since she was to teach by the direct method entirely in English. Her age, they thought, should be about fifty, but Dr. Stoddard persuaded them that she might well be younger. She was to have a house, car, servants, secretary, and a salary of $2,000 a year, and the contract was to be made for one year, renewable by mutual consent.

Dr. Stoddard returned to the United States charged with the task of finding a "schoolmarm" for the Crown Prince. I read about it in the newspapers with interest. I thought that it might improve the lowly position of women in Japan if a woman were elevated to teaching the Crown Prince, not knowing that women had been given the vote in the spring of 1946, had flocked to the polls in great numbers and elected thirty-five women to the Diet. That I myself might be the tutor no more occurred to me than I might fly to the moon and back on Tuesday.

I was at that time working for the American Friends Service Committee, writing report, articles, and appeals. I am a Quaker, and every Quaker, I think, wants to work at some time for the Service Committee. Because its work is directed not only to the binding up of the wounds of war but to furthering the cause of peace through the healing of tensions and misunderstandings, I had chosen it as my war service to the country. Now the war was over and I was preparing to return to the ordinary work of my life, which was the writing of books for young people. I had a book blocked out and the summer planned.

One morning late in May Samuel Marble, now President of Wilmington College, Ohio, who was then organizing the Committee's relief project for Japan, came in to talk to me about an appeal we were preparing. After we had finished the business in hand he turned to me and said without preamble, "Would you consider having your name suggested as tutor to the Crown Prince of Japan?"

The idea was so extraordinary, so far from any plans I had ever made for myself, and I felt myself so inadequate and inappropriate, a quiet Philadelphia Quaker at the most elaborate and mysterious court in the world, that my instant reaction was to say no. Positively No.

"Wait and think it over, at least over the week-end," he urged.

That evening I told my sister about it as something so fantastic as to be almost amusing. The Highland Scottish element, which we both inherit but which is stronger in her than in me, was in the ascendant that night. Its forebodings, sometimes called second sight, though by no means dependable, are never to be quite ignored, and her swift realization of the seriousness of the proposal was very sobering to me.

In the end my answer was that if Friends thought I could be useful I could not refuse to have my name suggested but that I would not lift a finger to get the job. Clarence E. Pickett, then Executive Secretary of the American Friends Service Committee, wrote exactly that to Dr. Stoddard.

During the days that followed, my mind inevitably dwelt much on the question. The responsibility, the delicacy of the position, the demand on talents, abilities, and training which I felt I did not have, the giving up of my book, the separation from my sister, the difficulties of life in a land wholly unknown to me and one where I thought the bitter resentments of war and defeat would still be keen: all these considerations weighed on me so that I find written in my diary: "With all my heart I hope it doesn't come."

On the other hand, I wanted deeply to give myself to the cause of peace and reconciliation. That Japan had renounced war in her new constitution was to me immensely significant. Here perhaps was an opportunity to uphold the hands of those who were willing to risk greatly for peace, and to bring before the Emperor's son in his formative years the ideals of liberty and justice and good will upon which peace must be based if it is to endure. So it was that after a week I could write in my diary: "I reach the point of leaving it in God's hands."

Two weeks after the subject had first been broached, I went to Albany for an interview at Dr. Stoddard's request. He was then finishing his work as New York State Superintendent of Education preparatory to assuming the presidency of the University of Illinois.

We talked for most of an afternoon, Dr. Stoddard asking me questions and answering those I asked him. He was in himself very reassuring, a man of stature, moral and intellectual as well as

physical, calm, gentle, wise. He told me of the experiences of the
Education Mission, of the coöperation which they received from
the Japanese, the friendliness, the lack of bitterness, the eagerness
for help in building a new Japan. It was the first time I had heard
from one who actually had been there the report that often sur-
prises and puzzles as well as impresses Americans. War and the
militarists were thoroughly discredited; the Japanese were turning
toward democracy, were trying to understand and practise it.
It was an extraordinary opportunity to teach the son of the
Emperor . . .

That October day when I entered the Palace for the first time,
there were four Allied sentries, two American and two British.
When our passes had been inspected we went on to the Japanese
policemen beyond the Moat in the arch of the great tile-roofed
gate. They were expecting us and waved us through.

We came at once to a large modern building, once white, now
darkened and streaked by the protective paint with which all
light buildings had been covered during the war to make them
less visible from the air. In front of it was a little pond, surrounded
by beautiful dwarf pines. This was the Imperial Household Building, the administration center for what had been formerly one of
the most important divisions of the government. The Imperial
Household employees had numbered about seven thousand, the
Minister had had a Cabinet post. Now the employees were reduced
to less than one thousand, and the Minister had become the
Emperor's Grand Steward.

We swept under a porte-cochère and got out of the car, to be
greeted by gentlemen waiting on the steps, an official in the Department of Ceremonies, the Secretary of the Grand Steward, and
others.

Up two flights of marble steps we went, to the office of the
Grand Steward, which looked over the pond and the gate, the
Moat and the outer gardens, toward a line of tall office buildings in
the distance. I did not know till later that one of these buildings
was the headquarters of General MacArthur, nor did I hear till
very much later that the affectionate nickname for the General
in the Imperial Household was *Ohoribata*, Honorable Across the
Moat.

The Grand Steward at that time was Mr., formerly Viscount, Yoshitami Matsudaira. He was rather elderly and spare, scholarly-looking and courteous, a little nervous in his manner. He spoke excellent English, having studied at Oxford. The room seemed filled with people, many of whom were there no doubt to take a look at the Crown Prince's tutor.

After we had a cup of tea, the delicious green tea in handleless cups that accompanies any operation, important or trivial, in Japan, the contract was brought out. It was typed on white paper, beautifully lettered by hand on the cover, tied up with purple ribbon and sealed with the imperial sixteen-petaled chrysanthemum. It provided, besides the salary, "all necessary living expenses, including house rent and utilities, motor car, provisions, laundry, payment of employees (domestic servants and secretary) and traveling expenses in Japan," as well as travel from Japan at the expiration of the contract.

Though even in my first hasty reading of it I knew it was a generous contract, designed to provide in every way for my comfort and safety and to protect my interests, I did not realize until I had been there a long time how much more was given to me, the American tutor, than to the Japanese who served the Imperial Family or taught the imperial children in the schools. This is perhaps a good place to say two things. One, that in all my experience in Japan I was never aware of jealousy or resentment on the part of my Japanese colleagues who had less and worked more; and second, that in all their dealings in regard to the contract, financially and otherwise, I found the Japanese not merely prompt and scrupulous but generous as well . . .

Later that day I met Mrs. Tsuneo Matsudaira. No relation to the Grand Steward, she was the wife of the former Ambassador to Great Britain and to the United States and mother of the lovely Setsuko, who after her education at the Friends School in Washington, had returned to Japan to marry the Emperor's younger brother, Prince Chichibu. Mrs. Matsudaira, gray-haired, serene, humorous, and wise, truly deserves the title of "a great lady." She was to be of the greatest possible help and support to me, and I was to see her frequently. When I asked her for guidance in the intricacies of court etiquette and procedure, she said simply, "Just be yourself and don't worry," advice which proved not only reassuring but sound. It got me through. . . .

I saw the Crown Prince for the first time together with his father and mother. The occasion was without precedent.

It was a beautiful, mild October day, and I had been in Japan not quite forty-eight hours. Mr. Nagamitsu Asano, the round, genial secretary of the Peers' School who did so much to help me that first year, arrived to escort Tané Takahashi and me to the Palace. We left our house at two in order to be at the Imperial Household Building at two-thirty. About halfway there, Tané suddenly cried out in an anguished voice, "*Do shimasho!*" (What shall I do?—the first Japanese words I learned. The next one was *dozo*—please). The pass had been forgotten!

Back we went to get it, Tané and I abashed, Mr. Asano laughing merrily. Then he explained that we really didn't have to be there until two-fifty; he had made allowance for just such contingencies. So we reached the Palace in good time, and went as we had done the day before to the office of the Grand Steward.

I had brought from Philadelphia some chocolates for the imperial children, and I now produced them. They were taken away to be presented before the audience. While we waited I was introduced to Mrs. Tatsuo Takaki, who, with Mrs. Matsudaira, was to be a beloved friend and mentor. Mrs. Takaki had lived for many years in New York; where at least two of her children had been born. After her husband's death she had returned to Japan and for twenty years she had been a lady-in-waiting and interpreter to the Empress. A woman of quiet and compelling charm and great sweetness, she has made it her particular mission to bridge the gap between Americans and Japanese, and she had among the Occupation a host of admiring friends.

Presently Mrs. Takaki and an elderly, rather severe lady-in-waiting and I went to the audience chamber. As we walked down one long corridor after another, Mrs. Takaki explained that the big room formerly used had been destroyed during the war but that Their Majesties liked the smaller room better . . .

After a moment or two the door opened and we stood up. The Emperor, the Empress, and the Crown Prince came in. Mrs. Takaki presented me to each in turn. We all shook hands. Their Majesties said that they were glad that I had come and they had been looking forward to my arrival eagerly.

Now it was the Crown Prince's turn. I waited for the prepared speech. But Prince Akihito had a mind of his own. "Thank you for the candy," he said.

He was twelve years old then, a lovable-looking small boy, round-faced and solemn but with a flicker of humor in his eyes. He wore the dark blue uniform of all Japanese schoolboys, long trousers, a jacket high in the neck and hooked down the front under a line of braid. At the collar was the mark of his school, a small silver cherry blossom. Like all Japanese schoolboys, his head was shaven close to the scalp; his short black fur of hair was glistening and his skull was well shaped, without the bumps and hollows that make this haircut so unbecoming to many boys.

The Emperor waved his hand to indicate a chair to me and we all sat down.

My first impression of the Emperor was that he was a shy and sensitive man and a friendly one. The Empress was a beautiful woman with the rather long, aristocratic face seen in some of the old prints, though unlike them her face lights up with a most charming and infectious smile. She was not wearing the traditional kimono and *obi* (wide brocade sash) but the simpler court dress developed during the war. That day she wore one made of soft gray-green silk; it had a kimono top and a full long skirt, with a narrow belt tied at the waist. She had tiny satin slippers to match. Of a comfortable motherly figure, she still looked much younger than her forty-two or forty-three years.

The audience lasted half an hour, and its atmosphere was unstrained and natural. We chatted easily on a variety of subjects. Their Majesties speaking in Japanese and Mrs. Takaki translating so smoothly, so skillfully that it scarcely seemed to come through a third person. They inquired solicitously about my trip and the conditions of my house. Her Majesty regretted that it was furnished with "odds and ends," and I replied that the furniture was lovely and I thanked her for all that had been done for me.

I said that I had come to Japan with friendship in my heart and in hopes of making some small contribution to the cause of peace among nations; I spoke of the honor and privilege of teaching their son and of my determination to do my best for him. The Emperor replied politely that it was an honor for their son that an American lady of such knowledge and understanding should come to teach him.

The Emperor inquired after Dr. Stoddard and also after Esther Rhoads, of whose work with LARA he was informed. Both Their Majesties thanked me, as an American, for the food that had been sent to Japan by the United States government during the previous summer of severe food shortage. We spoke of the Emperor's trip to Europe as a young man and he regretted that circumstances had prevented his visiting the United States.

The Empress said she would be glad if I could teach the princesses not only English but other things as well, that they had had very little experience. I replied that I should like very much to have them come to my house and show them things that American girls enjoyed. Her Majesty said that was exactly what she wanted.

That day, October seventeenth, happened to be a holiday, the harvest festival. I asked the Crown Prince how they celebrated it at his school and he told me, in Japanese, that they had had a sports day, and described one of the games traditional in the Peers' School. Three boys form a horse and a fourth boy, perched on their shoulders, is the rider. Horse and rider then engage another horse and rider in combat, each rider trying to pull the other off his mount. I was interested that the Crown Prince was involved in this kind of rough and tumble and amused later when I heard that he had got thrown. A rather widely circulated account of the Crown Prince in an American magazine asserted that although he had playmates they were never allowed to defeat him in any game. This I found over and over to be untrue. He was often defeated and when he won he won fairly. He took both defeat and victory in good part, though like any other boy he preferred victory.

The audience was brought to a close by Their Majesties' saying that they hoped they would see me often. A great armful of pink and white cosmos was brought in and the Empress gave them to me, saying that she had grown and picked them herself. I expressed my thanks, we all shook hands, and the Imperial family withdrew.

Mrs. Matsudaira and Mr. Sumikura (a chamberlain and former secretary of Prince Konoye) both attended my first private lesson with the Crown Prince, sitting at the little table at one side of the room while the Prince and I sat at the big table in the center. That first day I took a volume of the *Book of Knowledge* and we looked at the pictures together and talked about them as far as the Prince's limited vocabulary would go, which was not far.

The theory of teaching English entirely in English is that the student, learning or guessing the new words without interpretation, comes to think of them in English, instead of thinking of them in his own language first and then translating. In the second place, if English is the only language used, then he must plunge in and use at as best he can. The trick is the teaching of new words in such a way that the pupil really understands them and the building up of a new vocabulary through explanations in terms of already familiar words.

It took time, a great many pictures, and considerable agility. Sometimes I drew pictures on the blackboard, often I made use of the *Golden Dictionary*, a simple picture dictionary, and sometimes I demonstrated a word by getting up and acting it.

One quality of the Crown Prince's that very soon became apparent under the stress of this kind of learning was his intellectual honesty. It would save time and often tiresome repetition to pretend to understand, for instance, the distinction between *bring* and *take* before one actually did, but the Crown Prince never took that short cut. Looking a little worried and puzzled, he would admit frankly that he did not understand, and we would go at the problem again from a different angle. Then suddenly his face would clear and a happy look spread over it, and I would know that he had it. If I labored the point any further, to make sure, he would raise his hand impatiently and say, "Yes, yes, yes," in a way so like my own father that I was flooded with reminiscent amusement.

The presence all that autumn and winter of Mrs. Matsudaira and a chamberlain hampered both of us. It makes one feel a little silly to wave one's arm in the air in a swimming motion or to demonstrate the difference between jumping and hopping before two serious, interested, dignified adult spectators, but I learned in time to forget them. The effect on the Crown Prince, I felt, was more serious. Before answering any question he looked hastily at the chamberlain, whether for reassurance or because he felt self-conscious about making mistakes in front of him I did not know. The fact that he was noticeably more relaxed in the presence of those chamberlains who did not speak English suggests that the latter explanation was the right one. But as I saw him oftener outside of lesson hours, I realized that he was turning in everything to the chamberlains for prompting. The simplest question he seemed unable to answer for himself without seeking their help. This dependence upon them seemed to me undesirable and I longed for him to have the experience of doing his work entirely on his own, of daring to make mistakes.

At the same time I realized that I was to him a very tall and possibly rather frightening stranger from America and that perhaps he needed the presence of the familiar attendant. I understood also that the chamberlains must wonder uneasily just what I was going to do to their adored Prince, and I was glad to have them see my methods and my subject matter.

After a month we had a lesson with only Mrs. Matudaira present, no chamberlain, and I find in my diary for that day: "The best lesson yet." As time went on, the chamberlains gradually ceased to attend the lessons and in April, 1947, for the first time Mrs. Matsudaira was not in the room. After that she attended the lessons only occasionally, in order to report to the Empress about the Prince's progress.

The great problem all the way through was to get reading material that would be simple enough English for the Crown Prince and yet mature enough to engage his interest. I prepared my lessons very carefully, trying to work in each time the words he already knew and to add new words and constructions in a logical way. As he would always answer questions to the best of his ability but never volunteered anything, either question or comment, I spent a good deal of time teaching him how to ask questions in English, and for a part of each hour he had to ask me questions of his own making.

I sought in every way to stimulate his desire to use English as a tool, to be so eager to say something that he would perforce put it into English since there was no other way to get it said. His chief interests at that time, I had learned, were fish, riding, and tennis, which he was just beginning to play.

On a visit to the International Cultural Association Library I had been given a pre-war picture book of Japanese fish, beautifully illustrated by Japanese artists and printed in full color with a simple text in Spanish. Fortunately my college Spanish was not too rusty, and so I translated the text into simple English, Tané typed it neatly and pasted it over the Spanish, and the Crown Prince and I discussed the life of fish, using the words that were useful also in other contexts: water, river, ocean, swim, live, fresh, salt, warm, cold, deep, shallow, and so on.

Another picture book which I rewrote was Jan and Zhenya Gay's *Shire Colt*. The beauty and integrity of those lithographs of the sturdy colt and its mother, the life of the Cotswold farm, and the universal quality of the colt's adventures in discovering an ever-widening world, make it appealing to any age, and the Prince seemed to enjoy it.

But my most successful venture during those early weeks was my invention of a tennis match played on paper and in English. I made a chart of a tennis court, and cut balls and rackets out of cardboard, and we played tennis in English, scoring, commenting on the game, and in the end walking to the net and shaking hands over it. The Prince had encountered the simple past tense before, but in the tennis match he was served the perfect tense with: You have won the game. I have lost the game. Who has won the game? Who has lost the game?

The lessons tended to follow a general pattern. We would have some free conversation. (*Free* is a technical term, for anything so slow, so labored, so stilted as those early questions and answers is not usually considered free. How are you today? Is your cold better? What day is today? Did you have a good time yesterday? Did you play tennis? Now you ask me some questions.) We would read and talk about what we read. We would do some simple exercises. The Prince always enjoyed the kind in which blanks were left in sentences to be filled in with a choice of words. We would have some dictation, some practice with new words. Sometime during each hour I found some reason for him to get up and walk about, to write on the blackboard or go to the window and look out and tell me what he saw, or some other excuse to ease the stiffness of sitting still so long.

After a while in order to stir up the passivity which tended to leave all decisions, all initiative, to others, I began to say, "What shall we do first, dictation, conversation, reading?" At first he would demur, "You say," but after being prodded, he would generally choose dictation, which he liked least.

People have asked me what I called him. *Denka*—Highness—was what the Japanese called him, both teachers and classmates. In his family and around the court, he was called *Togusama*, Honorable Eastern Prince, and by his father it was shortened to *Toguchan*, *chan* being the affectionate ending. Prince Akihito was the form considered suitable for foreigners, and that was what I called him, except in the lessons in school.

Before I went for the first time to meet my classes in the Gakushuin, I was asked if I wouldn't like to have a Japanese teacher sitting in the back of the room throughout my lessons to keep order. There had never been a woman teacher beyond the Primary School of Gakushuin before, and furthermore many students were interpreting this new "democrashy" to mean that they could do exactly as they liked, and the teachers were afraid that I would have trouble in controlling my classes. Remembering what fiends we were to the French and German conversation teachers when I was in school, I thought it quite probable that I might have difficulty, but I did not think that having a Japanese teacher as a policeman in the room was a satisfactory solution.

One of the most fertile sources of foreign-teacher-torture, I remembered, was derision in all its varied forms of the way in which they mangled our names in pronouncing them. So I thought that I would eliminate that hazard at any rate by giving all the boys English names. There were other reasons also for the decision. One was that in their English textbooks the names of the children were all Japanese—Taro, Jiro, Yoshiko, Fumiko—and I thought they ought to learn to pronounce the English names. Then too I wanted to establish during that one hour as much of the atmosphere of an American classroom as possible. In the third place I thought it would be a good experience for the Crown Prince for once in his life to be on exactly the same level as the other boys, with no title and no especial treatment at all.

Accordingly I made out a list of boys' names alphabetically arranged for each section, and I marched into Section A the first morning very calm outwardly but feeling a bit adventurous within.

The boys all stood up. "Good morning, boys," I said. "Good morning, sir," they replied with one voice. I laughed and they laughed. Then I told them that you said Sir to a man but you called a woman by her name. The boys sat down and looked very expectant, their black eyes shining.

"My name is Mrs. Vining," I said, and turned to the boy who sat at the first desk on the right-hand side. "What is your name?" He told me.

"That is your real name," I conceded, "but in this class your name is Adam."

He looked surprised, as well he might.

"Now," I announced, "I am going to give you all English names." I went back to the first boy. "In this class, your name is Adam. Please say Adam. Please say, 'In this class my name is Adam.' " It took a little while to get the ideas over, and in the process we had some practice with pronouns. Your name is Adam. My name is Adam. His name is Adam. I wrote it on the blackboard. Adam wrote it in his notebook. I went on to the next, whose name became Billy.

The second boy caught on more quickly and the third boy jumped up eagerly to get his name. As I worked toward the Prince, who sat in the exact center of the room, I could see the others cutting their eyes around at each other, all agog to see what I was going to do about that situation.

I reached the Prince and said, "In this class your name is Jimmy." There was no particular reason for Jimmy, except that it just happened to be one of my favorite names.

He replied promptly, "No, I am Prince."

"Yes," I agreed cordially. "You are Prince Akihito. That is your real name. But in this class you have an English name. In this class your name is Jimmy." I waited, a little breathless.

He smiled cheerfully, and the whole class beamed. I realized that he probably had thought I hadn't recognized him, seeing him for the first time among the other boys. Also I think that he had always been identified in his own mind with his princeship and was unable at first to think of himself as a boy among other boys.

The other names went off quickly, and we passed on to the practice of prepositions. Near the end of the hour, Dr. Hozumi, Mr. Kikuchi, and a chamberlain tiptoed in to see how things were going. By that time the boys were answering to their names and the Crown Prince was raising his hand and responding to "Yes Jimmy?" just like any other schoolboy.

The observers tiptoed out again. When I joined them in the chamberlains' waiting room for a cup of tea between classes they all appeared pleased. Afterwards I heard that there was a flurry among some of the boys' parents, who were not pleased, but Mrs. Matsudaira stood up for me loyally and it passed over. I used the same names for about two years. By that time I knew all their real names and could pronounce them reasonably correctly, and as they were growing up rapidly I felt that they were beyond that sort of play and I dropped it. Some of them, however, still sign their letters when they write to me with the names I gave them then.

I told nobody outside our closed circle about all this, for I was in terror that the newspapermen would get hold of it and headlines would appear in the *Stars and Stripes*: "Tutor Calls Emperor's Son Jimmy." The secret never got out—among westerners. The Japanese knew and, evidently, approved. Only a short time after it was done, a newspaper in Ibaraki Prefecture came out with an editorial about me, in which "Vining Fujin" was urged to take "her Jimmy" with her to school in the United States when it should become possible.

Incidentally, I never had any trouble with discipline . . .

As the winter went on, it became obvious to me that the Crown Prince was happiest and most himself when he was with the other boys. I saw him in the classroom between classes, always in a knot of other boys, laughing, alert, and interested. Sometimes I would see him racing down the corridor to the room where they played ping-pong. There were three tables, and he awaited his turn to play, like anybody else, roaming the aisles between tables, picking up the balls that went astray and tossing them back, commenting on the game. The boys called him *Denka*—Highness—and outside the school they bowed to him and kept their distance, but in the school building and on the playground he was one of them, and the difference in his demeanor and his whole expression showed how that normal and happy relationship fed and watered his soul.

For this reason and to increase the opportunities for contact outside the schoolroom, I was eager to have two of his classmates join one of his private lessons each week, and when a new term began in April this was done. I chose the boys myself in consultation with the chamberlains and English teacher and, privately, with the Prince, and each term new ones were selected. I was always interested in the Prince's comments on his classmates, for he had a keen sense of character and he sometimes suggested boys whom I would not myself have thought of; in one case it was because he thought it would help the boy. The basis for choice was, first, character and personality, and second, at least a moderate ability in English. I liked to have one whose English was a little better than the Prince's and one whose English was not quite so good. The Prince himself stoutly resisted anyone who could speak very much better than he!

That first winter especially, people outside our immediate circle were interested in what I was teaching the Crown Prince and had large ideas of what I might accomplish. One February afternoon the Women's Committee of the United Christian Church gave a tea for me and presented me with a beautiful piece of handwoven tapestry in a design of mandarin ducks. This was an expression of the hope which many Christians felt and which others put to me in far more blunt terms, that I should convert the Crown Prince to Christianity.

There were also other misconceptions of the purpose of my work there. A prominent editor, for instance, asked me if there was any resistance to my democratization of the Imperial Family.

This was not what I had been invited for. I had been asked simply to teach the Crown Prince English. But early in my stay in Japan, Grand Steward Matsudaira said to me, "We want you to open windows on to a wider world for our Crown Prince." It seemed to me then that through the medium of English I could present to him the ideals of the western world and help him to understand the essential spirit of that democracy which Japan was embracing with a hasty and bewildered sort of zeal in reaction from her great disillusionment with military dictatorship.

I never tried to indoctrinate him with any specific dogma. I tried only to expose him to the best that I knew. Religion, I have always felt, must be caught before it can be taught, and democracy is learned at least as much through living and doing as through an intellectual understanding of its theory. There were some to whom this point of view was a great disappointment. I reminded them that the Crown Prince's English at that time encompassed no more than a simple discussion of the pictures in the d'Aulaires' *Abraham Lincoln* and a folk story, "The Monkey Wants Its Tail," which appeared in an American first grade reader, and recommended patience to them.

Much earlier I had realized that I must clarify my own ideas of the essentials of democracy, not only for the sake of the Crown Prince but for others who asked me. The first essential, I thought, was respect for the worth and dignity of the individual. The second I found best expressed by William Penn when he said, "That government is free to the people under it where the laws rule and the people are a party to those laws."

As a Quaker, I believe in regard to the first, that humanism is not enough, that the individual's worth and dignity derive from the light of the divine within his soul, and that when George Fox, the first Quaker, told his young followers to "walk cheerfully over the earth answering that of God in every man," the kind of *answer* he had in mind was social justice for everyone and a peaceful environment in which each soul can live out its fullest potentialities. So it was natural that my aspirations for the Crown Prince should take the form of a prayer, which I wrote during that first winter and which was a comfort to me when there seemed so little that I could do for him but to pray. It went like this:

"Heavenly Father, bless this child to whom some day will come great responsibility. Grant him free and happy growth to his fullest capacities of mind, body, and spirit. May he learn to know and trust Thy light within his own heart and come to respect its presence in his fellow men. Endow his teachers and chamberlains with wisdom and courage and grant that we may serve single-heartedly his best development, putting aside all selfish interests and desires. For His sake who gathered the children about Him, Amen."

★ *No one ever teaches well who wants to teach, or governs well who wants to govern.*

PLATO

★ *The object of teaching a child is to enable him to get along without his teacher.*

ELBERT HUBBARD

THE TEACHER

by Leslie Pinckney Hill

LORD, WHO AM I TO TEACH THE WAY
To little children day by day,
So prone myself to go astray?

I teach them KNOWLEDGE, but I know
How faint they flicker and how low
The candles of my knowledge glow.

I teach them POWER to will and do,
But only now to learn anew
My own great weakness through and through.

I teach them LOVE for all mankind
And all God's creatures, but I find
My love comes lagging far behind.

Lord, if their guide I still must be,
Oh, let the little children see
The teacher leaning hard on Thee.

GRADE 5B AND
THE WELL-FED RAT

by Frances Gray Patton

"Dear parent," said the mimeographed letter from the Parent-Teacher's Association of the Oaklawn School, "In this atomic age the future safety of civilization depends upon a truly scientific atmosphere. The boys and girls of today will be the men and women of tomorrow. At our meeting, Wednesday November 14, Miss Oates' grade, 5B-1, will take over the program to show we parents how our little folk are progressing in this direction."

Mrs. Potter sighed when she read it. Her daughter, Elinor, was in grade 5B-1.

Mrs. Potter made a point of staying away from schools. They depressed her. The very odor of their halls was an undertow to her spirits. It sucked her back into that nervous dullness of childhood from which she, by the grace of time, had thankfully escaped.

Her first two children were boys. They seemed fond of their mother, and not abnormally ashamed of her. They accompanied her on bird-walks in the woods, and sometimes even to a movie—though they did not sit with her there because, they explained, they could see better from the front row. They talked openly to her about sex and tropical fish and airplane motor frequency. But they did not discuss their school affairs. And the rare occasions when she was obliged to come to their school (to bring forgotten notebooks, for instance, or raincoats when the weather had changed unexpectedly), their embarrassment was pathetic. They greeted her vaguely, like people who "know the face, but can't recall the name." It suited Mrs. Potter.

But Elinor was different. To Elinor school was the stuff of life, and she brought it home with her. She remembered in detail the appearance of her teachers. She discovered, somehow, their private histories and philosophies. She recounted everything at the dinner table.

"Miss Oates had lipstick on her teeth again today," Elinor would remark. "It was probably her mother's fault. Miss Oates lives with this old, old mother, and sometimes she beats Miss Oates to the bathroom in the morning and she stays in there so long—you know how old people are!—that Miss Oates doesn't have time to fix herself up before school. Poor Miss Oates! I don't like lipstick on teeth."

Or she would lean forward, pudding spoon halfway to her mouth, and announce solemnly:

"Miss Bangs, our new music teacher, loves God. She really *loves* Him."

Elinor liked, also, to share her homework with her family. Her eyes shone as she recited the multiplication table or the trials of the Jamestown Colony. Her voice was full of proud emotion when she read her compositions aloud. One of these ended with a fine, confident flourish:

"After reading this chapter in *Tales of Distant Lands*," declared Elinor, "I know that if I woke up tomorrow morning in the middle of the Desert of Sahara, I would feel perfectly at home."

(She probably would at that, thought Mrs. Potter. Anybody who feels at home in a public school would feel at home anywhere.)

It was entertaining. It might have been entirely charming if Elinor had not begun urging her mother to visit the school. Other mothers came all the time; wasn't her mother interested in education?

Miss Oates thinks the school and the home should co-operate," said Elinor. "And besides," she added, "everybody wants to see you. I've told them you look like a pin-up girl."

This bit of flattery was irresistible. Mrs. Potter, though well-preserved, was on the shady side of thirty-five. She promised Elinor that next time her class was on the program she would attend the P.-T.A. meeting. It had seemed then something faraway and rather unlikely to happen.

Now, with the letter in her hand, she knew she was caught.

On the morning of the appointed Wednesday Mrs. Potter awoke with a heaviness, like a cold, undigested pancake, on her stomach. Then she heard her husband, Professor Potter, gargling in the bathroom and she took heart. Maybe, she thought, he was coming down with a strep throat, and she would have to stay home and nurse him. But he said he was all right—he was just gargling as a precaution because there were some colds among his students.

"I guess this is it," she said bleakly, and went down to the kitchen to start the cereal.

Elinor was too excited to eat much breakfast. She was to make the longest speech of all. She had not said the speech at home because she wanted it to be a surprise for her mother, and now she was afraid she didn't know it. She stared down at her plate and kept mumbling something about rats.

"Mama," one of the boys said at last, "don't let her go crazy right here at the breakfast table. She takes my appetite away."

"Suppose I forget something," said Elinor, trembling, "before those thousands of people!"

"I don't suppose there'll be many people," murmured Mrs. Potter soothingly.

It was the wrong thing to say.

"You mean we won't have a good audience?" demanded Elinor. In a gesture of despair she clapped her hand to her head. "My hair!" she moaned, holding out a yellow wisp in her fingers. "Oh, I wish I had some glamour. I have to get up there on that stage—without any glamour!"

She moaned again as she gathered up her books. But it was a moan, Mrs. Potter knew, made half of ecstasy.

"Wear your new girdle, Mama," said Elinor, "and use enough lipstick. Don't get it on your teeth."

Before the meeting Mrs. Potter went downtown for a shampoo

and a manicure. She disliked painted fingernails, but this time she permitted the manicurist to give her a brilliant polish called *Frozen Flame*. She was not going to let Elinor down. Then she went to a department store where she bought a red rayon carnation to pin on her coat. She thought she looked very nice. She almost believed she was going to enjoy the meeting.

After all, she told herself, her attitude of aloofness toward her children's education was self-indulgent and anti-social. More than that, it was ignorant; it was based upon some infantile fixation of her own. Times had changed. The public school must have changed with them, and—witness Elinor's enthusiasm—for the better.

But when she went into the school it did not smell very different. It did not look different, either. The walls were painted the same pale tan—a faintly nauseating color—and on the wall the same peasant girl still listened to her lark. As she walked down the concrete hall Mrs. Potter heard the echo of her own footsteps tapping behind her, like some hopeless monotony that would shadow her all her life.

At the door of the auditorium she was welcomed by Miss Oates. Her teeth, Mrs Potter. saw with relief, were clean as the proverbial hound's. Miss Oates, when Mrs. Potter introduced herself, exclaimed in evident surprise: "Are you *Elinor's* mother?" She gave her a long look, equally appraising and disappointed.

Mrs. Potter found a seat among the score of other mothers who were, she saw, as carefully coifed, as resolutely complacent as she herself. There was time only for the briefest interchange of compliments on one another's "darling children" before Miss Bangs began playing the piano. (Mrs. Potter found herself thinking irreverently that God might have rewarded that lady's devotion with the gift of greater talent!) Thirty children filed out upon the stage, singing "We march, we march, to vic-to-ree," in fresh, tuneless voices.

The children all looked healthy and clean. The boys wore white shirts and dark knickers. The bright, starched dresses of the girls belled out like field flowers. Their eyes were steady and serious, as if some transcendent emotion arose to sweep the least trace of frivolity from them. They made a touching picture.

Her Elinor, Mrs. Potter observed, was pale. She looked as if she had been crying and had just washed her face. But she seemed composed. She stood primly, with her hands crossed, like little limp fish, over her middle. When she caught her mother's glance, she shot her a swift, tremulous smile.

Miss Oates mounted the rostum. She was a thin, tall woman. She curved her body a little from the waist, as if to reduce the impression of its length. She fingered her pearls as she talked, and her features assumed the languid lines of patronizing whimsy. But her prominent blue eyes were coy and restless. Mrs. Potter felt sorry for her, and sorry, too, that she did not like her.

"*Ave!*" said Miss Oates cheerfully. "In this day of racial unrest and the atom bomb—"

Mrs. Potter shivered. Suddenly the pretty children on the platform looked unsubstantial, doomed, like the overbright figures in a nightmare. What earthly relevance had the race problem to the matter in hand, and why drag in the bomb at this juncture? The woman was a plain fool. Mrs. Potter bowed her head in vicarious shame.

"In this atomic age," Miss Oates continued, "this time of changing val-yews, we must dare to change our methods also. Therefore, when the fifth graders took up the study of nutrition, we did not give them dead books, but live, vibrant material. The Health Department kindly donated two white rats. We named one of them Wiffles, and the other one Squiffles."

She paused, smiling graciously. The audience made a sound that Mrs. Potter supposed might be called "an appreciative titter."

"Wiffles," said Miss Oates, "had his private cage, and Squiffles had his. But while Wifflles was fed milk and eggs and vegetable stew, Mr. Squiffles received only cookies and coca-cola. At first we thought Squiffles was the lucky rat, but we soon changed our minds. Wiffles began to look like a great big Marine sergeant, and Squiffles was just a poor little 4-F. But I'm going to let our young scientists tell you the rest. I know you want to hear, in their own little words, just what they've learned with their honest, inquiring little minds. So, ladies and gentlemen," here she dimpled at the principal, a bald, sleepy-looking man, "and mothers of the fifth grade, I want to introduce somebody you already know—The Class of Five B One."

Miss Oates retired into the wings. Everybody clapped. A stout, pink-cheeked boy came forward. He gave his bulging pants a hitch, and began to talk in a challenging monotone.

"In this atomic age, he said, "we must all be scientists.""

Mrs. Potter did not listen closely to him. She did not pay much attention, either, to the girl who maintained that, since the discovery of the airplane and the atom bomb, it was necessary to learn the rules of health. Mrs. Potter was waiting for Elinor.

Elinor, whose job was to sum up the results of the class experiment, was the last to speak. Mrs. Potter thought she was infinitely better than the others. In the first place, she looked exactly the way a ten-year-old girl ought to look. Even her straight hair, with its bothersome cowlick, had all the weedy grace of childhood; it made the ringlets of the other girls look artificial. And she spoke her piece in a rapid, businesslike way, without any hesitation or any fancy frills.

"The characteristics of the well-fed rat," said Elinor, "are different from the characteristics of the poorly-fed rat. The well-fed rat is heavier. The fur of the well-fed rat is soft and creamy. The poorly-fed rat has sore eyes, and his fur is very ratty. The poorly-fed rat is maladjusted, and he also has a bad disposition. He is ready to dart out of his cage whenever the door is opened. The well-fed rat has a calm, kind disposition. He is contented with his surroundings and does not wish to leave his cage. His tail is pink and waxy."

After the program was over Mrs. Potter stayed to congratulate Miss Oates upon the performance of her pupils. The children were marching off the stage through a back door, but Elinor darted from the line (like the poorly-fed rat, thought Mrs. Potter), and bounced over the footlights to her mother's side. Miss Oates came down, too, but by the steps.

"We're glad to see Mummy, aren't we, Elinor?" she said. There was something subtly menacing in her tone.

"It was really remarkable, Miss Oates," said Mrs. Potter. "I'm sure we were never so poised in the fifth grade." Then, in an attempt to add a friendly, adult note to the conversation, she added flippantly: "But it's sad, isn't it, that the well-fed rat liked his cage. Is the desire for freedom only the desire for food?"

Miss Oates curved her lips slightly. It was the sort of smile, Mrs. Potter remembered, that teachers kept for parents who tried to be clever.

"That's what the chart told us," Elinor said. "It said the well-fed rat liked his cage. It wasn't that way with our Wiffles."

She gulped on the last word. Miss Oates gave her an uneasy look.

"But, Elinor," said Mrs. Potter, "I thought you said in your report—"

"You see, Mrs. Potter," said Miss Oates, "the Health Department furnished us with a chart on rat nutrition to help us find our facts, but the rats didn't always co-operate. Squiffles, *our* poorly-fed rat, just cowered in a corner—"

"With a blank expression on his face," said Elinor contemptuously.

"—while Wiffles, who was supposed to feel all comfy, was forever trying to get out. Once he did escape, didn't he, Elinor?"

"Yes, Miss Oates," said Elinor, "and bit the blood out of Randy Adams when he caught him."

"We disinfected Randy's finger with iodine," Miss Oates said quickly.

Mrs. Potter was honestly puzzled.

"I thought," she said, "that the class just observed the rats firsthand, and drew its own conclusions."

"That's right," said Miss Oates patiently, "we observed them for a month. We fed and weighed them every day. Then, with the chart as a guide, we made out our reports."

"I see," said Mrs. Potter. But she wondered if she did.

"But," said Miss Oates, "when we compared our findings with those on the chart we saw that something, somewhere, had gone wrong. Maybe there was something funny about the rats to begin with. Or maybe we didn't follow directions properly. I don't know." She shrugged helplessly. "Frankly, I've never been good at science. I was always more the esthetic type."

"I know," said Mrs. Potter vaguely.

"Anyhow," said Miss Oates, "our results weren't exactly what we'd expected. We had promised to give this program and we simply didn't have time to do the experiment all over again. But we knew from the Health Department what facts we *ought* to have found, so—well, we just decided to take the bull by the horns and go ahead and find them! In this atomic age, we can't afford to be narrow about facts, can we? I mean we have to realize their broader implications. And after all," she finished, on a note of inspiration, "things often don't turn out right the first time—even at Oak Ridge."

"Indeed they don't," agreed Mrs. Potter.

"Now," said Miss Oates briskly, "I've dissipated long enough. I must go see what my class is doing. I believe in trusting children, you know. In times like these they have to learn self-reliance. And then I check up on them. Elinor, would you like to spend five whole minutes alone with Mummy? Be sure to ask her to come again."

"Maybe Elinor could show me the rats," suggested Mrs. Potter.

A glint of something like exasperation shone in Miss Oates' eyes.

"I do wish she could," she said, "but the truth is we've had a minor tragedy in our midst. When we took the covers off the cages this morning we found something that made us all feel dreadfully blue." She pursed her mouth ruefully and dropped her voice. "The well-fed rat was dead."

She began to back off with her eyes fixed warily on Elinor.

"Bye-bye," she said, and was gone.

"I hate her," said Elinor, grinding her words between her teeth. "She is a cold, black-hearted woman."

Mrs. Potter was dismayed.

"Oh no, darling—you don't!" she cried. "You don't *hate* anybody."

"I hate Miss Oates," said Elinor flatly. "She wouldn't even let us have a funeral for him."

"But she was so busy," said Mrs. Potter. "And she has that poor old mother!"

"I feel sorry for Miss Oates' mother," said Elinor. "Imagine thinking you were going to have a nice baby, and it turning out to be Miss Oates! She has no feeling for children or rats or anything. Mama, I loved Wiffles. He was a sweet rat."

"Maybe he's happy somewhere," said Mrs. Potter. It seemed the only thing to say.

"He didn't look happy," said Elinor. "He looked awful dead. He was lying on his back with his feet up in the air. His body was still warm." She began to sob quietly. "We wanted to cremate him like we read in the paper Jerome Kern was cremated. We were going to build a funeral pyre on the playground, and dance around it singing hymns. But ole Quaker Oats wouldn't let us. Do you know what she said?"

"What did she say?" asked Mrs. Potter, aware of an ignominious sympathy for Miss Oates,

"She said: 'In this atomic age we have no time to play funeral with rats.' And then—" Elinor's voice shook with grief and scorn— "she picked him up, by his pink, waxy tail, and gave him to the janitor."

Mrs. Potter kissed Elinor and patted her on the shoulder. She wiped her wet cheeks with a handkerchief.

"I guess you'll have to go now, baby," she said. "It was a lovely program, anyhow." She fished a nickel out of her purse. "After school get yourself an ice-cream cone—or a coca-cola."

As she saw Elinor's face brighten, Mrs. Potter felt like crying. The quick shift of a child's mood, like sunlight running up the beach on the heels of a cloud, had always been a thing to move her deeply. She had an impulse to snatch Elinor out of these cloisters of pious confusion and set her free in the simple light of day. But of course she did no such thing. She only smiled and watched her little girl skip jauntily off to Miss Oates' home room.

And a minute later when she, herself, walked down the hall, Mrs. Potter felt comforted. The old smell of chalk and peanuts, the hollow, reverberating sound of her own shoes, the pastoral rapture—expressed in sepia—of Millet's rustic, all managed to put reality smugly in its place. Life seemed inept and innocent and debonair. Even the split atom lost its terrors for the moment and became just something people talked at P.-T.A. meetings.

★ *William R. Webb, famous Tennessee schoolmaster, was invited to speak at a conference at Pomona College on 'The Place of Humanities in Education.' The man who preceded him didn't think much of the humanities and emphasized the importance of practical education. "What I want my son to know how to do, for example, is to milk a cow."*

"That is a very good idea," said Webb when his turn came. "A very good idea. I want my son able to milk a cow, but I'd also like him able to do some things that a calf can't do better!"

Dr. Remsen D. Bird

'Fun Fare,' a Reader's Digest Treasury of Wit and Humor
(Copyright 1949 by The Reader's Digest Association)

"Who Writes This Stuff?"

THE FIFTY-FIRST DRAGON

by Heywood Broun

O F ALL THE PUPILS AT THE KNIGHT SCHOOL GAWAINE LE CŒUR-Hardy was among the least promising. He was tall and sturdy, but his instructors soon discovered that he lacked spirit. He would hide in the woods when the jousting class was called, although his companions and members of the faculty sought to appeal to his better nature by shouting to him to come out and break his neck like a man. Even when they told him that the lances were padded, the horses no more than ponies and the field unusually soft for late autumn, Gawaine refused to grow enthusiastic. The Headmaster and the Assistant Professor of Pleasaunce were discussing the case one spring afternoon and the Assistant Professor could see no remedy but expulsion.

"No," said the Headmaster, as he looked out at the purple hills which ringed the school, "I think I'll train him to slay dragons."

"He might be killed," objected the Assistant Professor.

"So he might," replied the Headmaster brightly, but he added, more soberly, "We must consider the greater good. We are responsible for the formation of this lad's character."

"Are the dragons particularly bad this year?" interrupted the Assistant Professor. This was characteristic. He always seemed restive when the head of the school began to talk ethics and the ideals of the institution.

"I've never known them worse," replied the Headmaster. "Up in the hills to the south last week they killed a number of peasants, two cows and a prize pig. And if this dry spell holds there's no telling when they may start a forest fire simply by breathing around indiscriminately."

"Would any refund on the tuition fee be necessary in case of an accident to young Cœur-Hardy?"

"No," the principal answered, judicially, "that's all covered in the contract. But as a matter of fact he won't be killed. Before I send him up in the hills I'm going to give him a magic word."

"That's a good idea," said the Professor. "Sometimes they work wonders."

From that day on Gawaine specialized in dragons. His course included both theory and practice. In the morning there were long lectures on the history, anatomy, manners and customs of dragons. Gawaine did not distinguish himself in these studies. He had a marvelously versatile gift for forgetting things. In the afternoon he showed to better advantage, for then he would go down to the South Meadow and practise with a battle-ax. In this exercise he was truly impressive, for he had enormous strength as well as speed and grace. He even developed a deceptive display of ferocity. Old alumni say that it was a thrilling sight to see Gawaine charging across the field toward the dummy paper dragon which had been set up for his practice. As he ran he would brandish his ax and shout "A murrain on thee!" or some other vivid bit of campus slang. It never took him more than one stroke to behead the dummy dragon.

Gradually his task was made more difficult. Paper gave way to papier-mâché and finally to wood, but even the toughest of these dummy dragons had no terrors for Gawaine. One sweep of the ax always did the business. There were those who said that when the practice was protracted until dusk and the dragons threw long, fantastic shadows across the meadow Gawaine did not charge so impetuously nor shout so loudly. It is possible there was malice in this charge. At any rate, the Headmaster decided by the end of June that it was time for the test. Only the night before a dragon had come close to the school grounds and had eaten some of the lettuce from the garden. The faculty decided that Gawaine was ready. They gave him a diploma and a new battle-ax and the Headmaster summoned him to a private conference.

"Sit down," said the Headmaster. "Have a cigarette."

Gawaine hesitated.

"Oh, I know it's against the rules," said the Headmaster. "But after all, you have received your preliminary degree. You are no longer a boy. You are a man. To-morrow you will go out into the world, the great world of achievement."

Gawaine took a cigarette. The Headmaster offered him a match, but he produced one of his own and began to puff away with a dexterity which quite amazed the principal.

"Here you have learned the theories of life," continued the Headmaster, resuming the thread of his discourse, "but after all, life is not a matter of theories. Life is a matter of facts. It calls on the young and the old alike to face these facts, even though they are hard and sometimes unpleasant. Your problem, for example, is to slay dragons."

"They say that those dragons down in the south wood are five hundred feet long," ventured Gawaine, timorously.

"Stuff and nonsense!" said the Headmaster. "The curate saw one last week from the top of Arthur's Hill. The dragon was sunning himself down in the valley. The curate didn't have an opportunity to look at him very long because he felt it was his duty to hurry back to make a report to me. He said the monster, or shall I say, the big lizard?—wasn't an inch over two hundred feet. But the size has nothing at all to do with it. You'll find the big ones even easier than the little ones. They're far slower on their feet and less aggressive, I'm told. Besides, before you go I'm going to equip you in such fashion that you need have no fear of all the dragons in the world."

"I'd like an enchanted cap," said Gawaine.

"What's that?" answered the Headmaster, testily.

"A cap to make me disappear," explained Gawaine.

The Headmaster laughed indulgently. "You mustn't believe all those old wives' stories," he said. "There isn't any such thing. A cap to make you disappear, indeed! What would you do with it? You haven't even appeared yet. Why, my boy, you could walk from here to London, and nobody would so much as look at you. You're nobody. You couldn't be more invisible than that."

Gawaine seemed dangerously close to a relapse into his old habit of whimpering. The Headmaster reassured him: "Don't worry; I'll give you something much better than an enchanted cap. I'm going to give you a magic word. All you have to do is to repeat this magic charm once and no dragon can possibly harm a hair of your head. You can cut off his head at your leisure."

He took a heavy book from the shelf behind his desk and began to run through it. "Sometimes," he said, "the charm is a whole phrase or even a sentence. I might, for instance, give you 'To make the'—No, that might not do. I think a single word would be best for dragons."

"A short word," suggested Gawaine.

"It can't be too short or it wouldn't be potent. There isn't so much hurry as all that. Here's a splendid magic word: 'Rumplesnitz.' Do you think you can learn that?"

Gawaine tried and in an hour or so he seemed to have the word well in hand. Again and again he interrupted the lesson to inquire, "And if I say 'Rumplesnitz,' the dragon can't possibly hurt me?" And always the Headmaster replied, "If you only say 'Rumplesnitz,' you are perfectly safe."

Toward morning Gawaine seemed resigned to his career. At daybreak the Headmaster saw him to the edge of the forest and pointed him to the direction on which he should proceed. About a mile away to the southwest a cloud of steam hovered over an open meadow in the woods and the Headmaster assured Gawaine that under the steam he would find a dragon. Gawaine went forward slowly. He wondered whether it would be best to approach the dragon on the run as he did in his practice in the South Meadow or to walk slowly toward him, shouting "Rumplesnitz" all the way.

The problem was decided for him. No sooner had he come to the fringe of the meadow than the dragon spied him and began to charge. It was a large dragon and yet it seemed decidedly aggressive in spite of the Headmaster's statement to the contrary. As the dragon charged it released huge clouds of hissing steam through its nostrils. It was almost as if a gigantic teapot had gone mad. The dragon came forward so fast and Gawaine was so frightened that he had time to say "Rumplesnitz" only once. As he said it, he swung his battle-ax and off popped the head of the dragon. Gawaine had to admit that it was even easier to kill a real dragon than a wooden one if only you said "Rumplesnitz."

Gawaine brought the ears home and a small section of the tail. His school mates and the faculty made much of him, but the Headmaster wisely kept him from being spoiled by insisting that he go on with his work. Every clear day Gawaine rose at dawn and went out to kill dragons. The Headmaster kept him at home when it rained, because he said the woods were damp and unhealthy at such times and that he didn't want the boy to run needless risks. Few good days passed in which Gawaine failed to get a dragon. On one particularly fortunate day he killed three, a husband and wife and a visiting relative. Gradually he developed a technique. Pupils who sometimes watched him from the hilltops a long way off said that he often allowed the dragon to come within a few feet before he said "Rumplesnitz." He came to say it with a mocking sneer. Occasionally he did stunts. Once when an excursion party from London was watching him he went into action with his right hand tied behind his neck. The dragon's head came off just as easily.

As Gawaine's record of killings mounted higher the Headmaster found it impossible to keep him completely in hand. He fell into the habit of stealing out at night and engaging in long drinking bouts at the village tavern. It was after such a debauch that he rose a little before dawn one fine August morning and started out after his fiftieth dragon. His head was heavy and his mind sluggish. He was heavy in other respects as well, for he had adopted the somewhat vulgar practice of wearing his medals, ribbons and all, when he went out dragon hunting. The decorations began on his chest and ran all the way down to his abdomen. They must have weighed at least eight pounds.

Gawaine found a dragon in the same meadow where he had killed the first one. It was a fair-sized dragon, but evidently an old one. Its face was wrinkled and Gawaine thought he had never seen so hideous a countenance. Much to the lad's disgust, the monster refused to charge and Gawaine was obliged to walk toward him. He whistled as he went. The dragon regarded him hopelessly, but craftily. Of course it had heard of Gawaine. Even when the lad raised his battle-ax the dragon made no move. It knew that there was no salvation in the quickest thrust of the head, for it had been informed that this hunter was protected by an enchantment. It merely waited, hoping something would turn up. Gawaine raised the battle-ax and suddenly lowered it again. He had grown very pale and he trembled violently. The dragon suspected a trick. "What's the matter?" it asked, with false solicitude.

"I've forgotten the magic word," stammered Gawaine.

"What a pity," said the dragon. "So that was the secret. It doesn't seem quite sporting to me, all this magic stuff, you know. Not cricket, as we used to say when I was a little dragon; but after all, that's a matter of opinion."

Gawaine was so helpless with terror that the dragon's confidence rose immeasurably and it could not resist the temptation to show off a bit.

"Could I possibly be of any assistance?" it asked. "What's the first letter of the magic word?"

"It begins with an 'r,'" said Gawaine weakly.

"Let's see," mused the dragon, "that doesn't tell us much, does it? What sort of a word is this? Is it an epithet, do you think?"

Gawaine could do no more than nod.

"Why, of course," exclaimed the dragon, "reactionary Republican."

Gawaine shook his head.

"Well, then," said the dragon, "we'd better get down to business. Will you surrender?"

With the suggestion of a compromise Gawaine mustered up enough courage to speak.

"What will you do if I surrender?" he asked.

"Why, I'll eat you," said the dragon.

"And if I don't surrender?"

"I'll eat you just the same."

"Then it doesn't make any difference, does it?" moaned Gawaine.

"It does to me," said the dragon with a smile. "I'd rather you didn't surrender. You'd taste much better if you didn't."

The dragon waited for a long time for Gawaine to ask "Why?" but the boy was too frightened to speak. At last the dragon had to give the explanation without his cue line. "You see," he said, "if you don't surrender you'll taste better because you'll die game."

This was an old and ancient trick of the dragon's. By means of some such quip he was accustomed to paralyze his victims with laughter and then to destroy them. Gawaine was sufficiently paralyzed as it was, but laughter had no part in his helplessness. With the last word of the joke the dragon drew back his head and

struck. In that second there flashed into the mind of Gawaine the
magic word "Rumplesnitz," but there was no time to say it.
There was time only to strike and, without a word, Gawaine met
the onrush of the dragon with a full swing. He put all his back
and shoulders into it. The impact was terrific and the head of
the dragon flew away almost a hundred yards and landed in a
thicket.

Gawaine did not remain frightened very long after the death of
the dragon. His mood was one of wonder. He was enormously
puzzled. He cut off the ears of the monster almost in a trance.
Again and again he thought to himself, "I didn't say 'Rumplesnitz'!"
He was sure of that and yet there was no question that he had
killed the dragon. In fact, he had never killed one so utterly. Never
before had he driven a head for anything like the same distance.
Twenty-five yards was perhaps his best previous record. All the
way back to the knight school he kept rumbling about in his mind
seeking an explanation for what had occurred. He went to the
Headmaster immediately and after closing the door told him what
had happened. "I didn't say 'Rumplesnitz,'" he explained with
great earnestness.

The Headmaster laughed. "I'm glad you've found out," he said.
"It makes you ever so much more of a hero. Don't you see that?
Now you know that it was you who killed all these dragons and
not that foolish little word 'Rumplesnitz.'"

Gawaine frowned. "Then it wasn't a magic word after all?"
he asked.

"Of course not," said the Headmaster, "you ought to be too old
for such foolishness. There isn't any such thing as a magic word."

"But you told me it was magic," protested Gawaine. "You said
it was magic and now you say it isn't."

"It wasn't magic in a literal sense," answered the Headmaster,
"but it was much more wonderful than that. The word gave you
confidence. It took away fears. If I hadn't told you that you might
have been killed the very first time. It was your battle-ax did the
trick."

Gawaine surprised the Headmaster by his attitude. He was obviously distressed by the explanation. He interrupted a long philosophic and ethical discourse by the Headmaster with, "If I
hadn't of hit 'em all mighty hard and fast any one of 'em might
have crushed me like a, like a—" He fumbled for a word.

"Egg shell," suggested the Headmaster.

"Like a egg shell," assented Gawaine, and he said it many times. All through the evening meal people who sat near him heard him muttering, "Like a egg shell, like a egg shell."

The next day was clear, but Gawaine did not get up at dawn. Indeed, it was almost noon when the Headmaster found him cowering in bed, with the clothes pulled over his head. The principal called the Assistant Professor of Pleasaunce, and together they dragged the boy toward the forest.

"He'll be all right as soon as he gets a couple more dragons under his belt," explained the Headmaster.

The Assistant Professor of Pleasaunce agreed. "It would be a shame to stop such a fine run," he said. "Why, counting that one yesterday, he's killed fifty dragons."

They pushed the boy into a thicket above which hung a meager cloud of steam. It was obviously quite a small dragon. But Gawaine did not come back that night or the next. In fact, he never came back. Some weeks afterward brave spirits from the school explored the thicket, but they could find nothing to remind them of Gawaine except the metal parts of his medals. Even the ribbons had been devoured.

The Headmaster and the Assistant Professor of Pleasaunce agreed that it would be just as well not to tell the school how Gawaine had achieved his record and still less how he came to die. They held that it might have a bad effect on school spirit. Accordingly, Gawaine has lived in the memory of the school as its greatest hero. No visitor succeeds in leaving the building to-day without seeing a great shield which hangs on the wall of the dining hall. Fifty pairs of dragons' ears are mounted upon the shield and underneath in gilt letters is "Gawaine le Cœur-Hardy," followed by the simple inscription, "He killed fifty dragons." The record has never been equaled.

★ *A parent gives life, but as parent gives no more. A murderer takes life, but his deed stops there; a teacher affects eternity; he can never tell where his influence stops.*

HENRY ADAMS

from

THE BLACKBOARD JUNGLE

by Evan Hunter

THE DAY RICK BROKE THROUGH WAS DECEMBER TWENTY-FIRST, two days before the Christmas Assembly. It happened in a class for which he had prepared no lesson at all. He had meant to work out lesson plans over the weekend, it being a short week which would be terminated by the commencement of the Christmas vacation on Thursday.

But he'd got home late Friday night after the dress rehearsal. He'd spent all day Saturday at being a husband, devoting more time to Anne than he had in the past month. On Sunday, Anne's parents dropped by, staying for supper, and Rick never did get to attack his lesson plans.

So on the bus Monday morning he hastily scanned the text, picking out a yarn he thought was titled The Fifty-First Dragoon. *This is a war story* he thought. He had never read the story before, but war stories were sure-fire with these kids. He'd read it to them, and then try to lead the conversation around to his own war experiences, and that would, he hoped, kill the period.

He greeted 21-206 with the announcement that he was going

to read a story to them, and the kids accepted the knowledge gratefully.

Rick opened the text, cleared his throat, and discovered that the story was written by Heywood Broun. He also learned that it was not a war story titled the Fifty-First Dragoon.

It was, instead, a story titled The Fifty-First Dragon, and Rick felt a twinge of panic as he began reading aloud. The story told of a young knight named Gawaine le Coeur-Hardy who was enrolled at a knight school but who did not exhibit the proper spirit or zest for such knightly pursuits as jousting. In fact, Gawaine's lack of enthusiasm may very well have been termed cowardice. . . .

He was delighted with the story because it was a new experience to him as well as to the boys. But he was sorry in a way that it was not a war story, because it was decidedly allegory, and allegory was probably far-above the heads of these kids.

He faced the unusually silent class and wondered just what he should do next.

"Well," he said, "that was a pretty good story, wasn't it?"

"Yeah," the kids said, and he could tell they meant it.

"All about a knight who kills dragons, right?" he asked.

Finley, a kid near the back of the room, said, "He didn't really kill those dragons."

"What do you mean, Finley?"

"He was cheatin'," Finley said. "He had a magic word."

"What was the magic word?" Rick asked, and the class chorused, "Rumplesnitz!"

"It wasn't no magic word," Bello shouted. "He was just killin' the dragons his own self."

"Now, I don't understand that," Rick said, pleased with the response. "If it wasn't a magic word, why'd the headmaster give it to him?"

The class was silent for a few minutes, and then Shocken said, " 'Cause Gawaine was scared. He was a coward."

"But he *did* kill fifty dragons, and you just told me Rumplesnitz wasn't a magic word."

"So what?" Finley sneered. "He *thought* there was a magic word."

"Yes," Rick said, beginning to get a little excited now, surprised that they had garnered so much from the story. "That's just it. Gawaine thought it was a magic word. And did that help him kill the dragons?"

"Sure," White said, "He was scared of the dragons. If he don't have the magic word, he run away. He thinks it's magic, so he feels strong. He thinks he can kill any old dragon and the dragon can't touch him. That's why he needs it. Otherwise, he's a coward."

"How do you know that?" Rick asked the class.

"Well, once he finds out the word ain't magic," Daley said, "he gets et up."

"And is that why the headmaster gave him this magic word?" Rick asked, praying the response would continue. The kids were alive today, and he responded to them the way they were responding to him.

"That principal, he's a smart cat," Davidson said. "He knows Gawaine need something."

"What does Gawaine need?" Rick asked. "What's the word for it?"

"Con—" Daley started.

"Yes?"

"Confidence," Daley said triumphantly.

"Ah-ha, that's it," Rick said. "Confidence." He paused and made a sour face. "But that doesn't seem real," he said. "I mean, do you really think a word could give someone the confidence he needed?"

"Yeah, sure," Speranza said billigerently.

"How?"

"Well . . . like sometimes I'm scared before we take a test or something, an' I say three Hail Mary's, and I feel O.K. after that."

"It gives you confidence, is that right?"

"Yeah, sure," Speranza said.

"But still . . . a word like Rumplesnitz. I mean, after all, Hail Mary is a prayer. Rumplesnitz isn't a prayer."

"I don't think," Padres said slowly, "thees word means that. I mean, I don't think Rumplesnitz ees suppose to be nothing. You know what I mean?"

"Not exactly," Rick said. He was tense and tight, and he knew now that the kids were really discussing this thing the way it should be discussed. He heard Padres say:

"Thees Rumplesnitz, thees ees a fake, you know? The Hail Mary, that's real. Rumplesnitz, it don't mean nothing. Thees Gawaine, he fooling heemself."

The kids were squirming because they all had something to say.

They didn't call out because they wanted this lesson to proceed in an orderly fashion. They were enjoying this, and they felt something of the same thing Rick was feeling, and they wanted to express their ideas.

"But I thought this story was all about a knight who kills dragons," Rick said. His watch told him there were three minutes left to the period, and he wanted to round it out, wanted them to realize that the story said one thing while it meant another. "Was it?" he asked.

"Yeah, it was," Finley said.

"And only that? Just a knight who kills dragons?"

"Well, you could twist it around," Price said. "Then it becomes everybody, and not just Gawaine."

"You mean the story has a message?" Rick asked.

"Sure. It tells about fake words, and how you don't need them. If you're strong and quick, you can kill dragons—not really, but like that, you know?"

"Yes," Rick said, "exactly. And is the story a better one because it tells a second story, because it gives a message, and because it's not only about a cowardly knight?"

"It's a good story," Bello said.

"And will you remember the word for a story that tells two stories at the same time, a story that gives a message?"

"What is it?" Speranza asked.

"An allegory," Rick said, and wrote the word on the board. Someone behind him said, "That was a damn good story," and then the bell sounded.

He sat at his desk, thinking, *I've broken through, I've broken through*, and watching the kids mill around his desk while the kids in his second-period class filed in. He was too stunned to try a repetition of the same story in his second-period class, so he let it go, thinking all the while, *I've broken through, I've broken through to them. I've reached them.*

And when he walked to his hall patrol at the end of the second period, he was stopped by kids in his seventh-term classes. He was stopped at least a dozen times on his way down to the first floor, and each kid made the same request: teach us about the fifty-first dragon. . . .

TO THE TEACHERS OF AMERICA

by Oliver Wendell Holmes

TEACHERS OF TEACHERS! YOURS THE TASK,
Noblest that noble minds can ask,
High up Aonia's murmurous mount,
To watch, to guard the sacred fount
　　That feeds the streams below;
To guide the hurrying flood that fills
A thousand silvery rippling rills
　　In ever-widening flow.

Rich is the harvest from the fields
That bounteous Nature kindly yields,
But fairer growths enrich the soil
Ploughed deep by thought's unwearied toil
　　In Learning's broad domain.
And where the leaves, the flowers, the fruits,
Without your watering at the roots,
　　To fill each branching vein?

[110]

Welcome! the Author's firmest friends,
Your voice the surest Godspeed lends.
Of you the growing mind demands
The patient care, the guiding hands,
   Through all the mists of morn.
And knowing well the future's need,
Your prescient wisdom sows the seed
   To flower in years unborn.

———————————

★ *What greater or better gift can we offer the republic than to teach and instruct our youth?*

CICERO

★ *Love of power is the chief danger of the educator, as of the politician; the man who can be trusted in education must care for his pupils on their own account, not merely as potential soldiers in an army of propagandists for a cause.*

BERTRAND RUSSELL

YOU GIVE THE ANSWER

by Fred L. Brooks, Jr.

GETTING TO BE A WELL-LIKED TEACHER IS NO EASY MATTER.

If we require large assignments of home work, they say we are cruel.

If we don't, they say we are soft and easy.

If we try to instill aesthetic values into them, we are called erratic.

If we don't, we do not know how to teach.

If we drill in grammar, "boring" is the word they use.

If we don't, we do not teach thoroughly enough.

If we let our hair down in the classroom, we are not acting like a teacher should.

If we don't, we are hard, dry, and almost inhuman.

When we look up a word in the dictionary, we should not—for—

We should know all the words, and every meaning, also.

We ask Johnny to recite, but he just forgot—that very very minute.

We ask for a short story and the next day, the answer—"I wasn't in the mood to create."

From *Mississippi Educational Advance*, 1955.

When we don't smile, "Why don't you smile some time?"
If we do—"What are you smiling at?"
We try, we try—we have studied for years, but that teenager
is far "smarter" than we.
We repeat: "Getting to be a well-liked teacher is no easy matter.
You give the answer."

★ *Stephen Leacock, the Canadian professor and humorist, once
wrote an anecdote about the elective system at its extreme. He
had, he reported, met an American student during the summer
vacation. He asked him what he was going to take in the way
of courses that autumn. "Turkish, music and architecture," the
student promptly replied. "Do you expect to be choirmaster
in a Turkish cathedral?" Mr. Leacock asked. "No," said the
student, "those courses come at 9, 10 and 11 o'clock."*

IRWIN EDMAN
'To Teach Men to Know How to Be Free'
(The New York Times Magazine)

ALFRED NORTH WHITEHEAD

by Felix Frankfurter

FROM KNOWLEDGE GAINED THROUGH THE YEARS OF THE PER-
sonalities who in our day have affected American university life,
I have for some time been convinced that no single figure has had
such a pervasive influence as the late Professor Alfred North
Whitehead. Certainly so far as this applies to the country's oldest
university, my statement will hardly be disputed. I should like to
try to describe the nature of the ferment imparted by a thinker
whose philosophic speculations were mostly beyond the capacity
of those whom he touched.

That our universities have grave shortcomings for the intellectual
life of this nation is by now a commonplace. The chief source of
their inadequacy is probably the curse of departmentalization.
Among students, as well as among teachers, there has been a
tendency to regard courses as something which exist in nature,
instead of artificial simplifications for the mastery of what are
complicated organisms, whether of nature or reason or society.
Professor Whitehead exerted powerful influence to break down
this separation in the various departments of the university.

From the time that he came to Harvard in 1924 he infused an understanding of interdependence among the various disciplines, to use the current jargon. For all who came within the range of his infectious personality, arid professionalism was quickened into exhilarating meaning and the universe expanded. Such was the quiet, almost shy magic of his qualities that his influence imperceptibly but quickly permeated the whole university.

The need for breaking down sterlizing departmentalization has been widely felt. Unfortunately, however, a too frequent way of doing it has been, wittily but not too unfairly, described as the cross-sterilization of the social sciences. That is a tendency by which a difficult problem, say of the law, is solved by relying on the formulation of a dubious truth in some other field.

Professor Whitehead's insistence on understanding through realization of the interdependence of thought and ideas and institutions was quite otherwise.

He was fiercely on guard against the illusions of verbalization and did not confuse certainty with certitude. In short, he was tough-minded because he felt the universe as illimitable. He distrusted closed systems because they imprison the creative possibilities of insight and experience. He was relentlessly exacting of accurate responsible thinking, precisely because he knew that even the most rigorous thought cannot achieve fullness of comprehension.

It was not by courses or lectures that he ignited to deeper understanding and more beautiful visions the minds and feelings of hundreds of students, alike youngsters fresh from high schools and colleagues themselves eminent. He did this predominantly through informal and unpremeditated talk, mostly in his modest apartment, which gave even the most timid freshman the sense of participation in an exciting adventure. Everything of distinction contributed toward these unfailing memorable occasions. Not to mention Mrs. Whitehead would be to omit enveloping loveliness.

Professor Whitehead had a benign and beautiful presence, a voice and diction that made music of English speech, humor that lighted up dark places, humility that made the foolish wiser and evoked the wisdom of the taciturn. For twenty years Professor Whitehead exercised this great and radiating influence. He did so at Harvard because he was there. He did so beyond because he was what he was. People came to Harvard because he was there. People read his books who had no background for understanding them. This partly explains why he is said to be so hard to read. No one who is ready to read serious books can fail to find luminous charm in his non-technical writings, like his recently published *Essays* and his *Adventures of Ideas*.

To dwell, however inadequately, on the qualities of a teacher like Alfred North Whitehead is important if our universities are important. They are important if the institutions specially charged with the accumulation of the intellectual capital of the world are important to a society. Who will deny that Professor Whitehead was right in his belief that the fate of the intellectual civilization of the world today is to no inconsiderable extent in the keeping of our universities? "The Aegean Coastline had its chance and made use of it; Italy had its chance and made use of it; France, England, Germany had their chance and made use of it. Today the Eastern American states have their chance. What use will they make of it? That question has two answers. Once Babylon had its chance, and produced the Tower of Babel. The University of Paris fashioned the intellect of the Middle Ages."

The awful question that confronts American universities is, What are they doing with their power and their duty?

★ *In my own work at universities I have been much struck by the paralysis of thought induced in pupils by the aimless accumulation of precise knowledge, inert and unutilized. It should be the chief aim of a university professor to exhibit himself in his own true character—that is, as an ignorant man thinking, actively utilizing his small share of knowledge.*

ALFRED NORTH WHITEHEAD

ROBERT M. HUTCHINS
BEFORE A HOUSE COMMITTEE

by William O. Douglas

D R. ROBERT M. HUTCHINS, FORMERLY PRESIDENT OF THE UNI-
versity of Chicago, testified as follows before a House Committee
in 1952:

"Now, a university is a place that is established and will function
for the benefit of society, provided it is a center of independent
thought. It is a center of independent thought and criticism that is
created in the interest of the progress of society, and the one reason
that we know that every totalitarian government must fail is that
no totalitarian government is prepared to face the consequences of
creating free universities.

"It is important for this purpose to attract into the institution
men of the greatest capacity, and to encourage them to exercise
their independent judgment.

"Education is a kind of continuing dialogue, and a dialogue
assumes, in the nature of the case, different points of views.

"The civilization which I work and which I am sure every
American is working toward, could be called a civilization of the
dialogue, where instead of shooting one another when you differ,
you reason things out together.

From *An Almanac of Liberty*, by William O. Douglas. Copyright 1954 by
William O. Douglas. Reprinted by permission of Doubleday & Co., Inc.

"In this dialogue, then, you cannot assume that you are going to have everybody thinking the same way or feeling the same way. It would be unprogressive if that happened. The hope of eventual development would be gone. More than that, of course, it would be very boring.

"A university, then, is a kind of continuing Socratic conversation on the highest level for the very best people you can think of, you can bring together, about the most important questions, and the thing that you must do to the uttermost possible limits is to guarantee those men the freedom to think and to express themselves.

"Now, the limits on this freedom cannot be merely prejudice, because although our prejudices might be perfectly satisfactory, the prejudices of our successors, or of those who are in a position to bring pressure to bear on the institution, might be subversive in the real sense, subverting the American doctrine of free thought and free speech."

★ *What every conscientious teacher yearns for, is only that his pupil's mind shall hold within it some ideas that are clearly his own, that have been understood in his head because worked out there.*

NATHAN M. PUSEY

THE LITTLE BLACK BOYS

by Clara Laidlaw

THE LITTLE BLACK BOYS, SAMUEL AND HAMUEL, WERE THE FIRST, indeed the only, Negro children I'd ever had in my classes in Northford. I remember very well the first time I saw them, on Wednesday, the second day of school, when my freshman math class assembled for the first time.

They sidled into the room shyly, after all the white children had rushed in to begin disputing noisily over the choice of seats in the back of the room. The black boys hesitated just inside the door, looking around in a bewildered way, and then they slid quickly into two empty front seats. I couldn't help noticing how bent and shriveled and small their bodies were. Obviously they were twins, but even the usual physical retardation of twin children did not explain all their difference from the robust white children. There was hunger in the shallowness of their chests, and their thin, bent shoulders told of hard work beyond their years. When they sat down the seats were almost ludicrously large for them.

The white children buzzed and tussled until I called them to order, but the little black boys sat like twin statues, their eyes gleaming white as they stared at me, their round, fluted lips sober and still. They had cheap new dime-store tablets before them on their desks, and penny pencils, the dull brown ones with pointed erasers wedged into the tops.

When I asked them, as I had the others, if they wanted to be called by their full names or by nicknames, the frozen stillness of their faces broke for the first time, and the one nearest the blackboard said, his white teeth flashing, "I'm Sammy. He's Hammy."

Some of the little girls behind him began to giggle. I nodded hurriedly and said, "All right, boys. Sammy and Hammy it shall be," and turned quickly to take up the first lesson.

As the days and weeks went by I paid little attention to the twins. They were quiet and sober and good. They never whispered to anyone and no one whispered to them. I grew used to seeing their black faces staring blankly up at me, or their kinky black heads bent laboriously over their work. With diminished penny pencils clutched tightly in skinny black fingers, they worked hour after hour to produce grubby papers covered with painfully worked problems, all wrong. The class was a slow one; but of all the group, Sammy and Hammy were the slowest. If, after weeks of work, they became finally convinced that if A and B, working alone, could each do a piece of work in six days, working together they could do it in three, then the next day they would be equally certain that, if one tablet cost ten cents, two would cost five.

I used to find myself scolding them occasionally, and they would look up at me with remorse in their liquid black eyes, their mouths drawn down into a mask of guilty grief.

Once I said, "Oh, Sammy and Hammy, what am I to do with you?" and Hammy said, "We're sorry we's so dumb, Miz Carey." Then he smiled and Sammy smiled, like two bad little dogs trying to be ingratiating. So we were friends again, and I began writing on their papers, to their innocent delight. "This is better than yesterday's paper," or "Fine! You had two problems right today," instead of the bare 0's and 20's they really earned.

One day I found a paper of Hammy's from which the comment I had written had been neatly cut.

"We saves them," Hammy said shyly when I questioned him. "Our mammy pastes 'em in a big book we got from the tailor shop. She say—'tain't every boy gets him so many nice words said to him—least, not every black boy."

"Those twins!" the other teachers groaned. Poor little black boys, they couldn't do anything at all. The other children shunned them too, it seemed, and their days would have been sad indeed had they not had each other for company. Each day they brought their dinners and sat alone on the steps eating their plain bread from a paper sack, while the other children ate and played noisily in the lunchroom.

Sammy and Hammy would sit watching the antics of their fellows with eager interest and delight, whispering to each other, chuckling companionably at whatever pleased them, but never offering to join the fun. Their apparent contentment in their isolation puzzled me until one day Sammy said, concerning another matter, "Our mammy say—you twins, so you be twins together," and I understood what the mother was doing for them: making the gulf between white and black be their choice, guarding them thus from fear and from desire for what they couldn't have, making them self-sufficient in their twoness.

Still, their aloofness bothered me. I didn't want to make an issue of it, but when two or three boys or girls would come in to discuss class politics or the play, or to get news for the paper, or just to visit, I'd begin in a roundabout way to talk about democracy and the American dream and the Golden Rule, and finally, as offhandedly as I could, by way of illustration, I'd bring in Sammy's and Hammy's need of friends. The boys and girls would say, "Yes, Miss Carey," "Of course, Miss Carey," but the shadow would come down over their faces. They would look secretive and stubborn, and I knew they'd been talked to at home.

In a way, you couldn't blame their parents. The twins lived alone with their mother in an old shack 'way down at the shore. At first the black woman had gone about asking for work for herself and her boys, and she had done washing for a few ladies until it had got around that Cash Benson, the town's ne'er-do-well, had been seen hanging around the shack. Now she and the boys managed to live with no apparent means of support, and lately when the woman came to town everyone could see that she was visibly big with child. "Cash's nigger woman," the men on the street corners called her, guffawing as she passed. No wonder white parents kept their children from making friends with her boys.

She had gone to the Swedish Baptist Church twice when she had first come to town, taking the boys, stiff and clean in their patched Sunday suits. "I been baptized and bred up pure Baptist," she had told Reverend Swanson proudly, hesitantly accepting his proffered hand as he had bade her good day at the door of the church. Behind her the Swedish Baptist ladies had whispered and stared. The next Sunday, when she and the boys had taken their

seats humbly in the last pew, there had begun a rustling as, one
by one, some irately, some shamefacedly, the white ladies had risen
and left the church. The black woman had stayed for the service,
though Sammy and Hammy, watching her face, had begun to cry.
She had never come again.

The way things were, there didn't seem much I could do except
be especially nice to Sammy and Hammy, and that was hard too,
because I certainly couldn't praise their work, and to treat them
differently from the others would have antagonized the white
children and made things still harder for the twins.

Toward spring it came time to have the annual freshman party.
We had a class meeting, and the youngsters decided to charge
twenty-five cents a ticket to pay for the lunch, and to have dancing
and a program. Miss Carey, of course, was to help with the program. I always got that!

"Mr. President," I said. (We try to teach them to observe
parliamentary procedure, heaven help us!) "Mr. President, may I
say a word?"

"Keep still, you kids," the class president yelled gallantly. "Miss
Carey's got sumpin to tell you."

When approximate quiet had finally been achieved I said, "The
program committee and I are going to need help, so if you can
play a musical instrument, or sing, or dance, or recite, or stand on
your head"—(Hoots from the class. "Miss Carey made a joke!
Listen to her!")—"why, come and tell us. We need talent for our
program."

Then, before the tumult could get under way again, I added,
remembering the time I had missed the eighth-grade picnic because
my mother had been away visiting and I had been too proud to
borrow from the neighbors, "And another thing—sometimes
twenty-five cents is hard to get hold of, so if there's anyone who
wants to go to the party but who hasn't the money at the time,
why, you just come to me, privately, and we'll see if we can't fix
it up."

The next day, after school, I was correcting papers when the
door opened and the twins sidled in. My heart sank. After all,
did it matter what one apple cost if a dozen cost twenty-five cents?

Sammy's black face glistened, and he moistened his lips with a
pale tongue. "Us—us——" he whispered.

"We's got us each a box," said Hammy quickly from over
Sammy's slight shoulder. His eyes rolled toward his brother fear-

fully. Obviously it was not what they had intended to tell me.

"A box?" I echoed, a little relieved that the bewildering price of apples was not in question.

"A gittar," explained Sammy, his black face deadly serious. "We each got us a gittar. We plays us gittar music."

"Also, us—we sings," nodded Hammy enticingly. They obviously wanted me to say something. Their eyes begged me to say it, but I could not imagine what it was. It somehow never occurred to me that the two black boys would be coming to see me about the party.

But that was it. Sammy and Hammy wanted to go to the party, and, moreover, they wanted to be on the program.

"But I ain't got no two bits," said Sammy, his mouth drooping sadly.

"Nor me," echoed Hammy. "You said—come to you, Miz Carey . . ." His voice died away plaintively.

"We'll work for you—hard," offered Sammy.

Their eyes held mine apprehensively, like spaniels' eyes, hoping for a kind word.

"That's fine," I said with unnecessary vigor. "Fine! I'll put you down for the program. And don't you worry about the money. Your music will pay your way."

It was the wrong thing to say. I knew it when the boys stiffened into black statues and their faces hardened into expressionless masks.

"Our mammy say—work for what you gets," Hammy said at last, adding with sober dignity, "So we works for you."

"Yes," I said quickly, "maybe you'd better, so the others won't be jealous and think I like you best."

A look of blind adoration came into Sammy's face, and Hammy grinned in a pleased sort of way.

So it was fixed. I gave the boys the tickets, ostentatiously taking fifty cents out of my purse and putting it ceremoniously into the "party box." The work was to be done later, when I needed something done.

As the day for the party approached, excitement began to run high in the freshman class. The twins whispered to me that they had been "practicing up," and the sight of their raptly pleased faces intensified in me a little feeling of doubt I'd been trying to suppress. What, I thought, if the white children should be unkind to the black boys? What if the others on the program should refuse to appear with them? And what about the dance? What little girl would dance with them—and would I want her to, if she would?

I needn't have worried about the program. Apparently no parental ultimatum had been laid down. Perhaps no one had mentioned that the black boys were to make music, or perhaps the hours of the party were to be a sort of secular Truce of God wherein even black boys with a bad mother could have their hour of fun.

The party was to begin at eight, and at seven-thirty the gym was almost filled with children, all the little girls in bright new party dresses, with their hair tortured into elaborate beauty-parlor curls, sitting shyly on one side of the decorated gym, while all the little boys, dressed uncomfortably in new suits, with their damp hair brushed to alarming neatness, were seated on the other. The problem of the first half of the evening, as far as we teachers were concerned, was to coax the two groups, much against their wills, to consent to dance together, while the problem of the last half was to pry them apart and get them home before irate parents began telephoning.

But first came the program. Promptly at eight, since everyone had already been there for at least a half hour, the curtain went up, after several false starts and muffled grunts from the laboring stagehands.

Mary Ellen Adams and Jo Anne Merrill gave their usual military tap dance, which, since Mary Ellen is short and fat and lazy, and Jo Anne tall and thin and active, was rather far from the military effect desired. Little Genevieve Johnson sang "Ciribiribin," which she pronounced "See-ree-bee-ree-bean" for some unknown reason, and, with practically no encouragement, graciously added the encore "Blues in the Night." Glen Tillman played an excruciating violin solo, during which, mercifully, one string broke, so that the rest of the solo was, by anybody's mathematics, only three fourths as bad as the first. Benny Norton gave a reading in Swedish dialect with occasional lapses into Irish, Yiddish, and just plain American.

Then the twins came out from the opposite side of the stage, hesitating, looking dwarfed and lonely under the floodlights, black faces glistening and fearful, patched Sunday best pressed within an inch of its life. They clutched their cheap "gittars," looked out uncertainly at the darkened gym, struck a few chords, and then they sang.

I don't remember much else, not even what they sang. There

was stamping of feet when they finished, and shouting. They sang
song after song. They sang as the class danced, when it did dance.
They sang with the Capehart and without it. They sang while the
lunch was passed out until the class president himself brought them
two heaped plates and clapped each of the boys on the shoulder
by way of congratulation, while the class cheered through mouth-
fuls of sandwich and cake and waved pop bottles in the air.

They never left the stage all evening. Now, at last, something
was well with them: the little black boys, for whom 3 x 8 was a
variable, could sing.

After that, school was their heaven. Boys and girls who couldn't
play with them outside of school never failed to call: "Hi, Ham!
Hi, Sam!" in school. Math homework papers grew mysteriously
accurate though tests still revealed the most abysmal misconceptions
concerning mathematical practice. Even the seniors had them sing
at their class party. They made the senior glee club, though they
had feared before to try out for the junior one.

And they haunted my footsteps with a doglike persistence that
came near to wearing me out.

"When we going to work out that fifty cents, Miz Carey,
ma'am?"

"When the frost is out of the ground," I explained for the tenth
time. "I want you to spade my flower garden."

A day later: "When that frost get outa that ground?"

"Not for two weeks, at least."

Two days later: "That frost gone yet, Miz Carey?"

"Not yet," patiently.

"My! My! Sure stays a long time—that frost!"

When at last the frost did depart the two black boys attacked
my little garden spot with a vigor it had never known before. They
trailed quack-grass roots to their remotest hiding places and
exterminated them forever. They spaded and weeded and spaded
again.

"That's a great deal of work for fifty cents," I teased at last,
a little troubled at the sight of their thin bent backs stooping over
my garden so long.

"Our mammy say—work good," Sammy said firmly, and
Hammy's monkey-thin face echoed the stubborn set of his brother's
jaw.

"You give us those seeds—we plant 'em," Hammy called
pleadingly.

They planted my seeds, they hovered over the new little shoots, they weeded and watered and tended. I tried to give them extra pay, but they stiffened with hurt pride.

"Our mammy say—you take good care o' Miz Carey's garden, for she been purely good to you."

So I gave up in despair and let them do as they wished. I did all I could to get my neighbors to give them odd jobs, but only a few did, for the black boys' mother had had her baby, a girl baby, almost white, old Dr. Bates said, with hair like Cash Benson's.

In school the boys still haunted my room after class. They'd sit staring at my face, saying never a word until I had finished my work, and then not much unless I set the pace.

One afternoon I'd been reading a volume of Blake's poems, and on an impulse I asked them if they'd like me to read them a poem about a little black boy. I didn't think they'd understand a word of it, but I love to read poetry aloud, even if it's only to myself. Only after I had started to read did it occur to me that the black boys might read into it something that Blake had never intended, that I might be shaking their protective unawareness, might be emphasizing their difference in a way bad for them. But I had started and I had to go on.

They sat still as statues while I read:

"My mother bore me in the southern wild,
    And I am black, but oh, my soul is white!
White as an angel is the English child,
    But I am black, as if bereaved of light.

"My mother taught me underneath a tree,
    And, sitting down before the heat of day,
She took me on her lap and kissed me,
    And, pointing to the East, began to say:

" 'Look on the rising sun,—there God does live,
    And gives His light, and gives His heat away;
And flowers and trees and beasts and men receive
    Comfort in morning, joy in the noonday.

" 'And we are put on earth a little space,
    That we may learn to bear the beams of love;
And these black bodies and this sunburnt face
    Are but a cloud, and like a shady grove.

" 'For, when our souls have learned the heat to bear,
  The cloud will vanish, we shall hear His voice,
Saying: "Come out from the grove, My love and care,
  And round My golden tent like lambs rejoice.' "

"Thus did my mother say, and kissed me;
  And thus I say to little English boy.
When I from black, and he from white cloud free,
  And round the tent of God like lambs we joy,

"I'll shade him from the heat, till he can bear
  To lean in joy upon our Father's knee;
And then I'll stand and stroke his silver hair,
  And be like him, and he will then love me."

I watched their faces as I finished. They were still and solemn, but radiant.

"Our mammy say—heaven's like that," Hammy said softly at last.

"Who that man say all that?" Sammy whispered in an awed voice.

"William Blake, a very great poet."

"He a preacher, Miz Carey, I bet?" Hammy asked, looking at me hopefully.

"No, not exactly," I answered, and saw the radiance in their faces dim at my words. Impulsively I added, "But he was a man who thought he spoke with angels, and—and he wrote 'as one having authority, and not as the scribes'!" And I found myself telling them how Blake, dying, sang of the glories of heaven opening before his dimming eyes.

Hammy's face shone, and his teeth flashed in a grin of solemn delight.

"He sure knew—that white man!"

"God sure told him sumpin," Sammy affirmed, nodding deeply.

"Read it again, please, Miz Carey," said Sammy suddenly.

I read it again, and they both sighed with one accord.

"That's better'n music," Hammy whispered. "Read it once more again? Huh? Please?"

I laughed and shut the book. "No, twice is enough. Some other day, perhaps."

But I never read it to them again.

As he went out of the door Sammy turned. "You like rock gardens, Miz Carey?"

"Why, yes, of course," I said, "but if you're thinking——You've done altogether too much——"

"We knows a place," Hammy was saying dreamily, "a place where there's moss like a feather bed an' little white violets that's sweet as Jesus' breath——"

That was the last I was ever to see them. They rowed across to the place they knew after supper that night, a marshy island not very far offshore. Folks who saw them start said the water was choppy as they were going over. Coming back the boat overturned, and before the men could get to them they were drowned.

I heard the next morning in school.

The late May sun was warm on my hair that day, when school was over and I was plodding along the beach toward the Negro woman's shack. The silvery sand filtered into my slippers and dribbled out with each difficult step. Under the slanting sun the smooth blue waves lapped the shore and retreated in little slipping movements, as if they had never known storms or death.

Around the shack the rank shore grasses had been cleared away with scrupulous care, and in the shifting sand a few drooping plants gave evidence of the twins' efforts to make a garden of their own.

She opened the rough, tar-paper-covered door when I knocked —a thin, worn woman of about forty, with the fine features and liquid eyes one sometimes sees in people of her race. Her lined black face was masklike in its calm, but the eyes themselves were alive and tragic.

I don't remember what inadequate thing I said to her, but she must have felt my sorrow reaching out to hers, for she thanked me with something of the boys' doglike look in her eyes.

"They loved you so, Miz Carey," she said strangely, and I had the feeling that behind her simple words there was something strong and seeking, something she wanted of me—wanted badly, if only I could find out what it was.

She asked me in with homely courtesy and pulled out a rough chair for me to sit on.

The one room was painfully neat and bare. In a broken tumbler on the table a small bunch of short-stemmed white violets was beginning to droop, and on the ledge of the one window I saw the purple tulips I had given Hammy two days before. A table, three old chairs—one with no back—a small camp stove, and two camp cots were the only furnishings. The floor, rough and splintered from much scrubbing, was immaculate.

That space of floor seemed to me that day to be waiting mutely —waiting for the boys, who hadn't yet been brought back in their cheap little coffins. People never knew until long afterward that it was Cash Benson who had paid for it all, giving them the best funeral he could afford. That, at least, is to his credit, though he went off the next week and never came back. Reverend Swanson, too, came, the good old man, although he had to face the disapproval of the Swedish Baptist ladies to do it. I've thought of it often since and blessed the kindness of his gentle old heart.

But that day there were just the two of us. I sat by the table, and the afternoon sun through the only window threw the shadow of Hammy's tulips across the bare floor.

The boys' mother stood by the other side of the table, black and monumental and unweeping, staring at me with that queer tense look, seeming about to speak and then closing her lips gravely.

The baby began to cry, and she went over and picked the little thing up from the bed, blindly, as if she hardly knew what she did. After a moment she sat down opposite me, rocking the child gently in her arms.

Awkwardly I tried to comfort her, saying it was good she had the girl baby to fill a part of her heart. She looked at me strangely across the sun-mottled oilcloth, her ugly black face sharp with pain.

"But they was my true-born child'en," she said, as if reasoning with one who was dull of understanding. Slowly she looked down at the whimpering infant in her arms. "She white man's child, poor little thing."

Then she looked me straight in the eyes, not doglike but womanlike.

"I was all alone," she said simply.

I tried to speak, but there was nothing to say now.

When I started to go at last, it was with the feeling of how very futile my visit had been, of how empty sympathy and words of sympathy were to this woman.

She rose reluctantly when I did, saying softly, "You was good as they said you was to come." Then she added pleadingly, as if she feared I would misunderstand, "But it ain't fitten you come no more. Besides——" Her voice caught but she swallowed and went patiently on, "Besides it be best you remember Hamuel and Samuel as they was—yestiday."

I nodded mutely, and she seemed satisfied that I had not misunderstood or taken offense.

But on the doorstep she stopped me again, hesitating, uncertain, and I knew that the thing that was haunting her was still unsaid. I could feel the conflict of urgency and fear in her, the tension and the longing, but I had to watch her helplessly, hoping she would speak, afraid to ask for fear what I might say would be wrong.

She drew a deep breath then, throwing her head back nervously. Her eyes were shining and fearful, and the words, when they came, were slurred and hurried breathless.

"Last night—suppertime—Hammy 'n Sammy, they full of some word song you read 'em. They say—it better'n music. They go away singin' it to them two——Something about—black boys? You remember, Miz Carey, ma'am?"

Her breast rose and fell in agitation, and the child, awakening again, began to cry.

"I'll send you a copy," I said thickly. "A poem I read to them."

She shook her head. "You say it to me, please? I never did learn book reading."

I turned my head away, thinking of the scrapbook of "nice words" she had kept for her boys.

What I could remember, garbled, imperfect, half forgotten, I tried to say, remembering the two thin black faces lifted to mine in the quiet of the dusty schoolroom.

She was very still when I had finished, but her face was bright with a faith I could never know.

"My Hammy and Sammy?" she said wonderingly. "Maybe they God's white lambs today?"

And then she wept, putting her face down against the baby in her arms. "Oh, bless God," she whispered brokenly. "Blessed God, make it so. Sweet Jesus, make it so."

I touched her hand silently in farewell and went away. At the gate, when I turned and looked back, she had lifted her head, and I saw that she was looking far out over the water, gazing across at the distant shore line of that green, marshy island where the moss is like a feather bed and the little white violets are as sweet as Jesus' breath.

THE DIARY OF A FRESHMAN

by Charles Macomb Flandrau

T HE CRASH HAS COME, AND THE DEAN AND MY ADVISOR, TWO OR three instructors, some of the fellows at the table, and even Berrisford (this last is a little too much), have all taken occasion to inform me regretfully that they foresaw it from the first. This is the sort of thing that makes a man bitter. How did I know what was ahead of me? If they all realized so well that I was going to flunk the hour exams, why didn't they let me know then? It might have done some good if they had told me three weeks ago that they thought me stupid; but I fail to see the point of their giving me to understand at this stage of the game that they themselves all along have been so awfully clever. Yet, that's just what they've done; all except Duggie. And strangely enough it was Duggie that I most dreaded. As a matter of fact he has scarcely mentioned the subject. When I went into his room one night and stood around for a while without knowing how to begin and finally came out with,—

"Well, I suppose Berri's told you that I didn't get through a single exam?"—he merely said,—

[131]

"That's tough luck; I'm darned sorry;" and then after a moment he added: "Oh, well, there'll be some more coming along in February; it isn't as if they weren't going to let you have another whack at things."

"Of course I know it isn't my last chance," I answered drearily; "but I can't help feeling that the fact of its being my first makes it almost as bad. It starts me all wrong in the opinion of the Dean and my advisor and the college generally." Somehow I couldn't bring myself to tell Duggie what I thought, and what, in a measure, I still think—namely, that the marks I got were most unjust. There's something about Duggie—I don't know what it is exactly —that always makes you try to take the tone, when you're telling him anything, that you feel he would take if he were telling the same thing to you. This sounds rather complicated, but what I mean, for instance, is that if he got E in all his exams and thought the instructors had been unjust, he would probably go and have it out with them, but he wouldn't complain to any one else. Of course it's simply nonsense even to pretend, for the sake of argument, that Duggie could flunk in anything; but, anyhow, that's what I mean. . . .

My advisor is a young man and seems like an appreciative, well-disposed sort of person (he offered me a cigar after I had sat down in his study), so I didn't have any difficulty in telling him right off what I had come for.

"I've heard from my hour examinations," I said, "and I find that I have been given E in all of them." (I was careful not to say that I had failed or flunked, or hadn't passed, as that was not the impression I wished to convey.)

"We have met the enemy and we are theirs," he answered pleasantly. "Yes, I heard about that," he went on, "and I hoped you would come in to see me." Then he waited awhile—until the clock began to get noisy—and at last he glanced up and said,—

"What was it doing when you came in? It looked like snow this afternoon." But I hadn't gone there to discuss meteorology, so I ignored his remark.

"I can scarcely think I could have failed in everything," I suggested.

"It *is* somewhat incredible, isn't it?" the young man murmured.

"I never stopped writing from the time an examination began until it stopped," I said.

"What did you think it was—a strength test?" he asked brutally.

"I told all I knew."

"Yes," he acknowledged; "your instructors were convinced of that."

"And I don't think I got enough credit for it. If I had the books here, I feel sure I could make this plain."

"Well, let's look them over," he answered readily; and much to my astonishment he went to his desk and brought back all my blue-books.

I confess I hadn't expected anything quite so definite as this, but I tried to appear as if I had hoped that it was just what might happen. We sat down side by side and read aloud—first an examination question (he had provided himself with a full set of the papers) and then my answer to it.

" 'Explain polarized light,' " he read.

" 'The subject of polarized light, as I understand it, is not very well understood,' " I began; at which my adviser put his hands to his head and rocked to and fro.

"If you don't mind," I said, "I think I'd rather begin on one of the others; this physics course is merely to make up a condition, and perhaps I've not devoted very much time to it; it isn't a fair test." So we took up the history paper and read the first question, which was: "What was the Lombard League?" My answer I considered rather neat, for I had written: "The Lombard League was a coalition formed by the Lombards." I paused after reading it and glanced at my adviser.

"It was a simple question, and I gave it a simple answer," I murmured.

"I am afraid you depreciate yourself, Mr. Wood," he replied. "Your use of the word 'coalition' is masterly."

"But what more could I have said?" I protested.

"I don't think you could have said *anything* more," he answered inscrutably.

I read on and on, and he interrupted me only twice—once in the philosophy course to point out politely that what I constantly referred to as "Hobbes' Octopus" ought to be "Hobbes' Leviathan," and once in the questions in English Literature, to explain that somebody or other's "Apologia Pro Vita Sua" was not—as I had translated it—"an apology for living in a sewer." (I could have killed Berrisford for that—and it sounded so plausible, too;

for any one who lived in a sewer would naturally apologize.) He let me proceed, and after a time I couldn't even bring myself to stop and contest the decisions as I had done at first; for I dreaded the way he had of making my most serious remarks sound rather childish. So I rattled on, faster and faster, until I found myself mumbling in a low tone, without pronouncing half the words; and then I suddenly stopped and put the blue-book on the table and stared across the room at the wall. He didn't express any surprise, which, on the whole, was very decent of him, and after a minute or two of silence, during which he gathered up the evidence and put it back in his desk, we began to talk football and our chances of winning the big game. He said some nice things about Duggie, and hoped the rumor that he was overtrained wasn't true. I told him that I lived in the same house with Duggie and knew him very well, and feared it was true. He seemed glad that I knew Duggie. I stayed for about fifteen minutes so as not to seem abrupt or angry at the way my visit had turned out, and then left. We didn't refer to the exams again, so I don't see exactly how I can ever right the wrong they have done me. If my advisor were a different kind of man, I could have managed it, I think.

I haven't seen very much of the fellows lately, except, of course, at meals—that is to say, at luncheon and dinner, for I can't stand their comments at breakfast. They greet me with "Hello, old man —what's this I hear about your trying for the Phi Beta Kappa?" "Is it true that you're going to get your degree in three years?" "I shouldn't go in for a *summa cum* if I were you; a *magna* is just as good;" and all that sort of thing. They evidently find it very humorous, for it never fails to make them all laugh. I've taken to breakfasting at the Holly Tree, as I don't often meet any one I know there. I did one morning, however, come across the little instructor who had charge of the Freshman registration and made quavering remarks at me in a kind of Elizabethan dialect. He's a most extraordinary person. As he doesn't say more than half he means, and as I don't understand more than half he says, I find conversation with him very exhausting. But I like him, somehow.

I was reading a newspaper when he came in and didn't realize that he was standing near me until I heard a slow, tremulous, reproachful voice saying,—

"Who's been sitting in *my* chair?" It seems that he always has his breakfast at the same table in the chair that I, in my ignorance, had taken. I jumped up, of course, and after he had sat down and leaned back, he murmured feebly, "I'm an old man; but I know my place." I didn't know why he said this, as he isn't an old man at all; he can't be more than thirty-six or thirty-seven.

"I'm a young man, but I seem to know your place, too," I laughed, as I looked around for another chair.

"You clever boys chaff me so," he replied mournfully. "You mustn't chaff me; I'm only a simple villager." Just then the waitress appeared at a hole in the buff-colored fence that deludes itself into thinking it differentiates the kitchen from the dining-room, and the little man pounded softly and gently on the table, exclaiming,—

"What ho—Katy; some sack—some sack!" A request that Katy evidently understood better than I did, for she withdrew and came back in a moment with a cup of tea.

"How now, Sir John—is not my hostess of the tavern a most sweet wench?" the instructor inquired of me; which caused Katy —who had lingered to hear what we wanted for breakfast—to twist a corner of her apron around her finger and gurgle ecstatically,—

"Now, Mr. Fleetwood, you stop."

We sat there talking for more than an hour, and I don't know when I've had so improving a conversation. We talked mostly about books and plays. Mr. Fleetwood seems to care a great deal about both and discussed them differently from the way most people do. At our table at Mrs. Brown's, for instance, a book or a play is always either "rotten" or a "corker." But Fleetwood has no end of things to tell about them. He seems to know all the people who do the writing and acting, and remembers all the clever remarks they've made to him at various times, and the even cleverer ones he made in reply. Finally, when I got up to go he relapsed suddenly into his more doleful manner and said,—

"You will come to my Wednesday Evenings—won't you?" I felt as if I ought to have known what they were; but I'd never heard of them, so I suppose I looked mystified.

"The lions roar at my Wednesday Evenings," he explained,

turning on the tremolo in his voice, "but they won't hurt you—because they like me. They'll like you, too, if you'll come." I said I should like to come very much.

"When do you have your Wednesday Evenings?" I asked; for he was so dreadfully vague. He looked at me vacantly, and then stared at the ceiling awhile, as if trying to think.

"On Wednesday evenings," he at last petulantly quavered; and I left, for I began to think I was losing my mind. . . .

★ *The Proper Bostonian reserves his highest regard for something which is not located in Boston at all, but is a few miles up the Charles River in Cambridge, and which he calls Hahvud. Since all First Family sons repair there he wishes it to be recognized as the only college there is. "If a man's in there," one Bostonian used to say, tapping the catalogue of Harvard graduates, "that's who he is. If he isn't, who is he?"*

CLEVELAND AMORY
'The Proper Bostonians,' quoted by 'Fun Fare'
(Copyright 1949 by The Reader's Digest Association)

THE BERLITZ AFFAIR

by Emily Kimbrough

I CAN'T GO TO ITALY," I SAID ALOUD TO MYSELF ONE MORNING last March, "without knowing something of the language." And at that instant I knew I was going to Italy.

An hour earlier I had listened to considerable promotional talk on the subject from my friend, Sophy, who lives in Havenford, but shares my apartment when she is New York. Sophy is a very busy woman. She is Vice President of the National Urban League and an active participant in several other organizations. She is a vigorous campaigner and a great one for planning. Her hair is curly and has been gray since she was thirty-five. When she brings it on end by running her hands through it and says, "Now darling . . .," you know you're involved in a campaign and a plan, and it's a ninety to one bet that as of that minute, you're a goner.

Shortly after I made my decision, I announced it impressively to Sophy. "I'm signing up at the Berlitz School," I said, "for Italian lessons. You can't go to Italy without knowing something of the language."

Sophy pondered this. "I'll join you," she said at last. "I won't be so good as you, because you've got a much better musical ear than I have, though I know more about music than you do. However, I'll try not to hold you back."

I was magnanimous. She wouldn't hold me back at all, I promised, and I'd be glad of her company.

The following morning, Sophy and I, around nine-thirty, enrolled in the Berlitz School. The address is Rockefeller Center, that part of it with an entrance on Fifth Avenue. Immediately inside this entrance, we confronted a double flight of escalators, one going up and, directly beside it, the descending flight. Sophy was all for boarding the upgoing one. When I asked for what purpose, her answer was there didn't seem to be anything at the bottom.

With all the bustle we had just left on Fifth Avenue, there was, curiously, not a soul in this large, dark foyer. I released my grip on Sophy's arm in order to look for someone, and she immediately started up the steps.

I walked to the right of the stairway and almost at once came upon a large show window containing a display of the workings of the Berlitz School. A cardboard figure of a stylish gentleman dwarf dominated the scene. He wore a morning coat, gray trousers, his collar was exceptionally high. I thought he was a dwarf because the size of his head made the rest of him seem of diminutive proportions. But perhaps this was intended only to convey an outsize intellect, further indicated by an extra large pair of black, horn-rimmed spectacles and total lack of hair on his head. The figure carried a long pointer of the sort teachers use at a blackboard. This was directed to a cardboard sign listing a series of languages headed by French. Another cardboard sign nearby read, "Enroll Today." It was only after I had studied at some length the awesome prospect behind this invitation that I came upon, in small type, the information that the School itself was on the fifth floor.

There was no possibility of sharing with Sophy this discovery. She had long since passed beyond my view.

I did not know how to reach the fifth floor, since the escalator in the center seemed to end within sight directly above me. Several people came in from the street. I asked one of these if he knew where the elevators were. He directed me to their hiding place behind the escalator.

When I left the conveyance at the fifth floor, I saw almost at once a metal sign, labeled "Berlitz," pointing in the direction of the

School. The first person I saw as I came through the indicated door was Sophy, standing at a long counter, her back to me, talking to a young woman on the other side of the counter. I joined them.

"We're together," I told the young woman.

Sophy turned. "Oh, I'm glad you got here," she said. "Find someone to tell you the way?"

I continued talking to the young woman, explaining a brilliant idea that had occurred to me the evening before. "My daughter, B," I said, speaking each word slowly and distinctly in order not to confuse her with rapid English, "took a course in French from your school, but she didn't finish it. We lived in Philadelphia then, and this was five years ago. Do you think the credit could be transferred—unless there is a time limit on it? Perhaps you don't understand what I'm saying, but if you will let me speak to the manager here, I'm sure I could—"

Miss Berlitz interrupted me. "There will be no trouble about the credit," she said briskly, and her accent was as Middle Western as mine, "as long as you get permission from your daughter."

I stared at her. Sophy made a disagreeable sound, much like a snicker.

"Why," I said incredulously, "I don't believe you do understand. *I* paid for the course. I'm her mother."

My vis-à-vis was patient.

"It was your daughter who went to the classes. *She* registered. Therefore, it's for her to say whether at some time she wishes to continue the lessons and complete the course, or transfer to you those remaining. If you will give me her name and address, I'll have our office write to her asking for a release to you."

"She's gone to California with her baby on a month's visit to my parents," I reported. "She's been married since she took that course."

Sophy broke in. "I don't believe the Berlitz School is getting up a dossier on B," she told me. "Just your family's address will do."

I delivered the address and the young woman wrote it down. She then took my registration; Sophy's, I found, had already been taken care of. We were to have a lesson every morning, sharing a teacher, but with no one else in the class.

"You may start now, if you wish," our registrar said, and gathered up the papers we had signed, "Classroom L."

As we walked down the hall in the direction she had indicated,

I admitted my irritation. "It's silly," I said, "but I'm irked by such nonsense. What on earth has B got to do with *my* Italian? I paid for her lessons and she was too lazy to finish them. Now *she* gives *me* permission to take Italian. What I really mind is that she's going to think it very, very funny. It's almost put me off the whole idea."

Sophy asked me if I'd feel better just to pay for my lessons and forget the credit. Obviously this was nonsense; I said nothing more.

There was considerable traffic up and down the corridor, men and women, young girls and boys, most of them carrying notebooks, textbooks, pencils. I had a sudden wistful fantasy that I was back at college again, and wondered how it would be if I stopped some of these people to ask if they had seen the dean to arrange their courses and what were the professors like. But such snatches of conversation as I overheard were in foreign languages, no two of them the same and not one of them English. I felt suddenly shy and scuttled after Sophy, who, as usual, was ahead of me. She turned into a room on the left, stopping to look at the letter on the door. I followed her across the threshold and there I was, in a classroom like classrooms the world over, except that this was smaller than most. Three rows of chairs, each with a wide right arm on which to put books and notebook for writing, a desk by the door where the professor would sit. The room, at the moment, was empty. Sophy was standing still, looking around her, like me.

"It takes me back thirty years," I said. "I feel kind of queer."

Sophy nodded.

We took off our coats and gloves, and piled them on chairs in the back row. We selected places on the front row and sat down side by side, though there was plenty of space in which to spread ourselves more comfortably. Neither of us seemed to find anything more to say to the other.

On the threshold I had noticed vaguely that the walls were hung with pictures. I took more careful note of them while we waited for the professor. And of all the story-telling pictures I have ever seen, these held the record for content.

The one on the wall directly in front of me included, looking from left down around the border and up to the right-hand corner: a ferryboat on a blue ocean; a group of people on a beach, the ladies dressed in suits of the Annette Kellerman period; a hooded wicker bath-chair. Next, the skyline of New York, a dirigible floating overhead, a four-masted schooner in the harbor, an ocean liner with a tug pulling it and a hydroplane settling down just alongside. A bathroom came next, with tub and basin, soap, sponge, comb, pair of scissors, tube of toothpaste.

By this time I realized the purpose of these pictures was to teach the names of the objects in whatever language we were studying. It occurred to me that if this were the objective, it was a badly timed sense of delicacy that excluded the one object in a bathroom for which one undoubtedly would have the most urgent need in the language of the country one was visiting.

A bedroom scene balanced the bathroom; very quaint, with a ruffled canopy over the bed and around the dressing table. I made a mental note I would not tax my intellectual capacity with the Italian for ruffles.

I had not yet come to the borders. When I reached my scrutiny of these I knew at once Mr. Berlitz was going to ask more of me than I would be able to give him. Down the left border in order were a squirrel, a peacock, a frog, a duck, a beetle, and a pair of duelists matching swords. Across the bottom, a bee, a boiled egg in a cup, a pig, a cheese under glass, a glass of beer—that was all to the good—two roosters, a patch of mushrooms, an artist sitting at an easel; next, a roll of sausage, a loaf of bread, and, cantering up the opposite side, an ostrich followed by a swan, a caterpiller, a butterfly, an owl, a typewriter, a telephone, a stork, a parrot, an eagle, three fish, of to me unknown species, and a large wolf in a snowdrift.

I turned to Sophy to tell her I intended to take a stand on how wide an area I wished my Italian to cover, when a voice from the doorway said, "*Buon giorno.*"

I swung around with a start to see, bowing gracefully at us from the doorway, a handsome young man, obviously Italian, with black hair in a waving pompadour and large brown eyes.

Out of the corner of my eye I saw Sophy, rather red in the face, give a stiff little nod. I heard her mutter, but I doubt that it reached the young man, "*Buon giorno.*"

I tried to make my acknowledgment somewhere between Sophy's nod and the young man's bow. I found myself unable, because I felt silly, to produce a "*Buon giorno,*" but I gave out something in the nature of a whinny with a smile.

The young man seated himself at the desk by the door. He was carrying a book and two large white cards. He pushed these on top of the desk, bent over, looked at the cards, picked up one of them, and looking from it to each of us in turn said inquiringly, "*Signora Kimbrough?*"

"*Moi*," I answered loudly as if faulty hearing on his part were the stumbling block between us, and I pointed to my chest. With the instant realization, however, that my remark did not sound Italian, I added stiffly, "I am Mrs. Kimbrough."

The young man shook his head and pointed to me. "*Lei e Signora Kimbrough.*" He put the palm of his hand against his chest. "*Io sono Signor Grammatico.*" He repeated this back and forth several times, then turned to Sophy.

"*Signora Jacobs?*" he inquired.

"*Io sono Signora Jacobs*," Sophy replied.

"*Brava, brava*," said Signor Grammatico, and they smiled at each other.

I had a deplorable impulse to give her a kick in the ankle.

Signor Grammatico picked up his book. "*Il libro*," he said, pointing to it. "*Il lapis*," he picked up the pencil; "*la tavola*," he patted the table; "*la penna*," he showed us his fountain pen; "*la sedia*," and he bounced to indicate what he was sitting on; "*il muro*," he indicated the wall; "*il soffitto*," he pointed to the ceiling.

He lifted the book and looked inquiringly at me. "*Que e?*" he said with a rounding infection and I gathered he wanted me to tell him what it was.

"*Le libro*," I answered, and tried not to sound smug.

He shook his head, "Il *libro*," he corrected me.

We went on to the other objects. I gave these back to him in Italian with no hesitancy. I made only one other error. I confused "chair" with "ceiling." "*La soffitto*," I said, and bounced in my concentration on doing exactly what he had done.

"Il *soffitto*," he corrected, and pointed upward. "*La sedia*," and indicated when I had bounced.

I had already regretted the bouncing and was doubly mortified it had taken place on "the ceiling."

He turned to Sophy.

Sophy rattled off the objects with the rapidity of a chattering squirrel, and ending up with, "*il libro*," drew out the vowel and gave the "r" the kind of roll Caruso used to send out into the auditorium from the stage of the Metropolitan. My delivery had been uncompromisingly Muncie, Indiana.

I slewed around in my chair at right angles to my previous position and stared at my companion. She was leaning forward, her cheeks flushed, her eyes sparkling and fixed on Signor Grammatico.

"*Bravissimo,*" I heard Signor Grammatico murmur, and I resumed my former position facing him. Not that he was aware which way I was facing. He and Sophy were exchanging staccato nods of mutual congratulation.

There is an old hymn that begins, "I am a stranger here." This latter I waved aside as not applicable. But for the first line, spiritually speaking, the writer of that hymn and I were in precisely the same spot.

The lingual tour of the room continued, Signora Jacobs and Signor Grammatico leading the way, the rolling r's cascading behind them. I tagged along like an unwanted kid sister they'd been told to look out for. Sometimes the Signor tossed an inquiry at me, and Sophy would repeat the word to me helpfully, much in the way adults question a child learning the rudiments of speech. "Where is baby's nose?" says one, and the other echoes, "Nose, darling?" But Baby Kimbrough was by this time too addled to respond. In the end Signor Grammatico and Sophy evidently decided it was kinder to leave me alone. And so while I sat muttering to myself the two or three words I had managed to capture early in the hour, they trilled their r's and glided their vowels, from pocketbook to handkerchief to dress, suit, hat, shoes, and so on.

A bell ringing was the first familiar sound I had heard in sixty minutes. I know what it meant, too, and that in itself was a comfort. The bell was a surprise to Sophy and Signor Grammatico. They stopped the rondo on which they were engaged and shook their heads in a spontaneous expression of disappointment that such a pleasant hour had sped away. I was already at the chair in the back of the room where I had placed my coat and gloves. For fifty-five minutes I had been far, far in the rear. But sixty minutes and thirty seconds from the time I had entered that room found me going out of it, coated and gloved.

"*Arrivederci,*" or some such nonsense Signor Grammatico called after me. But I was safely across the threshold.

"Good-by," I said.

Passing the main desk in the hall, I was hailed by the girl who had taken my registration, the one who was going to ask my daughter's permission for me to be taught Italian on credit. I was in no mood for any further trafficking with that young woman and would have gone on my way but she called after me. "I think you will want to buy a book. They're on sale here."

I approached her and her book cautiously. I was not prepared to say whether or not I wanted a book, because I was not sure my brief association with the Berlitzes and their doings was going to continue. The young woman, however, held out invitingly to me a slim volume and I took it. Sophy joined me while I was examining it and immediately asked for one for herself.

On the way to the elevator she prattled about how exhilarating the hour had been, how her rusty old brain had come alive again, making her realize how much she had always loved languages. Once we were out on Fifth Avenue, I parted from her and her exhilaration. I did not see her again until evening.

By that time, however, I had made up my mind to go on with Mr. Berlitz and Signor Grammatico and all the rest of them, because I had said that one shouldn't go to Italy without knowing something of the language. This was what had really started me on the trip and I had better keep going, if one could call what I had accomplished to date "going" anywhere.

Sophy was spending weekdays in New York at my apartment, returning to her own house in Haverford for weekends. She had volunteered to plan with the travel agency our itinerary in Italy and see about renting a car.

She was very busy planning the trip and I did not see her during the daytime. The evening following my stumble into Italian, however, she was at the apartment poring over her map. I wanted to pore over the Italian book that had been put into my hand by the registration clerk but I was embarrassed. I waited until she had gone to her room and I was safely in my bed before I turned its pages. My dogged purpose, if it took me all night, was to catch up to where Sophy and Signor Grammatico had rested at the ringing of the bell.

At intervals during the day I had looked forward to this catching up. It would be like cramming for an exam. Many was the night, I reminded myself, I had put a wet towel around my head and studied right through until the dawn, pausing only for an occasional cup of strong, black coffee. I drink Sanka now, and that, I thought, would be the only difference. I leaned back happily against my pillow and opened to page one.

I had no need of a wet towel to help me. I had no need of the book itself, certainly no use from it, because it contained not one single word of English; just a listing of the words I had supposedly learned in my *lezione primo*. I could read the words, but of what good was that to me when I had no means of telling a *scapola* from a *denaro?*

Before I went to sleep, however, I could say every word on the list of the *lezione primo* like a parrot. The only ones I could pick out at random were *porta*, *finestra*, and *libro*, because they were the only ones to which I could attach a meaning. But I had the complete list down pat so long as it remained in sequence.

I tried them over the next morning the minute I awakened, and was pleased to find I still could rattle them off, though I was not yet up to drawn-out vowels and rolling r's.

On our way to the school I said nothing to Sophy about my last night's accomplishment. I intended it to be a surprise.

We had a new teacher that morning, a gentleman, but not so dashing as Signor Grammatico; his was a steam-roller model. We moved slowly but inexorably into counting and numbers. There was no foolish skittering around over the ground we had covered the day before. Not once was I given opportunity to recite my word poem made up from the *lezione primo*. Counting from one to one hundred was our routine for the day, and I was fine up to five. Five in Italian is spelled *cinque* and pronounced "*chin-que*." Since five in French is spelled *cinq* and pronounced "*sank*," I gave that pronunciation to *cinque*. I was corrected. The next time round I said "*sank-que*." I was corrected. The following time I gave "*chank-que*."

This evidence of imbecility was doubly exasperating to me because, for a long time I have thought and even said to anyone who might be interested that I get a far greater number of impressions by ear than I do by sight. I pick up music fairly easily. I even play by ear. The execution is bad but I render the tune accurately

All these things I said to myself with fury while Sophy flashed up and down from one to five, and five to one.

After that we moved on, starting with six, and I was what I please to call a humdinger until we reached fifteen. Fifteen is spelled *quindici* and pronounced as in *"quince."* I accepted that and returned it with no difficulty, and we moved on to twenty. But at twenty we stopped and went back to one, and at five I was at the old standstill again; *"sank," "sank-que," "chank-que,"* and now added to it a possible *"quin-que,"* et cetera.

The professor was kindness and patience itself. Sophy was kind and patient, too. I would have given anything to return to the spirit of indifference to me that had prevailed the preceding day. The most soothing sound of the entire hour was of Sophy's getting stuck the second time around and on succeeding ones, at seventeen.

When the bell rang I was in the eighties, but still wobbly at any number with a five in it. I stopped at the sound of the bell. The professor put up his hand arresting my motion of getting up to leave. He rose from his desk, walked over to my chair, and bent over me, first giving a furtive look over his shoulder toward the door. "You're going to Italy, aren't you?" he asked in a little more than a whisper.

The sound of my own tongue delivered in this conspiratorial fashion so startled me I drew back and could only nod in reply.

"Well, then," and his voice strengthened a little with urgency, "get those fives. You don't want to be gypped, do you?"

I thanked him in a whisper for his concern.

Each day following brought a new teacher, except for a repeat with Signor Grammatico. Sophy gave him a dazzling performance, to which he responded with enough *bravos* to fill a page. They even embarked on little sallies of witty repartee. I suppose that is what they were because of the mutual happy laughter each sentence brought. I would not have been surprised to see the Signor and the Signora push back the chairs and treat themselves to a little waltz turn.

On the last day of the course we had a lady teacher. She was somewhat elderly, rather frail, and was catching a cold. She wore a shawl around her shoulders and in addition to the inevitable book and cards, carried a box of Kleenex. Evidently the cards produced on the first day were handed to each succeeding teacher, because I could see them gradually being filled, the professor of each day adding to the contents left by his predecessors. Some wrote more than others. Signor Grammatico's notes, I had noticed, were brief, but the Signora of our last day wrote fully after each recitation. Between times she used a Kleenex apologetically.

We were into sentences now, she posing a question to each and eliciting a fully phrased response. At least that was her intention and it was fulfilled by one of us. She worked hard and earnestly; she was an excellent teacher. When the bell rang she was writing on one of the cards. At the sound she looked up. *"Molte bene,"* she said to Sophy, *"molte, molte bene."*

She took a fresh Kleenex from the box, held it to her nose, and turned to me. *"Coraggio, Signora,"* she said, *"corraggio e avanti."*

"That means 'courage,'" Sophy said, "'courage and keep going'."

★ *A chemistry professor asked his class what they considered the most outstanding contribution chemistry had made to the world. The first student to answer shouted: "Blondes."*

CHUB DE WOLFE
in Toledo Blade, quoted by 'Fun Fare'
(Copyright 1949 by The Reader's Digest Association)

FULBRIGHTING IN GREECE

by George R. Stewart

TIME WAS WHEN TEACHING IN A UNIVERSITY MEANT FIRST TERM and then second term, and perhaps a summer session, on the same campus, squeezed in before the beginning of next-year's first term. Once in a life-time the professor might go somewhere else to teach for a year. All that is greatly changed now, and if you ask what has changed it, you may receive a variety of replies, but you may also be answered with the single cryptic word, "Fulbright." Let my own case serve as example.

The telegram came on August 5, 1952. It asked whether I would go, for the coming academic year, to the University of Athens as Professor of American Literature and Civilization. I cleared with my own university and wired back that I could accept the appointment but for the first term only. On August 19, governmental red tape having been cut with surprising rapidity, I received official and final notice. (At the same time my loyalty must have been established, in such a short time as to suggest that my life has been blameless to the point of insipidity.) Ten days later—having rented the house, bought clothes, organized lecture notes, secured reservations, and settled all other business, as with lawyers, dentists, and doctors—my wife and I left home, on August 30.

I should hasten to add that this procedure, while it well illustrates the new element of sudden change that has entered academic life, is by no means typical of the way in which Fulbright appointments are handled. There was an emergency in the Greek situation, someone unable to go at the last moment. Moreover, although I had not applied for the appointment, I was considering an application for the following year, and this was known to various people.

In any case, we drove across the country and sailed from New York on September 12. After more than the ordinary vicissitudes of travel, and some resultant delays, we arrived in Athens on October 18.

The term "Fulbright" echoes the name of Senator J. W. Fulbright of Arkansas, himself a former Rhodes scholar, and therefore sensitive to international cultural relations. In 1946 he sponsored Public Law 584, Seventy-ninth Congress, commonly called the Fulbright Act. As Department of State Publication 3197 declares succinctly, this legislation was inspired by "two compelling factors: (1) the need for broader international understanding and (2) the shortage of dollars." In certain foreign countries, after the war, there was much valuable property of the United States. The foreign countries were eager to buy these supplies, but lacked our currency. Public Law 584 permitted them to buy the surplus property, not by expending dollars, but by bringing American scholars and students to those countries where they could be paid in domestic currency. A so-called "reverse Fulbright" has also been made possible—that is, the sending of scholars and students from the participating country to the United States. The ultimate aim, as expressed in another official document, is "to further goodwill and understanding between the United States and other countries through the exchange of students, teachers, lecturers, research scholars, and specialists." Moreover, although the same statement emphasizes scholarship, the most significant factor of the individual's participation is stated to be his continuing effects or influences "in the direction of ultimate World Peace."

Under the act, agencies known as United States Educational Foundations have been set up in the participating countries. These boards are generally composed of members in equal numbers from the United States and from the respective foreign country. On their recommendation the funds are expended, the programs established, and the candidates appointed.

Appointments fall under the three general heads of Visiting Lecturers, Research Scholars, and Special Categories. The first are generally professors of established reputation in some American university. Research scholars may range from people who might equally well be Visiting Lecturers to modestly compensated "Junior Fulbrights," who are young graduate students. Under Special Categories fall librarians, social workers, and specialists in many other fields. Teachers, typically at the secondary-school level, are also sent.

The arrangements are now in effect with no less than twenty-six countries, although those with China and Korea have recently been (for obvious reasons) suspended. Even at the risk of compiling a mere catalogue, the countries should be listed, for by their very names they display the far-flung nature of the enterprise, and suggest the importance of this two-way cultural influence. In Europe the participating countries include Austria, Belgium and Luxembourg, Denmark, Finland, France, Germany, Greece, Italy, the Netherlands, Norway, Sweden, and the United Kingdom. In Asia the alphabetical list runs from Burma, through Ceylon, India, Iran, Iraq, Japan, Pakistan, the Philippine Islands, and Thailand, to end with Turkey. Australia and New Zealand both participate. The continent of Africa, with only Egypt and the Union of South Africa included, might seem to be slighted, but actually most of it is brought within the range of action because the colonial dependencies of participating countries are included.

The arrangements are in general set up on a twenty-year basis, of which about fifteen years are left to run in most countries. The number of appointments varies with the countries, being affected by a number of factors. It is highest, as might be expected, for the United Kingdom, France, and Italy. In 1951-2 the program for the first of these countries, including its colonial dependencies, called for thirty-two Research Scholars and twenty-eight Lecturers and Specialists. The figures for France were thirty and twenty; for Italy, twenty-three and twelve. Some of the smaller countries, however, took unexpectedly large quotas. Egypt accommodated eight and fifteen; Norway, seven and ten. Greece, too, ranks higher in the list than one would expect of a country with a population of seven and one-half millions, smaller than that of New York City.

In Athens I found a university valiantly struggling to recover from the ravages of war, and a program in American studies which had to be created rather than continued. But, as Scott puts it, " 'twere vain to tell" the petty excitements and confusions of meeting my colleagues, calling upon the Dean with an interpreter, scheduling classes, and locating rooms. It ended by my having three classes, for nine hours of teaching, and one public lecture weekly. At least this was no sinecure! On the other hand, the late date of starting, Christmas vacation, and a special vacation on account of the Greek elections, all reduced the number of teaching weeks to such a small figure that I can lay no claim to having been overworked.

Almost immediately I discovered that most of the students did not know English well enough to do much reading in literature. I therefore decided to emphasize the "civilization" rather than the "literature" of my double-barreled title, and was thus put into the paradoxical position of trying to teach civilization to the Athenians. I ended up by devoting most of my time to American geography and history, because of the obvious utility of these subjects when the students should become teachers of English in Greek secondary schools.

The students themselves were delightful. They were about equally men and women, some older ones, but most of them about the age to be expected of American freshmen and sophomores. They could of course, like any students, be irritating at times. Greeks like to talk, and periodically, in response to some petty stimulus, the whole class would break into floods of an unintelligible tongue. Then I would have to struggle to get them back into English. The language problem was always a difficult one and made every hour's teaching the equivalent in labor of two or three at home. The students had learned English by all sorts of means, one of them merely by listening to radio broadcasts from London. The amazing thing was that they could handle the language at all, not that they had difficulty with my American speech. But they were in general eager, polite, and intelligent. One American assured me, "There are no dumb Greeks!" While I distrust even complimentary generalizations about a whole race, my experience at the University of Athens would lead me to confirm this particular one.

I soon saw that, considering how few weeks were available to me, the actual amount of teaching that I could do would not be very

important. Of greater moment would be the organizing of a program and the establishment of good relations with the students, both
of which I could pass on to my successor.

So, as part of this plan and after some hesitation, I decided to
invite each of the classes to a Sunday afternoon at my house, with
refreshments. This was a somewhat revolutionary procedure, and
might not even have been approved by the university authorities
if they had known of it. In Greece, the continental tradition holds,
and a professor is a thing apart from and above his students. Moreover, the straitened postwar finances of the country are reflected in
low salaries for professors, and most of them simply cannot afford
to entertain.

Each of the afternoons turned out to be a tremendous success.
In spite of his postwar poverty, the Greek never omits to be polite,
and so my wife and I were greatly touched when on each Sunday
morning a huge bunch of flowers was delivered with the compliments of the class. At the proper hour the students arrived,
almost wholly in a body. After a few moments of stiff formal
conversation in English, we showed them into the dining-room, and
like true students everywhere they fell upon the food. They also
drank moderately of the mild Greek wines and liqueurs. When the
food had been consumed—I speak literally—we returned to the
other room. Now things had loosened up, and the conversation was
more animated and easy. They looked at pictures of our house in
the United States and of our children. It ended by their sitting on
the floor singing Greek folksongs in magnificent voices and with a
full distribution of parts.

Upon my final departure from Greece I was again much touched
—remembering their poverty—when each of the classes presented
me with a farewell gift. The small framed watercolor of the temple
of Zeus hangs now in my living room, and the copy of a little Greek
vase stands nearby.

As the weeks passed, I gradually came to know more about the
whole Fulbright set-up in Greece. The U. S. Educational Foundation had its headquarters in Athens, and from the office of its
chairman, Maurice S. Rice, the lines of its influence radiated outward. Besides myself, there were six lecturers at work. One of these
was Merle Rife of Muskingum College, my colleague at the University of Salonika, and two others in specialized work in Athens.
Three Americans held research appointments—a numismatist, a his-

torian, and a New Testament scholar. There were seven at the graduate-student level. In addition, thirty Americans were variously distributed in other kinds of work—as librarians, in connection with the YMCA and YWCA, and, mostly, as teachers in schools of the secondary level. Some of these last were attached to the four private schools that have always been under considerable American influence, but eight teachers were actually functioning in the Greek public-school system. As someone put it, "Scratch a cultural activity, and find a Fulbrighter."

Actually the work of the foundation did not even cease at this point. No less than $70,000 was expended in the course of the year on scholarships for Greek students at the four private institutions already mentioned. The education of some 250 young Greeks was thus facilitated. And at the same time, under sponsorship of the foundation, sixty-eight Greek students were studying in the United States.

Of all these varied activities the one that seems the boldest and to call the most for special comment is the new practice of sending American secondary-school teachers to the gymnasia in various smaller Greek cities. It was a bold experiment and might well have failed. Most of the provincial Greek towns are very dull, few people speak English, the standards of living are vastly different from our own. There was a very good chance that a young American suddenly isolated in such an environment simply could not take it. But, on the whole, the program turned out to be a brilliant success. The work of these teachers has made certain that some contact with the United States has been made, not only by the Athenian (who is a good deal of an international anyway), but also by the grass-roots Greek of the provinces. As Justice Douglas pointed out in *Beyond the High Himalayas*, really to get at a people we must work at the village level. These Fulbrighters in Greece were not quite in the villages, but they have shown that Americans can successfully move in that direction.

In similar fashion one phase of my own work took me away from Athens and into the provinces. I had scarcely arrived when William Weld, the cultural attaché and a member of the Educational Foundation, approached me with the idea of giving lectures in various Greek towns. I took a dim view of the matter. I had been advised by friends that the project was scarcely worth my energy; like most professors, I knew how outside lectures can sap a man's time and strength and generally seem to accomplish little.

In the end I let myself be persuaded, more because the novelty of the adventure appealed to me than in the expectation of accomplishing any great good.

First, I had to write a lecture. I took as my subject "The Influence of Greece upon the United States." My idea was not to talk of the general influence of Greek civilization upon the Western world, but rather upon its specific influences in the United States, such as the effects upon our architecture, names, and literature. The language raised a particular problem. My audiences would know little English, and my own Greek was definitely at the stage of "This-is-the-pen-of-my-father." So we had my lecture translated, and then with my teacher I worked at perfecting myself well enough to read the first ten minutes of it in Greek. This was about as artificial as learning a part in a play, but I thought it worthwhile to make the gesture, because Greeks are not accustomed to having Americans try to learn their language, and would be correspondingly pleased.

Then, just before Christmas—armed with manuscripts in Greek and English and with interpreters arranged for—I set out on the Greek circuit. My schedule called for Patras and Pyrgos in the southwest; Rhodes in the Dodecanese off the coast of Turkey; and Kaballa and Salonika in the north. I ended by feeling not only that these lectures were among the most interesting of all my doings as a Fulbrighter, but also that they were perhaps the most useful.

Twice I read the lecture altogether in English, presenting a paragraph or two, and then pausing while the Greek interpreter read from his text. Three times I read my introductory section in Greek, and here I shall state (recalling Churchill's immortal tetrad) that if I have never shed blood or tears in the cause of Greek-American amity, I have at least expended a great deal of toil and sweat. I certainly hope my audiences appreciated the gesture. It was the hardest working gesture in which I ever indulged. One Greek-American friend paid me a high compliment upon my performance. He said, "I understood every word you said, and sometimes it sounded like Greek."

My experience at Pyrgos was the most interesting, and perhaps the most typically Greek. The others can be considered as variations.

Pyrgos is a town of some fifteen thousand people, in the ancient territory of Elis, close to Olympia. It is not a prosperous town even for Greece, and this means that by our standards it is indescribably poor. As usual, the U. S. Information Service had sponsored the lecture, and had made efficient arrangements in advance.

We made a long day of it by visiting Olympia first, and finally pulling into Pyrgos about five o'clock. It was a chilly, drizzly day, and the town offered little in the way of hotel or restaurant. So we had been invited to take tea with one of the leading families. Their hereditary business was the export of currants, but they had recently shifted to rice, which is now being grown in the district as the result of the work of American agricultural experts.

Tea-time was a memorable experience. There was real Greek courtesy and consideration, and plenty of real Greek food. The nomarch, Greek equivalent of a state governor, came to have tea also, and proved highly intelligent and agreeable. All four of the grown-up children spoke English, and the younger son, in his lieutenant's uniform, made the world shrink even beyond its proverbial smallness. We Californians met him in Pyrgos where he had just returned from being attached to an American division in Korea.

Then we all went to the lecture-hall. It was the best place in town, a very bare and barn-like room indeed, but seating about two hundred, on benches. It was full, and people were standing. Their clothes showed the poverty that is all but universal in Greece. They were mostly men; even yet, oriental customs have a strong hold in provincial Greece.

All the local dignitaries were there. The nomarch sat on the platform to make the introductory speech. The mayor was there too, along with the interpreter and Nelson Stephens, the U. S. Information Service representative for that area of Greece. In the front row sat that most important person in a Greek town—the bishop, magnificent with long black beard, flowing robes, and colorful insignia.

First the nomarch spoke. Being a true Greek, he spoke fluently and at length. My wife, in the balcony, whispered to one of the daughters we had met at tea-time: "What's he saying?" The reply was: "He is telling what your husband has done." Ten minutes later my ever-loyal spouse whispered again: "Well, he can't still be talking about my husband; George hasn't done that much!"

However that may be, I eventually got the floor. Scarcely anyone in the audience understood English, and they soon developed a routine. When the interpreter talked, they listened intently. As soon as I began, they relaxed with an audible rustle, and began—

quite naturally and not at all disrespectfully—to clear their throats and blow their noses. The exceptions were a few young boys, whom I took to be students of English. They were scattered here and there, generally seated between parents who turned proud eyes on their progeny during the periods of my own speaking. From the strained looks on those youths' faces I doubted whether they understood much, but at least they could pick up the Greek that followed, and so the parental pride need not be deflated.

I concluded, and then the interpreter concluded, and then came the applause. I thought it was over, and was ready to make my break from the platform. But the bishop was on his feet. He was speaking formally and with great dignity. I could not follow his Greek, but the occasion reminded me so much of the awarding of a degree to a commencement speaker at the university that I momentarily imagined I was being created an honorary archdeacon. I believe, however, he was only giving some kind of official commendation and thinks.

Finally we adjourned to the balcony and there the town notables assembled for a slight collation with Greek brandy and ouzo. (If you have been to Greece you will know ouzo; if not, it doesn't matter.)

In retrospect, I have decided the lectures served a good purpose. Whether, considered as high-level propaganda, they helped to prevent anyone's conversion to communism or to aid his reconversion, I would not know. They showed a certain number of Greeks, however, that an American professor was willing to take the trouble to come to speak in their towns, and Greek respect for a professor is very high. Such lectures—others of the Fulbrighters also gave them—may likewise help to show that the United States is interested in other things than the purely material ones.

The reception of the lectures was flattering. The halls were full; sometimes people were standing, and at Patras and Pyrgos a number had to be sent away for lack of even standing room. Local dignitaries turned out regularly, and some of them always sat on the platform along with the American representatives. At Kaballa— not far from the Bulgarian border and a Communist center—the major-general commanding the area attended, and a large number of officers. At Rhodes the local YWCA added its sponsorship. At Salonika the patriarch himself, although unable to attend, was careful to send his regrets.

The lectures were well reported in the local papers. In one city the demand was so great that the U. S. Information Service had the Greek text mimeographed for distribution. In another city the text was published in the newspaper.

A thoughtful man can scarcely return from Greece without feeling that the Fulbright program there is tremendously important and successful. Granted it has some shortcomings and some individual weak spots, the general conclusion can stand.

As elsewhere, the program in Greece works in two ways. It enables Americans to know Greece and Greeks, and it enables Greeks to know Americans. The contacts, moreover, are deeper than those of the tourist level. In the course of months they are established as living contacts, cultural contacts, and working contacts. In such international relationships the danger is always, of course, that the result may be bad, not good. In getting to know each other, people of two nations may only develop frictions, and end in dislike and lack of mutual respect. Too often some such distressing situation has resulted, or seems to be developing, in countries where large numbers of Americans have been engaged on missions of various kinds—thus giving the Communist propagandists their excuse to raise the cry of "the American occupation."

Our missions—economic, military, and other—have done incalculable good in reconstituting the war-shattered systems of many nations, but they have also piled up a stupendous debit of bad personal feeling. Proud peoples have too often felt themselves treated like "natives." American colonies have fenced themselves in with invisible wire—ridden in their own buses, bought at the PX, eaten in their own restaurants, sent their children to American schools, learned not a word of the language of the country, gathered in their own clubs. While I was in Athens a story circulated about an American woman who had been there for a year or more and had never seen any Greek money. When someone showed her a bill and said it was worth ten-thousand drachmae (except that he probably said "dracks," in the usual American fashion), she replied, "What are *they?*" I cannot vouch for the accuracy of the story, but it may well be true. It would certainly be possible, for in Greece many Americans are paid in dollars and spend them at the Post Exchange and the snack-bar in the Tameion Building.

On the other hand, the Fulbrighter—by the very terms of his appointment—is largely kept out of such an artificial situation.

He is paid in drachmae and rarely sees a dollar. In Athens we called ourselves the members of a mythical alphabetical set-up—the AWOP's, meaning Americans Without Privileges. We could not use the Army Post Office. We could not use the PX, actually a considerable financial hardship. We could not use the Mission buses, except by bluffing with our American clothes to get on, hoping we would not be thrown off. I developed something of a Greek's feeling about the snack-bar, and never even drank a coffee there, though I might have broken one of the six dollar bills I carried in my wallet. (Besides, when in Greece, I would rather sit in a street café and drink Greek coffee.)

Such a situation may have a tendency to develop a slight paranoia in the Fulbrighter, but at least it helps develop a sympathy with the people of the country. In addition, the Fulbright ranks are recruited from teachers and scholars, those classes which are most carefully trained to appreciate other people's points of view and to be interested in their customs and history.

The Fulbrighters, if they have not remade economies and armies, have at least spread good will, and—I think—very little bad will. They have not been primarily missionaries or do-gooders. If they had been or had attempted to be, they would have been less successful. On the other hand, they have not been exploiters. In contrast to the salaries and living-allowances received by many Americans abroad, the Fulbrighter draws a modest stipend in the currency of the country, and sometimes ends the year with a deficit, which he has to make up expending whatever dollar-savings he may have had at home.

If you ask various Fulbrighters why they are on their jobs, you will get various answers. Those on research appointments can simply say they are doing their own research and are essentially working in line with their own careers. The teachers will most likely say they want the experience of living and working abroad, that they want to get out of their rut at home, that they enjoy learning about a foreign people. Rarely will one of either kind say that he wanted to "help" the foreign country, carry on propaganda against communism, or spread American ideals. Largely, I think, because he is not a professional in any of these departments, he actually manages to accomplish a considerable amount in all of them.

O WHAT HARPER COULD WORTHILY HARP IT,
　Mine Edward! This wide-stretching wold
(Look out *wold*) with its wonderful carpet
　Of emerald, purple and gold!
Look well at it—also look sharp, it
　　　　Is getting so cold.

The purple is heather (*erica*);
　The yellow, gorse—call'd sometimes "whin."
Cruel boys on its prickles might spike a
　Green beetle as if on a pin.
You may roll in it, if you would like a
　　　　Few holes in your skin.

You wouldn't? Then think of how kind you
　Should be to the insects who crave
Your compassion—and then, look behind you
　At yon barley-ears! Don't they look brave
As they undulate—(*undulate*, mind you,
　　　　From *unda, a wave*).

The noise of these sheep-bells, how faint it
　Sounds here—(on account of our height)!

And this hillock itself—who could paint it,
  With its changes of shadow and light?
Is it not—(never, Eddy, say "ain't it")—
            A marvelous sight?

Then you desolate eerie morasses,
  The haunts of the snipe and the hern—
(I shall question the two upper classes
  On *aquatiles*, when we return)—
Why, I see on them absolute masses
            Of *filix* or fern.

How it interests e'en a beginner
  (Or *tiro*) like dear little Ned!
Is he listening? As I am a sinner
  He's asleep—he is wagging his head.
Wake up! I'll go home to my dinner.
            And you to your bed.

The boundless ineffable prairie;
  The splendor of mountain and lake
With their hues that seem ever to vary;
  The mighty pine forests which shake
In the wind, and in which the unwary
            May tread on a snake;

And this wold with its heathery garment—
  Are themes undeniably great.
But—although there is not any harm in't—
  It's perhaps little good to dilate
On their charms to a dull little varmint
            Of seven or eight.

WILLIAM LYON PHELPS

by Sinclair Lewis

I RATHER THINK THAT OF ALL PEOPLE I HAVE KNOWN, PROFESSOR
William Lyon Phelps—"Billy" Phelps—has, with the possible exception of Gene Debs, the greatest love of human beings and,
with the possible exception of Arnold Bennett, the greatest love of
novels and of plays. These twin affections have made him the
greatest of teachers, as well as the most agreeable of companions;
and his Yankee efficiency and shrewdness of vision have made him
more efficient than the sentimental Gene, just as a youthful liveliness
has made him more lustily amusing than ever was Arnold.

Not that he has not had sentimentalities. I would like to tackle
the impossible and keep a little out of the booming Yale-bull-dog
chorus of adulation which has always followed Billy; to try, a
little, to duck out back of the massed admirers of old grads who
keep reminding you, quite accurately, that Billy remembers the
faces and the names of more Yale alumni, more presidents of
women's clubs, more booksellers, more theater ushers, more actors,
and more Yale novelists than ten Jim Farleys put together. I would

like it clear that Billy has often been overenthusiastic about ephemeral bits of cleverness, about all the pixie descendants of Peter Pan, and that he has always covered too much ground. Yet with all this he remains the one man in his generation of college teachers who has been most able to inoculate students, even quite stupid ones, apparently formed only for the purpose of falling with virile grunts upon pigskin ovoids, with his own passion for the secret joys of good literature.

With this, as teacher and human being and college officer, he has stood conspicuously for changing the old caste-ridden army-like, fear-gripped university into a friendly concourse of human beings interested in learning. For over forty years, he has been to each generation of college students the Best Neighbor, the kindliest older friend, of the whole faculty. Here is an example of it, from days even before mine—and I graduated from Yale thirty-one years ago.

At that time, Chauncey Brewster Tinker, now Yale's proudest English scholar, was a timid Freshman from the outlands of Colorado, and Billy a bounding young instructor, not always too well liked by his superiors, because of his embarrassing doctrine that even undergraduates were human. By a mistake in marking, young Tinker (the most zealous of attendants on pious services) was put down as having too many chapel cuts. He protested to the dean, and was told to take his medicine like a little man, and not try to lie out of it.

Tinker had never met Phelps, then, but he had heard of him as a sort of St. Francis who sensibly gave more attention to Freshmen than to those loftier creatures, the sparrows. He barged in on Billy, told his story, was instantly perceived as an honest cub, and reassured. What then happened between the cocky young Instructor Phelps and the awe-robed Dean nobody knows, but Tinker was exonerated. And nobody ever will know what happened, because when I told this story to Billy, he himself had utterly forgotten it. Why should he remember a mere hourly incident like saving the whole career of a shining young scholar?

My own first bright experience with Billy was when I had to make up for several months of absence by what are jocularly known as "examinations." In other subjects, I took painful written But Billy, in ten minutes of amiable talk, really did find out what tests which revealed nothing whatever except a natural glibness.

I knew about seventeenth century poetry (which, in those days, when I was young and educated, was a good deal).

As at this moment of writing I am a member of Equity and touring with a play, I may be understood as being complimentary when I say that in everything Billy Phelps is a great actor. He is like none of the traditional pedagogues—the long-faced and dry and disapproving, the bushy and hearty, or the dapper and cynical. He has the handsome, square, mobile face of an actor; the quickly changing, bountifully feeling eyes of the actor; and the actor's natural gracefulness, and natural authority among duller and less imaginative men. I have long felt that it was only chance that kept Billy from being a truly great actor-manager—another Beerbohm Tree or Henry Irving or Sacha Guitry, or Noel Coward. He would have roared just his most lion-like as Othello, and then between acts have had an ant-like delight in the tiniest detail of the theater—why the deuce the hot-water tap didn't run in Miss Eglantine Devereux's dressing-room, and how in the name of Garrick it had been possible for George Jarndyce, the character man, to miss his cue by a whole .00007 of a second, and throw an entire scene. He would have reveled in the new musical score, in the scene designer's blueprints, in the patient diligence of the director.

As it is, Billy had enlivened the whole dismal realm of university grind by bringing to it some of the perverse charm of the theater, and when he incredibly greets a whole regiment of old boys each by his name at an Alumni Dinner (in Tarrytown or Tucson or Tuscany), in his gay friendliness there is an eagerness and warmth which, on the stage, would have enchanted thousands.

With such gifts, Billy has not, like a considerable percentage of teachers, been afraid to stalk out from the secure mock-battles of the campus into the real war of mature life. I have seen him with bishops and generals and turtle-mouthed steel magnates and whole seethings of professional writers as their peer, their much-prized friend. I think of another well-known teacher of English who has been a value and comfort to generations of would-be writers in college but who, once they escape from his admonitions, begins to belittle them, with a paternal jealousy and a certain uneasy provincialism. Not Billy, ever. No one would be happier than he that one of his brood should outdistance him in fame. And, thus liberated from village envy, he has, without losing one of the disciplined standards of the schoolroom, for many years been able to see the passing show and passing showmen of French and English and American life as one familiar with the great.

What a kind, good, innocent, sweet life Billy Phelps's has been! Yet all his kindness and sweetness have not been the protective virtues of a timid man, but the easily worn adornments of a strong man, a cosmopolitan man, a man veritably of the world!

★ *If one is fortunate enough to have attended a good school and a high-grade college, that is well. But it is better to have really educated oneself without these advantages than to have had the advantages and missed the opportunities.*

WILLIAM LYON PHELPS

GOOD TEACHERS
AND BAD PUPILS

by Gilbert Highet

O NE OF JESUS' TWELVE CHOSEN PUPILS WAS JUDAS ISCARIOT, WHO
helped the Jewish authorities to carry out his arrest. Jesus knew it,
too. At the Passover supper he spoke of it without mentioning the
name of the traitor: although we do not hear that he said or knew
anything of it until the last few hours.

This is a memorable case of one of the most important and
difficult questions in teaching. Why does a good teacher have bad
pupils? Jesus was one of the best teachers, and he had one of the
worst pupils. Why?

It was not that Judas simply fell short of the best in Jesus. He
did not try to understand the teaching of Jesus and then fail in all
good will, as the others sometimes did. He did not break down in a
crisis, like Peter. He turned his back and went the other way,
resolutely and effectively. To prove this, think of the method he
chose to single Jesus out for the police. His master's chief lesson
was that all men should love and trust one another. So Judas, instead of pointing to him with his hand or standing beside him, went
up and kissed him.

Spectacular as the Judas case is, it is only one of many. Socrates had a number of outstandingly bad pupils. The best known is the most brilliant—Alcibiades, who loved Socrates dearly and admired him fervently, and who also betrayed his country, went over to its enemies the Spartans and then betrayed them, returned to Athens and left it once more, and was killed after a career which included such other exploits as the seduction of the Spartan queen and blasphemy against his country's religion. But there were others —such as Critias, who became one of the Thirty Tyrants put in by Sparta after the defeat of Athens and who tortured and murdered hundreds of his fellow-citizens in a savage attempt to crush out the rule of the people. The real impetus behind the condemnation of Socrates was the people's hatred for the men he had taught to hate democracy. He had other pupils, certainly, but the revolutionaries were among the most brilliant. We cannot be quite sure how Socrates himself regarded them. Plato tells us that he thought they were potentially good young men who had been misled by other influences; and of course once they were fully embarked on their bad careers, he had little to do with them. But he seems to have been closely associated with them for a long time. Why did they go so very far wrong? Was he the best teacher in Greece, as Plato and others believed, or was he a man who, as the accusation read, corrupted the young?

The history of education is dotted with such terrible failures, as the chart of a difficult channel is starred with wrecks. Move on into the Roman empire and you will find others. Nero is one. He was the son of a princess who managed to get him adopted by her second husband, the reigning emperor, Claudius. As an heir to the throne, he was educated with great care. He was handed over to Seneca, a brilliantly clever talker and writer and an experienced courtier, who was also a philosopher attached to Stoicism—which means that he upheld a stern moral code based on the primacy of Duty, but was not unrealistically rigid about it. Seneca, assisted by an experienced soldier and administrator, worked over the young prince for years, with all the care and subtlety he could command. He gave him a thorough grounding in moral philosophy, and a considerable knowledge of literature and art. It was not all hard work and ethical principles either. After the old emperor died, Seneca wrote an outrageously funny skit about his trying to get into heaven and being kicked out, which was apparently meant to be read at Nero's coronation party; and he wrote nine blood-and-thunder tragedies which (according to one theory) were specially designed for the stage-struck young emperor to produce in his private theater, with himself as a star. The results of all this care were very good, to begin with. The first five years of Nero's reign were universally admired. Social justice, sensible financing, big public works, and much else were due to Nero's own enthusiasm and the guidance of his advisers. Then he began to deteriorate. From the age of twenty-two or so he got worse every year. He retired his tutor Seneca. He divorced, and then executed, his wife. He executed, or murdered, his mother. He started a career of absurd and foul debaucheries. He threw off every good influence, neglected his duties, ruined the empire, provoked it to revolt against him, and even then had scarcely the courage to commit suicide. And Seneca, his tutor? Several years earlier, Nero had condemned Seneca to death, like everyone else who had ever benefited him.

But why did he go wrong? Was it simply that the limitless power of an emperor was too much for anyone to bear? No, because others used it sanely. Or did it come too suddenly upon him? No, because he had been carefully trained for it by experts for years. Or was he badly trained—did Seneca perhaps encourage him to loose living so that he would be easier to handle? No, we do not hear that he did. On the contrary, all the evidence is that Nero was well educated, on a high moral standard.

There are many more like him in history, on a smaller scale: hundreds; thousands; tens of thousands of young men and women who had talent, and health, and security, who were trained by teachers who understood them, who were surrounded by people who loved them, and who threw the whole thing away. The mediocrities do not matter so much—the expensively educated girls who turned out to be bumpkins or bridge-fiends, the privately tutored and hand-tailored youths who went on the Grand Tour and returned without an idea in their sleek narrow heads. Chesterfield's son is a good example of that sort of unimportant failure. They are simply bald patches, thin and sandy gardens, depressed areas. No, the important problem is why really talented people with the best of teaching should turn out fatally, damnably bad: like Nero, like Judas.

This is a very hard problem for teachers, and for parents. To solve a question so tough as this, there are two devices that we can use. One is to find out what answers have already been suggested, and to think them over, comparing them together and filling up one by the help of others. The second is to ask whether the same problem appears in any other shape, to see what answers are given to it then, and to apply them.

Not many useful answers are given to our question. Why did Judas betray Jesus? Why did Nero kill his own teacher? Why did Alcibiades destroy so much that Socrates admired—integrity, purity, patriotism? Judas himself did not know. After he had finished, he knew he had done wrong. He knew it could not be put right; and he knew it had nothing much to do with the bribe he was paid; but he could not tell why he had done it.

As for Nero, he said Seneca was mixed up in a plot against him, but did he believe it in his heart? When he forced Seneca into retirement and disgrace, was he only safeguarding himself against assassination—against a plot made by the old man who could have killed him at any time for years?

Alcibiades has left no record except his acts. But his fellow-pupil Plato gives a valuable explanation of the problem, evidently written with him in mind. He says in effect that all sorts of pupils go wrong, including many mediocrities. But, he adds, philosophy is an exceptionally difficult type of education. It takes unusual talent to be a good pupil of Socrates. Therefore, when such a pupil goes wrong, he goes spectacularly wrong, by applying his unusual gifts to bad purposes. Remember that Plato was not thinking only of brain-power, but also of the other strengths that make up an exceptional personality—physical and spiritual energy, rapid and strong will-power, social adaptability and charm, bodily dexterity and beauty. When a young man or woman so richly endowed goes wrong, he or she goes very far wrong.

Plato adds another solution, which is certainly true in part. It is, he says, fearfully difficult to teach such a gifted pupil efficiently, because evil influences compete much harder for his attention. This is certainly true, so far as it goes. Obviously if Seneca had been able to train Nero under laboratory conditions he would have made a better thing of it. But he could not watch the young prince all the time. Even if he could, it would have been ill-advised to do so. And how can you teach self-control when every pretty slave-girl in the palace contrives to catch the master's eye and brush against his head? How can you repress his extravagance when the rooms are full of courtiers anxious to sell everything they possess and procure whatever the master fancies? Can anyone learn clemency, even from Seneca, when vile whispers slander every decent man at court, suggest confiscations of great wealth, describe the pleasures of inflicting torture?

True in part . . . but is this the only explanation? Is it all the truth? Do we feel that it explains everything?

No, we do not. We feel that men like Judas and Nero who turn against their teachers are not merely led aside by other influences. They do not simply wander off the path. They turn right round and go in the direction opposite to their guides. They do not merely drop their teachers, forget lessons and personalities. They deliberately attack their teachers, trying to annihilate them and all they stand for. And the problem we have to solve is: why does this so often happen to teachers of exceptional brilliance and goodness?

★ *The feeling that it is undemocratic to single out the best pupils is one which leads to a great waste of good material.*

BERTRAND RUSSELL

★ *Throughout education, from the first day to the last, there should be a sense of intellectual adventure.*

BERTRAND RUSSELL

THE SCHOOLTEACHERS

by Charles Péguy

IN A COMMUNITY, THE SCHOOLTEACHER MUST NOT BE THE REPRE-
sentative of the government. It is fitting that he should be the
representative of humanity. It is not a prime minister, no matter
how important a prime minister may be; it is not a majority that
the schoolteacher should represent in the community. He is the
born representative of less fleeting personages, he is the only and
priceless representative of poets and artists, of philosophers and
scholars, of the men who have made and maintained humanity. He
must ensure the representation of culture. That is why he cannot
assume the representation of politics, because he cannot hold two
offices, two representations.

If this is to be, we must have the courage to repeat to schoolteachers how indispensable it is that they should cultivate themselves. To teach at random is not the question. One must know
what one teaches, that is, one must have begun by first teaching
oneself. The most eminent men never cease cultivating themselves;
or rather, the most eminent men are those who have never ceased,
who ceaselessly continue their culture, their work. Nothing is
obtained without pains, and life is perpetual work. Education cannot be conferred: it is obtained by work, and it is communicated.
It is by reading that a man shapes himself and not by reciting handbooks. And it is also by working modestly.

THE COLLEGE TOWN

by Henry Seidel Canby

I REMEMBER FIRST THE COLLEGE TOWN. SURELY IT IS AMAZING that neither history, nor sociology, nor even fiction, has given more than passing attention to the American college town, for it has had a character and a personality unlike other towns. And quite as surely, its imprint of small-town respectability, convention, and common sense is deeper upon American education than has ever been guessed. With the rarest exceptions the home of the college has been a small town, even if that town was a suburb or a section, self-contained, of a city. There were hundreds of such towns in the period of which I write, and all with a family resemblance.

Cleaner, neater than other towns, with green spaces somewhere toward the center, and white spires or Gothic towers or windowed dormitories half hid by trees, they were the little capitals of the academic states. As trading or industrial centers their life might be indistinguishable from towns or cities of a like size, but in their social consciousness there was always some recognition of peculiarity. For the heart of the community was a college. Its subtle influences were as pervasive if less noticeable, than the quite unsubtle symbols of college life—playing fields, cafés, and collegiate clothing.

And in the early nineteen-hundreds the college town was no luncheon stop for automobiles. It was secluded, even if it was a town within a city, like the Yale section of New Haven; it knew its boundaries and kept them; it was jealous of its distinctions; if it was uneasy, it was also proud. The campus and the college buildings dominated its architecture like the temple and citadel of a Greek city-state, a difficult relationship since there was always some doubt in the minds of the town folk whether the college was an asset or a parasite. The town with its college was like a woman's club committee with a celebrity in tow, a credit to them but also an embarrassment and sometimes a nuisance; it was like a French village built upon a Roman camp to which tourists resort; it was like the mistress of an actors' boarding house, pleased by the notoriety but worried by the manners, or the morals, of her boarders; it was like almost anything but a town without a college. And many a college town was like a resentful mother who, expecting a quiet and manageable infant, had given birth to a Gargantua that swallowed whole streets and squares in its gigantic growing. I do not wish to be fantastic, yet only such similes will express how very unlike the rest of the United States was the college town.

New Haven, as I first knew it in the late nineties, was a decorous and beautiful town set in the midst of a sprawling industrial city of slums, factories, and long, undistinguished avenues. The college town was old New Haven, with its Green, its bordering business streets, its campus and blocks of residences north-stretching into park and country beyond. The elm-shaded streets of this old town were lined by sedate houses which in various modes still kept the impress of the Greek revival of the early nineteenth century. Eight out of ten had a portico of wood with two Doric columns painted brown or gray or white. Down the length of shady streets these columns made a pleasant arcade, broken here and there by high brick mansions of the eighties, or charming green-shuttered, white-walled reminder of the better proportions of a Colonial day.

It was a guarded town, very unlike the ample if ugly spaciousness of the mansarded avenues of my youth, where broad porches and open gates welcomed relatives and friends. There were no open doors in the New England college town. Behind the twin Doric columns, which might have been labeled Respectability and Reserve, two squint lights seemed always to be looking down their noses at the passer-by, fearful lest he should wish to enter. The college town, unlike the rest of America, was jealous of privacy, and doubtful of casual relationships.

Lights went out early in these bosky streets, often to be relit in upstairs studies. When the chapel bell rang ten, and the undergraduate navigating homeward across the Green filled the night with shouts and melody, the prim town pulled up its covers, shut its ears, or burrowed deeper in a book. Nights in the college town were consecrated to sleep or work.

Along these town streets, professors lived, students wandered, but also the social and professional leaders of the city sought residence, because, after all, it was the college that gave tone to the community. Academic society was therefore both town and gown, and had a double flavor which recalled in homely fashion the atmosphere of those small European courts where both prince and bishop had their following. It was not an exciting society, yet certainly it was not dull. New Haven had never forgotten that it was once a colony, all of itself, and it might have been a state had it not sheltered republicans and regicides. There was a stiff, aristocratic quality in the old families, now entirely lost there as elsewhere in America. From their harsh stalks sprouted personalities of extraordinary independence, so that it was hard to tell sometimes whether decorum or eccentricity was the dominant note of the town's society. These families belonged to the college world, yet were not wholeheartedly of it. They arranged its finances, fought its lawsuits, supplied a president or a professor now and then, were mysteriously powerful sometimes in academic affairs, yet in general their attitude of respectful but slightly contemptuous toleration of learning, so characteristic of America, was tempered only by the belief that the college belonged to them and put them a cut above the aristocracies of Hartford or Springfield, and made them able to take rank even in New York. Hence the teacher, who in this money-making age lived on the edge or beyond of society, in the college town might have a definite place, though he was not society himself. Wealth and position did not so much stoop to him as restrain their privileges so that he could enter. By a self-denying ordinance tacitly understood, the rich in the college set (and no other society counted) spent only a part of their incomes at home, eschewed butlers, denied themselves broughams, and later, for a while, automobiles, kept dues low in the clubs, and, if they did spend, put their money into that good wine and costly food which the scholar has always enjoyed. And he responded with an unexpected geniality which was sometimes grateful and sometimes lumbering, and sometimes only a courteous irony.

Thus the college was priveleged socially, not only in the hand-picked sons of the cultivated or the well-to-do that came as students, but in the close contacts between the faculty and the aristocracy of the college town. But it was conditioned also by the life of a small-town community, which, no matter how good its traditions, how admirable its character, how genuine its culture, was, by definition, a little provincial, a little priggish, and very much inbred. And yet there was a raciness in this mingling of town and gown that gave its own flavor to the college society, and was some compensation for the gustier airs which blew through capitals and metropolises.

I can see now a characteristic "reception" in a great house behind the broad sweep of the elms of Hillhouse Avenue, which was to the college town of New Haven what Fifth Avenue once was to New York—a terminus of social pride. Tables were laden with heavy, mind-satisfying food, champagne bubbled on the sideboards, stiff-backed professors were trying to relax, while their wives with the curious pursed mouth of the academic woman, showed more concern for their dignity than for the entertainment. Among them moved the grandes dames of our town society, soothing vanities by a kind word, snubbing with a vacant look the strange uncouth creatures that science was bringing into the university, but not too emphatically, since one never knew nowadays who might become famous. And with them were our town eccentrics, women usually of old families, too sure of themselves to bother about social distinctions. Worse dressed than the professors' wives, they had a confident distinction of ugliness which lifted them above our small-town limitations, and they spoke the language of the academic world with understanding and tolerance, like missionaries among an Indian tribe. Trailing behind them, yet always heading back toward the champagne, were our faculty "characters"—the great hearty souls that scholarship which is not pedantry creates in its happier moods, men whose broadcloth might be shiny and spotted, their linen none too clean, yet with minds and faces of the great world, known in Europe and conscious of it, witty often, sarcastic usually, ill-mannered, inclined to lash out at this pompous bourgeois society, which nevertheless gave them their only chance to eat, drink, and be merry with their own kind. There was our famous Chaucerian scholar, Lounsbury, his sparse wide beard wagging under his rapid tongue, his eyes a little bleary, an epigram worth quoting with every glass of champagne. "Why do they want to inscribe old Whitney's name on the Court House wall? All he knew was Sanskrit. What did he ever do for New Haven?" says a banker. "Do!" Lounsbury shoots back, "By Gorry! It's enough that he lived here!"

There were subtle jealousies between town and gown which could not be assigned to differences in income. The town had inherited a Yankee distrust of ministers who talked about God but made no money, and now that ministers were less and professors more it transferred this distrust with increments. It was irritated by its own deference to an institution that did not make for profits. Energy that in other communities was organizing machine tools or life insurance, here in this college community leaked away in a trickle that sometimes carried sons and heirs with it into the academic world where it was transformed into the teaching of adolescents or into books that nobody but professors read. The town derived a goodly share of its income from the rapidly increasing expenditures of the college and its students, and this, too, it resented, feeling that it was committed to an approval of what the college was doing. It endured the noisy night life of the students, the untidy boarding houses that crowded its streets, the frequent arrogance of the academic mind, but it disliked the haunting sense of inferiority which came from knowing that it was celebrated because of the college. It listened to the endless shoptalk of the faculty and pretended to take the "big men" of the undergraduate world at their face value, but it could not entirely respect, still less understand, the creature upon which it lived and which it believed it had created. Not until the expansive twenties when alumni, enriched by the war and prosperity, upset their applecarts of gold into the college coffers, and made education, or at least the side-shows of education, a big business, was the town convinced that the college, its own college, was worthy of its birthplace. No Commencement orator was ever so persuasive as gifts in the millions and a building program that was a major industry.

And yet, as with Christians and Infidels living together in old Spain, there was more interpenetration than appeared on the surface. The college taught the town to discuss ideas; it taught also friendship and a delight in the companionship of like-minded men. The two blended in the adult life of the community, for the habit of the undergraduate fraternity persisted in dozens of little clubs of talkers which flourished throughout the town because their members had learned clubability. It was a rash hostess who gave a dinner party on Wednesday or Friday nights, their favorite meeting times. In these clubs scholar, lawyer, and business man ate, drank, and read papers explaining their jobs or their social philosophy. Ideas spread through the college town, freed from that taboo on abstractions which was the curse of the small town elsewhere in America, and many a scholar was saved from pedantry, or a paralysis of the emotions in the arid wastes of specialist theory, by his contacts with men whose daily task was the handling of men. Even the women became clubable; and indeed it was in New Haven that by happy inspiration Our Society was born, whose inestimable privilege after the meeting was to inspect every closet in their hostess's house. But it was a man's town.

Still another institution the college gave to the society of the town, the college widow. I knew two of them in their old age and profited greatly from my friendships. For the college widow had a depth and richness of emotional experience never developed in American life of that day outside of the few metropolises, and seldom there. She began at sixteen or eighteen as a ravishing beauty, the darling of freshmen; she passed on in the years of her first blooming from class to class of ardent youngsters, until, as her experience ripened, she acquired a taste, never to be satisfied by matrimony, for male admiration abstracted from its consequences; and more subtly for the heady stimulant of intimacy with men in their fresh and vigorous youth. By her thirties she had learned the art of eternal spring, and had become a connoisseur in the dangerous excitement of passion controlled at the breaking point, a mistress of every emotion, and an adept in the difficult task of sublimating love into friendship. The students lived out their brief college life and went on; she endured, and tradition with her, an enchantress in illusion, and a specialist in the heart. Twenty, even thirty years, might be her tether; and when suddenly on a midnight, a shock of reality, or perhaps only boredom, ended it all, she was old—but still charming and infinitely wise. To smoke a

cigarette with her when cigarettes were still taboo for women, and
drink her coffee and liqueur, was a lesson in civilization.

Yet in fostering in its midst the sprawling infant, gray-headed
but still growing, which was the college, the town sacrificed its
own youth. There was childhood and maturity in a college town,
but no youth in between. Youth male was absorbed into the undergraduate community and came home only on Sundays, youth
female was usually sent off perforce to school or woman's colleges,
away from the dangerous glamour of college streets. Hence the
young folk in the college town settled back in their home environment only their mid or late twenties, and then only did social
life in a community begin for them. There were no calf loves in the
society of the college town, no gawkish immaturity, no giggling,
no rebellious escapes. And since the young had reached the earning and marrying stage in a society where the scale of living was
based upon an instructor's salary, their pleasures were necessarily
simple. Relative poverty was regarded as a virtue, doing without
was a pride. One walked, not rode; went to concerts rather than to
the theater; danced to a piano and a cornet; gave books not jewelry;
sat down four at a table, not eight; kept married instead of toying
with expensive ideas about lovers and divorce.

The results for the college town were by no means ill. The tittle-
tattle of a small town had little fuel here. It was an educated
society, and since it could not afford to be frivolous, and both
puritan custom and economy held the passions in check, every opportunity was given to vivacity and ideas in conversation. Talk
was cheap, which did not prevent it from being good. It was often
stiff with convention and sometimes pedantical, yet the fun was
more civilized than country-club horseplay, the wit, when any,
aware of the nature of wit.

And yet it was all a little arid. The young people had come together too late. They had no sentimental memories to share, and
thanks to the restrictions of what was, after all, a small town, and
to the official nature of their college society, and to relative poverty,
the sex in relationships was weak. Every emotion had its inhibition.
Like the columns of the houses, the twin shrines in every heart were
Reserve and Respectability.

The college town was thus the imperfect resultant of two worlds
in a physical merger where souls and minds remained desperate.
Even this understates the difficulty. The undergraduates belonged

to the faction of the gown, but had themselves come in a vast majority from uncollegiate small towns, and so in ideas and attitudes toward learning were far closer to the Philistines of the streets than to the Israelites of the campus faculty. Their relations with the faculty could too often be described as passive resistance, usually with the sneaking sympathy of both parents and town. Hence, there was a split in the college itself, so that in my days not a duality but a trinity—town, gown, and sweater—would have best described our community.

I have written of the college town with pleasure because I was happy there, and excited, and amused, and also cabin'd, cribb'd, confined; yet also with a very definite purpose. For it is impossible to think of the college of that day without its encircling town. This was the air the professor breathed, and which the student absorbed from his freshman year onward. For him the town often provided his first experience in adult social life. Nor in discussing the internal conflicts of the college itself which have been so decisive in shaping the type known as the college graduate, is it right to forget for a moment the influence of these nests of puritan respectability, given tone by the American aristocracy that clung to them for shelter from the make-money world outside. Here is a factor in education and in the faiths and prejudices of the educated and educator which has escaped the theorist and the statistician alike. We have forgotten that the types we analyze so readily—professors, alumni, humanists, scientists, scholars—were in their conditioning period American boys in a small college town.

★ *There are obviously two educations. One should teach us how to make a living, and the other how to live.*

JAMES TRUSLOW ADAMS

AN ELEGY ON EZEKIEL CHEEVER

by Cotton Mather

You that are *Men*, & Thoughts of *Manhood* know,
Be Just now to the *Man* that made you so.
Martyr'd by *Scholars* the stabb'd *Cassian* dies,
And falls to cursed Lads a Sacrifice.
Not so my CHEEVER; Not by *Scholars* slain,
But Prais'd, and Lov'd, and wish'd to *Life* again.
A mighty *Tribe* of Well-instructed Youth
Tell what they owe to him, and Tell with Truth.
All the *Eight parts of Speech* he taught to them
They now Employ to *Trumpet* his Esteem.
They fill *Fames Trumpet*, and they spread a Fame
To last till the *Last Trumpet* drown the same. . . .
   A Learned Master of the *Languages*
Which to Rich Stores of *Learning* are the *Keyes*
He taught us first *Good Sense* to understand
And put the *Golden Keyes* into our Hand,
We but for him had been for Learning *Dumb*,
And had a sort of *Turkish Mutes* become.
Were *Grammar* quite Extinct, yet at his Brain

[180]

The *Candle* might have well been lit again.
If Rhet'rick had been stript of all her *Pride*
She from his *Wardrobe* might have been Supply'd,
Do but Name CHEEVER, and the *Echo* straight
Upon that Name, *Good Latin*, will Repeat.
A *Christian Terence*, Master of the *File*
That arms the Curious to Reform their *Style*.
Now *Rome* and *Athens* from their Ashes rise;
See their *Platonick Year* with vast surprize:
And in our *School* a *Miracle* is wrought;
For the *Dead Languages* to *Life* are brought.

His *Work* he Lov'd: Oh! had we done the same:
Our *Play-dayes* still to him ungrateful came.
And yet so well our *Work* adjusted Lay,
We came to *Work,* as if we came to *Play*.

Our *Lads* had been, but for his wondrous Cares,
Boyes of my Lady *Mores* unquiet Pray'rs.
Sure were it not for such informing *Schools,*
Our *Lat'ran* too would soon be fill'd with *Owles*.
Tis CORLET's pains, & CHEEVER's, we must own,
That thou, *New-England*, art not *Scythia* grown.
The *Isles* of *Silly* had o're-run this Day
The *Continent* of our *America*.

Grammar he taught, which 'twas his work to do:
But he would *Hagar* have her place to know.

The *Bible* is the Sacred *Grammar,* where
The *Rules of speaking well*, contained are.

He taught us *Lilly,* and he *Gospel* taught;
And us poor Children to our *Saviour* brought.
Master of Sentences, he gave us more
Than we in our *Sententia* had before.
We Learn't Good things in *Tullies Offices;*
But we from *him* Learn't Better things than there,
With *Cato's* he to us the *Higher* gave.
Lessons of JESUS, that our Souls do save.
We Constru'd *Ovid's Metamorphosis,*
But on our selves chang'd, not a *Change* to miss.
Young *Austin* wept, when he saw *Dido* dead,
Tho' not a Tear for a *Lost Soul* he had:
Our Master would not let us be so vain,

But us from *Virgil* did to *David* train,
Text or Epistles would not *Cloathe* our Souls;
Pauls too we heard; we *went to School at Pauls.* . . .
Death gently at the *Stalk*, and kindly laid
Him, where our God His *Granary* has made.
    Who at *New-Haven* first began to Teach,
Dying *Unshipwreck'd*, does *White-Haven* reach.
At that *Fair Haven* they all storms forget;
He there his DAVENPORT with Love does meet.
    The *Luminous Robe*, the *Less* whereof with *Shame*
Our Parents wept, when *Naked* they became;
Those Lovely *Spirits* wear it, and therein
Serve God with *Priestly Glory*, free from Sin.
    But in his *Paradisian Rest* above,
To *Us* does the Blest Shade retain his Love.
With *Ripen'd thoughts* Above concern'd for Us,
We can't but hear him dart his Wishes, thus.
    "*TUTORS*, Be *Strict*; But yet be *Gentle* too:
Don't by fierce *Cruelties* fair *Hopes* undo,
Dream not, that thy Who are to Learning slow,
Will mend by Arguments in *Ferio*.
Who keeps the *Golden Fleece*, Oh, let him not
A *Dragon* be, tho' he *Three Tongues* have got.
Why can you not to Learning find the way,
But thro' the Province of *Severia?*
Twas *Moderatus*, who taught *Origen;*
A *Youth* which prov'd one of the Best of men,
The Lads with *Honour* first, and Reason Rule;
Blowes are but for the *Refractory Fool*."

★ *You cannot teach a man anything; you can only help him to
find it within himself.*

                                                    GALILEO

"COPEY"

by Rollo Walter Brown

I T IS NOT POSSIBLE TO WRITE ABOUT CHARLES TOWNSEND COPELAND without speaking in the first person. For "Copey" had the mysterious vitality to be found in every great teacher: you could not have acquaintance with him without thinking of him in relation to yourself.

My personal acquaintance with him was long deferred. When I first arrived in Harvard Square, fresh from what Barrett Wendell called "the wilds of Ohio," it was early July, and Harvard Summer School students were everywhere. As I moved about with much free time ahead of me into September, I noticed one morning in shop windows and on bulletin boards that "Mr. Copeland" was to read on a certain evening in Sever Hall. The wording of the announcement led me to feel that here was to be something unlike the lectures I had heard in the little college from which I had just come.

Although my roommate and I went early, we found the lecture hall overflowing into the main corridor of the building. Near us, three official-looking youngish men conferred seriously, and they

From *Harvard Yard in The Golden Age*, by Rollo Walter Brown. Copyright 1948 by A. A. Wyn, Inc. Reprinted by permission of the publisher, A. A. Wyn, Inc., New York.

decided to "go over and tell him" that he just had to read where
there was more room—in the New Lecture Hall. When they
started we trailed along close behind, in the hope of gaining advance information and securing seats.

From one of the upper windows of an ancient-looking dormitory
a serious little man with cropped dark mustache and magnificent
forehead looked out into the quiet of the Yard. One of the three
hurried up. The man at the window vanished, and then the man
who had gone up came to the window. "He does not wish to read
in the New Lecture Hall."

"But tell him that the people simply cannot get in."

Then the man himself reappeared. "I wish to read in Sever."

"But already the hall is overflowing into the corridor."

"That is the way I want it."

We followed back to Sever Hall. By this time the audience—
chiefly schoolma'ams in bright summer dresses—reached all the
way through the corridor, down the entrance steps, and out into
the Yard. While the men conferred anew—we learned that one of
them was President Eliot's secretary—the stern little man we had
seen at the window came trudging along the path with books under
his arm.

It would be difficult to imagine a less academic-looking person
than he was as he came up. He was small and shrunken, and he
wore a checked suit, a collar of material that had a figure in it, and
a black derby hat that seemed larger than his head, though it was
not. He was then still under forty-five—I came later to know—
but a shuffling walk and some vast disapproval in his face made
him seem older. No one ever saw a professor who looked like this.
He might have been an actor—as he was. For he seemed well
enough aware that he was the cause of all the flurry, and that he
was being looked at with some awe.

The men spoke to him with respect—one of them addressed him
as "Mr. Copeland"—but with great earnestness. "You can see for
yourself how it is."

"Let them crowd in."

"They are already standing everywhere, and sitting in the
windows."

"Let them sit in the windows!"

Some of the crowd began to move nearer.

The three men sought to make themselves impressive. These

Summer School students had paid their fees and were entitled to hear him—and could, if only he would be obliging enough to change his plans.

"Very well," at last he said dourly, "I suppose if I must, I must —damn it!"

He moved off toward the New Lecture Hall. Quickly the crowd had the news, and followed. As he marched along with great deliberateness, he was like a dark comet with a long spreading tail of a thousand bright dresses in the twilight.

When the last stragglers were in and the last woman had dropped her handbag and Copey had said warningly, "Now if you ladies will get a firm grip on everything," he was ready to read. But the mosquitoes bothered him, and he tried also to make war on them. While he sat with his eyes intent upon the page, he slowly lifted an open palm until it was poised just above his head, and read in a resonant, deliberate voice:

In the spring a young man's fancy lightly turns to thoughts of love . . .

Smack! And on into the next stanza.

He noticed the titters and suppressed laughter, and in the course of the next poem, he lifted his hand again, and the titters spread all over the hall. But this time he did not bring his hand down. And after he had finished the poem and was leafing ahead in the volume for the next one, his face revealed the faintest trace of a smile.

Clearly enough, I was in the presence of some sort of extraordinary person. I went to hear him whenever he read. But for months I regarded him only from afar.

Then one day when the frosts of autumn were upon the Yard and gusts of wind were denuding the old buildings of their brilliant ivy, a friendly professor suggested that Copey might be able to help me with some seventeenth-century letters in which I had become interested. The next afternoon at four o'clock I climbed the stairs in Hollis Hall to Copey's rooms. I knocked. I heard no one. I knocked again. Then I heard what seemed to be shuffling slippered feet, and the turning of the lock in the door. Then the door swung open, and there stood Copey like a thundercloud.

"Damn it, young man, don't you know that I never see anybody until after ten in the evening? Why do you disturb me at this time of day?"

I drew desperately upon my resources: I explained that I had really been sent by one of his colleagues, who had said nothing about hours.

"Well, then, since you are here, come on in. But you must be brief. I have only five minutes. Sit down there and tell me what your errand is."

I stumbled through a hasty explanation of my interest in the letters.

"Oh! Oh!" And I could see the cloud stealing from his face. "So that is it." And the deliberate voice became almost intimate. "But I am not at all sure that I can be of the least help."

Then for an hour I listened to the most illuminating and brilliant talk my provincial young ears had ever heard. He completely forgot that I had come at the wrong time.

When I was ready to go and was making a floundering effort to express my appreciation, I said, "But you gave me no chance to tell you my name. It is Brown."

"Mine's Copeland!" he replied in his resonant platform voice, and then smiled as if we both must know that that was pretty good.

"And now since we have been properly introduced, why don't you come and see me some evening after ten o'clock? Just look for a light in that window over there in the corner. And if you see it, come on up."

It was the beginning of a friendship destined to be without end. And as I saw more and more of Copey I came to understand how almost anything said about him by anyone who had ever seen him might express one facet of truth. For his stringent exterior and his quick sallies of wit and sarcasm were capable of such proportioning that he could be casually interpreted almost as one chose. He repelled many, and with such energy that they became eloquent. To these he was cranky; he was artificial, even in voice; he was a charlatan in the world of scholars. George Santayana, in speaking of his own official career at Harvard, referred to Copey as an "elocutionist" who "by declaiming" provided a "spiritual debauch" for "the many well-disposed waifs at Harvard living under difficult conditions."

Those who became Copy's followers were the ones who by friendly intuition or fortunate chance were led to see that Santayana and Copey constituted a head-on collision in philosophies. Santayana, by his own confession on various occasions, preferred to remain in the quiet backwaters and watch the mainstream of very imperfect human beings go by. The "well-disposed waifs" at Harvard did not interest him deeply. And they did interest Copey —the ones who would not be scared off. These found themselves getting excited over discoveries that Copey helped them to make. They found themselves feeling adequate to discover thereafter whatever they needed or much wished. And they were filled with a robust gratitude. Copey's eccentricities became for them matters of affectionate regard; the undergraduate indignities suffered at his hands had to be talked about, and matched, and laughed at again and again as so many embellishments of the less obvious and greater Copey—until he became one of the company of picturesque legendary figures in three centuries of Harvard history.

Of course his followers had to linger long over his wit. Henry Ware Eliot wrote in *Harvard Celebrities:*

If wit and madness be as like as Pope and others tell,
Then Copey by the merest squeak escapes the padded cell.

Copey criticized the lines by reminding Eliot that it was not Pope, but Dryden. Eliot thought that was only a technicality. "Dryden" would not fit into the line.

And every Copey disciple knew that Eliot was right. The fundamental truth was there: Copey was full of wit—of his own special brand. Or if it could not always be called wit, it could be called whatever one liked. It was the expression of Copey.

There were countless examples—without drawing upon anything aprocryphal. There was, for instance, that story—in many versions, but grounded solidly in fact—about Copey's reply to his sister's maid. When he went to see his sister, Mrs. Dunbar, on Highland Street in Cambridge, and the Irish maid unexpectedly ran into him, threw up her hands in consternation, and exclaimed, "Jesus!" Copey very calmly replied, "No, no! Just Mrs. Dunbar's brother." When a student who felt sure that he would never become a writer asked Copey somewhat worshipfully how many of his former students had dedicated books to him, Copey proudly gave him the number—a large one. Then he added: "But Bill, I can tell you something else. I have had six kids named for me. So if you cannot qualify in one respect, perhaps you can in another." He was afraid that much graduate study in English was only a process in de-education. So when he was told that a man who was seeking an assistantship in English already had his Ph.D., Copey turned and asked in stentorian voice: "And does he have the Ph.D. death rattle?"

Sometimes students found it difficult to appreciate his notions of what was amusing. When an undergraduate who was one of my friends arrived five minutes late at his first conference with Copey, Copey asked severely, "What are you doing here at this hour, my young man? I have no conference with anyone at 3:05." The "young man" apologized very humbly, and Copey used up the remainder of the time in telling him what students might expect in his courses if they undervalued promptitude. The next time the student arrived early, and Copey asked, as though puzzled: "What can I do for you, young man?"

"I came for my conference."

"But I have no conference with anyone at 2:55."

"It is for 3:00, but I didn't want to be late this time."

"Well just go out and walk under the elms until 3:00."

A senior who all in all had an excellent college record, but had been careless in his course under Copey, and was in danger of failing, and therefore losing his diploma, went to Copey somewhat too belatedly, somewhat too desperately. He came away with a brief report: "Copey called me a toad."

Sometimes he attached to his own experience a uniqueness that his most devoted friends did not find in it. Many years after my own university days were over I stopped at Hollis Hall to see Copey for a few minutes when he was having a year of leave. He lay upon a couch with a heavy towel that had been dipped in ice water on his forehead, and with his hands folded so neatly that he looked like a corpse.

"Do you suppose I am ever to be well again?" he asked.

"Of course you are, just as soon as you get away from here and quit thinking about students and lectures and themes and conferences."

"But you must remember that I am sixty-three years old."

"Now let me see," I replied in an effort to be comforting, "that is just twenty-six years younger than President Eliot, isn't it?"

The corpse sprang up, full of furious life. "My God! Don't you dare mention that man to me! The Lord just made him to show to people!"

Five minutes later I met Dean Briggs in the Yard, and he asked, "Have you seen Copey recently?"

"Just now." And I told him what Copey had said about being sixty-three years old.

"Why," the Dean replied with a tolerant, beaming smile, "there have been several other people as old as that."

Nor did Copy hesitate to let it be known that he welcomed appreciation, and praise, and the widest possible publicity for anything he had done, or was doing, or was contemplating. He once told me that he had heard I meant to write a sketch of him, and asked me why I hadn't done it. I explained that I had had such a pleasant project in mind, but had deferred to a common friend who wished to write the sketch if ever he could get to it—though he did not. "But," Copey asked reprovingly, "would it be calamitous if both of you should write about me?"

Always there were stories about how this or that person had outshone Copey in brightness—about the class in English at Radcliffe that put twenty-three glasses of water (one for each girl) on his desk at the next meeting after he had requested one of the girls—"as though she were just a Harvard student"—to go and find the glass of water which he always required; about the girl dressed for tea when she came late to his afternoon course whom he asked, "One lump or two, Miss Smith?" and who retorted, "I'll have two, thank you, and no lemon"; about the tailor required by Copey to make him a new checked coat to take the place of one that had suffered a speck of damage in the course of pressing, who had the new coat delivered by a Negro boy wearing Copey's old coat of identical pattern; about the sharp-eyed little woman who had been scolded out of the audience by Copey because she could not stop coughing, who slipped in early to his next reading and sprinkled cayenne pepper all over the top of his desk and evened the score. Some were only what somebody had thought of the next day or the next week and wished he had said or done on the spur of the moment. But whether they were the ones based on fact or the ones only savored with the reminiscent wish that it had been like that, they were truthful comments on the man for whom they were intended.

All such things were part of the miscellany that in one way or another revealed something of Copey. But they were no more the complete expression of him than the stories of Whistler's wisecracks were the complete expression of Whistler the artist. Essentially

Copey was in earnest. He enjoyed participating in the mighty enterprise of awakening young men. When once a student had discovered that, and had begun to know his own part in the experience he looked upon Copey as an eccentric but devoted revealer of gifts from heaven.

There were conditions to be met. Everyone within the circle of his life had come to full alertness. He required undivided attention, and would resort to any expedient, even a theatrical one, in order to get it. When he went, for instance, to one of his Summer School courses—open to men and women—and found a great body of pleasant but casual-looking students waiting for him, he wondered —very eloquently—if some of them had not got into the wrong room. After other preliminaries designed to create expectancy, he remarked, "My Uncle Toby once said"—and then he cast a commanding eye over the room and asked, "But who is 'my Uncle Toby'?"

He waited for a few seconds, displayed impatience, and then became impetuous. "Am I to understand that no one here knows 'my Uncle Toby'?"

A young man lifted his hand timidly and ventured: "*Twelfth Night?*"

"No! No! My God, no! Not *Twelfth Night!* Where did you go to college—tell me!"

The man told him.

"And you mean to say that you never heard about 'my Uncle Toby'? Who were your teachers of English?"

After a fearful silence, a young woman in the rear of the room lifted her hand, and Copey noticed.

"And will you tell us where 'my Uncle Toby' is?"

"In Sterne's *Tristam Shandy*."

"Why, of course! Of course! Of course! Here is a young lady who can tell us who 'my Uncle Toby' is. And where did you go to college?"

"Radcliffe."

"Radcliffe! The young lady who tells us where to find 'my Uncle Toby' is from Radcliffe! And did you have any courses with me while you were there?"

She mentioned two.

"Now you see! It is one of my own Radcliffe students who is able to tell us about 'my Uncle Toby.'"

And with an atmosphere of humility and awesomeness filling the room, he was ready to proceed into the hour and on into all the hours of the summer session.

He had become master of two seemingly simple yet difficult means of teaching, and his chief hold upon students was through these: he read literature to them—in large groups; and he talked to them—one at a time, or in small groups. The era had not yet come when professors asked, "But if I use my time in talking to students, when am I to get my work done?"

Copey's own commentary in his classroom lectures seemed never to be claiming his entire concern, though he was witty and discerning. But when he pushed aside the few sheets of lecture notes and took up the literature itself to read, he came to full life. His reading was so vivid, so complete an expression of the author read, that nobody could forget it. Men listened to him and wondered how they had in their own reading been so incompletely present. And that was precisely how Copey had planned to have it worked out.

He liked the literature that read well aloud—and eventually compiled an enormous anthology called *The Copeland Reader*. In consequence, men went about in the Yard—and after—with their heads ringing with Dr. Johnson, and Blake, and Wordsworth, and Scott, and Lamb, and George Borrow, and Tennyson, and Dickens, and Hardy, and Stevenson, and Conrad, and Francis Thompson, and Kipling, and Walter de la Mare, and Masefield, and Abraham Lincoln, and Thoreau, and Whitman, and Mark Twain, and many and many another.

Such lecturing and such reading constituted only the workaday giving of courses. But when Copey announced a special evening reading, an hour that had for its sole purpose the giving of delight through profound or subtle revelation, that was an event in academic annals.

Of course there were certain to be amusing preliminaries and accompaniments. These were expected. Many a student would have felt cheated if Copey had sat down becomingly and read. At the appointed hour somebody had to lock the door against late-comers; somebody had to open a window—or close it—or open one and close another—or open or close two or three; somebody had to see that a glass of water was on the desk just the right distance away—and in the right direction; everybody had to choke off all coughing; and Copey himself had to readjust the reading light time after time.

To the uninitiated these matters were artificial and sometimes annoying. But where was there another man who could fill a lecture hall to overflowing with university students of every degree of sophistication, just to hear him read? They knew that they were not being deceived. Copey read so imaginatively, he was so vivid himself, that students had the enjoyable feeling of seeing luminously what they had before been wholly unaware of, or had felt but vaguely. It was something to see: a hall packed with students listening intently to a man read for an hour from the Old Testament, and finding themselves moved to the verge of tears as he closed:

"And the king was much moved, and went up to the chamber over the gate, and wept: and as he went, thus he said, O my son Absalom, my son, my son Absalom! would God I had died for thee, O Absalom, my son, my son!"

One could not forget his reading. Yet it was in his other means of bringing students to aliveness, his talking to them in his conference room or study, that many found the chief good of his teaching. In his course in writing, after a student had done all else that was required, he sat in Copey's presence and read his theme, broke out in a cold sweat to see how less than perfect it was, now that he read it in the presence of the Mighty Conscience, and heard the criticism that Copey dictated and that he himself wrote on the outside of the theme. "And put down an *A* with a long minus." Or it might be "a *B* with a big plus," or "two *B*'s."

But in his talk as well as in his reading it was when he was half or wholly away from the workaday that he became most completely unforgettable. When the light was in the window after ten o'clock, men made their way up the wooden stairs that had thus resounded to the tramp of feet since before the building had been used as barracks in the Revolutionary War, past rooms that had been occupied by a long succession of men more or less known in America, and finally to a room in which Ralph Waldo Emerson had broken the ice in the washbasin on winter mornings one year while he was in college.

Sometimes Copey welcomed them personally. Sometimes he was already sitting erect in the good-sized chair close to one side of the fireplace—where he always seemed to be on a dais—and an earlier student opened the door, or hurried back into the next room to bring out one more chair.

"Sit right there!" Copey would command from his place of eminence, and the late arrival would obey.

One evening a hesitant freshman ventured in when the only chair left was a small painted one opposite Copey almost in the fireplace. "Right there!" Copey directed. "Sit right there!"

His brilliance that evening was extraordinary even for him, and everyone sat intent and inquiring. Suddenly he broke off in the middle of a sentence with a "My God, young man!"

The fire had steadily grown hotter, the paint on the chair was smoking and blistering, and the freshman's face looked as if he himself were in danger of bursting into flame.

"You do know how to hold the fort, don't you?" said Copey.

Very privately some of Copey's followers believed that he kept the little painted chair there close against the fireplace as an initial test of loyalty. Men who could stand such a scorching would be sure to come again.

No one—not even Copey himself—knew the direction the talk might take. It might begin in some such conventional way as, "And where are you from?"

"From Ohio—southeastern Ohio."

"But you do not have the Midwestern guttural r-r-r-r-r!"

"Half of my family came over the mountains from Virginia."

"Ah! That explains it." And since regions all over the United States were represented in the bright room, the interesting question of migrations and regional speech might claim the greater part of the evening.

But students were always hoping that the talk could be turned to Copey's own experience—to literary gossip, to the great actors and actresses that Copey had come to know when he was writing for the *Boston Post* before he came to Harvard. He had written a life of Edwin Booth in the "Beacon Biographies" series, and always somebody was ready to ask him about Edwin Booth and John Wilkes Booth—if there were a half chance. And Ellen Terry, and Duse, and Bernhardt, and Mrs. Fiske—would Maude Adams and Julia Marlowe ever equal them? Or somebody started him off on the Harvard men of only yesterday who were already distinguished—a heavy percentage of them, it seemed, Copey's own students. Teddy Roosevelt had to be considered also, and what he was doing with the big stick. And did everybody know that the tall young Roosevelt in the Yard at the time was Teddy's cousin? And who were some of the recent poets who deserved to survive?

Sometimes Copey had to take down two or three volumes and read a little to make clear just why he believed as he did.

In such talk, in the presence of a dozen men who had come because their own enthusiasm had brought them, Copey's mind and tongue were freed. But almost more interesting still, the students began to find their own minds and tongues freed, so that they expressed themselves with a clearness and a certainty that until a moment ago they did not know they could command.

Before midnight some of those nearest the door slipped very unobtrusively away. After a time, when several had gone in this manner in order not to break the current of the conversation, all the others were standing and having—or hearing—a final word, and saying good-by. One or two carried the chairs back and put them where they belonged; and then there was a bulge of cheerful voices on the stairs as the last of the group descended.

Thus the procession of Copey's awakened ones grew and reached farther and farther until it had spread all over the United States and more or less over the world. In such a center as New York City they became so numerous that they felt called upon to have Copey come to them. At first he refused. To a man who had never been "farther west than Philadelphia, or farther south than Philadelphia," even New York seemed remote. But one day in the Yard at the north-west corner of University Hall, the same man who had once prevailed upon Copey to give up Sever and go to the New Lecture Hall to read, prevailed upon him to go to his former students in New York.

It became an annual pilgrimage—a kind of royal progress, since each year the committee in charge tried to outdo the committee of the preceding year in devising sumptuous ways of expressing appreciation. Copey rode in state; he saw what he wished to see; he refused to see whatever he thought he would not care for; he was let alone when he wished to have quiet; and then at a grand dinner in the Harvard Club, he read to the men who had named themselves "The Charles Townsend Copeland Association." Before many spring sessions had passed, men were traveling from other regions to the New York meeting—down from Boston and up from Philadelphia and Washington.

Especially after he had retired from the faculty at Harvard— where late he was elevated to the Boylston Professorship of Rhetoric and Oratory to succeed Dean Briggs, in a succession that began with John Quincy Adams—did his former students crowd in upon him on special occasions, and remember him on his birthday as if he were a President of the United States. He was happy to hear from so many, to know with great certitude that he had been influential in so many lives—and no small number of them very distinguished lives.

But he hated to have to remember that he was growing old. Being a retired teacher was not quite the same as being a teacher. He missed the cheerful voices on the resounding stairs of Hollis Hall. He missed Hollis itself—after he had moved into a complicated apartment house equipped with all such contrivances as door telephones, elevators, and garbage incinerators.

He had preoccupations that were revealed in unpredicated ways. He had never met Edwin Arlington Robinson, though both were from Maine. Once when "E.A." was coming to our house on his way through Boston and Cambridge I arranged to take him to Copey's apartment. It would be interesting just to sit back and hear these two discuss poetry and poets.

As we crossed the Cambridge Common, Robinson said, as if he might be the least bit nervous, "I wish I were a good talker— like Frost—for I know Copey is. But I am not, and never was. So I've just tried to put the best of myself into my poems and let it go at that."

Copey, however, made everything easy. He greeted us at the door with, "Now no introduction is necessary. Come right in, and sit right down, for we must have all the time for talk."

But the talk took a strange direction. Copey told us that he had been sitting there reading something that his mother had written when she was well toward fourscore years old. She was in a calm frame of mind, she said, yet she saw there in the room with her at the moment her own mother, who had been dead many years.

"Now what do you make of that?" Copey asked Robinson. And they were away on a lively discussion of immortality that occupied the entire evening. Not one word was said about any literary matter until just as we were leaving. "Here, come back for a moment," Copey commanded, "and write your name opposite this poem of yours that I like particularly."

The years advanced, and Copey did not like the fact. He was

resistant. One morning when he was taking his accustomed walk in Cambridge Common, I said when I met him: "Why, Copey, I haven't seen you looking so well in ten years."

"Yes, I know," he replied, "but you see, I am eighty-two years old—and God damn it!"

Yet he lived right on, and had a pretty good time, thank you. Always there were his students—those countless expressions of something that at least in small part was himself. I met them wherever I went—and covered the backs of envelopes with messages to Copey. On a train between San Francisco and Seattle the man across the table in the dining car was reading a book—an interesting book. "A teacher I had in college started me off at this," he explained, "and I have never stopped." It came out that the teacher was Copey. In Southern France one afternoon while I basked in the sun on the mountainside above Montpellier with a man whom I had not met until that morning—a man of importance today in the world of letters—he told me that when he was not finding it easy to earn food and shoe soles in college, he had a great friend in a professor who could say to one, "Well, God bless you, my boy," and slip two or three five-dollar bills into one's palm with his firm handshake and never cause the slightest twinge of embarrassment. And a man back from the Aleutians said, "Funny thing, though I imagine there must be others who have had the same experience; but I always got a bit of a lift just from being with Copey."

If one could see the map of the world as it is, there would be unbreakable and shining threads running back from spots of Copey's influence everywhere to Cambridge, Massachusetts. Nobody knows this better than Copey himself. That is how he lives. He does not need to peruse what someone has written in a book about the abiding satisfactions of life.

★ *According to a former student, William James "sometimes . . . would put his hands to his head and say, 'I can't think today, we had better not go on with the class,' and he would dismiss us."*

THE MIND OF PROFESSOR PRIMROSE

by Ogden Nash

My story begins in the town of Cambridge, Mass.,
Home of the Harvard Business and Dental Schools,
And more or less the home of Harvard College.
Now, Harvard is a cultural institution,
Squandering many a dollar upon professors,
As a glance at a Harvard football team makes obvious;
Professors wise and prowling in search of wisdom,
And every mother's son of them absent-minded.
But the absentest mind belonged to Professor Primrose.
He had won a Nobel award and a Pulitzer Prize,
A Guggenheim and a leg on the Davis Cup,
But he couldn't remember to shave both sides of his face.
He discharged the dog and took the cook for an airing;
He frequently lit his hair and combed his cigar;
He set a trap for the baby and dandled the mice;
He wound up his key and opened the door with his watch;
He tipped his students and flunked the traffic policeman;

He fed the mosquitoes crumbs and slapped at the robins;
He always said his prayers when he entered the theater,
And left the church for a smoke between the acts;
He mixed the exterminator man a cocktail
And told his guests to go way, he had no bugs;
He rode the streets on a bicycle built for two,
And he never discovered he wasn't teaching at Yale.
At last one summer he kissed his crimson flannels
And packed his wife in camphor, and she complained.
"My dear," she ordered, "these *contretemps* must cease;
You must bring this absent mind a little bit nearer;
You must tidy up that disorderly cerebellum;
You must write today and enroll in the Pelman Institute."
He embraced his pen and he took his wife in hand,
He wrinkled a stamp and thoughtfully licked his brow,
He wrote the letter and mailed it, and what do you know?
In a couple of days he disappeared from Cambridge.
"For heaven's sake, my husband has disappeared,"
Said Mrs. Primrose. "Now isn't that just like him?"
And she cut the meat and grocery orders in half,
And moved the chairs in the living room around,
And settled down to a little solid comfort.
She had a marvelous time for seven years,
At the end of which she took a train to Chicago.
She liked to go to Chicago once in a while
Because of a sister-in-law who lived in Cambridge.
Her eye was caught at Schenectady by the porter;
She noticed that he was brushing off a dime,
And trying to put the passenger in his pocket.
"Porter," she said, "aren't you Professor Primrose?
Aren't you my husband, the missing Professor Primrose?
And what did you learn at the Pelman Institute?"
"Mah Lawd, Maria," the Porter said, "mah Lawd!
Did you say *Pelman?* Ah wrote to de *Pullman* folks!"

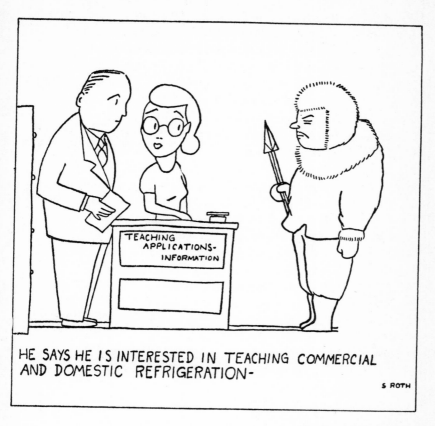

HE SAYS HE IS INTERESTED IN TEACHING COMMERCIAL AND DOMESTIC REFRIGERATION-

S ROTH

(Courtesy of High Points.)

PNIN GIVES A PARTY

by Vladimír Nabokov

T HE 1954 FALL TERM HAD BEGUN. AGAIN THE MARBLE NECK OF A homely Venus in the vestibule of Humanities Hall, Waindell College, received the vermilion imprint, in applied lipstick, of a mimicked kiss. Again the *Waindell Recorder* discussed the parking problem. Again in the margins of library books earnest freshmen inscribed such helpful glosses as "Description of nature," "Irony," and "How true!" Again autumn gales plastered dead leaves against one side of the latticed gallery leading from Humanities to Frieze Hall. Again, on serene afternoons, huge amber-brown monarch butterflies flapped over asphalt and lawn as they lazily drifted south, their incompletely retracted black legs hanging rather low beneath their polka-dotted bodies.

And still the college creaked on. Hard-working graduates, with pregnant wives, still wrote dissertations on Dostoevski and Simone de Beauvoir. Literary departments still labored under the impression that Stendhal, Galsworthy, Dreiser, and Mann were great writers. Word plastics like "conflict" and "pattern" were still in vogue. As usual, sterile instructors successfully endeavored to "pro-

[200]

duce" by reviewing the books of more fertile colleagues, and, as usual, a crop of lucky faculty members were enjoying or about to enjoy various awards received earlier in the year. Thus an amusing little grant was affording the versatile Starr couple—baby-faced Christopher Starr and his child-wife Louise—of the Fine Arts Department, the unique opportunity of recording postwar folk songs in East Germany, into which these amazing young people had somehow obtained permission to penetrate. Tristram W. Thomas ("Tom" to his friends), Professor of Anthropology, had obtained ten thousand dollars from the Mandeville Foundation for a study of the eating habits of Cuban fishermen and palm climbers. And another charitable institution had come to the assistance of Dr. Bodo von Falternfels, to enable him to complete "a bibliography concerned with such published and manuscript material as has been devoted in recent years to a critical appraisal of the influence of Nietzsche's disciples on Modern Thought."

The fall term had begun, and Dr. Hagen, Chairman of the German Department, was faced with a complicated situation. During the summer, he had been informally approached by an old friend about whether he might consider accepting next year a delightfully lucrative professorship at Seaboard University, a far more important seat of learning than Waindell. This part of the problem was comparatively easy to solve—he would accept. On the other hand, there remained the chilling fact that the department he had so lovingly built would be relinquished into the claws of the treacherous Falternfels, whom he, Hagen, had obtained from Austria, and who had turned against him—had actually managed to appropriate by underhand methods the direction of *Europa Nova*, an influential quarterly Hagen had founded in 1945. Hagen's proposed departure, of which, as yet, he had divulged nothing to his colleagues, would have a still more heart-rending consequence: Assistant Professor Timofey Pnin must be left in the lurch. There had never been any regular Russian Department at Waindell, and my poor friend Pnin's academic existence had always depended on his being employed by the eclectic German Department in a kind of Comparative Literature extension of one of its branches. Out of pure spite, Bodo von Falternfels, who had grudgingly shared an office with Pnin, was sure to lop off that limb, and Pnin, who was only an Assistant Professor and had no life tenure at Waindell, would be forced to leave—unless some other literature-and-language department agreed to adopt him. The only department that was flexible enough to do so was that of English. But Jack Cockerell, Chairman of the English Department, disapproved of everything Hagen did, and considered Pnin a joke.

For Pnin, who was totally unaware of his protector's woes, the new term had begun particularly well; he had never had so few students to bother about, or so much time for his own research. This research had long entered the charmed stage when the quest over-rides the goal. Index cards were gradually loading a shoe box with their compact weight. The collation of two legends, a precious detail of manners or dress, a reference checked and found to be falsified by incompetence or fraud, the spine thrill of a felicitous guess, and all the other innumerable triumphs of *bezkoristniy* (dis-interested, devoted) scholarship had corrupted Pnin and made of him a happy, footnote-drugged maniac.

On another, more human plane, there was the little brick house that he had rented on Todd Road, at the corner of Cliff Avenue. The sense of living in a discrete building all by himself was to Pnin something singularly delightful, and amazingly satisfying to a weary old want of his innermost self, battered and stunned by thirty-five years of homelessness. One of the sweetest things about the place was the silence—angelic, rural, and perfectly secure, and thus in blissful contrast to the persistent cacophonies that had surrounded him from six sides in the rented rooms of his former habitations. And the tiny house was so spacious! (With grateful surprise, Pnin thought that had there been no Russian Revolution, no exodus, no expatriation in France, no naturalization in America, everything—at the best, at the best, Timofey—would have been much the same: a professorship, perhaps, in Kharkov or Kazan, a suburban house such as this, old books within, late blooms without.) It was—to be more precise—a two-story house of cherry-red brick, with white shutters and a shingle roof. The green plat on which it stood had a frontage of about fifty arshins and was limited at the back by a vertical stretch of mossy cliff with tawny shrubs on its crest. A rudimentary driveway along the south side of the house led to a small whitewashed garage for the poor man's car Pnin owned. A curious basketlike net, somewhat like a glorified billiard pocket—lacking, however, a bottom—was suspended for some reason above the garage door, upon the white of which it cast a shadow as distinct as its own weave but larger and in a bluer tone. Lilacs—those

Russian garden graces, to whose springtime splendor, all honey and hum, my poor Pnin greatly looked forward—crowded in sapless ranks along one wall of the house. And a tall deciduous tree, which Pnin, a birch-lime-willow-aspen-poplar-oak man, was unable to identify, cast its large, heart-shaped, rust-colored leaves and Indian-summer shadows upon the wooden steps of the open porch.

A cranky-looking oil furnace in the basement did its best to send up its weak, warm breath through registers in the floors. The living room was scantily and dingily furnished, but had a rather attractive bay at one end, harboring a huge old globe, on which Russia was painted a pale blue. In a very small dining room, a pair of crystal candlesticks, with pendants, was responsible in the early mornings for iridescent reflections, which glowed charmingly on the side-board, reminding my sentimental friend of the stained glass that colored the sunlight orange and green and violet on the verandas of Russian country houses. A china closet, every time he passed by it, went into a rumbling act that also was somehow familiar from dim back rooms of the past. The second floor consisted of two bed-rooms, both of which had been the abode of many small children, with incidental adults. The floors had been chafed by tin toys. From the wall of the chamber Pnin had decided to sleep in he had untacked a pennant-shaped piece of red cardboard with the enigmatic word "Cardinals" daubed on it in white, but a tiny rocker for a three-year-old Pnin, painted pink, was allowed to remain in its corner. A disabled sewing machine occupied a passage-way leading to the bathroom, where the usual short tub, made for dwarfs by a nation of giants, took as long to fill as the tanks and basins of the arithmetic in Russian schoolbooks.

Timofey was now ready to give a housewarming party. The living room had a sofa that could seat three, and there were a wingback chair, an over-stuffed easy chair, two chairs with rush seats, one hassock, and two footstools. He had planned a buffet supper, which he would serve in the dining room. All of a sudden, he experienced an odd feeling of dissatisfaction as he checked, mentally, the little list of his guests—the Clementses, the Hagens, the Thayers, and Betty Bliss. It had body but it lacked bouquet. Of course, he was tremendously fond of the Clementses (real people—not like most of the campus dummies), with whom he had had such exhilarating talks in the days when he was their roomer;

of course, he felt very grateful to Herman Hagen for many a good turn, such as that raise Hagen had recently arranged; of course, Mrs. Hagen was, in Waindell parlance, "a lovely person;" of course, Mrs. Thayer was always so helpful at the library, and her husband, of the English Department, had such a soothing capacity for showing how silent a man could be if he strictly avoided comments on the weather. While visiting a famous grocery between Waindellville and Isola, he had run into Betty Bliss, a former student of his, and had asked her to the party, and she had said she still remembered Turgenev's prose poem about roses, with its refrain "*Kak horoshi, kak svezhi*" ("How fair, how fresh"), and would certainly be delighted to come.

But there was nothing extraordinary, nothing original, about this combination of people, and old Pnin recalled those birthday parties in his boyhood—the half-dozen children invited who were somehow always the same, and the pinching shoes, and the aching temples, and the kind of heavy, unhappy, constraining dullness that would settle on him after all the games had been played and a rowdy cousin had started putting nice new toys to vulgar and stupid uses. And he also recalled the time when, in the course of a protracted hide-and-seek routine, after an hour of uncomfortable concealment he had emerged from a dark and stuffy wardrobe in the maid's chamber only to find that all his playmates had gone home.

Pnin, returning to his unsatisfactory list of guests, decided to invite the celebrated mathematician, Professor Idelson, and his wife, the sculptress. He called them up and they said they would come with joy but later telephoned to say they were tremendously sorry —they had overlooked a previous engagement. He next asked Miller, a young instructor in the German Department, and Charlotte, his pretty, freckled wife, but it turned out she was on the point of having a baby. The party was to be the next day and he was about to ask the Cockerells when a perfectly new and really admirable idea occurred to him.

Pnin and I had long accepted the disturbing but seldom discussed fact that on any given college staff one was likely to find at least one person who was the twin, so far as looks went, of another man within the same professional group. I know, indeed, of a case of triplets at a comparatively small college, and I remember that among the fifty or so faculty members of a wartime "intensive language school" there were as many as six Pnins, besides the genuine and, to me, unique article. It should not be deemed surprising, therefore, that even Pnin, not a very observant man in everyday life, could not help becoming aware (some time during his ninth year at Waindell) that a lanky, bespectacled old fellow with scholarly strands of steel-gray hair falling over the right side of his small but corrugated brow, and with a deep furrow descending from his sharp nose to each corner of his long upperlip—a person whom Pnin knew as Professor Thomas Wynn, head of the Ornithology Department, having once talked to him at a garden party about golden orioles and other Russian countryside birds—was not always Professor Wynn. At times he graded, as it were, into somebody else, whom Pnin did not know by name but whom he classified, with a bright foreigner's fondness for puns, as "Twynn" or, in Pninian, "Tvin." My friend and compatriot soon realized that he could never be sure whether the owlish, rapidly stalking gentleman whose path he would cross every other day at different points of progress between office and classroom was really his chance acquaintance, the ornithologist, whom he felt bound to greet in passing, or the Wynnlike stranger who acknowledged Pnin's sombre salute with exactly the same degree of automatic politeness that any chance acquaintance would. The moment of meeting would be very brief since both Pnin and Wynn (or Twynn) walked fast; and sometimes Pnin, in order to avoid the exchange of urbane barks, would feign reading a letter on the run, or would manage to dodge his rapidly advancing colleague and tormentor by swerving into a stairway and then continuing along a lower-floor corridor; but no sooner had he begun to rejoice in the smartness of the device than upon using it one day he almost collided with Tvin (or Vin) pounding along the subjacent passage.

By great good luck, on the day of the party, as Pnin was finishing a late lunch in Frieze Hall, Wynn, or his double, neither of whom had ever appeared there before, suddenly sat down beside him and said, "I have long wanted to ask you something—you teach Russian, don't you? Last summer I was reading a magazine article on birds. ["Vin! This is Vin!" said Pnin to himself, and forthwith perceived a decisive course of action.] Well, the author of that article—I don't recall his name; I think it was a Russian one—mentioned that in the Skoff region (I hope I pronounce it right?) a local cake is baked in the form of a bird. Basically, of course, the symbol is phallic, but I was wondering if you knew of such a custom."

"Sir, I am at your service," Pnin said, a note of exultation quivering in his throat, for he now saw his way not only to carry out his brilliant idea but also to pin down definitely the personality of at least the initial Wynn, who liked birds. "Yes, sir. I know all about those *zhavoronki*, those *alouettes*, those—We must consult a dictionary for the English name. So I take the opportunity to extend a cordial invitation to you to visit me this evening. Half past eight, post meridiem. A little house-heating soirée, nothing more. Bring also your spouse—or perhaps you are a Bachelor of Hearts?" (Oh, punster Pnin!)

His interlocutor said he was not married and he would sure love to come. What was the address?

"It is 999 Todd Rodd—very simple! At the very, very end of the rodd, where it unites with Cliff Ahvnue. A little brick house with a big black cliff behind."

That afternoon, Pnin could hardly wait to start culinary operations. He began them soon after five and only interrupted them to don, for the reception of his guests, a sybaritic smoking jacket of blue silk, with tasselled belt and satin lapels, won at an émigrè charity bazaar in Paris twenty years ago. (How time flies!) This jacket he wore with a pair of old tuxedo trousers, likewise of European origin. Peering at himself in the cracked mirror of the medicine chest, he put on his heavy tortoise-shell reading glasses, from under the saddle of which his Russian potato nose smoothly bulged. He bared his synthetic teeth. He inspected his cheeks and chin to see if his morning shave still held. It did. With finger and thumb he grasped a long nostril hair, plucked it out after a second hard tug, and sneezed lustily, an "Ah!" of well-being rounding out the explosion.

At half past seven, Betty Bliss arrived to help with the final arrangements. Betty now taught English and History at Isola High School. She had not changed since the days when she was a buxom graduate student. Her pink-rimmed, myopic gray eyes peered at you with the same ingenious sympathy. She wore the same Gretchenlike coil of thick hair around her head. There was the same scar on her soft throat. But an engagement ring with a diminutive diamond had appeared on her plump hand, and this she displayed with coy pride to Pnin, who vaguely experienced a twinge of sadness. He reflected that there was a time he might have courted her—would have done so, in fact, had she not had a servant maid's mind, which he soon found had remained unaltered, too. She could still relate a long story on a "she said-I said-she said" basis, and nothing on earth could make her disbelieve in the wisdom and wit of her favorite women's magazine. She still had the curious trick—shared by two or three other small-town young women within Pnin's limited ken—of giving you a delayed little tap on the sleeve in acknowledgement of, rather than in retaliation for, any remark reminding her of some minor lapse. You would say, "Betty, you forgot to return that book," or "I thought, Betty, you said you would never marry," and before she actually answered, there it would come—that demure gesture, retracted at the very moment her stubby fingers came into contact with your wrist.

"He is a biochemist, and is now in Pittsburgh," said Betty as she helped Pnin to arrange buttered slices of French bread around a pot of glossy-gray fresh caviar. There was also a large plate of cold cuts, real German pumpernickel, a dish of very special vinaigrette where shrimps hobnobbed with pickles and peas, some miniature sausages in tomato sauce, hot *pirozhki* (mushroom tarts, meat tarts, cabbage tarts), various interesting Oriental sweets, and a bowl of fruit and nuts. Drinks were to be represented by whiskey (Betty's contribution), *ryabinovka* (a rowanberry liqueur), brandy-and-grenadine cocktails, and, of course, Pnin's Punch, a heady mixture of chilled Château Yquem, grapefruit juice, and maraschino, which the solemn host had already started to stir in a large bowl of brilliant aquamarine glass with a decorative design of swirled ribbing and lily pads.

"My, what a lovely thing!" cried Betty.

Pnin eyed the bowl with pleased surprise, as if seeing it for the first time, and explained that it was a recent present from young Victor, his former wife's son by a second marriage. Victor was at St. Bartholomew's, a boarding school at Cranton, near Boston, and Timofey had never met the boy until last spring, when his mother, who lived in California, had arranged to have Victor spend his Easter vacation with Pnin at Waindell. The visit had proved a success and was followed by the arrival of this bowl, enclosed in a box within another box inside a third one, and wrapped up in an extravagent mass of excelsior and paper that had spread all over the kitchen like a carnival storm. The bowl that emerged was one of those gifts whose first impact produces in the recipient's mind a colored image, a blazoned blur, reflecting with such emblematic force the sweet nature of the donor that the tangible attributes of the thing are dissolved, as it were, in this pure inner blaze, but suddenly and forever leap into brilliant being when praised by an outsider to whom the true glory of the object is unknown. Timofey was using the precious bowl for the first time tonight, he told Betty.

A musical tinkle reverberated through the small house, and the Clementses entered with a bottle of French champagne and a cluster of dahlias.

Dark-eyed, long-limbed, bob-haired Joan Clements wore an old black silk dress that was smarter than anything other faculty wives could devise, and it was always a pleasure to watch good old bald Tim Pnin bend slightly to touch with his lips the light hand that Joan, alone of all the Waindell ladies, knew how to raise to exactly the right level for a Russian gentleman to kiss. Her husband, Laurence, a nice fat Professor of Philosophy in a nice gray flannel suit, sank into the easiest chair and immediately grabbed the first book at hand, which happened to be an English-Russian and Russian-English pocket dictionary. Holding his glasses, he looked away, trying to recall something he had always wished to look up, and his attitude accentuated his striking resemblance, somewhat en jeune, to Jan van Eyck's ample-jowled, fluff-haloed Canon van der Paele, seized by a fit of abstraction in the presence of the puzzled Virgin to whom a super, rigged up as St. George, is direct-ing the good Canon's attention. Everything was there—the knotty temple, the sad, musing gaze, the folds and furrows of facial flesh, the thin lips, and even the wart on the left cheek.

Hardly had the Clementses settled down when Betty let in the man interested in bird-shaped cakes. Pnin was about to say "Pro-fessor Vin" but Joan—rather unfortunately, perhaps—interrupted the introduction with "Oh, we know Thomas! Who doesn't know Tom?" Pnin returned to the kitchen, and Betty handed around some Bulgarian cigarettes.

"I thought, Thomas," remarked Clements, crossing his fat legs, "you were out in Havana interviewing palm-climbing fishermen?"

"Well, I'll be on my way after mid-years," said Professor Thomas. "Of course, most of the actual field work has been done already by others."

"Still, it was nice to get that grant, wasn't it?"

"In our branch," replied Thomas with perfect composure, "we have to undertake many difficult journeys. In fact, I may push on to the Windward Islands. If," he added, with a hollow laugh, "Senator McCarthy does not crack down on foreign travel."

"Tom received a grant of ten thousand dollars," said Joan to Betty, whose face dropped a curtsy as she made that special grimace consisting of a slow half bow and a tensing of chin and lower lip that automatically conveys, on the part of Bettys, a respectful, congratulatory, and slightly awed recognition of such grand things as dining with one's boss, being in *Who's Who*, or meeting a duchess.

The last to arrive were the Thayers, who came in a new station wagon and presented their host with an elegant box of mints, and Dr. Hagen, who came on foot, and now triumphantly held aloft a bottle of vodka.

"Good evening, good evening," said hearty Hagen.

"Dr. Hagen," said Thomas as he shook hands with him. "I hope the Senator did not see you walking about with that stuff."

The good Doctor, a square-shouldered, aging man, explained that Mrs. Hagen had been prevented from coming, alas, at the very last moment, by a dreadful migraine.

Pnin served the cocktails. "Or better to say flamingo tails—specially for ornithologists," he slyly quipped, looking, as he supposed, at his friend Vin.

"Thank you!" chanted Mrs. Thayer as she received her glass, raising her eyebrows on that bright note of genteel inquiry that is meant to combine the notions of surprise, unworthiness, and pleasure. An attractive, prim, pink-faced lady of forty or so, with pearly dentures and wavy goldenized hair, she was the provincial cousin of the smart, relaxed Joan Clements, who had been all over the world and was married to the most original and least liked scholar on the Waindell campus. A good word should be also put in at this point for Margaret Thayer's husband, Roy, a mournful and mute member of the Department of English, which, except for its ebullient chairman, Cockerell, was an aerie of hypochondriacs. Outwardly, Roy was an obvious figure. If you drew a pair of old brown loafers, two beige elbow patches, a black pipe, and two baggy eyes under hoary eyebrows, the rest was easy to fill out. Somewhere in the middle distance hung an obscure liver ailment, and somewhere in the background there was "Eighteenth Century Poetry," Roy's particular field, an over-grazed pasture, with the trickle of a brook and a clump of initialled

trees; a barbed-wire arrangement on either side of this field
separated it from Professor Stowe's domain, the preceding century,
where the lambs were whiter, the turf softer, the rills purlier, and
from Dr. Shapiro's early nineteenth century, with its glen mists,
sea frogs, and imported grapes. Roy Thayer always avoided talking
of his subject, and kept a detailed diary, in cryptogrammed verse,
which he hoped posterity would someday decipher and, in sober
backcast, proclaim the greatest literary achievement of our time.

When everybody was comfortably lapping and lauding the
cocktails, Professor Pnin sat down on the wheezy hassock near his
newest friend and said, "I have to report, sir, on the skylark—
'zhavoronok,' in Russian—about which you made me the honor
to interrogate me. Take this with you to your home. I have here
tapped on the typewriting machine a condensed account with bibliography. . . . I think we will now transport ourselves to the other
room, where a supper à la fourchette is, I think, awaiting us."

Presently, guests with full plates drifted back into the parlor.
The punch was brought in.

"Gracious, Timofey, where on earth did you get that perfectly
divine bowl!" exclaimed Joan.

"Victor presented it to me."

"But where did he get it?"

"Antiquaire store in Cranton, I think."

"Gosh, it must have cost a fortune!"

"One dollar? Ten dollars? Less, maybe?"

"Ten dollars—nonsense! Two hundred, I should say. Look at it!
Look at this writhing pattern. You know, you should show it to
the Cockerells. They know everything about old glass. In fact,
they have a Lake Dunmore pitcher that looks like a poor relation
of this."

Margaret Thayer admired the bowl in her turn, and said that
when she was a child, she imagined Cinderella's glass shoes to
be exactly of that greenish-blue tint, whereupon Professor Pnin
remarked that, primo, he would like everybody to say whether
contents was as good as container, and, secundo, Cendrillon's shoes
were not made of glass but of Russian squirrel fur—vair, in French.
It was, he said, an obvious case of the survival of the fittest among
words, "verre" being more evocative than "vair," which, he submitted, came not from "various," variegated, but from "veveritsa,"
Slavic for a certain beautiful, pale winter squirrel fur, having a

bluish, or better say *sizïy*—columbine—shade. "So you see, Mrs. Fire," he concluded, "you were, in general, correct."

"The contents are fine," said Laurence Clements.

"This beverage is certainly delicious," said Margaret Thayer.

By ten o'clock, Pnin's Punch and Betty's Scotch were causing some of the guests to talk louder than they thought they did. A carmine flush had spread over one side of Mrs. Thayer's neck, under the little blue star of her left earring, and, sitting very straight, she regaled her host with an account of the feud between two of her co-workers at the library. It was a simple office story, but her changes of tone from Miss Shrill to Mr. Basso, and the consciousness of the soirée's going so nicely, made Pnin bend his head and guffaw ecstatically behind his hand. Mrs. Thayer's husband was weakly twinkling to himself as he looked into his punch, down his gray, porous nose, and politely listened to Joan Clements, who, when she was a little high, as she was now, had a fetching way of rapidly blinking or even completely closing her black-eyelashed blue eyes. Betty remained her controlled little self, and expertly looked after the refreshments. In the bay end of the room, Clements kept morosely revolving the slow globe as Hagen told him and the grinning Thomas a bit of campus gossip.

At a still later stage of the party, certain rearrangements had again taken place. In a corner of the davenport, Clements was now flipping through an album of "Flemish Masterpieces," which Victor had been given by his mother and had left with Pnin. Joan sat on a footstool at her husband's knee, a plate of grapes in the lap of her wide skirt. The others were listening to Hagen discussing modern education.

"You may laugh," he said, casting a sharp glance at Clements, who shook his head, denying the charge, and then passed the album to his wife, pointing out something in it that had suddenly provoked his glee. "You may laugh," he continued to the others, "but I affirm that the only way to escape from the morass—just a drop, Timofey; that will do—is to lock up the student in a sound-proof cell and eliminate the lecture room."

"Yes, that's it," said Joan to her husband under her breath, handing the album back to him.

"I am glad you agree, Joan," said Hagen, and went on, "I have been called an *enfant terrible* for expounding this theory, and perhaps you will not go on agreeing quite as lightly when you hear me out. Phonograph records on every possible subject will be at the isolated student's disposal—"

"But the personality of the lecturer," said Margaret Thayer. "Surely that counts for something."

"It does not!" shouted Hagen. "That is the tragedy. Who, for example, wants *him?*" He pointed to the radiant Pnin. "Who wants his personality? Nobody! They will reject Timofey's wonderful personality without a quaver. The world wants a machine, not a Timofey."

"Why, Timofey is good enough to be televised," said Clements.

"Oh, I'd love that," said Joan, beaming at her host, and Betty nodded vigorously. Pnin bowed deeply to them with an "I-am-disarmed" spreading of both hands.

"And what do *you* think of my controversial plan?" asked Hagen of Thomas.

"I can tell you what Tom thinks," said Laurence, still contemplating the same picture in the book that lay open on his knees. "Tom thinks that the best method of teaching anything is to take it easy and rely on discussion in class, which means letting twenty young blockheads and two cocky neurotics discuss for fifty minutes something that neither their teacher nor they know. Now, for the last three months," he went on, without any logical transition, "I have been looking for this picture, and here it is. The publisher of my new book on the Philosophy of Gesture wants a portrait of me, and Joan and I knew we had seen somewhere a stunning likeness by an Old Master but could not even recall his period. Well, here it is. The only retouching needed would be the addition of a sports shirt and the deletion of this warrior's hand."

"I must really protest—" began Thomas.

Clements passed the open book to Margaret Thayer, and she burst out laughing.

"I must protest, Laurence," said Tom. "A relaxed discussion in an atmosphere of broad generalizations is a more realistic approach to education than the old-fashioned formal lecture."

"Sure, sure," said Clements.

At this point, Joan scrambled up to her feet and Mrs. Thayer looked at her wristwatch, and then at her husband. Betty asked Thomas whether he knew a man called Fogelman, an expert on bats, who lived in Santa Clara, Cuba. A soft yawn distended Laurence Clements' mouth. The party was drawing to a close.

The setting of the final scene was the hallway. Hagen could not find the cane he had come with; it had fallen behind the umbrella stand.

"And *I* think I left my purse where I was sitting," said Mrs. Thayer, pushing her husband ever so slightly toward the living room.

Pnin and Clements, in last-minute discourse, stood on either side of the living-room doorway, like two well-fed caryatids, and drew in their abdomens to let the silent Thayer pass. In the middle of the room, Professor Thomas and Miss Bliss—he with his hands behind his back and rising up every now and then on his toes, she holding a tray—were standing and talking of Cuba, where a cousin of Betty's fiancé had lived for quite a while, Betty understood. Thayer blundered from chair to chair, and found himself with a white bag, not knowing really where he picked it up, his mind being occupied by the adumbrations of lines he was to write down in his diary later in the night:

We sat and drank, each with a separate past
locked up in him, and fate's alarm clocks set
at unrelated futures—when, at last,
a wrist was cocked, and eyes of consorts met. . . .

Meanwhile, Pnin asked Joan Clements and Margaret Thayer if they would care to see how he had embellished the upstairs rooms. They were enchanted by the idea, and he led the way upstairs. His so-called *kabinet*, or study, now looked very cozy, its scratched floor snugly covered with the more or less Turkish rug that Pnin had once acquired for his office in Humanities Hall and had recently removed in drastic silence from under the feet of the surprised Falternfels. A tartan lap robe, under which Pnin had crossed the ocean from Europe in 1940, and some endemic cushions had disguised the unremovable bed. The pink shelves, which he had found supporting several generations of children's books, were now loaded with three hundred and sixty-five items from the Waindell College Library.

"And to think I have stamped all these," sighed Mrs. Thayer, rolling up her eyes in mock dismay.

"Some stamped by Mrs. Miller," said Pnin, a stickler for historical truth.

What struck the visitors most in the bedroom was a large folding screen that cut off the fourposter bed from insidious drafts, and the view from the four small windows: a dark rock wall rising abruptly some fifty feet away, with a stretch of pale, starry sky above the black growth of its crest. On the back lawn, across a reflection of a window, Laurence strolled into the shadows.

"At last you are really comfortable," said Joan.

"And you know what I will say to you," replied Pnin in a confidential undertone vibrating with triumph. "Tomorrow morning, under the curtain of mysteree, I will see a gentleman who is wanting to help me to buy this house!"

They came down again. Roy Thayer handed his wife Betty's bag. Herman Hagen found his cane. Laurence Clements reappeared.

"Goodbye, goodbye, Professor Vin!" sang out Pnin, his cheeks ruddy and round in the lamplight of the porch.

"Now, I wonder why he called me that," said T. W. Thomas, Professor of Anthropology, to Laurence and Joan Clements as they walked through blue darkness toward four cars parked under the elms on the other side of the road.

"Our friend employs a nomenclature all his own," answered Clements. "His verbal vagaries add a new thrill to life. His mispronunciations are mythopoeic. His slips of the tongue are oracular. He calls my wife John."

"Still, I find it a little disturbing," said Thomas.

"He probably mistook you for somebody else," said Clements. "And for all I know you *may* be somebody else."

Before they had crossed the street, they were overtaken by Dr. Hagen. Professor Thomas, still looking puzzled, took his leave.

"Well," said Hagen.

It was a fair fall night, velvet below, steel above.

Joan asked, "You're sure you don't want us to give you a lift, Herman?"

"It's only a ten-minute walk," he said. "And a walk is a must on such a wonderful night."

The three of them stood for a moment gazing at the stars. "And all these are worlds," said Hagen.

From the lighted porch came Pnin's rich laughter as he finished recounting to the Thayers and Betty Bliss how he, too, had once retrieved the wrong reticule.

"Come, Laurence, let's be moving," said Joan. "It was so nice to see you, Herman. Give my love to Irmgard. What a delightful party! I have never seen Timofey so happy."

"Yes, thank you," said Hagen absent-mindedly.

"You should have seen his face when he told us he was going to talk to a real-estate man tomorrow about buying that dream house," said Joan.

"He did? You're sure he said that?" Hagen asked sharply.

"Quite sure," said Joan. "And if anybody needs a home, it is certainly Timofey."

"Well, good night," said Hagen. "So glad you could come. Good night."

He waited for them to reach their car, hesitated, and then marched back to the lighted porch, where, standing as on a stage, Pnin was shaking hands a second or third time with the Thayers and Betty.

"I shall not forgive you for not letting me do the dishes," said Betty to her merry host.

"I'll help him," said Hagen, ascending the porch steps and thumping upon them with his cane. "You, children, run along now."

There was a final round of handshakes, and the Thayers and Betty left.

"First," said Hagen as he and Pnin reëntered the living room, "I guess I'll have a last cup of wine with you."

"Perfect, perfect!" cried Pnin. "Let us finish my *cruchon*."

They made themselves comfortable and Dr. Hagen said, "You are a wonderful host, Timofey. This is a very delightful moment. My grandfather used to say that a glass of good wine should be always sipped and savored as if it were the last one before the execution. I wonder what you put into this punch. I also wonder if, as our charming Joan affirms, you are really contemplating buying this house."

"Not contemplating—peeping a little at possibilities," replied Pnin with a gurgling laugh.

"I question the wisdom of it," continued Hagen, nursing his goblet.

"Naturally, I am expecting that I will get tenure at last," said Pnin rather slyly. "I am now Assistant Professor nine years. Years run. Soon I will be Assistant Emeritus. Why, Hagen, are you silent?"

"You place me in a very embarrassing position, Timofey. I hoped you would not raise this particular question."

"I do not raise the question. I say that I only expect—oh, not next year, but, example given, at hundredth anniversary of Liberation of Serfs—that Waindell will make me Associate."

"Well, you see, my dear friend, I must tell you a sad secret. It is not official yet, and you must promise not to mention it to anyone."

"I swear," said Pnin, raising his hand.

"You cannot but know with what loving care I have built up our great department," continued Hagen. "I, too, am no longer young. You say, Timofey, you have been here for nine years. But I have been giving my all for *twenty-nine* years to this university! And what happens now? I have nursed this Falternfels, this poltergeist, in my bosom, and he has now worked himself into a key position. I spare you the details of the intrigue."

"Yes," said Pnin with a sigh, "intrigue is horrible, horrible. But, on the other side, honest work will always prove its advantage. You and I will give next year some splendid new courses which I have planned long ago. On Tyranny. On the Boot. On Nicholas the First. On all the precursors of modern atrocity. Hagen, when we speak of injustice, we forget Armenian massacres, tortures which Tibet invented, colonists in Africa. The history of man is the history of pain!"

"You are a wonderful romantic, Timofey, and under happier circumstances . . . However, I can tell you that in the spring term we *are* going to do something unusual. We're going to stage a dramatic program—scenes from Kotzebue to Hauptmann. I see it as a sort of apotheosis—But let us not anticipate. I, too, am a romantic, Timofey, and therefore cannot work with people like Bodo von Falternfels, as our trustees wish me to do. Kraft is retiring at Seaboard, and it has been offered me that I replace him there, beginning next fall."

"I congratulate you," said Pnin warmly.

"Thanks, my friend. It is certainly a very fine and very prominent position. I shall apply to a wider field of scholarship and administration the rich experience I have gained here. Of course, my first move was to suggest that you come with me, but they tell me at Seaboard that they have enough Slavists without you. It is hardly necessary to tell you that Bodo won't continue you in the German Department. This is unfortunate, because Waindell feels that it would be too much of a financial burden to establish a special Russian Department and pay you for two or three

Russian courses that have ceased to attract students. Political trends in America, as we all know, discourage interest in things Russian."

Pnin cleared his throat and asked, "It signifies that they are firing me?"

"Now, don't take it too hard, Timofey. We shall just go on teaching, you and I, as if nothing had happened, *nicht wahr?* We must be brave, Timofey!"

"So they have fired me," said Pnin, clasping his hands and nodding his head.

"Yes, we are in the same boat," said the jovial Hagen, and he stood up. It was getting very late.

"I go now," said Hagen, who, though a lesser addict of the present tense than Pnin, also held it in favor. "It has been a wonderful party, and I would never have allowed myself to spoil the merriment if our mutual friend had not informed me of your optimistic intentions. Good night. Oh, by the way, I hope you will participate vitally in the dramatic program in New Hall this spring. I think you should actually play in it. It would distract you from sad thoughts. Now go to bed at once, and put yourself to sleep with a good mystery story."

On the porch, he pumped Pnin's unresponsive hand with enough vigor for two. Then he flourished his cane and marched down the wooden steps.

The screen door banged behind him.

"*Der arme Kerl,*" muttered kind-hearted Hagen to himself as he walked homeward. "At least, I have sweetened the pill."

From the sideboard and dining-room table Pnin removed to the kitchen sink the used china and silverware. He put away what food remained into the bright arctic light of the refrigerator. The ham and tongue had all gone, and so had the little pink sausages, but the vinaigrette had not been a success, and enough caviar and meat tarts were left over for a meal or two tomorrow. "Boom-boom-boom," said the china closet as he passed by. He surveyed the living room and started to tidy it up. A last drop of Pnin's Punch glistened in its beautiful bowl. Joan had crooked a lipstick-stained cigarette butt in her saucer; Betty had left no trace and had taken all the glasses back to the kitchen. Mrs. Thayer had forgotten a booklet of pretty multicolored matches on her plate; it lay next to a bit of nougat. Mr. Thayer had crumpled into all kinds of weird shapes half a dozen paper napkins. Hagen had quenched a messy cigar in an uneaten bunchlet of grapes.

In the kitchen, Pnin prepared to wash up the dishes. He removed his silk coat, his tie, and his dentures. To protect his shirt front and tuxedo trousers, he donned a soubrette's dappled apron. He scraped various tidbits off the plates into a brown-paper bag, to be given eventually to a mangy little white dog, with pink patches on its back, that visited him sometimes in the afternoon—there was no reason a human's misfortune should interfere with a canine's pleasure.

He prepared a bubble bath in the sink for the crockery, glass, and silverware, and with infinite care lowered the aquamarine bowl into the tepid foam. Its resonant flint glass emitted a sound full of muffled mellowness as it settled down to soak. He rinsed the amber goblets and the silverware under the tap and submerged them in the same foam. Then he fished out the knives, forks, and spoons, rinsed them, and began to wipe them. He worked very slowly, with a certain vagueness of manner, which might have been taken, in a less methodical man, for a mist of abstraction. He gathered the wiped spoons into a posy, placed them in a pitcher, which he had washed but not dried, and then took them out one by one and wiped them all over again. He groped under the bubbles, around the goblets and under the melodious bowl, for any piece of forgotten silver, and retrieved a nutcracker. Fastidious Pnin rinsed it, and was wiping it, when the leggy thing somehow slipped out of the towel and fell like a man from a roof. He almost caught it—his fingertips actually came into contact with it in midair, but this only helped to propel it into the treasure-concealing foam of the sink, where an excruciating crack of broken glass followed upon the plunge.

Pnin hurled the towel into a corner and, turning away, stood for a moment staring at the blackness beyond the threshold of the open back door. A quiet, lacy-winged little green insect circled in the glare of a naked lamp above Pnin's glossy bald head. He looked very old, with his toothless mouth half open and a film of tears dimming his blank, unblinking eyes. Then, with a moan of anguished anticipation, he went back to the sink and, bracing himself, dipped his hand deep into the foam. A jagger of glass stung him. Gently he removed a broken goblet. Victor's beautiful bowl was intact.

Pnin rubbed it dry with a fresh towel, working the cloth very tenderly over the recurrent design of the docile glass. Then, with both hands, in a statuesque gesture, he raised the bowl and placed it on a high, safe shelf. The sense of its security there communicated itself to his own state of mind, and he felt that "losing one's job" dwindled to a meaningless echo in the rich, round inner world where none could really hurt him.

★ *The following story is told about the late George Santayana. About forty years ago the philosopher came into a sizable legacy and was able to relinquish his post on the Harvard faculty. The classroom was packed for his final appearance, and Santayana did himself proud. He was about to conclude his remarks when he caught sight of a forsythia uncurling in a patch of muddy snow outside the window. He stopped abruptly, picked up his hat, gloves, and walking stick, and made for the door. There he turned. "Gentlemen," he said softly, "I shall not be able to finish that sentence. I have just discovered that I have an appointment with April."*

BENNETT CERF
'Laughter Incorporated'
(Garden City Publishing Co., 1950)

★ *It was once remarked of a venerable Oxford don who refused to resign, that he had all the Christian virtues except resignation.*

BLISS PERRY
from 'And Gladly Teach'

"He is friendly and democratic in his student relations."

"He understands the problems met by the students in their work."

"He takes broad, not departmental views of education."

"He is emotionally stable and mature."

the 'ideal' professor

"His behavior reflects high ideals."

"He inspires students to express themselves sincerely."

THE PH.D. OCTOPUS

by William James

SOME YEARS AGO WE HAD AT OUR HARVARD GRADUATE SCHOOL A very brilliant student of Philosophy, who, after leaving us and supporting himself by literary labor for three years, received an appointment to teach English Literature at a sister-institution of learning. The governors of this institution, however, had no sooner communicated the appointment than they made the awful discovery that they had enrolled upon their staff a person who was unprovided with the Ph.D. degree. The man in question had been satisfied to work at Philosophy for her own sweet (or bitter) sake, and had disdained to consider that an academic bauble should be his reward.

His appointment had thus been made under a misunderstanding. He was not the proper man; and there was nothing to do but to inform him of the fact. It was notified to him by his new President that his appointment must be revoked, or that a Harvard doctor's degree must forthwith be procured.

Although it was already the spring of the year, our Subject, being a man of spirit, took up the challenge, turned his back upon literature (which in view of his approaching duties might have seemed his more urgent concern) and spent the weeks that were left him, in writing a metaphysical thesis and grinding his psychology, logic and history of philosophy up again, so as to pass our formidable ordeals.

When the thesis came to be read by our committee, we could not pass it. Brilliancy and originality by themselves won't save a thesis for the doctorate; it must also exhibit a heavy technical apparatus of learning; and this our candidate had neglected to bring to bear. So, telling him that he was temporarily rejected, we advised him to pad out the thesis properly, and return with it next year, at the same informing his new President that this signified nothing as to his merits, that he was of ultra Ph.D. quality, and one of the strongest men with whom we had ever had to deal.

To our suprise we were given to understand in reply that the quality *per se* of the man signified nothing in this connection, and that three magical letters were the thing seriously required. The College had always gloried in a list of faculty members who bore the doctor's title, and to make a gap in the galaxy, and admit a common fox without a tail, would be a degredation impossible to be thought of. We wrote again, pointing out that a Ph.D. in philosophy would prove little anyhow as to one's ability to teach literature; we sent separate letters in which we outdid each other in eulogy of our candidate's powers, for indeed they were great; and at last, *mirable dictu,* our eloquence prevailed. He was allowed to retain his appointment provisionally, on condition that one year later at the farthest his miserably naked name should be prolonged by the sacred appendage the lack of which had given so much trouble to all concerned.

Accordingly he came up here the following spring with an adequate thesis (known since in print as a most brilliant contribution to metaphysics), passed a first-rate examination, wiped out the stain, and brought his college into proper relations with the world again. Whether his teaching, during that first year, of English Literature was made any the better by the impending examination in a different subject, is a question which I will not try to solve.

I have related this incident at such length because it is so characteristic of American academic conditions at the present day. Graduate schools still are something of a novelty, and higher diplomas something of a rarety. The latter, therefore, carry a vague sense of preciousness and honor, and have a particularly "up-to-date" appearance, and it is no wonder if smaller institutions, unable to attract professors already eminent, and forced usually to recruit their faculties from the relatively young, should hope to compensate for the obscurity of the names of their officers of instruction by the abundance of decorative titles by which those names are followed on the pages of the catalogues where they appear. The dazzled reader of the list, the parent or student, says to himself. "This must be a terribly distinguished crowd,—their titles shine like the stars in the firmament; Ph.D.'s, S.D.'s, and Litt.D.'s, bespangle the page as if they were sprinkled over it from a pepper caster."

Human nature is once for all so childish that every reality becomes a sham somewhere, and in the minds of Presidents and Trustees the Ph. D. degree is in point of fact already looked upon as a mere advertising resource, a manner of throwing dust in the Public's eyes. "No instructor who is not a Doctor" has become a maxim in the smaller institutions which represent demand; and in each of the larger ones which represent supply, the same belief in decorated scholarship expresses itself in two antagonistic passions, one for multiplying as much as possible the annual output of doctors, the other for raising the standard of difficulty in passing, so that the Ph. D. of the special institution shall carry a higher blaze of distinction than it does elsewhere. Thus we at Harvard are proud of the number of candidates whom we reject, and of the inability of men who are not *distingués* in intellect to pass our tests.

America is thus as a nation rapidly drifting towards a state of things in which no man of science or letters will be accounted respectable unless some kind of badge or diploma is stamped upon him, and in which bare personality will be a mark of outcast estate. It seems to me high time to rouse ourselves to consciousness, and to cast a critical eye upon this decidedly grotesque tendency. Other nations suffer terribly from the Mandarin disease. Are we doomed to suffer like the rest?

Our higher degrees were instituted for the laudable purpose of stimulating scholarship, especially in the form of "original research." Experience has proved that great as the love of truth may be among men, it can be made still greater by adventitious

rewards. The winning of a diploma certifying mastery and marking a barrier successfully passed, acts as a challenge to the ambitious; and if the diploma will help to gain bread-winning positions
also, its power as a stimulus to work is tremendously increased.
So far, we are on innocent ground; it is well for a country to have
research in abundance, and our graduate schools do but apply
a normal psychological spur. But the institutionizing on a large
scale of any natural combination of need and motive always tends
to run into technicality and to develop a tyrannical Machine
with unforeseen powers of exclusion and corruption. . . .

To interfere with the free development of talent, to obstruct
the natural play of supply and demand in the teaching profession,
to foster academic snobbery by the prestige of certain privileged
institutions, to transfer accredited value from essential manhood
to an outward badge, to blight hopes and promote invidious
sentiments, to divert the attention of aspiring youth from direct
dealings with truth to the passing of examinations,—such consequences, if they exist, ought surely to be regarded as drawbacks
to the system, and an enlightened public consciousness ought to be
keenly alive to the importance of reducing their amount. Candidates themselves do seem keenly conscious of some of these evils,
but outside of their ranks or in the general public no such consciousness, so far as I can see, exists; or if it does exist, it fails to
express itself aloud. Schools, Colleges, and Universities, appear
enthusiastic over the entire system, just as it stands, and unanimously applaud all its developments.

I beg the reader to consider some of the secondary evils which
I have enumerated. First of all, is not our growing tendency to
appoint no instructors who are not also doctors an instance of
pure sham? Will any one pretend for a moment that the doctor's
degree is a guarantee that its possessor will be successful as a
teacher? Notoriously his moral, social and personal characteristics
may utterly disqualify him for success in the class-room; and of
these characteristics his doctor's examination is unable to take any
account whatever. Certain bare human beings will always be
better candidates for a given place than all the doctor- applicants
on hand; and to exclude the former by rigid rule, and in the end
to have to sift the latter by private inquiry into their personal
peculiarities among those who know them, just as if they were
not doctors at all, is to stultify one's own procedure. You may say

that at least you guard against ignorance of the subject by considering only the candidates who are doctors; but how then about making doctors in one subject teach a different subject? This happened in the instance by which I introduced this article, and it happens daily and hourly in all our colleges? The truth is that the Doctor-Monopoly in teaching, which is becoming so rooted an American custom, can show no serious grounds whatsoever for itself in reason. As it actually prevails and grows in vogue among us, it is due to childish motives exclusively. In reality it is but a sham, a bauble, a dodge, whereby to decorate the catalogues of schools and colleges. . . .

———————————

★ *The wife of the great physicist, Robert A. Millikan, happened to pass through the hall of her home in time to hear her maid answer the telephone. "Yes," Mrs. Millikan overheard, "this is where Dr. Millikan lives, but he's not the kind of doctor that does anybody any good."*

★ *Portia: I can easier teach twenty what were good to be done than be one of the twenty to follow my own teaching.*

SHAKESPEARE
'Merchant of Venice'

from

THE DEVIL'S DICTIONARY

by Ambrose Bierce

BRAIN (n.) An apparatus with which we think we think.

CHILDHOOD (n.) The period of human life intermediate between the idiocy of infancy and the folly of youth—two removes from the sin of manhood and three from the remorse of age.

EDUCATION (n.) That which discloses to the wise and disguises from the foolish their lack of understanding.

IGNORAMUS (n.) A person unacquainted with certain kinds of knowledge familiar to yourself, and having certain other kinds that you know nothing about.

LEARNING (n.) The kind of ignorance distinguishing the studious.

THE BOY WITH THE LOW I.Q.

by Fulton Oursler

ONE OF THE WORST EVILS OF TODAY IS THE EXAGGERATED IMPORT-
ance given to so-called intelligence tests. Many other qualities
besides agility in answering trick questions go into the making
of human personality. A man can fail all the tests and make a
wonderful life. Let me tell you what happened to a young Canadian
boy.

Call him Johnnie Marvin. He was the son of a carpenter, and his
mother worked as a housekeeper. They lived frugal lives, saving
their money for the day when they could send their son to college.
Johnnie had reached the second year in high school when the blow
fell.

A psychologist attached to the school called the young man,
just reached sixteen, into his private office, and this is what he said:

"Johnnie, I've been studying your marks and I've gone over
your various tests in motor and sensory impressions—your physical
examination. I've made a very careful study of you and your
achievements."

"I've been trying hard," put in Johnnie.

"That's just the trouble," said the psychologist. "You have
worked very hard indeed—but it has not helped. You just don't

seem able to get ahead in your studies. You're just not cut out for it, and for you to remain in high school would, in my opinion, be a waste of your time."

The boy buried his face in his hands.

"This will be hard on my mother and father," he said. "Their one idea is for me to be a college man."

The psychologist laid a hand on the boy's shoulder.

"People have different kinds of talents, Johnnie," he said. "There are painters who were never able to learn the multiplication table, and engineers who can't sing on key. But every one of us has *something special*—and you are no exception. Someday you will find what your special gift is. And when you do, you will make your parents proud of you."

Johnnie never went back to school. Jobs were scarce in the town, but he managed to keep busy mowing the lawns of the house-holders and puttering in their flower beds. And then a curious thing happened. Before long his customers began to notice that Johnnie had what they called a "green thumb." The plants he tended grew and blossomed, and the rose trees bloomed. He fell into the habit of making suggestions for rearranging the tiny front-yard landscapes. He had an eye for color and could make surprising combinations that pleased the eye.

One day while he was downtown he happened to notice a stretch of unused land behind the city hall. Chance or fate or whatever you may like to call it brought one of the town's selectmen around the corner just at that moment. Impetuously the boy said: "I can make a garden out of this dump if you'll let me."

"This town's got no money for frills," said the selectman.

"I don't want any money for it," said the boy. "I just want to do it."

The selectman, being a politician, was astounded to find anyone who did not want money, under any and all circumstances. He took Johnnie into an office, and when the young man came out he had the authority to clean up the public eyesore. That very afternoon he borrowed extra tools and seeds and soil. Someone gave him a few young trees to plant. When others heard of it they offered rosebushes and even a hedge. Then the town's leading manufacturer heard of it, and he volunteered to supply some benches.

Before long the dreary old dump had become a little park. There were grassy lawns and little curving walks and restful seats and little houses for the birds. All the townspeople were talking about what a lovely improvement the young man had made. But it was also a kind of show window for Johnnie. People saw the result of his skill and knew him for a natural landscape gardener.

That was twenty-five years ago. Today Johnnie is the head of a prosperous business in landscape gardening. His customers extend into neighboring provinces.

Johnnie still cannot speak French or translate Latin; trigonometry is unknown to him. But color and light and lovely prospects are his bread and butter. His aging parents are proud of Johnnie, for he is not only a success—a man of affairs and a member of the best clubs in town—he has also made his part of the world a lovelier place to live in. Wherever he and his men go, they spread beauty before the eyes of people.

★　*And in the world, as in the school,*
I'd say, how fate may change and shift;
The prize be sometimes with the fool,
The race not always to the swift.

THACKERAY
'The End of the Play'

THE FACULTY *INTIME*

by Henry Noble MacCracken

Why DOES THE COMMUNITY OF SCHOLARS HOLD SO LITTLE IN common? Why does each scholar bear the company of others reluctantly, and scatter each to his cell at the first release? The question is something musty.

"In "Religio Magistri," an *Atlantic Monthly* essay which I wrote soon after coming to Vassar, I set forth that the good teacher believes in his subject, in his scholar, and in himself. Students were fired by the burning enthusiasm of their teacher for the subject taught. They would forgive almost any lack but that.

But the same zeal that inspires the teacher may not make for harmony in faculty life, if it is pushed to excess, for then intolerance accompanies it.

> For virtue, growing to a pleurisy,
> Dies in his own too much.

At Harvard I knew, as all other students did, about the quarrels in the Harvard faculty. W. A. Neilson never disguised his active contempt for W. H. Schofield, the playboy of the English teachers. Copeland admitted he was in the doghouse because he insisted that poems were meant to be read aloud rather than studied. Intolerance is the faculty hot sauce.

At Yale I knew A. S. Cook's isolation in an unhappy eminence of Anglo-Saxon scholarship. I had known the hostility of some of my colleagues, when in an unlucky moment I ventured the suggestion that the Graduate Students Club should be allowed to run itself without the interference from the professors. I never recovered from the shock. Once I went in my discomfiture to Uncle Toby Cross, my departmental head, for consolation. He said: "Noble, you'll just have to learn that there are people who dislike you, and get along with the knowledge as well as you can. You can't be friends with everybody."

When Tucker Brooke, my warm friend of Oxford days, had come to Yale on my recommendation and was in danger of being dropped from the faculty after his first not too successful year, my interference with a plea for him met with keen resentment. So I knew something about tensions within the charmed circle of academic life. I was not prepared, however, for the intricacy or the intensity of such problems at Vassar. On the second day of my term there entered my office Miss Abbie Leach, Professor of Greek, bearing a satchel which she emptied upon my desk.

"These documents," she said, "constitute the basis of my charges against Miss Macurdy, the other member of my department."

It had all begun, apparently, with an iota subscript. Miss Leach, entering Miss Macurdy's classroom one day, had found upon the table some corrected papers. She glanced at them, and was horrified to see that her colleague had failed to correct the missing iota in a masculine dative. That was enough. From that time she had been certain that Grace Macurdy was no scholar.

I stood up, gathered the papers solemnly, replaced them in Miss Leach's bag, and placed it by her side.

"Miss Leach, take back these papers, and never let me see or hear of them again. My administration began yesterday. It will never review what happened yesterday or the day before that. Any attempt to the contrary will entail the most serious consequences."

There was a moment tense with electric frequencies in the academic air. Miss Leach looked ready to explode. Then the air cleared, and ozone could be sensed.

"At least we know where we stand," she said, and departed. I never heard the subject mentioned again by her.

Not that the matter was ended. When I recommended Grace Macurdy for promotion, as I did at the end of the semester, it was without Miss Leach's approval. In its place, I had a dozen letters from scholars of equal eminence in the faculty. Miss Macurdy won her way to eminence as a scholar, writer, and teacher, and today is remembered as one of the most distinguished professors in Vassar's long list. Her wonderful collection of Greek art is now a part of Vassar's Classical Museum.

Let it be said at once that Miss Abbie Leach was also a distinguished woman and teacher of no common quality. After her death I recognized it by placing her name on a tablet in Vassar's memorial hall as one of five famous scholars in the earlier days of the college, and as the "nucleus" of Radcliffe College. Her insistence on instruction in classics had been the agent that mobilized the women who won Harvard's reluctant consent to its "Annex." To her further credit be it recorded, that when she knew of her own mortal illness, she arranged to pay a formal call upon Miss Macurdy in her chambers, and drank the tea of reconciliation with her. It was a heroic act, worthy of Thermopylae.

Two days after the encounter with Miss Leach, Miss Lucy Salmon, famous head of Vassar's History Department, came in with a similar complaint against Dean McCaleb. More voluble than Miss Leach, she was harder to cork, but I managed at last, with more rudeness, I am afraid, to drive in the stopper. I would not listen to a word of it. It was long before she forgave me.

She was not too easy in social ways. At our first reception to the faculty, she blocked the whole line with an interminable discussion, and finally pulled me out of the receiving party altogether, to continue it. This was too much for Marjorie, my wife, whose patience gave out. She stood up bravely to the redoubtable professor, and I came meekly back to the appointed task of shaking hands.

Not long after that Marjorie had a quite unintentional revenge. She invited Miss Salmon and Mr. Mills to the same dinner party, and placed them next to each other, blithely unconscious that they had not spoken to each other for years. Back in 1890 economics had been started at Vassar as a branch of history, with Mr. Mills in charge. This separation of the two subjects was fiercely contested by Miss Salmon, and the controversy had lasted twenty-five years. But Marjorie's innocence turned the trick, and the embarrassed professors, feeling all eyes upon them, were forced into polite conversation. The awful moment passed without fisticuffs.

This was not the only conflict between woman and man in the faculty, as I was soon to learn. Some of them were caused by the man's attitude. George Shattuck, Professor of Geology, was a magnificent physical figure. He had been, while at Amherst, intercollegiate champion in the half-mile run, and there was about him always an air of abounding animal vigor, intolerable to some of the quiet, tired ladies of the faculty. His temperament, however, belied his physique. He suffered from lack of competitive life, and became a kind of chaperone, trying to protect tender females from the rough side of life. The females might be tender, but they resented his escort.

One of my first sights was a scene at the door of Main. Out from its portal came Miss Macurdy, dressed for a suffrage parade in Poughkeepsie, and proudly wearing a silk band across her bosom, emblazoning the awful suffrage colors, and *Votes for Women* shamelessly displayed. Mr. Shattuck met her. "I implore you, Miss Macurdy," he cried, "Don't go down there among that rough crowd. It isn't safe. You will be assaulted. You don't know what may happen."

"Out of my way, Mr. Shattuck," cried the embattled Amazon, and off she marched.

The men of the faculty numbered about a quarter of the whole body, and nearly all of them were heads of departments. Naturally, therefore, in this women's college there ensued a strife of the insubordinate bloc against the imposed domination of the male.

Sometimes the unexepected self-assertion of women professors came from the same dynamic that makes professors absent-minded —devotion to truth in one's special field. Among my best friends on the faculty was Miss Martha Beckwith, who held at Vassar the chair of Folklore, a rare if not unique position. In her researches she had lived with Hawaiians of the older stock, Negroes in Jamaican highlands, and reservation Indians.

"Come, Miss Monnier," she said one day. "The paper advertises a genuine Hawaiian hula at the theater. I want to see it. A car just went by with a big poster, too. Genuine hula, think of it!"

Miss Monnier's protests were of no avail. Off they went to the theater on Main Street. At the door the usher asked for tickets. "Nonsense," said Miss Beckwith, "I am an authority." Awed and puzzled, the doorman let them through. They marched down to a central seat. The vaudeville was on, and the "hula" girls, from West Forty-second Street of course, capered on.

"This is unscholarly," said Miss Beckwith, "I must protest."

"Please, Martha, don't make a scene. What is the use?"

Martha Beckwith arose and addressed the audience. "In the interest of truth," she said, "I must denounce this performance. It has nothing about it that in any way represents the true hula except the skirt, and even that is artificial. You are being taken in."

The theater was in uproar. "Go ahead, old lady. Speak your mind. Tell us about the hula! Sit down!" Miss Martha did not sit down. She told them what the true hula was, until the petrified manager came to life, and started off the "hula" once more.

"Come, Mathilde," said the scholar. "We will not stay for such an unscholarly performance."

Miss Monnier followed Miss Beckwith's stately withdrawal while the customers cheered.

Sometimes woman's aggression came from the sudden recognition of newly acquired powers. A young instructor one evening returned from her last lesson in judo in the faculty recreation class. At the door of Main Building she was accosted by a man who was waiting in the darkness. The thought flashed: "my judo." She extended her hand which the surprised stranger grasped. A quick turn, a powerful yank, and the stranger went flying over her head and into a big barberry bush which flanked the walk. Our heroine dashed for the door and got safely in.

"But did he speak to you?"

"Oh yes, something about how to get a taxi."

That's all there is. It is however pleasing to dwell upon the feelings of the stranger as he withdrew from the bramble bush, no doubt with his eyes scratched in again.

One of the kindest and most generous of the men, walking with me round the flower circle one evening improvised this parody:

> "What though the Easter breezes
> Blow soft round Vassar's pile
> Where every prospect pleases
> And only *man* is vile."

He soon after sought and found an excellent post at a men's college.

In general, the men in self-defense became conservative, opposing every change, while a triumphant women's majority drove them from pillar to post in faculty reform. Departments with women heads sought to keep men from any posts in their field, and the men in return, notably in art and music, added men to their staff as time went on. I could not honestly recommend a man to apply for a place in any department headed by a woman.

Conflicts within departments were often the result of some sex antagonism. A woman who sought the favor of the masculine was pretty sure to incur the hostility of the other women, and was likely to lose her post when the man retired. One department was so split over this that no meeting of its members could take place, and I was forced to assume a temporary chairmanship to enable them to organize. Men by themselves were not wholly free from such squabbles. In the gentle subject of philosophy the temperamental differences of the two men were so acute that they never spoke to each other.

In three departments the man-woman tension led to a splitting of the departments into two independent ones where the subjects of instruction permitted it. Thus geography was separated from geology and became a social science, and botany left the shelter of zoology. Unhealed splits occurred in other departments which remained united in name only.

Faculty tensions were no joke, however. At times I began to feel as if war would break out any minute on the campus, as it threatened to do upon the national scene that spring. I was led to study the causes of all these tensions, and to try whether through changes in the way of living, some improvement might not follow in human relations. Occasionally, in later years, marriage solved the problem most happily, as when Professor Philip Davis married Professor Hallie Flanagan.

But the chief cleavage did not run along the sex line. The academical animal, it seemed to me, was rather sharply divided into two groups. The first group, and the more numerous, might be called the analytical. Its nature was reflective, studious, industrious, but not dynamic. It sought a leader and was content to follow guidance. It was disinclined to physical exercise. Poor health often dogged such teachers, and timidity and inferiority controlled their feelings. They tended towards group life, since low spirits love company. They worked well in chosen grooves, preserving the great tradition of learning, but they would never add much to it, or alter its course.

The other group might be called creative. They were active, independent, aggressive. They exercised, and had a surplus of energy with which to combat disease. They led faculty action, and loved the scent of battle. The college was too small a field for them. They left the protection of college rooms, and lived in town, where they participated strenuously in civic life. They worked for suffrage, against child labor, against economic inequality and other forms of injustice. It was whispered of one of them that she had defended the right of an unmarried woman to bear a child and rear it. One or two, it was darkly hinted, were socialists. One even dared to be a Unitarian. Dangerous women, all of them. They rejoiced in every conflict of ideas. The times were ripe for change. One of them, Miss Washburn, had been intrepid enough to invade the secret precinct of the men's smoker at psychological meetings. Marching uninvited into its midst, she had sat down and lighted a cigar. None questioned her privilege to enjoy the smoker thereafter.

When war came, Lily Taylor, a younger teacher of classics, went to Italy for the Red Cross, and worked there and in Yugoslavia. Another Latinist, Elizabeth Haight, chairmanned American studies in Rome, and became preëminent as an authority on classical narrative.

The creative group was as a whole superior to its station, the analytic group in danger of submitting to its handicaps. For the first my task seemed to be to further their projects, and support them with college funds or by special solicitation of aid. Thus, for the painter Chatterton, it was my task to find the money for a studio attached to his home. But it was the large group of analytics that became my particular charge. They were not all women, by any means. Indeed, in a college for women, the men who accepted posts were likely to leave soon for other fields if creatively disposed, leaving the analytics to carry on.

As I studied the situation, I found much in the college life that tended to worsen the status of the less active group. Whether they made the conditions, or the conditions made them, was of no consequence. A change was indicated as the treatment. The monotony of long years of teaching the same subject at the same dead level must be done away. One must have time to keep up to date.

Either by shifting to new courses, or by introducing new methods of instruction, the pure waters of learning must be freed from the sludge brought down by the years. The long-studied private enterprises of research once started in high hope, but laid on the shelf for lack of encouragement, must be brought out and dusted. Grants for further study, for research, travel, and publications must be sought. The tired teacher must be made to feel that her college, with all its resources, was behind her and her own advancement.

So, when the time came to make an academic statute and to define the duties of the president, I wrote: "The function of the president is to conduct the administration with the purpose of advancing the interests of every department." I know of no better way of putting it; but I might add "and every teacher," which is tautologous but a little clearer.

To the teacher whose mind is centered on the relation of the college toward herself instead of her own impact on her world, nothing is so disappointing as the slow rate of promotion, and increase of pay. By taking a personal interest in the teacher, by pointing out the relation between activity and promotion, and often by suggesting a subject of study and the means of securing time for it, I was able to give the lift needed to the discouraged worker.

Many scholars of the analytic type have a good deal of the creative quality undiscovered. To probe for this and find it became my work. To imbue every teacher with a sense of responsibility not only for her courses but for the whole college was the first step. To accomplish this meant an early extension of faculty suffrage. The younger instructors became voting members and were added to important committees. I lived to see the time when the most vital faculty debates were led by a young instructor, who stood up to the Dean in open debate.

The decentralization of administrative work throughout the college, so that each teacher had an increased sense of her own value to the college, was the aim. I cannot say that it was ever fully attained, or that it was done quickly, but at least the centralizing tendency was checked. I tried my best to make a place in the work for the younger colleagues, and got a rich return in suggestions and cooperation.

The faculty as a parliament sat in an impossible room. It was on the third floor of old Main, given them because no one else wanted it. Dark and unventilated with two windows in corners, it was crowded when a hundred teachers met there. We moved to a lecture room in "Rocky," and as soon as it was possible, to the Aula, a hall of height and light, with comfort and dignity. It seemed to me, perhaps fancifully, that the quality of faculty debate became less bitter, more worthy of its nature, than in the old pesthole of a room, now made over into storage closets.

As individuals, the teachers had had but little care given them. To induce men with families to accept faculty posts, and to bring them into closer contact with the college, the trustees had constructed four houses for them, opposite the entrance on Raymond Avenue. Some devoted alumnae built a home for the librarian, Miss Wood, and others gave a home for Dean McCaleb. Dr. Hill built his own home on good terms, engaging to bequeath it to the college. This started a new plan, by which teachers could build their homes, selling them to the college on severance of the relationship by death or resignation. Three houses had been built under this plan. Further encouragement of it, in many cases by joining the college in the mortgage, has led to the erection of more than thirty houses by men and women of the faculty, on college land, at no rental fee. No house has been bought at less than original cost. Several of them are really two-apartment dwellings for the residence of two single teachers.

Fifty of the older teachers, all unmarried women, lived in single rooms in the student residence house. For them two apartment houses, Williams and Kendrick, were later built, the plans for them being started at once. Each was run on a club plan. Other small apartments were purchased. Garden plots were offered and eagerly exploited.

There was scarcely a single private office in Vassar for any of its teachers. My activity in hunting for unused space led for a time to the nickname of "Attic Philosopher." The search was long and toilsome, but well rewarded, some fifty offices being added here and there. New buildings for various sciences met the scientists' needs pretty well. With the removal of five of the larger departments from Rockefeller Hall, its overcrowded rooms and offices were found adequate for the rest.

When the chance came to add space in the library, twenty-five research studies were built for faculty use. These rooms, with an occasional borrowing of the larger student cubicles, have greatly improved the facilities for scholarly work.

These are prosy details, but the planning and labor that went into their completion was fully compensated for by the appreciation of those for whom I worked. It meant much to me that Professor Washburn, probably our most famous scholar and certainly our best lecturer, could at last have her own building when the Vassar Brothers Laboratory was vacated by the Physics Department.

"Miss Washburn, do you feel easy in conscience?" I asked her, when she sat at ease in her new Zion. "This building is limited by deed of gift to physics and chemistry, you know."

"Certainly," said she. "After all, psychology is just a kind of physics. It is a mode of motion."

Vassar Brothers Laboratory is no more. A trustee skilled in engineering reported against it, and the old hall was torn down, while Blodgett received the psychologists in fireproof quarters. But that was after Miss Washburn's death. She would have resigned before accepting quarters designated under the general name of euthenics. Once, while playing golf with her over the new golf course on Sunset Hill, I remarked to her, not without a spice of malice, "What a beautiful view of Blodgett you get from here."

"I never look at it," she solemnly replied.

Miss Washburn's creative life led to research in science, but she stopped short of its application. Yet she freely granted that from applied science came much new evidence which theoretical science must take into account. It was just not her duty to use it, and she feared lest students of applied science would be stifled by its routine, and lose their divinely given intellectual curiosity.

With all this work for the bettering of conditions, and with all these efforts to make work at Vassar more attractive, I never succeeded in eliminating faculty tensions. Some folks just do not like others. I came to two conclusions in the final consideration. The first is, that tension is inherent in intellectual life, when workers live too much to themselves. The mutinous emotions, left to themselves in the preoccupation with the intellect, take their revenge in breaking down the restraints which life in a wider community enforces! Lifelong association, at very close quarters, is not easy at best, as all apartment house tenants well know. Unlikeness and inequality of abilities tend toward friction, which a common love of scholarship does not succeed in overcoming.

Only something as strong as a common religion can remove

it; and even religion has not made monastery or convent life ideal, if we can trust the witness of their chronicles. Man was not meant to live alone, but it should be added that women were not meant to live together. Nor men either.

————————————

★ *When a girl applies for admission to Vassar, a questionnaire is sent to her parents. A father in a Boston suburb, filling out one of these blanks, came to the question, "Is she a leader?" He hesitated, then wrote, "I am not sure about this, but I know she is an excellent follower."*

A few days later he received this letter from the president of the college: "As our freshmen group next fall is to contain several hundred leaders, we congratulate ourselves that your daughter will also be a member of the class. We shall thus be assured of one good follower."

The Journal of Education
quoted in 'Fun Fare'
(Copyright 1949 by The Reader's Digest Association)

ELEGY FOR JANE

(My Student, Thrown by a Horse)

by Theodore Roethke

I REMEMBER THE NECKCURLS, LIMP AND DAMP AS TENDRILS;
And her quick look, a sidelong pickerel smile;
And how, once startled into talk, the light syllables leaped for her,
And she balanced in the delight of her thought,
A wren, happy, tail into the wind,
Her song trembling the twigs and small branches.
The shade sang with her;
The leaves, their whispers turned to kissing;
And the mould sang in the bleached valleys under the rose.

Or, when she was sad, she cast herself down into such a pure depth,
Even a father could not find her:
Scraping her cheek against straw;
Stirring the clearest water.

My sparrow, you are not here,
Waiting like a fern, making a spiney shadow.
The sides of wet stones cannot console me,
Nor the moss, wound with the last light.

If only I could nudge you from this sleep,
My maimed darling, my skittery pigeon.
Over this damp grave I speak the words of my love:
I, with no rights in this matter,
Neither father nor lover.

From *The Waking: Poems 1933–1953*, by Theodore Roethke. Copyright 1950, by Theodore Roethke. Reprinted by permission of Doubleday & Co., Inc.

A SLIGHT CASE OF ADJUSTMENT

by Muriel Resnik

IN THE FALL OF 1943 I MOVED WITH MY TWO SMALL SONS FROM A tiny fishing village in Connecticut to midtown New York. I anticipated long, happy days shopping for clothes, absorbing culture, and exploring the city, while my offspring were constructively occupied at a good school, returning to me at the end of the day newly able to share their toys and ready for a night of unbroken sleep.

Before we moved I conscientiously investigated several schools, finally choosing the one I felt to be properly sympathetic with my ideas on child training—which had been formed by studying the works of a master of a certain psychological school of thought on the subject.

Mike, the older boy, was then five years old, with a wistful face that belied his strong will. Hank, at three, was quite rotund and solemn, his owl-like quality accentuated by spectacles worn soiled and askew at the tip of his button nose. He was to enter the advanced nursery group. Mike was found to be eligible for the kindergarten. Advanced nursery, by the way, differed from primary nursery in that its members were expected to stand by themselves and "remain dry" a good part of the time. The school hours were the same for both boys, nine until three, with hot lunch, nap, and afternoon milk included.

The first day of school was brilliantly sunny and comfortably crisp. The park foliage was golden, the sky free of clouds, and a

brisk little wind blew us along the street. The schoolhouse was five
stories high, limestone outside, marble inside. Great double doors
of brass and iron and glass clanged behind us and we entered the
hall rather timidly. The shrill voices of children greeting each
other after the long holiday, the wailing of the little ones, the
scolding, soothing mother voices, the potpourri aroma of chalk
dust and soap, furniture polish and Lysol, woolens and vegetable
soup, the dankness of the mausoleum-like marble walls and floor,
produced in me that long forgotten first-day-of-school sinking in
the pit of the stomach. My sons hung on my hands, clasping them
convulsively.

I had been told by the billowing chatelaine of the establishment
to be prepared to "stay with them" for a short time the first day.
It was a difficult time for all of them, she told me, but particularly
for mine. She impressed upon me the grave dangers of the move
from our established home to a new environment so completely
different, and added that this plus a new school and routine might
result in great fears and insecurities. I felt like the next of kin who
has authorized an operation that is 90 per cent fatal.

We climbed the winding marble stairs and found Mike's room
at the top. It was a large room with a fireplace, wide windows
overlooking a garden, and a clean bare floor. Against the walls were
open shelves filled with a variety of fascinating toys. A blackboard
covered one wall, original drawings were tacked on the others,
and small chairs stood in friendly groups around the low tables.
The kindergarten students were busy hanging up jackets, donning
smocks, and looting the shelves with a grim single-mindedness.
Mike dropped my hand, grabbed his smock, and with a hurried
"g'by" to us, wrested a large steam shovel from a bewildered child
seated flat on the floor with legs straight out before him. "SEE?"
said Mike, manipulating the shovel.

Mike's teacher told us that Hank's group had gone to the roof,
so we stepped into the little elevator and rode haltingly to the top.
We emerged from the darkness of the hall into the brilliant sunlight. The floor of this playground was covered with gravel and
the entire area was enclosed in chicken wire like a large cage.
Two of the group sat solidly on tiny chairs. Three were crying
on their mother's laps. One small individualist was busily engaged
in throwing pebbles onto the street below, aiming at passers-by.

Hank's teacher, a pleasant young woman who asked us to call her
Joan, suggested that she tell a story. We drew our little chairs and

stools into a circle around her. Joan was a spellbinding storyteller.
In a short time the three mothers were able to slip away, unnoticed
by their offspring. I unfolded slowly, only to have a small hand
dart out to grab my skirt. I caught Joan's eye. She shook her head
at me and smiled at Hank. "Mother's here just as long as you
want her," she cooed. "Now you just listen to the rest of the
story." I settled myself as comfortably as possible on my little
stool, staring at the fresh run in my stocking. My back was beginning to ache.

After what seemed to me an interminable time, we all went down-
stairs to the classroom. Here Hank obligingly draped himself in his
little blue smock, smoothed it over his round front and sat down
in a small chair, gesturing me into the one next to him. I glanced
hopefully at Joan. "That's right," she smiled, "Mommy will sit next
to Hank. Isn't that nice?" I looked at my watch. It was ten-thirty.
I sat down.

The group sang a little morning song. The group did a little
dance of falling leaves. The group beat out a little rhythm on
drums, cymbals, a tambourine, and a triangle. Then the group
spread themselves around with great sheets of paper and pots of
finger-paints. During all this activity Hank and I sat quietly in
our chairs. When the mid-morning juice was served he roused from
his torpor for a moment. I rose only to be stopped by the tug
on my skirt. I sat down, shifting restlessly from haunch to haunch.
My legs were numb, my stocking was ruined, New York was
waiting. Finally I raised my hand. "Joan, I've got to go home," I
said. "I have so much to do. I can't stay here any longer."

"All right," she said smoothingly, "you go home now, Mother,
and Hank will stay with us—"

Hank rose.

"—and have lots to tell you when you call for him this afternoon—"

Hank hurled his smock to the floor and reached for my hand.
"No?"

Hank had reached the door, dragging me with him.

"Perhaps tomorrow then. We'll see." Joan waved and laughed
unconcernedly. "Byeeee. See you tomorrow."

We trudged down the marble steps and strolled out into the
street. A week later Joan suggested that perhaps if I showed an interest in the group activities.

Two weeks later I knew all the songs, had developed a definite flair for fingerpaints, had made an excellent adjustment to the group, co-operated well with my classmates, always shared my toys, and was by far the most graceful falling leaf. My son observed me with delight as he sat still as a little Buddha.

We went to school each morning and stayed until lunchtime. (That was as long as *I* was willing to stay.) We went directly back to our apartment where we had lunch and a brief rest period. Then we walked to the park where I perched restlessly on the working end of a seesaw.

My dreams of renewed culture were necessarily in abeyance, and I was uncomfortable when seated more than ten inches off the floor. I intimated to Joan that perhaps there might be another method of handling the problem. She murmured something vague about adjustment periods and how some took longer than others and The Move . . . but on my insistence she agreed that I could leave my child in the morning with the promise that if he were "unhappy" the school would call me and I would hasten to retrieve him.

I explained the new system to Hank. "Now that you're accustomed to school," I said, "beginning Monday I will leave you there in the morning and I will come home."

He dropped to the floor like a wounded bird and turned blue.

"If you are not happy at school," I continued rapidly, "Joan will call me on the telephone and I will come back for you. But you will be happy. Your group has such fun."

He released his breath slowly. His expression was thoughtful.

As soon as the big doors closed behind them that Monday morning I skipped lightheartedly down the street, loitering in front of shop windows to scrutinize their contents. I did some marketing, browsed my way through the neighborhood rental library for somehing to occupy my newly found leisure, and went home humming happily. As I put my key in the door I heard the phone ringing. I crossed the room slowly and picked it up. It was Joan. I think it was Joan. I could barely hear her voice over Hank's roars of grief and indignation.

"All right, all right," I said. "I'll be right there. Tell him I'll be right there."

When I arrived at the school Hank was seated comfortably in the reception room. He seemed calm enough. As soon as he saw me he slid off his chair and took my hand, pulling toward the door.

The teacher on duty smiled understandingly. "He was unhappy," she said, "so we thought . . ."

I nodded.

We went home, had lunch and rest period, and again I found myself in the park, bouncing viciously on the seesaw while Hank sat stolidly across from me. This became the pattern of my days. I would leave the boys at school each morning and, returning home, would find my phone ringing. I then retraced my steps to the school, exchanged a few bitter quips with the teacher guarding Hank, and took him home.

It was well on to November when I succeeded in cornering Joan. I suggested that it was up to her ingenuity to find some way to keep this child happily at school. We had made no progress, since, contrary to her expectations but not to mine. Hank refused to increase his waiting period. The duration of his school day was still approximately one half-hour.

Joan and I finally agreed to hold an after-hours conference.

Three days later we met at school in a small office. Joan assured me that Hank was everything charming, bright, unusual, and endearing, and I agreed, wondering how she knew anything of the child, having spent so little time with him.

I leaned back in my chair studying the dust on the files and the sweet potato growing rampant in the window, wondering about dinner . . . could anything attractive be done with leftover boiled cabbage? . . . listening absently to Joan weave her way in and out of the facts. The move, uprooting . . . young plants . . . tender care and nurturing . . . slowly. . . . The little room was warm and the late afternoon sun beat upon my head. I was fighting to keep my eyes open when I realized that she was waiting for me to reply to something she had just said about Stamford.

"Stamford," I repeated fuzzily.

Joan looked at me archly. "Hank has told me all about it, Mrs. Resnik."

"About what?"

"About the Stamford incident."

I straightened. "I'm sorry. I don't think I understand."

"I do feel quite certain," she continued after a moment, "that careful treatment will gradually eradicate the memory of the Stamford thing and that Hank will regain his feeling of security and faith in you."

I giggled nervously. "But what *are* you talking about? What Stamford—?"

"Mrs. Resnik." She leaned toward me and patted my knee. "My dear, Hank has told me everything. Everything. That you took him to Stamford and left him there promising to return for him, then you didn't and he became so very frightened. You see, his behavior pattern now is the result of your error at that time. Wherever you take him now and attempt to leave him, he will fight you, for he becomes frightened and does not believe that you will come back for him. Now if you will just—"

"Joan, this is incredible," I interrupted. "Hank has never been to Stamford. He's never been there. Hank has *never been* to Stamford."

Her eyes were accusing, fixed on mine.

"I've never gotten off the Parkway . . . we go right past it. I don't know anyone in Stamford." I could feel the warmth rising over my neck and my face was burning. I knew that I looked guilty. She continued to gaze at me with that "out of the mouths of babes" look. I felt even warmer. "But Joan," I faltered. Her expression was sympathetic, even kind, and disappointed. I knew she would never believe me. I stopped and waited for the blush to fade, studying the toe of my right shoe.

"This is not irrevocable," Joan remarked. "You have done harm, thoughtlessly perhaps, but we will be able to repair the damage. You must believe me, however, that the way back is a slow one. We will create a new behavior pattern. You *must* return to the school for him again and again and again until the child feels, eventually, that his faith in his parent is well-founded and he finds security once more. Until he *knows* that if you tell him you will return for him that you will be here. Therefore, that anything you say you will do, you will do, and that anything you say is so, *is* so."

I could hear someone running down a flight of steps with a great echoing clatter. A door opened, a snatch of song burst out, to be hushed when the door swung heavily to. I raised my eyes from my shoe to Joan. "How long"—I cleared my throat. "Excuse me. How long do you think this will take?"

"I really couldn't say. Maybe a month, two months, three"— she waved her hand expansively—"maybe right till the very end of the year."

I swallowed.

"But even if it does take right up to the very last school day, it will be a year well spent," she added enthusiastically, "if we accomplish nothing else. How much more important it is for a youngster to re-establish his faith in his parent than to become proficient in finger-painting or blocks . . . hummm?"

I returned her smile weakly. I thanked her and walked home slowly, thinking. When I closed the door quietly behind me I could hear Mike's voice in the boys' bedroom being very definite about something with the middle-aged sitter I had hired for the occasion. I hung up my coat and rubbed my numbed hands together. Hank came shuffling into the room, redolent of Johnson and Johnson, cheeks scarlet, light blue bathrobe belted tight across his fat middle, stepping on the feet of his dun-colored sleepers. He stopped dead and peered at me, gauging my mood. I studied his bland face. He whipped his glasses out of his bathrobe pocket, placed them atilt on the end of his nose, and stared up at me. I sat down in a large chair.

"Come here," I said.

He approached me willingly enough and leaned upon my knee, head on hand, fat cheeks pushed out of shape.

"You told Joan I took you to Stamford and left you there."

A small smile played fleetingly with the corners of his mouth.

"Hank, how could you? You know very well you've never been to Stamford. And when did I ever break my word to you? Never."

He remained immobile.

"What ever made you say such a thing?" I waited for his answer.

His lips were sealed but there was a gleam in the back of his eyes.

"All right," I said, finally. "It was not nice of you to tell Joan something that wasn't true. Not nice at all. You embarrassed me, but that's beside the point. It wasn't true and you know it and I know it."

He leaned harder.

"Now you listen to me. I am going to take you to school on Monday and leave you there. And I am not coming home. I will not be here if the telephone rings. It can ring and ring and ring and ring, but I will not be here to answer it."

He looked deep into my eyes.

"But I will come to school in the afternoon and bring you home when I bring Mike home and when all the other mothers and nurses bring the children home. It won't do you any good to say that you're unhappy, because I won't be around to *bring* you *home*."

He tried to stare me down but I refused to lower my eyes. He pulled himself erect with a sigh and stumbled into his room.

We spent a quiet weekend with no mention of the new routine. Monday morning I took my sons to school, fled back to my apartment. I jammed my key in the lock, burst inside, slammed the door, and leaned against it. There was no sound but the pounding of my heart. I sat down and waited. The phone didn't ring.

That afternoon when I called for the children at school I was quiet, relaxed, and content. I had spent the entire day window-shopping Madison Avenue.

Joan smiled at me over the heads of her class. She pushed toward me and whispered, "It worked."

I looked at her, startled.

"I told you," she said, "if you'd only be patient . . . and it happened much sooner than I had expected. Remember I told you it might take months? I am really amazed. Really. No trouble at all this morning. He seemed to be quite happy all day. Not terribly active, but happy." She put her arm around my shoulders. "Happy in his security, Mommy. His faith in you has been restored."

I smiled enigmatically and reached for Hank's hand. He placed it trustingly in mine.

★ *Princeton, N.J.—Parents of teenagers, said George Gallup in a report on a recent poll, are in favor of stricter schools.*

Almost 65 per cent of those questioned said that they felt that discipline in most of the schools throughout the country was not strict enough. And, they stated, this was the fault of the parents of the children for not allowing school officials to be stricter.

Parents were asked also whether children should be given more homework in order to keep them busy and to discourage juvenile delinquency. Only 8 per cent of those who answered thought that there was too much homework, 39 per cent that there was not enough, and 26 per cent that the amount was about right; 27 per cent expressed no opinion.

The Nation's Schools
(News Story, January, 1955)

DR. COIT OF ST. PAUL'S

by Owen Wister

THE FIRST HEADMASTER OF ST. PAUL'S SCHOOL WAS TWENTY-SIX when he opened it alone, and with three boys. Three hundred and thirty-nine were there, and thirty-six masters, on the winter day when he died, at the age of sixty-five; and a hush fell upon the hearts of those who had gone out of that school into the world. The master builder of their consciences and characters would never again look at them with his searching blue eyes. His marble effigy, recumbent in the School Chapel, is rightly clothed in a monastic gown, with a rope knotted round the waist. The sculpture knew that time had misplaced him, as an April day will sometimes appear in January. His well-known fellow churchmen and acquaintances, Phillips Brooks, Bishop Doane, and the three Bishops Potter, were at one with their epoch; he came as straight from the twelfth century as John Brown from the Old Testament, or Napoleon from the age when invaders could change the course of history.

His spirit was felt to be so remote from the present that to see him do some everyday thing, as when by a quick light touch from behind he knocked the cap over the eyes of a little new boy who had forgotten in his general timidity to take it off as he was entering the Chapel, never ceased to be incongruous; or as when, in the midst of reproving two boys who had together destroyed a

posted bulletin not to their liking, he pulled himself up short on
the brink of a joke:—

'Then I'm to understand that Tom tore it down, and Jack tore
it—to pieces.'

He adjusted himself to his age in little that was not needed for the
welfare of the school that he created, and in his creation he found
his context, the medium for his genius; during forty years he filled
every cranny of St. Paul's with his tremendous personality.

Few boys over whom his spiritual fire passed ever forgot it, or
the tall black figure in which it blazed. Whatever religious observ-
ance they may have dropped away from, whatever scruple of their
boyhood they got over, him they never got over. Twenty-five
years after he was dead, and three rectors had succeeded him, a
lady who came to live at the school found that she met his legend
at every turn; he was still present in the place, pervading it; while
out in the world he lived so deep in men of forty and fifty that
his formidable shape would appear to them in their dreams.

Henry Augustus Coit was born on January 20, 1830, seven
hundred years later than the days of his spiritual kin. Behind the
times he was not; he was keenly alive to them, found them little to
his liking, and withdrew from them to live devotedly in his work,
and deeply within himself, in perpetual communion with something
eternal. Had he come into the world at Assisi or Siena, when Innocent II was pope, instead of at Wilmington, Delaware, when
Andrew Jackson was president, it might well be that the calendar
would now include another saint, that another order would be
numbered with the Franciscans and Benedictines, and that his
portrait—possibly even his martyrdom—by Pinturicchio or Pietro
Vannucci would hang treasured in the hill-town cathedrals of
Italy. Instead, there is his photograph in the Alumni House: a stern
sad man in clerical black; a broad brow, a keen eye, the beard and
shaven upper lip of other days; obviously a man of war and a
captain; less obviously a prophet of poetic vision, and a tender,
very human heart; a true and vivid likeness of the man's aspect
in his full prime. To catch the vision and the heart, his youthful
face must be studied, his ardent face when he was twenty-four:
beardless, a brow that might be Shelley's, thick waving hair massed
above this, an eye of wide-open wistfulness, a mouth of marked
purpose, not yet chiseled by strife, and the fashion of choker and
collar to be seen round the neck of Daniel Webster. In this early

likeness noble and serious dreams can be read, dreams meant to come true through action; the face in the Alumni House has been hammered into austerity by forty years of fighting with the beasts at Ephesus, and the knowledge that nothing comes wholly true. He is reported to have said once that boarding schools were a necessary evil: if he ever did, it was a momentary flash, an overstatement of his feeling that the best he could do must fall short of what, in the beginning, he may have hoped to do. And possibly this, with his native bent for indignation at the evil in the world, rather than elation over the good, may have set stern sadness in the depths of his countenance, in spite of the drollery and humor which often played over its surface. His lightning perception of the ludicrous did little to help the mood that dwelt inmost in him.

At morning service in the Chapel, when he said, 'Man goeth forth unto his work and to his labour until the evening,' there was an overtone in his arresting voice which seemed to be almost fatalistic, almost to ask, 'And what does it all come to?'

When he gave out such hymns as 'Abide with me! Fast falls the eventide,' 'Weary of earth, and laden with my sin,' 'Lead, kindly Light, amid the encircling gloom,' and many another that bore upon the tragedy of life, the music of his utterance fitted those words closer than when he stood tall and majestic in the white amplitude of his surplice, and read, 'The day of resurrection! Earth, tell it out abroad!' or, 'The heavens declare the glory of God; and the firmament showeth his handywork.'

The spirit in exile, separated by seven centuries from its native epoch, could not sing the Lord's song in a strange land jubilantly, like Phillips Brooks, who was at home in his times, and splendidly buoyant, and could make it sound like a trumpet. 'Life is so simple!' Brooks exclaimed exuberantly, one Sunday morning in his pulpit. It was not simple to Henry Coit: better to hold aloof from it, and put armor on young souls to encounter it and prevail. Behind every sentence that he preached in Chapel, every page of Greek or Latin which he put with such grace into English for his stumbling boys, every game, that he countenanced outdoors and in, lived the unswerving purpose to equip young souls to meet a life that was mostly evil. In him, more than in any of his remarkable brothers, the heritage of Celtic twilight prevailed, and his New England ancestors held his stormy temperament in their grip. The sombre cast of

Puritanism dimmed the natural sun of mirth and humor that constantly struggled to shine out in him, and checked, too often to his own loss and the loss of those around him, the impulse of laughter and fun which bubbled up liberally in him. It almost seemed as if he felt it wrong to relax. In his spontaneous distrust of any indulgence, he was more like John Knox than like the converted troubadour of Assisi, at whose touch the rose tree lost its thorns: the discipline of the thorn was to him more desirable than the smell of the rose. He had never been converted, like Saint Paul, or Saint Francis, or Saint Ignatius; he had never needed conversion; the straight line of his life was from its beginning to its end without a break, and all his days he walked humbly in the sight of his God—but not much so in the sight of men.

His ecclesiastical chief, and affectionate friend, Bishop Niles, a trustee of the school, was explaining to him once why he could not attend the approaching functions and prize giving of Last Night; Last Night at his own school in Holderness came on the same date, and claimed his presence. And while he talked Dr. Coit kept his back turned in annoyance.

'Henry Coit,' said the Bishop at last, 'when I am speaking to you of serious things, you will please look at me.'

The trustees of the school, a chosen group of men capable in their various callings, were humorously aware that when they convened at the Rectory to discuss and decide upon whatever of importance had come up they were little more than what is termed rubber stamps, ratifying the decisions of their Headmaster. They sat and heard him; they learned what had been done, and what was to be done, and the reasons for it; in their submission they were not unlike boys being lectured in his study. The chief difference was that, being mature men, they recognized to the full the extraordinary quality of their Headmaster, his sagacity and integrity, the success he was making of his work—and so they were glad to give him his head. Such a way to conduct a complex institution could never last, except during the same exceptional state of things, as when some nation is ruled for a while by a benevolent despot.

'When our meeting is over,' said a trustee, Dr. Samuel Eliot, to a parent of one of the boys, 'Dr. Coit waves a hand toward the dining room, and tells us that we shall find sherry and cigars there. None of us ever dares to go in.'

His attitude about tobacco was something quite peculiar, and must be laid not alone to his innate distrust of any mere physical indulgence; a delicate and extreme fastidiousness marked his taste in a multitude of directions, and this the smell of tobacco evidently offended. In his summer holidays, late in life, when he sat with his family on the deck of some Canadian Steamer, and cigar smoke floated his way, he would give the characteristic wave of his hand to waft it off, and a sniff of his nose, and a blow with his lips, while the gleam of irony twinkled in his blue eye.

When Augustus Swift, who brought much-needed liveliness and liberality in living to the school early in 1874, came to establish his rooms full of good water colors, bright shelves of books, comfortable curtains and chairs, across the hall from the Doctor's austere study, and the doors of both rooms would be open, the Doctor would interrupt what he was saying to some boy by a turning of his head and a searching sniff, and, 'My dear, don't you notice an odor of nicotine?' And the ironic twinkle in the blue eye would follow, and win the delighted boy's confidence.

Less playful was his remark to his son when he appeared one day with a cigar in his mouth: 'And when did you assume that badge of manhood?'

That was the father; the most did not carry it so far. For the trustees cigars and sherry were always ready, and prejudice was waived for other guests. In the upstairs apartment of his son and daughter-in-law during the later days when they lived with him, the badge of manhood was allowed. And when a certain prelate was staying in the house the Doctor, after dinner, would say to his son, 'Take the Bishop upstairs and see that he has all the necessary apparatus.'

Dr. Coit's fastidiousness came out in his dress; never a wrinkle in his severe coat, or a fray in his white collar, or a speck on the polish of his long, narrow, well-made shoes. At his right hand on his desk lay always a row of pencils, symmetric and sharpened to the finest point; his swift handwriting, though traced by a flying pen, was exquisitely formed and delicate as a thread.

Fastidiousness came out in his choice of words, in his literary taste, in his severity or his laughter over the English into which the boys would put their Horace or their Euripides.

He was holding an oral examination in sixth- form Latin, and had invited an old boy, arrived from college for a visit, to sit beside him on the platform.

'You may scan the first line of this ode,' he said to one of the form.

'Vitas me hinnuleo similis, Chloe,' the boy read in correct rhythm.

'That will do. Now translate it.'

'You shun me, Chloe, like a mule.'

'Oh, my dear! A mule! Do you think calling her that would soften her heart?'

'It's in the dictionary, sir.'

'Didn't you notice any other word there? Didn't you see "fawn"? Well, go on; and remember it's a lover addressing a young lady.'

And while the boy continued the Doctor, quietly mirthful, turned to the visitor and said, 'You see, we're still going at it on all fours!'

II

Going at it on all fours under such discipline as Henry Coit's trained many a clumsy mind to go upright with a good carriage. This advantage has befallen youth before. Arnold of Rugby, Fellenberg of Hofwyl, and Muhlenberg, who taught Henry Coit—these were all of the race of great civilizers. Whenever you had Mark Hopkins at one end of a log and a student at the other, it was said that you had a university. Arnold not only licked drunken, lawless Rugby into shape; his work there reformed Harrow and Eton, and ordained a new decency in the brutal schools of Britain.

Henry Coit had nothing to reform; he had something to create out of almost nothing—a farm in the wilds, and three boys driven there with him in a carriage. He played on an old square piano to accompany them in their evening hymns; and, since Henry Coit, every preparatory school in America has had its eye on what he made out of that beginning in 1856.

Without pretensions to erudite scholarship, he gave young brains the secret of taste and discrimination, set intellects, when an intellect could be discerned, on the right road. Through the unerring felicity of his comments, Cicero, Horace, Homer, Euripides, set their seal upon every young intelligence that was congenitally capable of taking this impress; and the seal remained long after the syntax had evaporated.

St. Paul's boys were noted for their good use of English; it was recognized by the boys from other schools who met them at Harvard, where they anticipated the required course in the rhetoric without effort. Why did they find this so simple a matter? Because Dr. Coit's strict and delicate taste pervaded St. Paul's from top to bottom. Not alone his classes in Greek and Latin, but those of his assistant masters also were equally lessons in English. No going at it on all fours if the boy could be lifted to his feet; accuracy even to the last shade was demanded, but merely as the necessary root of the matter. This must bloom into the natural idiom of the Mother Tongue; it could not be left a dislocated jumble of gerunds and ablatives absolute.

> Sweet when she smiles my Lalage I'll love,
> Sweet when she talks to me,

is the English into which Dr. Coit turned two lines of Horace, as he sat with his sixth form. It was quite often his way toward the end of the hour to hold the book up, and lean back, and read to the boys his version of whatever Latin or Greek had been that day's assigned work; and once a boy returning from Harvard, disappointed with some readings of Homer to which he had listened there, begged him to write out and publish his own translation. The suggestion was whisked to the winds by a sweep of the thumb over the long fingers, and a sound in the throat, which could express every shade of disapproval from diverted irony to corrosive scorn, and at which the boy had frequently shaken in his shoes.

Personal questions, attempted compliments, brought instantly the whisk of the thumb and the sound in the throat. To that same boy, on another visit, the Doctor ironically narrated a conversation with a President of the United States, who had inquired by what methods he was so successful in impressing himself on his scholars. It was the Founder of Christianity, Dr. Coit had retorted, whose words and example he strove to teach; and to the alumnus he added, 'Impress one's self! As if one wanted a set of young apes!'

But when the alumnus broke into laughter at this a quick 'Pssh!' cut him short. At that sound he had also often shaken in his shoes.

To provoke mirth and cut it short was one of the strange traits of this strange man. It was as if his humor had escaped from him unaware, and was not to be countenanced. Yet he could relax in the heartiest laughter.

Two old boys came up to the Anniversary, and interpolated an Italian number in the concert programme. One, in a wild wig, sat pounding the piano, while the other, got up like an operatic prima donna, rushed about the school-study platform and shrieked scales and trills in a high falsetto. Dr. Coit, in one of the stalls at the end of the room, sat rocking backward and forward, and at last put his hand over his face.

When his humanity came uppermost, he could be like sunshine; the blue eyes ceased to pierce, and twinkled or shone with an understanding that warmed many a boy's heart to strive with all the strength that was in him. The appeal and the exhortation were in essence always religious; the same talk from other lips has left many a boy cold; it was the fiery spirit that burned in Henry Coit which opened young hearts and minds and touched to life the aspirations latent there.

With forty years of boys to deal with, nothing short of omniscience could have steered free of mistakes. Henry Coit's genius with youth did not save him from misreading some characters whom their contemporaries saw through easily. He thought too well of some, and of some not well enough. There was a boy who received the school medal, the crown of all honors, given in token of character, influence, loyalty, good standing. No one watched this boy walk up and get it with any hearty enthusiasm; the school knew better. Many years later, when the boy had come a good deal to the fore through exercise of the same assiduity, adroitness, and colorless adaptation which had won him the school medal, somebody arriving at the Rectory spoke of having seen him in a train.

'Poor potatoes,' remarked Dr. Coit.

Because of his never dropping his old boys out of sight, but always following up their careers, he had long since taken his former medal boy's true measure, and could be philosophic over the error.

Philosophy was not always at his elbow; he could treat a boy's translating Chloe into a mule lightly, but when fastidiousness was outraged he was at times less calm.

A small boy received a hamper from home. He must have been meant to share the good things in it; instead, he ate them all in his alcove, alone—candy, cake, pickles, and preserves. In the middle of the night terrible results followed; the whole dormitory was startled from its sleep, and every window had to be opened.

The small boy did not perish, but he was not at his desk in the schoolroom next morning; and another boy, on going to speak to Dr. Coit, found the door of the study closed, and stood outside, appalled by the words that came through it:—

'You will pack your trunk immediately. The carriage has been ordered to take you to the train. Your parents are expecting you. *Dirty little pigs like you shall not stay at this school.*'

The blast in those last words was described by the boy who heard them. It seldom broke forth, and only when Henry Coit had no time to think second thoughts. It fell once on the head of a graduate in his mid-twenties, who had been asked if he took the Sacrament regularly, and had told the truth, that he could take it no longer with sincerity. But on this occasion, when Henry Coit had talked himself out of his storm of disappointment and indignation, he quieted into affection and concern for the old boy's soul; and their relations thereafter became more close than they had ever been before.

The same graduate did not tell Dr. Coit the truth upon an earlier occasion, when he was being questioned too closely about some reported irregularities of one of his friends, a sophomore at that time. The sophomore, after being ejected from a Boston theatre, had spent the night in jail. The papers had mentioned the incident. The graduate did his best. He affected surprise, and was certain that nothing of the sort had happened. But Dr. Coit merely sat shaking his head.

'To think of those delicate little features relaxed in drunkenness!' was his only observation.

One momentous event became a legend through the stir it made. On his way from the schoolroom to recitation on the third floor, a fourth-former, loitering at the rear of his class, turned the key in the door of Dr. Coit's study on the second landing. The imprisonment lasted but a moment. A master happening to arrive and knock heard the quiet voice of the vice rector, Joseph Coit, telling him to unlock the door. Out of it Henry Coit issued, and is described as mounting the stairs three steps at a stride. The fourth form was hardly settled in its seats when the door burst open, and the black apparition, with blue eyes blazing, towered before the class. The revolutionary deed was announced amid petrified silence. Who had done this? No one spoke. After a pause, whoever had done it was commanded to stand up. There was no move, but only more silence.

'If the boy does not come to me by to-night,' said Dr. Coit, 'I shall dismiss ——, ——, —— (naming three boys in bad standing) to-morrow.' He went, leaving a right guess among those three picked out.

This stroke put on the screws. The recitation was adjourned, the fourth form held a meeting. Every name was called; each boy rose and absolutely denied it to his classmates. But the truth was known by two there. A fourth-former, still tardier than the culprit, had come up the stairs behind him. Wrung between telling tales on the guilty or seeing the innocent suffer, this witness broke silence at last. Among his peers, in their teens, he never recovered his standing: had he not gone back on the code? But hadn't the Doctor's threat forced him? Bated fourth-form breaths recovered themselves and argued fiercely. What right had the Doctor to make a threat like that? Well, didn't the Doctor have to keep his school going? They thrashed it back and forth. The telltale lost caste, still more the culprit who had serenely lied to his comrades; Dr. Coit came out of it justified, on the whole. Somehow their young eyes saw it as he saw it, that codes have to give way in given cases. It is interesting to remember that Arnold of Rugby would say to a boy, 'If you give me your word, of course I am bound to take it,' while to one boy, who happened to be telling the truth, Dr. Coit said, 'Between your word and a master's, I am bound to take the master's.' The boy never forgave him. All commanders must at times suffer from having to justify their means by their end.

III

When, like most temperaments of genius, he fell victim to his mood, the lightning might strike other victims. Close to the end of a school year, out of a clear sky, he sent for a fifth-form boy and ordered him to go home by the next train. The boy asked the reason. Merely that he was doing no good, was 'disloyal,' not with 'the spirit of the place'—words often used by Henry Coit. The boy left the study.

Later, when Joseph Coit was in the study with his brother, the boy's roommate appeared at the door.

'Well, sir?'

'Dr. Coit, you're sending H—— M—— away.'

'Yes, sir.'

The roommate knew that he was taking his life in his hands.

'Dr. Coit, the Anniversary is next week. In a month we shall all go home. If you expel him now, everybody at home will hear of it. To say that he was not satisfactory to you will make them all sure that something which cannot be told is the cause of his sudden dismissal so close to the end of the year. That will put a cloud on his character which will darken it for a long while. If you allow him to stay the term out, and he does not come back after the holidays, no one will notice it much, or think that he was guilty of something that he never did.'

Henry Coit sat awhile, looking at the roommate.

'Joseph,' he began to his brother at length, quite mildly, 'do you hear what the boy is saying? He says I mustn't send H—— M—— away.'

'Oh, let him stay!' said Joseph, always looking out of the window.

'My dear,' said Dr. Coit to the roommate, 'you may tell H—— M—— from me that he needn't go.'

Another boy braved him quite differently. He was seventeen, and saw college life drawing near. Although head of his form month after month, as good at his books as in his conduct, he had no intention of becoming a bookworm; his imagination was filled with the freedom which all his friends at college were enjoying. He alone in his form had hung back from being confirmed. The Doctor had hoped that he would join the confirmation class in his fourth form. He had steadily expressed his unwillingness for two years, and the chances of his ever consenting were coming to an end. Once again Dr. Coit sent for him and made his friendly, apprehensive, urgent appeal. When the boy stood before him unmoved, he gave it up, but dwelt earnestly upon the necessity of prayer night and morning, if the soul were to continue safe. It was all friendly, fatherly, and sacred; and the boy was deeply touched. At the end, Dr. Coit handed to him a slim book, saying that its daily use would be of help. It was entitled *Private Prayers for School Boys.*

In surprise at himself, and in trepidation, the boy said, 'If you please, Dr. Coit, I would rather make my own prayers.'

The Doctor received the book back from his hand and laid it down without a sign of anger.

'Certainly, my dear, you must do as you feel about it.' Then he looked at the boy with his charming smile. 'But take care about being too self-reliant.'

Another wrestling contest occurred in the sixth-form Greek.

The boys were seated around the room with the Doctor at the end of the long table.

'You may begin,' he said to a boy who ranked second in the form.

'Sit down, sir!' he interrupted imperatively after a few words had been translated. 'Take it up, next, and see if you can do it properly.'

The next boy repeated verbatim the translation of his predecessor.

'That is right,' said the Doctor. 'You may continue.'

'That's exactly what I said!' loudly blurted the first boy.

'Pssh!' went the Doctor, like the lash of a whip.

'It is, though,' the boy muttered.

No notice was taken of it. The *Alcestis* went on, while the boy smouldered over his injury.

At the end of the hour, as the form was leaving the room, the Doctor spoke to the boy, who stopped beside the chair.

'I had a curious dream last night,' said the Doctor, amicably. 'I dreamt that you were impertinent to me, and apologized.'

'Did you dream that I apologized?'

'I did.'

'It was a curious dream.'

And the boy, still a mere bomb of fury, left the Doctor sitting alone in the recitation room. He did not expect it to end there; in his state of mind he would have been expelled with pleasure. Nothing followed. In the Doctor's manner when they next met there was not a symptom of their collision. So this lion could be bearded in his den.

This same boy was Library poet. When his effusion appeared in the *Horæ*, the Doctor sent for him. It lay open upon his desk, near all the finely sharpened pencils; beside it lay a blue book, containing the boy's recent Latin examination.

'My dear,' said the Doctor, tapping the poem, 'this—well—it doesn't amount to very much. But here'—he touched the blue book—'is a true achievement. Such good work means something. But don't lie back on it. We should never remain entirely pleased with what we do, and—well—isn't that one of your dangers?' With his winning smile, the Doctor handed the blue book to the boy. It had received a perfect mark.

Upon whomsoever Dr. Coit bestowed full praise, it lived with him, one of the glowing moments of his school life. The threshold of the Doctor's study was like a gate of judgment. In the forty years of his reign, what thousands of hangdog steps crossed it, what thousands of fluttering hearts entered there, and issued heavy with their sentence, or lifted upon the wings of the morning! Only in the room where a man like that presides can be heard the words that scorch or heal beyond forgetting.

IV

There is no mystery about Henry Coit, save the eternal mystery of genius. His forefathers account for him; his blood had been two hundred years in the country when he was born, the second in a family of nine, his father a clergyman, and behind him other clergymen, and families of eight, nine, ten, and fathers who lived to eighty. John Coit came from Wales to Salem in 1636, and was a shipbuilder in New London in 1650. Shipbuilding Coits followed him; and a Coit commanding his regiment at Norwich; and graduates of Harvard, Columbia, and Princeton; merchants in Boston and New York, Congregational ministers. Their wives were mostly from New England. It is a typical case of energetic colonial blood. Henry's brothers were men out of the common; two of them—Joseph and Milnor—laid important stones in the edifice of St. Paul's, particularly Joseph.

With his descent, it is curious how little he suggested New England, save in his suspicion of all gayeties and pleasures not intellectual; but he had grown up in the Middle and Southern States, and this it must have been that abolished whatever else of New England might have lurked in him.

The asceticism was pretty steep when he began at St. Paul's at the age of twenty-six. On Sundays, those three small scholars might merely, by way of relaxation, walk sedately in the vicinity, hair brushed, hands washed, and in their Sunday best. One fall afternoon they met some sheep in a field, and forgot to be sedate. In the middle of the chase a tall black figure strode upon them over the field, and their hearts fainted away.

'Little boys, expedite!' commanded the figure; and herded them to their penance. It was heavy: three days without any play!

Although Henry Coit's asceticism mellowed as he matured, and his eyes were gradually opened to the good in cricket, and hockey, and rowing, and football, and track athletics, he never went further than approval; they stirred no chord in him. He watched them with a whimsical detachment.

It cannot be said that he was always genial in manner; the younger boys especially regarded him with awe, and his own sense of the intense seriousness of life and duty gave a sternness and austerity to his aspect which made many of his pupils afraid of him. He liked to encourage games and sports . . . his sympathy with these pursuits showed itself mainly in hasty and occasional visits to the playground. . . .

I should describe him as a great prophet among schoolmasters, rather than as an instructor or educator in the ordinary sense of the term. . . . The dominating idea . . . was that a headmaster is called of God to make his school a Christian school. . . . This idea pervaded not only his chapel sermons. . . . In his lessons, his study of history, his discipline, his exhortations addressed to . . . the whole school, he is felt to be always striving to infuse into the common life his own enthusiasm of Christian earnestness. . . .

It is not necessary that this should be a school for three hundred or even of one hundred boys, but it *is* necessary that it should be a school of Christian gentlemen.

Any St. Paul's boy who knew Dr. Henry Coit would recognize him in these paragraphs—which are quoted from a life of Arnold of Rugby.

This remarkable parallel is matched by one remarkable divergence. Arnold constantly spoke out on public questions, wrote numerous pamphlets, and took the chair of London University. In his sixty-five years Henry Coit wrote once to a newspaper, and once for a magazine. It is a piece of the cloistered, twelfth-century inner man, the haughty withdrawal from things temporal, the ardent dedication to things eternal. Fastidiousness plays a part in it, and social shyness as well. He was shy when he met parents; few of them ever saw the true man at his full stature, as he was in the pulpit, or on Thursday evenings in the schoolroom, or at times in his study, dealing with a difficult case.

'If a boy has set his mind to do nothing, but considers all the work here as so much fudge, which he will evade if he can, he is sure to corrupt the rest, and I will send him away without scruple.'

His voice can be heard in these words—but they are Arnold's.

Again the striking resemblance, but always inside the cloister. Henry Coit seemed unaware of the United States, and the President, and all others in authority, save when the Episcopal service obliged him to pray for them on Sunday mornings.

What had his attention been doing between 1830 and 1865? The clash of slavery and abolition began in the year of his birth. Bleeding Kansas, John Brown, King Cotton, John C. Calhoun, Lincoln and Douglas—the whole of the one great drama our history holds so far, the long tragedy that marked American faces with a spiritual depth now vanished, unrolled while Henry Coit was growing up in the Middle and Southern States. What had all this counted for him? Some thought his sympathies were with the South. If so, his conscience must have raked him fore and aft when Sumter was fired on. He offered himself for Union military service, and was rejected. Most Americans who lived through all this showed it till their deaths, referred to it almost daily. Never Henry Coit. Away off from it at St. Paul's School, it had been out of sight, and in after years seemed out of mind. It must be supposed that he turned the whole of himself like a burning glass upon one spot, and set that spot aflame; what lay outside the periphery of his mission did not count.

Although the founder and several of the other trustees lived in Boston, Boston sent but few boys; more came from both New York and Philadelphia, while the masters of the formative years were from Maryland, Pennsylvania, and New York. New England influence was negligible, if not nil; the High Church tradition, both sacred and secular, endowed St. Paul's with the full, unbroken inheritance of the Anglican liturgy and humanities, the flavor of England, Italy, and Greece, as transmitted through the Renaissance. Cromwellian dissent was as absent from the precepts as fish balls from the cuisine, and Henry Coit's asceticism neither held him back from Horace nor inclined him to Emerson.

'The man was good,' he remarked of Emerson one day, to an old boy. 'That is perfectly obvious. But do you know his poems, my dear? "And yielded myself to the perfect whole." The perfect whole! And what may that be? Well, perhaps they have them in Massachusetts.' The blue eyes twinkled, and the long leg, crossed over the knee, swung as the boy had seen it swing many a time in the study, when the voice had been saying 'It is perfectly obvious' about one thing or another.

V

That a flower so alien to the granite and pines of New Hampshire as St. Paul's School should bloom in their midst is due to the accident of the founder's first choice for his headmaster declining the invitation; and that Henry Coit, in soul a monastic of the twelfth century, should have sprung from six generations of New England shipbuilders, merchants, and divines must remain a mystery. Ecclesiastical as he was, yet he would not consent to the boys making auricular confession as part of their discipline, which it is said had been suggested to him. Father Hall's ritualistic services in the Church of the Advent went too far for him in that direction, while the liberal doctrines of Phillips Brooks went too far in the other.

He paid the schoolmaster's usual forfeit to his calling. Phillips Brooks expressed it once to a freshman who had come from St. Paul's to Harvard:

'When my classmate Dimmick took the Adams Academy at Quincy, of course we bade him good-bye as a companion. After a man has acquired the habit of talking to boys, real conversation with him is over for his old friends. Coit is a curious man,' Mr. Brooks added, and laughed jovially.

Whenever Phillips Brooks came up to make the Anniversary address in the Chapel, the sight of assembled youth lifted him above even his usual eloquence, and it poured out like a burst of sunshine. After service he was to be seen from afar, beaming and huge, moving about the grounds, Dr. Coit escorting him.

'A curious man!' he exclaimed to the freshman. 'He dislikes Harvard on account of the irreligious influence which he has seen it exert, and he consulted me as to what clergyman he should tell his Harvard boys to seek out for guidance. He said, "I don't quite wish them to go to Father Hall, and of course I can't send them to you." '

'Where did you tell him to send us?'

'How could I tell him? I said, "Well, Dr. Coit, it hardly looks as if I were the man to advise yu!" ' And again Mr. Brooks (he was not yet a bishop) laughed out jovially, with Christian tolerance for a great brother Christian.

For one so steeped in the classics, the great brother Christian showed by occasional flashes that Emerson was by no means the only contemporary writer of whom he had an opinion; he recommended *Balaustion's Adventure* very highly to his sixth form when they were reading *Alcestis* with him. On the other hand, he began one Thursday evening in the schoolroom:—

'I find little books lying about,'—and the thumb flicked slightingly over the fingers,—'little novels with all sorts of little titles.

"Red as a rose was she." Hmp! Black as a crow was he.' The school giggled. 'Pssh! When you read a novel, choose one that has something in it. Go to Thackeray. Go to Scott.' And the rest of that Thursday's discourse was on fiction, always with the background that any novel which did not hold up right living and Christian faith was 'poor.' Nothing said on Thursdays was ever said in the Chapel, nothing in the Chapel was ever said on Thursdays.

On his vigilant round one day, he leaned over a boy's shoulder, and saw *Atalanta in Calydon*.

'What's this, my dear?' He picked it up and turned the leaves back and forth, shaking his head. 'Yes—beautiful words: "Time with a gift of tears, Grief with a glass that ran." Hmp! He couldn't say "Grief with a gift of tears," because he preferred more alliteration to more sense. . . . My dear, don't read Swinburne. I'd much rather have you read Byron. Byron was a man.' He handed the book back. 'Don't lend this to anyone.' And with this mark of confidence he proceeded on his solitary walk.

He possessed the rapid eye that could seize the whole content of a page with a glance; and the booksellers of Boston knew him well. Whenever somebody else took morning Chapel, the boys understood that the Doctor was not at the school. They did not know that he timed these absences by the length of his hair. When it needed cutting and only then, he left his post and went straight to the Parker House. There, in quiet, he spent one night, his presence in Boston known only to the barber and certain shops. The booksellers described the tall, intent figure in black, circulating slowly among the shelves, picking up a volume, putting a volume down, and departing with an armful to read undisturbed, relaxed, in his room at the Parker House, and in the train next day. The train always rested him; and beside the books he would bring little tokens for the family.

Best to the family, and to the New Hampshire neighbors, was this affectionate side of him revealed. The farmers with their families became his devoted parishioners; he held special services for them, he won them to his faith. In times of illness and of grief he went to them and sat comforting them. He was to be met among the hills and the pines, driving his buggy to visit some home in need, often with special food cooked at the Rectory or a bottle of wine—a lonely figure, unforgettable, with something majestic about it.

When he spoke in a sermon of 'the eternal solitude of the

human soul,' that word came from the experience of his own soul; when in another sermon he said, 'Therefore we pray, Empty us of ourselves that we may be filled with Thee,' it was the heart of his attitude toward life. Besides the gentle and wise lady who was Mrs. Coit, and Joseph, his more equable and judicious brother, was there any other who served to steady him when the blasts of his temperament broke from the stern repression under which they were held? Who else was admitted to the privacy of his brooding meditations? To many a fortunate boy Joseph's warm heart gave the shelter and the anchor of his intimacy, and was a human providence to him at critical moments which he could never have brought himself to confide to Henry. It was well for St. Paul's School, very well, that Mrs. Henry Coit was there at the actual beginning, and that Joseph Coit went there only nine years later. The presence of neither caused bated breaths; when Henry appeared on the scene, awe came with him, leapfrog ceased, caps were touched in silence. His response often mystified some boy; what had he done now? Very possibly nothing to deserve the haughty coldness which had made him wonder; it is certain that Henry Coit sometimes was sunk in his inner mood, and unaware of the effect his manner produced. But this was never the case on Sunday nights, when he stood on the schoolroom platform after the Sunday evening hymn, and the whole school filed by to shake hands with him. Then indeed his good-night conveyed unmistakably his opinion of each boy's recent record. Mostly this was correct; sometimes utterly unjust.

Henry Augustus Coit may be said to have died in his boots, kept going by his will and his conscience after his vital fires had burned low, and an accident had lamed him, and the loss of his wife had plunged him in deeper loneliness. His vital fires burned out early in 1895. After three weeks at home for Christmas, the school returned to work. Dr. Coit had not left work. During those weeks he is said to have written five hundred letters. He had no secretary. One Sunday morning, after receiving the Sacrament at early celebration, he was seen to leave before the end of the service. He was found fainting in the vestry. For a few hours next day he struggled on in his study. That was the last of him. A few days later he was lying face to the wall, silent even to his brother Joseph, who was overcome in telling of this afterward. Henry Coit had no more to say to any man.

The news stunned the old boys of St. Paul's, scattered over the country. The Doctor was not their parent; he was their tribunal, still living in their conscience as their exalted and uncompromising mentor. They had never known any man like him; they were never to know any man like him again. Many started for the school, but the great tempest of that winter prevented their arrival. Nevertheless, some hundred of them got there, and followed in their carriages through the deep drifts. And so, while the gusts of snow raged, they stood watching the body being lowered into the ground.

On his birthday in after years, two old boys walked to the grave on the hill among the pines, and met there an old servant of the school, all alone, giving way to his grief. Upon their speaking to him, he slowly drew a gold piece from his pocket and held it out, and said:—

'He gave me that, forty-two years ago.'

★ *The nobler type of man has three sources of joy, and to rule the Empire is not one of them. That his parents are both alive, that his brethren are free from trouble—this is his first source of joy. That he need feel no shame in the presence of God, no embarrassment before his fellow men—this is his second source of joy. That it is his to train and teach the budding talent of the Empire—this is his third source of joy. Yes, the nobler type of man has three sources of joy, and to rule the Empire is not one of them.*

From 'The Book of Mencius' translated by Lionel Giles
(Copyright 1942 by John Murray, London.
Reprinted by permission of the publisher)

"I should think she'd be ashamed to let people
know the poor quality of her teaching!"

(Courtesy of *The Saturday Review*.)

THE JOLLY OLD PEDAGOGUE

by George Arnold

'T WAS A JOLLY OLD PEDAGOGUE, LONG AGO,
  Tall, and slender, and sallow, and dry;
His form was bent, and his gait was slow,
And his long, thin hair was white as snow,
  But a wonderful twinkle shone in his eye:
And he sang every night as he went to bed,
  "Let us be happy down here below;
The living should live, though the dead be dead,"
  Said the jolly old pedagogue, long ago.

He taught the scholars the Rule of Three,
  Reading and writing, and history, too;
He took the little ones on his knee,
For a kind old heart in his breast had he,
  And the wants of the littlest child he knew.
"Learn while you're young," he often said,
  "There is much to enjoy down here below;
Life for the living, and the rest for the dead!"
  Said the jolly old pedagogue, long ago.

With the stupidest boys, he was kind and cool,
  Speaking only in gentlest tones;

The rod was scarcely known in his school—
Whipping to him was a barbarous rule,
   And too hard work for his poor old bones;
Besides it was painful, he sometimes said:
   "We should make life pleasant down here below—
The living need charity more than the dead,"
   Said the jolly old pedagogue, long ago.

He lived in the house by the hawthorn lane,
   With roses and woodbine over the door;
His rooms were quiet, and neat, and plain,
But a spirit of comfort there held reign,
   And made him forget that he was old and poor.
"I need so little," he often said;
   "And my friends and relatives here below
Won't litigate over me when I am dead,"
   Said the jolly old pedagogue, long ago.

But the pleasantest times of all he had,
   Were the sociable hours he used to pass,
With his chair tipped back to a neighbor's wall,
Making an unceremonious call,
   Over a pipe and a friendly glass:
This was the finest pleasure, he said,
   Of the many he tasted here below.
"Who had no cronies had better be dead,"
   Said the jolly old pedagogue, long ago.

The jolly old pedagogue's wrinkled face
   Melted all over in sunshiny smiles;
He stirred his glass with an old-school grace,
Chuckled and sipped, and prattled apace.
   Till the house grew merry from cellar to tiles.
"I'm a pretty old man," he gently said,
   "I've lingered a long time here below;
But my heart is fresh, if my youth is fled!"
   Said the jolly old pedagogue, long ago.

He smoked his pipe in the balmy air
   Every night, when the sun went down;
And the soft wind played in his silvery hair,
Leaving its tenderest kisses there,

On the jolly old pedagogue's jolly old crown;
And feeling the kisses, he smiled, and said:
" 'Tis a glorious world down here below;
Why wait for happiness till we are dead?"
Said this jolly old pedagogue, long ago.

He sat at his door one midsummer night,
After the sun had sunk in the west,
And the lingering beams of golden light
Made his kindly old face look warm and bright,
While the odorous night-winds whispered, "Rest!"
Gently, gently, he bowed his head;
There were angels waiting for him, I know;
He was sure of his happiness, living or dead;
This jolly old pedagogue, long ago!

★ *Teachers should be held in the highest honor. They are the*
allies of legislators; they have agency in the prevention of
crime; they aid in regulating the atmosphere, whose incessant
action and pressure cause the life-blood to circulate, and to
return pure and healthful to the heart of the nation.

MRS. SIGOURNEY

HARVARD:
THE COCKPIT OF LEARNING

by Bliss Perry

LET US COME BACK TO WHAT ONE OF MY BROTHERS CALLED 'THE overarching of Harvard': a true Cockpit and Paradise of Learning, where petty flaws and neglected corners may be pardoned and forgotten. Its fascination for me, as a teacher, lay in its freedom. I do not mean merely that 'academic freedom' of thought and utterance which was defended so courageously by Presidents Eliot and Lowell. I had no subversive economic or social views to express, either in the classroom or in public. Whenever my good father made a vigorous speech against protective tariffs there were certain newspapers and public men who demanded that he should be deprived of his professorship; but times had changed, and no one cared much what a professor of English literature might be saying to relieve his mind. I disliked publicity, and avoided topics that might furnish "copy" for the newspapers. My classroom was "dukedom large enough," and I think few men were ever happier there. That very lack of co-operative team-work which my gloomy colleague criticized when he declared "We *have* no Department" left us free, as individuals, to teach in our own fashion and to try, within reason, any experiments we pleased.

I was supposed, for instance, to be lecturing to graduates on Political Satire since the Renaissance, but inasmuch as it was necessary to show them first what political satire was, I could take material, if I liked, from the Old Testament and from Aristophanes. Since the classic English school of satire was founded upon Roman models, I joined forces with Morris Morgan of the Latin Department and took my students in to hear him lecture upon Juvenal and Horace, and he brought his men into my room to hear about Dryden and Pope. I wish now that we had carried this collaboration in Comparative Literature courses much further than we did, particularly in studying international influences upon the development of types of fiction. But the point is that professors were free to seek out many inventions. I experimented for a while with 'pass' and 'honors' grades, determined by examinations of different degrees of difficulty, although based upon the same required reading; and as long as the grades were handed in promptly at University Hall, there was no one to say how they were determined. Instead of a regular lecture in the Emerson course I escorted the class, year after year, to Concord, to visit the Old Manse and the Emerson House and Sleepy Hollow, and I know that many boys learned more in those sunny afternoons than I could ever have taught them in Sever 11.

I was too preoccupied with my own classes to know much about what was going on in the University. Fortunately I had little committee work, and was quite out of touch with the complicated machinery of administration which was housed in University Hall. I fear I was jealous of University Hall, for it had developed the habit of robbing the English Department of some of our best men—Briggs, Hurlbut, Greenough, Murdock, and, for one year, Lowes—in order to utilize them as Deans. It is, I am told, an honor to become a Dean, but it is one dearly purchased if it means the temporary or permanent end of a scholar's productivity. The whole tendency of American institutions is to breed ten administrators to one real teacher. I used to pass University Hall with something of the small boy's dread of passing a cemetery: for teachers lay buried there under their roll-topped desks. Only once did I get a cheerful picture of it, and that was during a holiday in Florence in 1928. George W. Cram, the Recorder of the University, was likewise in Florence, and one day we tramped out to a hill-town beyond the Certosa to see the frescoes in the ancient church and incidentally to try a cup of the mulled wine for which the local restaurant was famous. In that one excursion I heard more amusing gossip about the machinery of University Hall than I had picked up in twenty years at Cambridge.

Likewise I was too ignorant of the personal history of the men whom I was trying to teach. One could place the graduate students roughly, for one knew the colleges from which they came and something about their records and their plans. But I never knew even the names of the majority of students in the big undergraduate courses, nor their preparatory schools nor their Harvard groupings and social affiliations. I had to leave all that to my assistants who read the blue-books and conferred personally with the men. I trust that my natural sympathies, like my father's were with the poor, the aliens in race, the 'untouchables'; but I did my best to treat each student precisely as I treated every other. I admit that when a boy came up to the desk one April, just as I was about to begin what I thought was an important lecture, and asked me confidentially what sort of trout-reel I considered the most reliable, I caught the lad's spring fever, and had no difficulty in remembering his name.

The response of these undergraduates to a teacher's efforts seemed to me wonderful. Many of them, naturally, had no particular interest in literary questions, and had elected one of my courses because the rules for 'distribution' obliged them to choose one course in Literature. But once inside the classroom, they met me halfway. The real work of the course had to be done by the student himself, in mastering the handbooks containing the facts essential to a knowledge of a given period, and in interpreting and reflecting upon the assigned masterpieces. The lectures were designed to assist in an intelligent approach to the writers chosen for study, and not as a substitute for what each boy was expected to discover for himself. It was the business of the assistants to find out through conferences and written tests exactly what each student was accomplishing; and it was the professor's business to superintend all that, and to make each lecture hour interesting and profitable to the whole class—an impossible but fascinating enterprise.

I imagine that very few of the students realized—if they happened to see the professor strolling down to the Yard for a 'nine-o'clock,' carrying a green bag full of books and lecture-notes, and smoking an after-breakfast pipe—how many hours he had given to the preparation of his lecture and how inordinately anxious he was that it might go well.

First, as to preparation, I will illustrate from 'English 41,' one of those survey courses which are supposed to be easy enough for an experienced teacher. We began with some reading from *Beowulf*, in translation, some English and Scottish ballads, and a little Chaucer; then some pre-Shakespearean drama, half-a-dozen of Shakespeare's plays, Spenser, a little Jacobean drama, then Bacon and Milton and so on down the centuries until we reached authors that were still living, like Kipling. It is obvious that upon each topic selected as the subject for a lecture in such a course, new biographical and critical material is constantly appearing. This new material may be too technical to mention in the classroom, but the teacher is bound by the honor of his profession to keep informed of it if he can. He distinguishes sharply however, between 'keeping abreast' of the new knowledge, and 'research,' which means adding to it oneself. Here, for instance, are some letters, just discovered, by Swift or Gray or Horace Walpole: a conscientious teacher feels that he should examine these letters before lecturing again upon the writers. That is merely 'keeping abreast,' although the mass of new material has now become so great that no one scholar can possibly be in touch with all of it. John Lowes's *Road to Xanadu*, on the other hand, is based upon true 'research' into Coleridge's reading and into the workings of a poet's mind. Even keeping abreast, a much more humble effort, is no holiday affair.

I choose for illustration four English authors on whom I happened to be lecturing at Williams in the eighteen-eighties, at Princeton in the eighteen-nineties, and at Harvard in the nineteen-twenties: Fielding, Byron, Thackery, and Browning. It is clear that the lecturer, at the outset, should have read the entire work of each author. Then comes the task of thinking, for, as W. C. Brownell used to say: 'To produce vital and useful criticism it is necessary to think, think, think and then, when tired of thinking, to think more.' The third stage is the selection and arrangement of such significant facts, conclusions, queries, as can be presented to a class in fifty minutes. All this is preparatory to the actual delivery of the lecture. But we will suppose, as in the case of the four authors just named, that the teacher continues to lecture upon these men, at intervals, for forty years. If he has had any vigorous intellectual life of his own, his opinion of the four authors is bound to change somewhat with each yearly reading. This or that aspect of their personality or their art gains or loses in significance; no one can read Byron at sixty-five with the eyes of twenty-five. The teacher has changed, and the mood of his classes changes with the years or with the shift in literary fashions. In the eighteen-eighties one could allude to a passage in George Eliot or in Tennyson and be fairly certain that the allusion would be understood; in the nineteen-twenties one was equally certain that the allusion would not be understood. It was safer to quote Hemingway or D. H. Lawrence. It is true that the teacher may find his old notes on Byron useful in certain respects, but chiefly as a record of the development of the teacher's critical sense of his classroom methods. I am by no means sure that I taught Byron any more effectively at sixty-five than at twenty-five, but I could not help teaching him differently.

Once, when I was going up to my library in the evening for two or three hours of final preparation for the next morning's lecture, one of my daughters protested. 'What are you going to talk about tomorrow?' she asked. 'Sir Walter Scott,' I answered. 'I suppose,' she remarked with fine sarcasm, 'that you never heard of Scott before?' But familiarity with the subject of the lecture was the very reason why I had to sharpen my senses afresh by re-reading his pages and by re-thinking my old conclusions before I could venture to re-shape another talk on the old and glorious theme.

Very likely I re-shaped too anxiously, in the dread of repeating myself. Dr. George Gordon told me that he never 'preached a sermon but once' and that was during the actual half-hour of delivery. When he had prepared what he had to say, he dismissed it from his mind until he reached the pulpit, and as soon as he had finished his discourse he could dismiss it from his mind again. I wish I could say that! I worry over a lecture for days and weeks beforehand, enjoy the actual hour of teaching enormously, and then suffer acute misery in reflecting how I might have bettered the instruction. Old John Sullivan, a guide on Lake Nicotaus, once paid me a great although undeserved compliment. The trout were coming in fast that morning, and John, regarding the process with shining eyes, exclaimed: 'I do like to watch a fellow fish who doesn't get *excited!*' But in reality I was deeply excited—too deeply to let John suspect it; and I have sometimes wondered whether my pupils realized the intensity of feeling which underlay a decorous classroom manner of dealing with certain books and men. Perhaps I gave myself away when I read poetry aloud.

How many of us conductors of courses there were, under the great hospitable roof of 'the overarching' Harvard, each one of us convinced, naturally of the transcendent importance of his own theme! We could never have gone on without that faith, and when a man loses it, it is time for him to stop teaching. Even though he does not and cannot lose his zest for his subject, the years take their toll of his physical energy, and he comes to realize that he should give place to younger men. 'I *retire*,' said Mark Hopkins when he gave up the Presidency of Williams at seventy, '*that it may not be asked why I do not retire.*' One need not have been a pupil and colleague of Mark Hopkins to recognize the old gentleman's wisdom. He knew his world.

When Samuel Johnson wrote his final *Idler* paper in 1760, he remarked: 'There are few things not purely evil, of which we can say, without some emotion of uneasiness, *this is the last.*' I cannot affirm that I faced my final lecture at Harvard in May, 1930, 'without some emotion of uneasiness,' but the kindness of my pupils carried me through the ordeal. They gave me some rare editions of books that I was known to like, and arranged to have a portrait painted for the University. I thanked them as well as I could. But I did not really need any fresh evidence of their regard, for I was sure of it already, and I cannot remember whether I told them in words that I was fond of them. They knew it, anyway.

Then I drove out to Milton with my son, and celebrated the new freedom with a round of golf. It was forty-nine years since I met my first class at Williams.

★   *It is a luxury to learn; but the luxury of learning is not to be compared with the luxury of teaching.*

ROSWELL D. HITCHCOCK

from

LUCIFER WITH A BOOK

by John Horne Burns

Do you read books, boy?

What use are books to a farmer? he said sullenly.

Education, boy, is not something to prepare you for life. That is a vulgar American error. . . It's something to take you *out* of life. Don't you want to have some small kingdom of your own that no one can take away from you? You have one now, but when you are older it will slip away from you, and you will never know why you are poor. . . That is what you can get from books. That is why everyone has the right to education, true education . . . Boy, the things on the printed page are at least as real as life. They last longer than life. And that proves that they have an independent existence that is deeper and longer than life . . . And every American (and you too, boy) owes it to himself to know much or little of what has been thought and said before him. Then he loses some of his sense of loneliness, which is our lot. Thus by education he merges with the whole, and will not be just a sore thumb . . .

from

SPRING

by James Thomson

DELIGHTFUL TASK! TO REAR THE TENDER THOUGHT,
To teach the young idea how to shoot,
To pour the fresh instruction o'er the mind,
To breathe the enlivening spirit, and to fix
The generous purpose in the glowing breast.

THE TEST OF
A GOOD COLLEGE TEACHER

by Donald H. Morrison

IF YE HAD A BOY WUD YE SIND HIM TO COLLEDGE?" ASKED MR. Hennessy. "Well," said Mr. Dooley, "at th' age whin a boy is fit to be in colledge I wudden't have him around th' house."

This fall, about two and a quarter million American boys and girls left the house and moved to college campuses. The parents of many scraped, saved, and denied themselves so that their children might gain an education. Each year the colleges spend millions of dollars, frequently needed for salaries and new buildings, so that young people of ability but without financial means may have the benefit of a college experience.

Does the return justify the effort of parents and colleges? Yes— *if*, as a result of their education, young people acquire habits of mind and ways of looking at their problems that enable them to live more effective lives. If college is worth the time, effort, and money it costs, its value is in the kind of place that it is—and especially in the quality of the teachers who work there.

In writing about the qualities of good teachers I am not thinking primarily about law, medical, or engineering schools or any other institution that is concerned chiefly with professional, vocational or technical training. My concern is the "liberal college," which has as its fudamental purposes the intellectual, moral, and social development of its students.

Much has been thought and written on the subject of effective teaching. No one is confident that he has *the* answer and many doubt that there is any prescription for good teaching. What follows is based upon reading, observation and experience. Undoubtedly there are some good teachers who do not have the qualities I am going to discuss. But I believe that there are few poorer teachers with these qualities.

What a teacher is, as a human being, is as important as what he knows or can learn. He must be a person of unquestioned character and integrity. A student intelligent enough to be in college cannot spend forty or more hours in a classroom without forming some judgment about the teacher's worth as a person and without being influenced by his approach to problems of fact and value. On a campus one often hears a student say, "From what I have heard of Professor X, I'd like to take a course from him. What is he teaching?" To these students, and they are frequently among the best, the important thing is not the *subject* but the *teacher*. In this judgment there is the beginning of wisdom.

A good teacher has a first-rate, orderly, creative mind. He should have abundant physical vitality and energy. Teaching is hard work and people are impressed by the zest and spirit with which a healthy, energetic person tackles a difficult but interesting job.

A teacher must be enthusiastic about his subject. If it does not interest him, if he does not consider it one of the most important things in the world, he is not likely to inspire young people, who have had many teachers and whose heads have a tendency to be full of things other than learning.

A sturdy personality is essential for good teaching. Popular books about peace of mind, the meaning of dreams and psychosomatic medicine have helped to set high public value on the qualities of "being well-adjusted" and of "having an effective personality." But one should pause over Peter Viereck's plea for the "Unadjusted Man." It is useful to be reminded that many of the ornaments of our culture were created by tortured human beings like Van Gogh and rebellious ones like Thoreau and Frank Lloyd Wright. Certainly a person can be unconventional—a non-conformist—and still be a good teacher.

But he must not use his classroom or his relations with students to compensate for personal inadequacies and frustrations. By the nature of his position, a teacher embittered by personal disappointment can hurt and repulse with corrosive wit the timid or groping student whose ability and accomplishments, though potentially good, he considers less than adequate. It is easy, too, for an excessively introverted or disturbed teacher to meet his class on schedule and afterwards retreat to the library, office, or home where he is inaccessible to those who need his help. And a teacher who lacks confidence in his own ability often gets satisfaction from the large enrollment attracted by an easy course or by antics or stories that amuse but do not instruct.

A good teacher teaches for the right reason. He has a friendly interest in and liking for young people. He believes that there is no more certain way to a better life for man than through the improvement of the young by means of education.

Unfortunately, dedication to *teaching* is not the only reason why men and women enter the profession. There are, for example, teachers honest enough to admit that they don't like students. Such people may be useful around an educational institution but their place is not the classroom. As teachers they are as misfit as the doctor who does not like to make sick people well or the business man who would rather lose than make money.

Some teach because as undergraduates they liked books and conversation and thought that as teachers they would have leisure time to read and converse. Others seem to give substance to Shaw's too glib characterization. "Those who can, do; those who can't, teach." That is, for some, teaching may be a way of avoiding the more competitive professions for which they are psychologically or physically ill-equipped. But the converse of Shaw's quip is also true and needs to be said, "Many of those who have done cannot teach." A man nearing retirement does not make a good teacher simply because he achieved distinction in the world of affairs, any more than skill in reading and writing makes a poet. The art of teaching is delicate, esoteric, and complex and cannot be mastered overnight by one who has given the best of his life and strength to another arduous profession.

A teacher is not likely to overcome the initial handicap of teaching for the wrong reason. Unlike olives, students are not an acquired taste. They cling tenaciously to the less endearing qualities of their elders and they have a talent for getting into mischief on their own. One who does not like them and believe that they are worth educating should find an occupation other than teaching.

Good college teachers have a constructive or affirmative philosophy of life. They believe that life is challenging and valuable and that the effort to live as effectively and as nobly as one can is worthwhile.

All about us are examples of the puniness of men and of the foolishness of their efforts to govern themselves, to create beauty, to live rationally, to make the most of their lives and the world. A teacher whose views are essentially cynical and whose teaching consists of the documentation and elaboration of the drabness and futility of man and his works is not likely to inspire young people to live as humanely as they can.

More likely than not, a good teacher believes that there is a difference between right and wrong and that man has a duty to try to choose, and to advance, the right rather than the wrong. He believes also that man has some control over his destiny, that only death is inevitable and even death may be postponed.

A good teacher is almost certain to have some view of life and the universe that to him "makes sense" and that is a part of his way of life. He is able to fit pieces of diverse knowledge into a pattern that unifies experience and enables him to face calmly—courageously if necessary—the things that he does not know. He has some firm convictions about what is worth living and dying for. He may or may not profess religious faith but he knows enough to have at least a reverent view of the universe.

These beliefs have a direct bearing upon the liberal colleges' goal to help students mature as whole and wholesome human beings. They are of particular significance in the teaching of young college students. The college years are years of rebellion, when boys and girls are trying to become adults in their own right and are struggling for independence from parents, homes, and values with which they have been closely knit. It is difficult to see how a teacher without a constructive philosophy can help them as they begin to formulate their own view of life.

The first requirement of a teacher is that he be competent in the subjects he teaches. Usually he has three or four years of graduate study beyond college, where his preparation begins. When he faces his first class, he is full of information that was carefully acquired under the guidance of the experts who were his graduate teachers. Consequently, he tries to do too much in the 45 or 50 minutes available in a single class. He knows more than he can teach.

As a good teacher develops, he finds that he is teaching more than he knows. Almost any subject worth teaching is a growing subject which man is only beginning to understand. Millions of dollars are spent each year by researchers in pursuit of more precise knowledge about the things that teachers and students are studying. The process is never-ending and the teacher can never catch up. In this dilemma of knowing and not knowing, what does the good teacher do? For one thing, he tries to show his students the relation between what was known, what is known, and what is unknown.

What is *known* today about nuclear physics, or the physiology of protoplasm, or the structure of the universe, or of man's nature and his behavior as an individual and in groups, is quite different from what was *known* twenty-five years ago. Although man goes ever more deeply in his search for truth, the ultimate answers have not been found. A good teacher has a decent respect for these mysteries and for the effort to solve them. He tries to infect his students with the excitement and the delight of exploring the boundaries of knowledge.

How do students learn? What can a teacher do to help? These are key questions in the art of teaching which good teachers answer for themselves.

Studies of the nature of the learning process indicate that learning is most certain when the student has a sense of needing and wanting to know, of experiencing and living himself what is being taught. This is also the testimony of students.

With this conviction about learning as a starting point, the good teacher tries to help students acquire critical and creative habits of mind by thinking about problems that have meaning, reality, and urgency for them. The memorizing of fact by the student is not enough and exposition of knowledge by the teacher is not enough.

The good teacher repeatedly asks, "What does my subject mean in terms of the student's experience and life? What can I do to help this young person to see the significance of these facts, this point of view, this method of tackling a problem? And when he sees the significance, how can it help him to lead a more effective life?" These questions are in the undergraduate's mind when he asks his succinct but challenging, "So what?"

The good teacher solves this problem of showing the continuing relevance of knowledge. He is always alert for illustrations that may excite the interest of a student. He uses the rich resources of a good daily newspaper and popular as well as scholarly publications. He finds in a book about a great symphony orchestra fascinating comment on the human factors in leadership and cooperative activity, and evidence of the value of music in nourishing and renewing the spirit. *The Caine Mutiny* and *War and Peace* provide in a palatable form other examples of human experience that may lead a student on to more elaborate, more precise studies of fundamental problems. The biography of a great scientist or artist is used to give insight into the philosophy, methods, and rewards of a creative life. History, poetry, novels, biography, newspapers—all the records of human experience are mined to enliven and enrich teaching for students.

It is of course basic that the only education worthy of the name is self-education. Good teaching, therefore, is measured by what goes on in the mind and heart of the student, not by what the teacher thinks or does. Education is a cooperative venture in which a student is stimulated and guided by a teacher. Consequently, a good teacher works hard to get students to work hard for themselves. Under his guidance the student is ashamed to do anything but his best work.

He uses whatever methods are suited to the subject and the student at the time. For one, it may be the ancient and well-tested device of the lecture. For another, it may be a discussion in which Socratic questioning leads the student to sharpen his thought and expression and ultimately to formulate a conclusion or a judgment which is his. Both methods are used to awaken curiosity, stimulate thought, fire imagination, nourish insight, season judgment. Always the objective is the *student's* curiosity, *his* thought, *his* imagination, *his* insight, *his* judgment—not the teacher's.

The good teacher uses the classroom for this purpose, not to display elegantly his own knowledge before a captive and passive audience. The eventual effect of this kind of teaching is to make the teacher unnecessary. Seeing a student reach this point of liberation and independence is perhaps the greatest reward of teaching. A religious leader may need constant disciples; a good teacher does not.

In the last analysis, good teachers need good students. However perceptive, however experienced he may be, the teacher cannot be certain what is going on in the student's mind. He can only guess what the student needs most to know. It is up to the student to ask the questions which help the teacher help him to learn.

This is the meaning in the admonition of Dartmouth's President, John Sloan Dickey, at the opening of college each year—"Your business here is learning and that is up to you. We'll be with you all the way." And in the dedication of Professor N. F. Cantor's *The Dynamics of Learning*—"to my students who have taught me how to learn to teach."

There are three principal ways to improve teaching:

(1) We need to assert and reaffirm the purpose of a liberating education. President Dickey has put this point briefly: "Our purpose is to develop in all the products of the College *both* the full capacity of individual power and the moral will to its decent use." When his purpose permeates all of a college's activities, when it drives teachers and students alike, teaching and learning are at their best.

(2) We need better prepared teachers. Graduate schools emphasize too little the significance and meaning for man of the subjects taken in preparation for teaching. The view that "the job of a chemistry professor is simply to teach chemistry" is only half right.

There is too little attention to the art of teaching. College teaching is perhaps the only great profession which does not use some form of apprenticeship in training the novice. A useful experiment in "teaching internships" is now being carried on by several colleges, including Dartmouth, with the help of the Fund for the Advancement of Education. Although programs vary somewhat, Dartmouth's is typical. The young instructor works in association with an experienced professor. They visit each other's classes and those of other professors, and they discuss what they have observed in terms of objectives and methods. The "interns" meet weekly to consider problems of college teaching. They try to seek light on the way students learn and on the usefulness of various teaching techniques. They try to think critically about why they are becoming teachers and how they can help others to learn. As one way of focusing down on student needs and problems, each "intern" acts as counselor for a few students in academic difficulty. The colleges participating in the internship program think that it may have a far-reaching impact on the quality of liberal arts teaching.

(3) Finally, we can get better teaching if we have better teachers. The qualities of a good teacher make for success in much better-paying jobs. Most colleges start a new instructor at about the salary paid by a successful firm to its office boys and stenographers. The significant competition for first-rate talent is between education and the other professions. As a result of low academic salaries, an increasing proportion of those who become teachers are entering the profession for the wrong reasons and lack requisite qualities for good teaching. As a practitioner of a noble profession, the teacher deserves better of his society than he is getting. He does not become a teacher to make money but he must support and educate his family and he should be able to buy the books and do the travelling that are a part of his business expense.

Ordway Tead, who has written as perceptively as anyone about teaching and learning, has said, "Next to the ministry with its concern for what was formerly called the saving of souls stands teaching with its concern for the creative guidance of mind and heart."

For such a vital purpose, the very best of human material should be available.

★ *Education means drawing forth from the mind latent powers and developing them, so that in mature years one may apply these powers not merely to success in one's occupation, but to success in the greatest of all arts—the art of living.*
                                                WILLIAM LYON PHELPS

AT SEA AROUND US

by Jacob C. Solovay

Because i had a love for youth,
    From *diem* on to tender *diem;*
And yearned to shed my light and truth,
    And make them noble just as I am—
I scorned to be a simple creature.
What happened? I became a teacher . . .

My baccalaureate I took,
    And never missed a single session;
And then my master's, book by book,
    To learn finesse for the profession.
And now, as everyone can see,
I daily get my *third* degree.

I know some twenty thousand facts,
    And have forgotten twice as many.
I've studied educational acts,
    From Aristotle to Jack Benny.
I must be of the cultured set,
To teach my class the alphabet.

I bring the world into my room,
    The pageantry of all the ages,
But in their intellectual gloom
    They squint at hieroglyphical pages;
They eye me with a tart derision,
And moan for jokes and television.

Now reading maketh a man full
    (That's not original but Bacon),
But when a fact I try to pull,
    My students visibly are shaken.
For minds will find it hard to spare
A fact when there is no fact there.

Defenseless colleagues, pray be kind
    And good to students—and so sweet.
No matter if they have no mind—
    They are with confidence replete.
And if you find that this is dull, sirs,
Things will pep up with peptic ulcers.

You see, the time is out of joint,
    And so are we, if I may mention.
Then briefly let me state my point
    For your meticulous attention:
Give pupils their degrees at ten,
    And let *us* go to school again!

★ *It is noble to teach oneself; it is still nobler to teach others—and less trouble.*

MARK TWAIN

"That so? I'm a teacher, too. What do <u>you</u> do for a living?"

MAN WITH A PIPE

by James Thurber

I HAD ONLY TWO MALE TEACHERS BEFORE I ENTERED OHIO STATE University, in the fall of 1913, one of them an amiable chemistry man named Gullum, who sympathized with my profound disinclination to make deadly bromine gas, even under a hood, in the high school laboratory, and the other a professor of physics, Mr. Hambleton, who used to stare out a window while I was reciting, as if the flight of a sparrow or the swaying of a poplar bough were more relevant to his subject than anything I could possibly say. One day, in the physics class, I proudly announced my own system of computing the rate of acceleration of a falling object. Mr. Hambleton impatiently tried out the elaborate Thurber method on the blackboard a couple of times, chewed one end of his mustache when he saw that it worked, and then turned his bleak smile on me and said, "Young man, you would go from New York to Boston by way of Detroit." Some years after that, I told this story to Joe Taylor, at the end of one of his English classes at the university, and he said, "A straight line can also be the dullest distance between two points." I had met a little late, but not too late, a male teacher who was not a captive of old, inherited exactitudes, and who never laid down a formal rule for getting to Boston, or to Kew, or to Carcassonne, or anywhere else.

I saw Joe Taylor for the last time more than twenty years ago. I had come out of a restaurant on Fifth Avenue with a colleague of mine, and I suddenly beheld Professor Taylor walking toward us hurriedly, with a distracted look on his face. We stopped and talked, and it came out that he had arrived in New York a week earlier for a meeting of the Woodberry Society. It was not his fault, but that of the late John Erskine, secretary of the society, who had sent out the invitations and got the date wrong. I wanted him to have dinner with me, but he said he had to pack and take a train back to Columbus. He wasn't sure that he would be able to return for the meeting the following week, but he made a tentative date in case he did come back. When he left us, my colleague turned to me and said, "Who is that wonderful man?" He didn't come back, and three years later he died, in Columbus, at the age of sixty-four.

I will always remember my first view of Joseph Russell Taylor, in one of his English classes at Ohio State, more than thirty-five years ago. He was round of face and body, with yellow hair, pink cheeks, and fine blue eyes. He usually wore a brown suit, and he always brought to class the light of the enchanted artistic world he lived in, of whose wonders he once said, "It is possible that all things are beautiful." He was a poet and painter as well as a teacher, and he believed that the materials of art were in all the activities of man. His classes were popular from the beginning, and in the nineteen-twenties as many as a hundred and twenty-five men and women crowded into his lecture room. On the opening day of one of his classes in 1914, he began by saying to us, "I do not expect you to take notes in this class." Forty of the fifty young men and women present wrote that down in their brand-new notebooks with their brand-new fountain pens. Standing at the lectern, possibly lost in contemplating two of his favorite fictional heroines, Henry James' Mme. de Vionnet and George Meredith's Diana— for whom he had named his own daughter Diana—he seemed oblivious of the aimless scratching in the notebooks. I don't know what experiment he was trying that day, but it didn't work. He should have known that the things he had to say were always worth recording. Some of his former students, after thirty years and more, still have at hand the notes they took in the courses, including that one in 1914.

His influence was not confined to students who hoped to become writers or teachers of English. A dozen years before my day at the university, he had tolerated the occasional classroom inattention of a young man who was given to drawing, in his notebook, prize-fighters without faces, and other unique figures. The student was a Columbus boy named George Westley Bellows, whose parents had been dismayed, rather than delighted, by their son's devotion to the idle practice of drawing pictures. Luckily for him, his professor not only was something of a painter himself but had taught draw-ing for several years before he became a teacher of English. Close students of Bellows' life have recognized Joe Taylor's lively and lasting interest in his young friend's talent, and most of them feel that without this encouragement the artist might never have be-come a professional. Joe Taylor was, for one thing, a friend of Robert Henri, Bellows' first influential teacher, and he seems to have brought the two men together. In the Gallery of Fine Arts in Columbus, there hung for a time an oil portrait of the sympathetic professor sitting in a chair and holding a pipe in his hand, done by his former student nearly forty years ago. When its subject was first shown the finished study, he said, "That is a painting of Joseph Russell Taylor by a young artist, but it will one day be known as Bellows' 'Man with a Pipe.' " He was a great pipe man, and once asked me, after I began to write for a living, if I smoked one when I worked. I told him that I did, although I didn't, and it seemed to please him mightily, for some obscure reason. "Good!" he said with satisfaction.

It may be that he tried to discourage note-taking on that far-off morning because, at the time, his appraisals of some authors were undergoing continual mutations. "Don't quote me outside class," he told us more than once, "because my judgments are subject to change." One of his significant reversals of literary opinion, in my years at the University, involved the novels of Joseph Conrad. "Conrad is merely a spinner of yarns," he said one day, and then some weeks later, "I have changed my mind about Conrad. He is Henry James in the waste places." I don't know for sure what con-tributed most to this critical shift, but it is likely that he had been impressed by the recently published "Victory," which many Conradians now consider the Master's finest work. It contained, in Lena of the faraway island, a lady highly suitable for Joe Taylor's gallery of beloved heroines. The fictional ladies of Thomas Hardy, on the other hand, never won his heart, but he later revised his early feeling that they were merely milkmaids in romances written for milkmaids.

Joe Taylor was a great feminist, and he liked Meredith for giving his women characters equal stature with his men, and Henry James for his high and subtle development of ladies in his novels. He was always referring to or quoting from Wordsworth's tribute to the "perfect woman, nobly planned; to warn, to comfort, and command." He used to write on the blackboard—not always in poetry class, either, because his lectures unconventionally over-lapped—the years in which Robert Browning and Elizabeth Barrett Browning had done their best work, and contend that their true excellence had flowered during their marriage and might otherwise have languished.

Even now and then, he would stray from the subject in hand, abandon his notes, and discuss what was uppermost in his mind, or fresh in the news, or going on around the campus. One day, he announced that Theda Bara, then at the height of her vampish fame, would have no effect upon him, emotionally or artistically, if she should bang into his presence with her great blue eyes bulging and her dark hair in exaggerated disarray. "You can't get passion into a story with exclamation points," he said. Sometimes he would bring a cheap novel to class and show how its hasty and careless author was trying to palm off "italics" for genuine emotion. "General Stonebridge was a man of iron," one of these novels began, and Professor Taylor then quoted some of the staunch fellow's vapid conversation and said, "A character of iron does not speak in words of tinfoil."

Ludwig Lewisohn, who in my time was teaching German and German literature at Ohio State, was disappointed to find no "vicious faces" on the campus. Joe Taylor, however, was interested not in a search for depravity but in finding signs of spiritual in-crease and of fine sensibility in the world about him, and he never gave up the wistful hope of instructing the unvicious in the litera-ture of living. Perceptive and congenial young minds can scarcely be said to have flourished like wild flowers in that time and region, but the good professor did his best, and he had a lasting effect on the minds and hearts of scores of men and women. Professor Lewisohn, who liked and admired few men at Ohio State, brought

Joe Taylor into his novel "Roman Summer." "But it must not be supposed that John Austin was a fool," the passage reads. "At college he had fallen under the influence of a teacher of intense but limited and stagnant tastes: a small ruddy gnome of a man who had, long ago, been a favorite pupil of George Edward Woodberry, a protégé of Richard Watson Gilder in the general days of the *Century* and had published a volume of late Victorian verse. His literary eminence was a legend in the city. Young Austin had taken all of the courses offered by his teacher. He was not unaware now of the man's limitations. What allied him to that teacher still was an unconquerable love of beauty and fitness and precision of speech." Lewisohn's years at Ohio State were unhappy ones and, coming from him, this qualified tribute is praise indeed.

"I know that some of you restless young men are eager to get to classes that teach you how to make a living," Professor Taylor said once, taking out his watch and laying it on the lectern. "It is now only ten minutes till economics, or chemistry, or engineering." Many a restless male student gave fresh attention to this kind of talk. They listened when he said that the word "beauty" could not be applied to campus cuties, because beauty in a woman cannot be purchased with the scant coin of twenty-one years of life. With local references like this, he deftly led the anti-literature boys and girls in and out of Meredith and James, quoting the former's "My heart is not made of the stuff that breaks" and the latter's "When she touches a thing the ugliness, God knows how, goes out of it" in support of his fond thesis that beauty in a woman is a product of maturity. If the interest of the male students began to wane, he might talk about Chic Harley, the great Ohio State halfback of the period, pointing out that Harley's graceful running with a football brought true beauty of line and motion to a game that had been, only a few years before, a turgid struggle of monolithic masses. If Theda Bara didn't snap the boys out of daydream or apathy, Chic Harley invariably did. Once, Joe Taylor fascinated his young listeners by comparing Charles Dickens to Billy Ireland, who was then cartoonist for the Columbus *Evening Dispatch*, and one of the best in the country. Dickens was to Joe Taylor—at least at that moment—only a greatly gifted caricaturist.

Professor Taylor went to all the football, baseball, and basketball games, and I had the good luck to have a seat near his in Ohio

Field the exciting day in 1920 when our team defeated Wisconsin by virtue of a fifty-yard pass from Workman to Stinchcomb, thrown just a second before the gun ending the game was fired. In the bedlam that instantly struck the stands like a hurricane, I caught sight of Mr. Taylor yelling at the top of his voice and slapping a strange man in front of him with his hat, time and again. He knew which of his students were varsity athletes, whether in football, baseball, basketball, or track, and many of them, including an old track man named Tracy Pittenger, remember him with special fondness. "My track career came to a sudden end out at Champaign, Illinois, when I was running at the Illinois Relay Carnival in March of 1922," Pittenger wrote recently. "I broke my leg, and along with it my heart. The following week, after I had my leg set in a cast and was hobbling from one class to another, I was about to pass Joe Taylor, going in the opposite direction. There was a moment of hesitation as we came almost face to face. I saw in his face, in just a split second, a look of complete understanding, and there were also two little tears (one in his eye and one in mine). What he did then will stand out forever in my memory. He lifted his hat and passed on his way. I will always be grateful that he didn't stop and tell me he was sorry, because what that little gesture told me was more than any words could have told. Especially when the gesture was performed by a man who never should have been required to remove his hat to any man."

The Pittenger story was written for a detailed history of Ohio State athletes and athletics, now in preparation at the university, where intercollegiate sports are rated of enormous importance. I can easily believe that Joe Taylor raised his hat to Pittenger that day—after all, A. E. Housman, one of Joe's idols, also had a warm and rueful affection for lightfoot lads—but I very much doubt the reality of the tear in his eye. Joe Taylor's eye was not made of the stuff that weeps easily. He had too much temper and toughness of spirit for the sentimental, and a fine way of getting mad, rather than merely sorry, when things went wrong. One day in 1917, I happened to look out a window of the Ohio Union Building and I saw my favorite professor practicing on a putting green about thirty yards away. He kept missing the cup by a wide margin, but he finally sent the ball to within a few inches of the hole. He went back several yards to try again, and I could see his confidence in his step and in the set of his shoulders. His next attempt was the worst of all, the ball swerving a good three feet to the left of its objective. Joe began to pound his putter on the ground, and then he walked to a tree and banged it six or eight times against the trunk. He then went back and kicked the ball, picked it up, and stalked away. Not long after this, incidentally, a young man named Robert Tyre Jones put on an identical tantrum at the Merion Cricket Club, outside Philadelphia, but he went on to the greatest glory in the history of the game. Joe Taylor, I must report, never got very much better at golf, but he was an excellent swimmer and played a good game of tennis.

Joseph Russell Taylor, born in Circleville in 1868, was so deeply attached to Ohio that no offer of fortune could have lured him away. He had no desire to win public renown, like Billy Phelps, of Yale, or Copey, of Harvard, and he was not flattered when his students began to call him Joey, in a mistaken attempt to institutionalize him. His ideal teacher, and one of the strongest influences in his life, was the late George Woodberry, in whose celebrated English literature classes at Columbia in the nineties young Taylor had sat enchanted. (Joe had entered Ohio State when he was only fifteen, and so he was still a youngster when he graduated.) Woodberry was not only a great teacher; he was also a poet, and he was interested in the athletes as well as the young literati who flocked to his classes. It was not easy to trace the Woodberry influence in the Taylor lectures. It showed up more in his profound and stubborn belief that he was, like Woodberry, first of all a poet. At Columbia he wore a Van Dyke beard, wrote poetry diligently in his spare time, and signed himself "J. Russell Taylor." He soon took off the beard and restored the "Joseph" to his name. Two skillful sonnets of his were published in a book called "Columbia Verse 1892-1897." After college, he sold poems to the *Atlantic Monthly, Harper's, Scribner's,* and *The Century,* and in 1903 they were published by Houghton, Mifflin in a volume called "The Overture." He later brought out several long poems, one of them wistfully entitled "Our Dancing Days."

He went to Europe twice, to visit places that made his heart leap up: the Nether Stowey of Coleridge, and Shelley's Tremadoc— where he had the luck one morning to hear a skylark singing—and, best of all, Tintagel, on the rocky coast of Cornwall, where the legendary ruins of King Mark's Castle stand, and Tarascon, in Province. Of Daudet's "Tartarin of Tarascon," he once wrote,

"It is, in my judgment, France's greatest contribution to literature in the nineteenth century." Tintagel was, for him, even more hallowed ground, because it was associated with Tristam, whose "I come from Lyonesse and a gentleman am I" he often quoted, in a dozen unexpected contexts of his own. He spent many years working, at night and in odd hours, on a monumental essay about Tristam, which I was privileged to read after his death. It ran to nearly half a million words, and was lighted and adorned by his own extensions and permutations of the great legends. He didn't believe that the poets, from Matthew Arnold to Edwin Arlington Robinson, had done full justice to the romantic figure of Sir Tristam, and he held that Wagner had made of him nothing more than a tenor. I can still hear Professor Taylor telling his classes that Tristam's lady, Iseult, was, beyond peradventure of doubt, a redhead. You didn't have to agree with him about this, or about anything else, and if, in written examinations, you set down judgments exactly opposed to his, it made no difference in your grades, as long as your points were sincerely argued.

He came back eagerly to Ohio from New York, or from Europe, for he was always, be sure (as he might have put it), a wandering and not too comfortable Ohioan wherever he went, forever remembering home. Since his dearest literary shrines and settings were so far away, his deep affection for his native state seemed to me at first a wonder unmixed (to use another of his phrases), but I came to realize that he had the true devotion of the poet to his own region, like Wordsworth's to the Lake Country of England, or Burns' to Scotland. Joe Taylor's notebooks and diaries show that he had roamed all over Ohio, painting streams and meadows, silver birches and scarlet oaks, and spotting birds by their songs and colors. On one weekend of rambling, he identified a hundred and seventy-five different birds, and he would not have exchanged the upland plover or the hermit thrush of the Middle West for Shelley's skylark, or for the nightingale whose autumnal song he once heard in the Boboli Garden, in Florence. He was familiar with Ohio's wild flora, from the fungus known as fairy ring to the purple-fringed orchis, and his home was bright in season with the flowers he collected in the woods and fields. His children remember his coming home at dusk one day bringing their mother a bouquet of bloodroot and anemones, around which he had neatly wrapped a damp handkerchief to keep it fresh.

When Joseph Russell Taylor was forty-one, Henry Holt published "Composition in Narration," his only textbook (if you could call it that)—a small volume of lyric essays on the art of writing, whose serenity has survived like a flower in a book. It came out in 1909, a year remembered by most men as the year Blériot flew over the English Channel. To Joe Taylor, it was the year Meredith and Swinburne died. The book was written so long ago that it is filled with quiet, old-fashioned scenes: a gentleman calling on a lady and presenting his card at the door; beaux taking their belles to dancing parties in sleighs or horse cabs; a balloon dreamily drifting over central Ohio in the race that started during the St. Louis World's Fair of 1904. "There were voices of children on the quiet air, and there was the good smell of the fires of autumn leaves; things of immemorial familiarity; and on the south of the evening passed what a voyager, a portent, the first sail on a new sea, the angel of tomorrow!"

Joe Taylor's book darts and wanders, intensely or at a leisurely pace, down the hundred pathways of his agile thought, but his poetic prose is carefully disciplined. "Art is revision," he wrote, and he must have lit his pipe a thousand times in rewriting his chapters. He brought impulsive feeling, rather than cold mental analysis, to everything he touched—he goes so far as to call intellect "the conventional part of imagination"—but he had the good writer's dissatisfaction with imperfect statement, and the book shows his constant wariness of certainties. "The only taste that is false is that which does not change," he wrote.

As a textbook, "Composition in Narration" must have puzzled professors looking for conventional rules and familiar rituals. It begins, "There are really only two kinds of writing: artistic, which is narration, and scientific, which is argument," and then starts off on a Taylor-guided tour of a hundred subjects. The author quotes from personal letters; talks about his father, who gave up teaching to become a minister; explores the difference between literal fact and literary truth; discusses painting and music; skillfully takes apart one of his own moods; describes a spectacular fire in Columbus, and the effect a small replica of the Venus de Milo had on him when he spent what must have been hours turning it slowly around in different lights. In the book's last section, called "References," he talks about authors he liked at the time: Henry James, above all and at greatest length; de Maupassant; Daudet;

Stevenson; Anthony Hope, for his "The Dolly Dialogues;" and, finally, "Mr. Wister." Joe must have loved "The Virginian," because the Far West always appealed to him; one of his long poems, called "Thirty Ponies," was about a tribe of Western Indians. There is also this note in "References," which I can't get out of my mind and probably never will: "It is almost true also that the most perfect Stevenson story was not written by him, but by Mrs. Stevenson; 'The Nixie,' the story remains still, as far as I know, buried in a magazine of the Eighties." That wonderful "almost true" is pure Joseph Russell Taylor, copyright 1909. It has given a lovely case of the nixies.

In spite of a critical taste that changed like the weather, Joe Taylor had his immutable convictions: that nothing genuine need fear the test of laughter (he thought the comic aspects of wearing a scarlet letter could have been exploited by Hawthorne); that youth cannot hold a candle to maturity (he was never entranced by Keats' celebration of young, or trivial, love forever imprisoned in shallow April); and that there is nothing prose can do that poetry can't do better. Since James' novel "The Ambassadors" seemed perfect to him, he actually persuaded himself that it was essentially poetry. (His contention that its dialogue was the very spit and idiom of its time was even more startling.) He also believed, all his life, that "the artist is the normal man," a cryptic judgment that none of his students who went on to write or teach has ever been able to follow very far without getting lost. In his later years, he kept assuring his classes that poetry should not be read aloud, and this I think I can perhaps explain. In my day, he used to read poetry aloud, with a peculiar and disconcerting lift of inflection on the last syllable in every line. Some of his students took to imitating this curious mannerism out of class. He never did get the hang of reading verse easily and effectively, and he must have come to the conclusion that it couldn't be done.

He firmly believed from his twenties into his sixties, that politics is an impermanent factor of life and has no valid place in art and literature. "Such things as love, life, and death, and people are the permanent things," he told his students. He said that Shelley was not a true poet, because he was a rebel; apparently you can't be both. In 1917, he said, "The Germans cannot win the war, because they are wrong," and he let it go at that. Communism was wrong,

too, and therefore couldn't win: "Improvement cannot be brought
about by any Bolshevist revolution, or socialistic redistribution of
property. We are not so desirous of an earthly paradise as to ap-
prove revolutionary and violent means of attaining it. What we
want is simply the privilege of going on—not perfection but the
privilege of striving." Politics, to be sure, did not include patriotism.
Joe Taylor was one of the most patriotic Americans I have ever
known. He never forgave Henry James for becoming a British
subject, and in the preface to a long, unpublished essay that, for his
private satisfaction and amusement, he called "Taylor on James,"
he held that the novelist could not get rid of his Americanism
merely by changing countries. He predicted in 1912 that James
would come back to his own land, and he must have been gratified
when he found out later that the book the Master was working on
when he died dealt with Americans in America, after a long series
of novels about Americans in Europe.

For the reassurance and guidance of any militant Ohio State
trustee who might figure that a man who had rejected politics must
have been a dangerous fellow, I reprint, from "Composition in
Narration," Joe Taylor's warm tribute to his country.

How should you answer if I should ask you, What is the
Nation? Where is it? Show it to me. Does it look like the statue
in New York Harbor? Is it the fleet that recently went round
the world, with peaceful guns and with dancing on the decks?
Is it the flag, is it the capitol, has it the President's many-
caricatured countenance? Where and what is the Nation? Is
there such a thing? You would answer that the Nation exists only
in the minds and hearts of men. It is an idea. It is therefore more
real than its courts and armies; more real than its cities, its rail-
roads, its mines; its cattle; more real than you and I are, for it
existed in our fathers, and will exist in our children. It is an idea,
it is an imagination, it is a spirit, it is human art. Who will deny
that the Nation lives?

He seems to have held himself aloof from campus politics and
scandals during his more than forty years at Ohio State, but in
1929 a grotesque tragedy reached out and touched him. A professor of veterinary medicine named James H. Snook murdered a
university coed, and after his execution university authorities de-
creed that the top half of every office door in all campus buildings

should be made of transparent glass. Joe Taylor was sixty-one at
the time, and it had been his custom, after his final class, to lie
down and rest in his office before going home. The Snook door,
which made a goldfish bowl of his privacy in the English building,
put an end to these periods of rest and had a disturbing physical
and emotional effect on him, which he found hard to shake off.
Two years later, he was sitting in his parked automobile on the
campus when it was struck and knocked over on its side by a
bus filled with agricultural students. He never fully recovered from
the effects of this accident, and in 1933 he died, of complications,
a few months before his sixty-fifth birthday. In his last year, he had
painted dozens of water colors of his beloved Ohio landscape, and
he must have written poetry, too, since it was such an important
part of his life. I doubt whether he found any joy in the American
novels of the nineteen twenties, except, of course, those of that
normal artist, Miss Willa Cather. His delight in James and Meredith
never declined and he kept going back to them at the end, and,
you may be sure, to Wordsworth's immortal "She Was a Phantom
of Delight." His friends thought of him as one of the permanent
things of life, and when we heard that he was dead, the light of
that day diminished.

★ *It is the supreme art of the teacher to awaken joy in creative
expression and knowledge.*

ALBERT EINSTEIN

★ *The man who can make hard things easy is the educator.*

EMERSON

A VETO BY
ALFRED E. SMITH

by William O. Douglas

In 1920, GOVERNOR ALFRED E. SMITH OF NEW YORK VETOED A BILL requiring each public school teacher to obtain a certificate from the Commissioner of Education that he is of good moral character, will support the state and federal constitutions, and is loyal "to the institutions and laws" of New York and the nation. The bill also gave power to the Commissioner to revoke the certificate if he found the teacher was not "loyal." The Governor said in a notable veto:

"The test established is not what the teacher teaches, but what the teacher believes. . . . It permits one man to place upon any teacher the stigma of disloyalty and this even without hearing or trial. No man is so omniscient or wise as to have entrusted to him such arbitrary and complete power not only to condemn any individual teacher, but to decree what belief or opinion is opposed to the institutions of the country.

"No teacher could continue to teach if he or she entertained any objection, however conscientious, to any existing institution. If this law had been in force prior to the abolition of slavery, opposition to that institution which was protected by the Constitution and its laws would have been just cause for the disqualification of a teacher. . . .

"Opposition to any presently established institution, no matter how intelligent, conscientious, or disinterested this opposition might be, would be sufficient to disqualify the teacher. Every teacher would be at the mercy of his colleagues, his pupils, and their parents, and any word or act of the teacher might be held by the commissioner to indicate an attitude hostile to some of the institutions of 'The United States' or of the State.

". . . The bill confers upon the Commissioner of Education a power of interference with freedom of opinion which strikes at the foundations of democratic education."

★ *This is the task of a liberal education: to give a sense of the value of things other than domination, to help to create wise citizens of a free community, and through the combination of citizenship with liberty in individual creativeness to enable men to give to human life that splendor which some few have shown that it can achieve.*

BERTRAND RUSSELL

FLOWER FOR A
PROFESSOR'S GARDEN OF VERSES

by Irwin Edman

A TEACHER SHOULD IMPART WHAT'S TRUE
At least what they allow him to;
A college teacher should not vex
His pupils with his thoughts on sex;
He should keep mum if he has odd
Views on the character of God.
He should dismiss as red inventions
All but the three well-known dimensions,
Not teaching logic, which might hurt
Young minds impeccably inert,
Nor even question any truths
Their nurses taught these darling youths.
No skepticisms—that might lead them
To use their heads if they should need them.
Only such views by housewives favored—
Be, teacher, be vanilla-flavored.
Make your lectures chocolate fudge
Fit to be nibbled by a judge;
Cookies sweet enough to dish up
Before a bon-bon loving bishop,
Or shall we say, an angel layer

To set before an upright mayor.
Then will your thoughts be sure to keep
Your students sound, and sound asleep.
And keep for you, though far from clever,
Your job—and what a job!—forever!

★ *William Lyon Phelps, on a pre-Christmas examination paper, found written, "God only knows the answer to this question. Merry Christmas." He returned the paper with the notation, "God gets an A; you get an F. Happy New Year."*

★ *Told by John Erskine: "At the end of my university studies when I was leaving for my first professional job, I went to say goodbye to my old teacher, William Peterfield Trent. 'I can give you no theoretical advice in pedagogy,' he said, 'but I'll tell you one thing from experience. It will frequently happen when you are holding forth that some boy in the class will disagree. He will probably shake his head violently. You will be tempted to go after him and convert him then and there. Don't do it. He is probably the only one who is listening."*

FRAME OF REFERENCE

by Frederick James Moffitt

AFTER ATTENDING A CONFERENCE OF SCHOOL FOLK LAST WEEK, writes W.L.G., I thought I had heard the last sesquipedalian word in pedagese and pedigobble. But, alas, I had little realization of the lengths to which school people will go to make themselves misunderstood.

In the current issue of a national education magazine (not *TNS*), I stumbled on the word "cafetorium," meaning, I suspect, that part of the school building which, owing to the economy program, serves as an assembly hall and the place in which the kids eat their lunches, to the detriment of both pleasant eating and competent dramatics.

This cafetorium business is a beautiful sample of our love of words. If cafetorium, why not auditeria? How about the gymnarium or the audasiam where basketballs splatter the unguarded windows? In the small school, a cafaugym after lunch becomes, presto, a gymauditeria in which the little ones merrily pelt the basketballers with leftover pie until the audigym is made ready for the evening meeting of the members of the Parent-Teacher Association.

There is no doubt that our school administrators will fully exploit all of these possibilities for a frame of reference for future Rotarations and Kiwanianastrophes!

The Neighbors

By George Clark

"Did I learn anything in school today, Miss Watts? Mom always asks."

(Chicago *Tribune*—New York News Syndicate, Inc.)

CANINE PRIMARY

by Robert Littell

O F COURSE I WANTED MY DOG TO HAVE ALL THE ADVANTAGES OF modern psychological pedagogy, so I entered him at the John Dewey Day Dog School, an institution said to be conducted under the auspices of Teachers' College. To be sure, he would meet the sons of more famous dogs at one of those church boarding schools, but I want my dog to be nonsectarian. Also, he is a mongrel, and the patrician dogs might make fun of him. I call him Nero after the well-known violinist. I am sure he is gifted in some direction, and it might as well be music.

"This is Nero," I said to the principal of Day Dog, "and I should like him to learn how to beg, give his paw, play dead, fetch a ball, point a bird, walk on his hind legs, carry a newspaper in his mouth, and lie down when I say *couche-toi*. And when I say *couche-toi* I mean *couche-toi*. I love my dog, but I want him to be versatile, and obedient."

"Progressive canine pedagogics," answered the principal, twiddling the Phi Beta Kappa key on his watch chain, "have arrived at the conclusion that there is no place in the curriculum for modern languages until close to the age of adolescence, let us say 18 months. And as for your other requests," he added, smiling with indulgent pity, "we cynologists of the new school believe in the fundamental approach. We do not teach formal subjects, such as begging and carrying newspapers, for some time. We begin by studying the dog's reactions until we understand his personality. We try to rehabilitate the dog's emotional attitudes, which are nearly always warped by faulty home environment. We attempt to bring out the suppressed traits of his character. A dog, if left alone with a number of objects, will choose that which most appeals to him . . ."

"Chew?" I interrupted timidly.

"No, choose. Our tests have selected a list of eleven hundred objects which appeal to one side or another of dog nature. Our teachers show the dogs how to play with those objects. For correct play habits are the foundation of character. Upon that foundation the normal dog builds with amazing rapidity. He learns to adapt himself to unusual situations and to the society of other dogs. He learns to abandon moping, day dreaming and isolationist or antisocial conduct. And he graduates, if we have been successful and if the dog's owner co-operates, a complete, well-rounded, psychically integrated and physically homogeneous dog."

"What does he know?" I asked.

The principal looked at me scornfully. "Knowledge is secondary," he said, "the main thing is to unfold the tiny buds of dog personality."

Then he showed me through the school. In one room a group of puppies were tearing shoes apart with their teeth. In another, full of older dogs, I saw a teacher crawling on all fours, holding a ball in her mouth and growling.

"At first," explained the principal, "the teachers have to talk to the dogs in very simple language." In a third room some of the dogs were chasing each other around, others were gnawing bones, scratching themselves and barking.

"Recess?" I questioned.

"Not at all," said the principal, rather acidly, "these dogs are learning to integrate their personalities."

So I left Nero, who whined pitifully as I went, at the Day Dog School. He came back wagging his tail, so I supposed everything was going splendidly. A few days later I received a letter from the school. "Little Nero," it said, "is an introvert. We have had a faculty meeting about him, and it seems best that his vitality should be built up by drinking extra milk in the middle of the morning." Enclosed was a bill for $10 for the milk, which I paid. Some weeks went by, weeks during which I was absorbed by the affairs of the world of men. Nero seemed quite as happy and lively as ever, but otherwise I could not notice any change in his play habits or personality, and he destroyed slippers, barked at strangers, slept on brocade sofas, just as before. Although I was very busy I called up the principal. "Nero," he said, "is becoming gradually externalized. His teacher considers him much less selfcentered. The dogs in his class are now studying dog biscuit. The classroom is full of samples of the materials that go into dog biscuit, the walls are hung with maps showing where dog biscuit is made. By observing familiar objects and tracing them back to their component sources do we lead the plastic canine mind out of Narcissism into the wonders of the objective universe."

The next day Nero refused to eat any dog biscuit and was caught munching a first edition of the poems of Edna St. Vincent Millay. The influence of the school had begun to tell. Already Nero was beginning to decide things for himself, or, in the words of a pamphlet on primary canine mentality lent me by the principal, to "opt."

Nero's first monthly report, while not brilliant, was satisfactory. "Nero," it said, "is adapting himself rapidly to the group, and is barking with the greater self-confidence, but lacks cooperative spirit and is more than normally destructive of materials." Enclosed was a bill for 13 pairs of shoes, which I thought rather high, but a footnote explained that Nero vastly preferred new shoes to old, and that the zest of novelty was a highly important educative factor. I was tempted to write back that Nero had just finished a home-study course in hook rugs, and enclose a bill for the rugs, but I hate arguing with people who know so much about psychology and so many long words. And anyhow Nero seemed very happy.

I have never received so many letters as I did from that Day Dog School since the time when in a moment of ghoulish curiosity I answered an advertisement for the Cliffview Mausoleum. First it was Owner's Week. "Next week is Owner's Week," wrote Nero's teacher, "and every owner will give his dog something for the dog to take back to school and present to the School Museum. It is suggested that the gift should be either fruit, flowers or something illustrating the Industrial Revolution in America." Then it was Woodchuck Week. "Your dog," said the mimeographed letter, "has been digging on his own initiative, along with other primary dogs, a deep hole in the Nature Study Yard. He will soon get to the bottom which is concrete. He expects to find something at the bottom when he gets there. If he doesn't find anything he will be disappointed and disillusioned, a hole-complex may form in his mind and he will tend to indulge in fantasies rather than action. The teachers and the older dogs think that it is imperative that every dog should find a woodchuck at the bottom of his hole. Unfortunately our woodchuck fund is exhausted. Won't you please send a live woodchuck to reach the school not later than Thursday?"

Then there was a bill for bus fare for taking all the pre-primary dogs on an expedition to the George Washington Bridge. Then another monthly report. "Nero is much more social-minded than when he came to Day Dog, and co-ordinates well for his age. He is already becoming an independent little mechanism. However, he is a highly sensitive dog, and cannot bear reproof. Perhaps this is because he is not admonished sufficiently at home. May we ask his owner to cooperate with us. Do not whip or slap Nero, but when he misbehaves show him what he has done and explain why it was a mistake. Reason with him as much as possible. . . . Scratching: excellent; Music: only fair."

Well, he can't be perfect. I would be the last person to wish for a regimented, under-individualized dog. And he is certainly making progress. The class has just been studying primitive wolf life. The wolf was the ancestor of the dog, and many dogs have wolf-like traits. It seems quite logical for them to study, through lantern slides and samples in little bowls, how wolves lived and what wolves ate. And wolf folkways are as good an approach as any to an understanding of our complicated civilization. One should study wolves imaginatively, from the inside. All the dogs are asked to pretend that they are wolves. If some of them develop howls or take to biting visitors, that's only the seamy side of a very beautiful and understanding educational carpet. On the whole I am satisfied with Day Dog. Nero lacks concentration, but is full of self-expression and curiosity. And curiosity, they say, is the mother of wisdom.

And yet somehow I am sorry that Nero has not learned how to

give his paw, or stand on his hind legs, or balance a piece of sugar on his nose. He can't do any of the normal useful dog tricks. He jumps all over people, his voice is shrill, and he talks all the time. When I say *"couche-toi"* to him he barks and runs around the room. Yet of course I would not want to have these things driven into him at the expense of a budding, blossoming, vital personality.

The principal of Day Dog says that the basic methodology of canine education could probably quite successfully be applied to children (though unfortunately no one has thought of doing so), but not to lizards. Lizards, it appears, have no personalities or emotional content worth integrating.

★ *Sam Levenson, the comedy star who once was a teacher, partici-*
pated in a program, 'What's Wrong with Our Schools?' He
made this contribution: "What's wrong with our schools is
that everybody is afraid of somebody. The teacher is afraid
of the principal, the principal is afraid of the superintendent,
the superintendent is afraid of the Board of Education, the
Board of Education is afraid of the parents, the parents are
afraid of the kids—and the kids aren't afraid of anybody."
'Clearing House,' January, 1956
Reported by Ben Lyon in The New York Post

THE PERFECT TEACHER

1. The education of a college president.
2. The executive ability of a financier.
3. The humility of a deacon.
4. The discipline of a demon.
5. The adaptability of a chameleon.
6. The hope of an optimist.
7. The courage of a hero.
8. The wisdom of a serpent.
9. The gentleness of a dove.
10. The patience of Job.
11. The grace of God.
12. The persistence of the devil.

PRIMARY EDUCATION

by Phyllis McGinley

PRIMARY EDUCATION

Pupils to Learn Tolerance Here Twice a Month
—Headline in the *New York Herald Tribune*

BY HOOK, BY CROOK, BY HAIR OF HEAD,
  By scruff of neck and seat of pants,
Our stubborn infants shall be led
  Along the paths of tolerance.

As bends the twigs, thus grows the el-em;
  As twists the thread, the spool unwinds;
So, twice a month, we're bound to sell 'em
  The doctrine of Impartial Minds.

Tagged, labeled, catalogued, and graded,
  Sitting submissive in a queue,
Fortnightly they shall be persuaded
  To entertain the larger view—

To stretch their hands across the ocean;
  To open their childish hearts
And love their neighbor with devotion,
  As per the diagrams and charts;

To call the foreigner their brother
  (Unless by chance he should indorse
Some heretic opinion other
  Than that included in the Course).

By rote, by rule, by text and primer,
  By maps and slides and lectures read,
We'll see that Truth is set to simmer
  In every tot's intolerant head.

Or so believes the Board of Ed.

★ *For a number of years, I taught in the Blue Ridge Mountain
schools of Virginia. Trying always to impress the virtue of
honesty upon my students, I required them to give a pledge
that they had neither given nor received help on their examinations. One young girl handed in her paper with this pledge on
it: "I haven't received no help on this exam, and God knows I
couldn't give any."*

S.E.L. WARWICK

'Fun Fare,' a Reader's Digest Treasury of Wit and Humor
(Copyright 1949 by The Reader's Digest Association)

GOOD-BYE, MR. CHIPS

by James Hilton

AND THEN THE ROW WITH RALSTON. FUNNY THING, CHIPS HAD never liked him; he was efficient, ruthless, ambitious, but not, somehow, very likable. He had, admittedly, raised the status of Brookfield as a school, and for the first time in memory there was a longish waiting list. Ralston was a live wire; a fine power transmitter, but you had to beware of him.

Chips had never bothered to beware of him; he was not attracted by the man, but he served him willingly enough and quite loyally. Or, rather, he served Brookfield. He knew that Ralston did not like him, either; but that didn't seem to matter. He felt himself sufficiently protected by age and seniority from the fate of other masters whom Ralston had failed to like.

Then suddenly, in 1908, when he had just turned sixty, came Ralston's urbane ultimatum. "Mr. Chipping, have you ever thought you would like to retire?"

Chips stared about him in that book-lined study, startled by the question, wondering why Ralston should have asked it. He said, at length: "No—umph—I can't say that—umph—I have thought much about it—umph—yet."

From *Good-Bye, Mr. Chips*, by James Hilton. Copyright 1934 by James Hilton. Reprinted by permission of Little, Brown & Co.

"Well, Mr. Chipping, the suggestion is there for you to consider.
The governors would, of course, agree to your being adequately
pensioned."

Abruptly Chips flamed up. "But—umph—I don't want—to retire. I don't—umph—need to consider it."

"Nevertheless, I suggest that you do."

"But—umph—I don't see—why—I should!"

"In that case, things are going to be a little difficult."

"Difficult? Why—difficult?"

And then they set to, Ralston getting cooler and harder, Chips
getting warmer and more passionate, till at last Ralston said, icily:
"Since you force me to use plain words, Mr. Chipping, you shall
have them. For some time past, you haven't been pulling your
weight here. Your methods of teaching are slack and old-fashioned;
your personal habits are slovenly; and you ignore my instructions in
a way which, in a younger man, I should regard as rank insubordination. It won't do, Mr. Chipping, and you must ascribe it to my
forebearance that I have put up with it so long."

"But—" Chips began, in sheer bewilderment; and then he took
up isolated words out of that extraordinary indictment. "*Slovenly*—
umph—you said—?"

"Yes, look at the gown you're wearing. I happen to know that
that gown of yours is a subject of continual amusement throughout the School."

Chips knew it, too, but it had never seemed to him a very re-
gretable matter.

He went on: "And—you also said—umph—something about—
insubordination—?"

"No, I didn't. I said that in a younger man I should have regarded it as that. In your case it's probably a mixture of slackness
and obstinacy. This question of Latin pronunciation, for instance—
I think I told you years ago that I wanted the new style used
throughout the School. The other masters obeyed me; you prefer
to stick to your old methods, and the result is simply chaos and
inefficiency."

At last Chips had something tangible that he could tackle. "Oh,
that!" he answered, scornfully. "Well, I—umph—I admit that I
don't agree with the new pronunciation. I never did. Umph—
a lot of nonsense, in my opinion. Making boys say 'Kickero' at
school when—umph—for the rest of their lives they'll say 'Cicero'

—if they ever—umph—say it at all. And instead of 'vicissim'—God bless my soul—you'd make them say, 'We kiss 'im! Umph—umph!'" And he chuckled momentarily, forgetting that he was in Ralston's study and not in his own friendly form room.

"Well, there you are, Mr. Chipping—that's just an example of what I complain of. You hold one opinion and I hold another, and, since you decline to give way, there can't very well be any alternative. I aim to make Brookfield a thoroughly up-to-date school. I'm a science man myself, but for all that I have no objection to the classics—provided that they are taught efficiently. Because they are dead languages is no reason why they should be dealt with in a dead educational technique. I understand, Mr. Chipping, that your Latin and Greek lessons are exactly the same as they were when I began here ten years ago?"

Chips answered, slowly and with pride: "For that matter— umph—they are the same as when your predecessor—Mr. Meldrum—came here, and that—umph—was thirty-eight years ago. We began here, Mr. Meldrum and I—in—umph—in 1870. And it was—um—Mr. Meldrum's predecessor, Mr. Wetherby—who first approved my syllabus. 'You'll take the Cicero for the fourth,' he said to me. Cicero, too—not Kickero!"

"Very interesting, Mr. Chipping, but once again it proves my point—you live too much in the past, and not enough in the present and future. Times are changing, whether you realize it or not. Modern parents are beginning to demand something more for their three years' school fees than a few scraps of languages that nobody speaks. Besides, your boys don't learn even what they're supposed to learn. None of them last year got through the Lower Certificate."

And suddenly, in a torrent of thoughts too pressing to be put into words, Chips made answer to himself. These examinations and certificates and so on—what did they matter? And all this efficiency and up-to-dateness—what did *that* matter, either? Ralston was trying to run Brookfield like a factory—a factory for turning out a snob culture based on money and machines. The old gentlemanly traditions of family and broad acres were changing, as doubtless they were bound to; but instead of widening them to form a genuine inclusive democracy of duke and dustman, Ralston was narrowing them upon the single issue of a fat banking account. There never had been so many rich men's sons at Brookfield.

The Speech Day Garden Party was like Ascot. Ralston met these wealthy fellows in London clubs and persuaded them that Brookfield was *the* coming school, and, since they couldn't buy their way into Eton or Harrow, they greedily swallowed the bait. Awful fellows, some of them—though others were decent enough. Financiers, company promoters, pill manufacturers. One of them gave his son five pounds a week pocket money. Vulgar . . . ostentatious . . . all the hectic rotten-ripeness of the age. . . . And once Chips had got into trouble because of some joke he had made about the name and ancestry of a boy named Isaacstein. The boy wrote home about it, and Isaacstein père sent an angry letter to Ralston. Touchy, no sense of humor, no sense of proportion—that was the matter with them, these new fellows. . . . No sense of proportion. And it was a sense of proportion, above all things, that Brookfield ought to teach—not so much Latin or Greek or Chemistry or Mechanics. And you couldn't expect to test that sense of proportion by setting papers and granting certificates. . . .

All this flashed through his mind in an instant of protest and indignation, but he did not say a word of it. He merely gathered his tattered gown together and with an "umph—umph" walked a few paces away. He had had enough of the argument. At the door he turned and said: "I don't—umph—intend to resign— and you can—umph—do what you like about it!"

Looking back upon that scene in the calm perspective of a quarter of a century, Chips could find it in his heart to feel a little sorry for Ralston. Particularly when, as it happened, Ralston had been in such complete ignorance of the forces he was dealing with. So, for that matter, had Chips himself. Neither had correctly estimated the toughness of Brookfield tradition, and its readiness to defend itself and its defenders. For it had so chanced that a small boy, waiting to see Ralston that morning, had been listening outside the door during the whole of the interview; he had been thrilled by it, naturally, and had told his friends. Some of these, in a surprisingly short time, had told their parents; so that very soon it was common knowledge that Ralston had insulted Chips and had demanded his resignation. The amazing result was a spontaneous outburst of sympathy and partisanship such as Chips, in his wildest dreams, had never envisaged. He found, rather to his astonishment, that Ralston was thoroughly unpopular; he was feared and respected, but not liked; and in this issue of

Chips the dislike rose to a point where it conquered fear and demolished even respect. There was talk of having some kind of public riot in the school if Ralston succeeded in banishing Chips. The masters, many of them young men who agreed that Chips was hopelessly old-fashioned, rallied round him nevertheless because they hated Ralston's slave driving and saw in the old veteran a likely champion. And one day the Chairman of the Governors, Sir John Rivers, visited Brookfield, ignored Ralston, and went direct to Chips. "A fine fellow, Rivers," Chips would say, telling the story to Mrs. Wickett for the dozenth time. "Not—umph—a very brilliant boy in class. I remember he could never—umph—master his verbs. And now—umph—I see in the papers—they've made him—umph—a baronet. It just shows you—umph—it just shows you."

Sir John had said, on that morning in 1908, taking Chips by the arm as they walked round the deserted cricket pitches: "Chips, old boy, I hear you've been having the deuce of a row with Ralston. Sorry to hear about it, for your sake—but I want you to know that the Governors are with you to a man. We don't like the fellow a great deal. Very clever and all that, but a bit too clever, if you ask me. Claims to have doubled the school's endowment funds by some monkeying on the Stock Exchange. Dare say he has, but a chap like that wants watching. So if he starts chucking his weight about with you, tell him very politely he can go to the devil. The Governors don't want you to resign. Brookfield wouldn't be the same without you, and they know it. We all know it. You can stay here till you're a hundred if you feel like it—indeed, it's our hope that you will."

And at that—both then and often when he recounted it afterward—Chips broke down.

I CONSIDER MR. CHIPS

by John P. Marquand

IF YOU HAVE NOT PREPARED FOR COLLEGE AT ONE OF THE OLDER and larger schools, with traditions and a recognized headmaster, you have missed a great experience. You have missed something fine in intimate companionship. You have missed that indefinable thing known as school spirit, which is more important than books or teaching, because it lasts when physics and algebra and Latin are forgotten. The other day I tried to read a page of Cicero and I could not get through a single line, although I got a B on my Latin entrance examination, but I can still remember the school hymn word for word. I am quite sure even today that I can tell, after a five minutes' talk with anyone, whether he attended a public or private school thirty years before. I believe that I can go even further than that. I can tell whether he went to a really good boarding school or to a second-rate one. The answer is always written in his voice and manner. That is why school is so enormously important.

I owe a debt of gratitude to my school, and I believe it was the best school then and it is the best school now. No matter what else has happened to me in the way of failure and disappointment

I am glad that I went to St. Swithin's. More than once the particular thing I learned there, which you can call manners or attitude,
for want of better words, has helped me in my darkest moments,
and I have Mr. Ewing to thank for it, my old headmaster.

"In order to be a leader," Mr. Ewing used to say in chapel,
"and to take the place which is made for you, you must learn
first to obey and serve."

This sort of thing is hard to express to anyone who has never
been there. I have tried to explain it to Bill King more than once.
I told him on one occasion that I was sorry that he had not gone
to St. Swithin's, that he would have been quite a different person
if he had gone there.

"You're damned well right I would have," Bill said, "but I like
to think I couldn't have stood it."

"You could have, Bill," I told him, "If you had started in the
First Form. The way to get the most out of school is to start at
the beginning. Very few boys are taken in after that, because they
don't get the most out of it."

"You mean, they have minds of their own," Bill said.

"That isn't what I mean at all," I told him. "The Skipper can't
do a proper job on a boy unless he has him all the way through."

"Skipper!" Bill said. "Can't you stop calling him the Skipper?"

"That's all right," I told him. "The graduates of any good school
have a nickname for the headmaster. I wish you really knew the
Skipper, Bill. If you really knew him you wouldn't indulge in so
many half-truths."

"I do know him," Bill said. "I crossed the ocean with him once."

"That isn't really knowing him," I said. "You can only know
the Skipper when he's up at school doing his job. He's different
anywhere else."

"Wherever that old jellyfish is," Bill said, "he's a conceited,
pandering poop."

"My God, Bill," I said, and I had to laugh. "You just don't
know the Skipper. He hadn't been more than a few years out
of Harvard when he came there. You should have seen him on
the football field! The Skipper's sixty now and he still plays games."

"Mr. Chips," Bill said. "*Good-bye, Mr. Chips.*"

"And what's wrong with Mr. Chips?" I asked.

"What's wrong with Mr. Chips?" Bill said. "Frankly, everything
was wrong with Mr. Chips."

"You aren't talking sense," I said. "I can think of nothing finer than Mr. Chip's last remark. 'Children? . . . I've had hundreds of them, and all of them are boys."

"Don't," Bill said. "You'll have to go away if you make me want to cry. Could anything be more unnatural than herding a lot of adolescent males together who ought to be with their parents and their sisters and their friends' sisters, learning the usual amenities of life?"

"The school wasn't unnatural," I said. "We were all able to see family life there, Bill, a good deal happier and more successful that what lots of us saw at home."

"How much did you see of it?" Bill asked.

"We used to see a lot of it," I said. "We were all brought up with the Skipper's children. Why, Mrs. Ewing always saw that every boy came in once a week for tea, and the Sixth Form always came in on Sundays for a pick-up supper."

"It sounds like a biological laboratory," Bill said. "It's like the neurologists at all those nervous-breakdown places. They have to have a happy married life or else they'll be fired. Well, go ahead. What did the Skipper teach you?"

"You can sneer at it all you like, Bill," I told him. "It doesn't affect me, because you don't understand. The Skipper had the guts to stand for what he stood for. That's more than either you or I have."

"We don't get a house and salary for it," Bill said. "We don't get paid for having guts. Don't get mad, Harry. You couldn't help it. Most of us were sent away from home somewhere and made to adjust ourselves to some arbitrary, artificial world that was built up by some positive and not intelligent individual. The only thing you can do is to try to snap out of it. Say good-by to it fast. Good-by, Mr. Chips."

"There are a lot of things you never say good-by to," I said, "if you go to a first-rate school."

"Yes," Bill said, "that's true. Not when they catch you young."

"You have to have standards to live," I said.

"Did you ever meet a poor boy there?" Bill asked. "Did you ever learn that people are abused and hungry, or what a minimum wage is? Did you ever get outside and go downtown? Did anybody ever teach you what the other ninety-nine percent of people think about?"

"You learn that later," I said. "I spent the happiest time of my life there, the most worth-while time. I wish I were back there now."

"The old subconscious desire," Bill said, "to crawl back into your mother's womb."

Now, I can be amused by people when they talk that way. I am even broad-minded enough to see their point of view, but there is nothing easier than to make fun of something that you do not understand.

I wish I might go back there again, because I did well at school. I was never one of the leaders. I never stood high in my form. I was too light for football, but of course I played it, because everyone had to play. I never did like baseball, but I wrote things for *The Crier*, the school paper. None of this meant very much, but I was an integral part of something—a part of a group.

I wish I could go back. Whenever autumn comes, even now, if I am in the country, I seem to be close to school. I still have all the indefinable sensations which mark the beginnings of a new year. I think of the fresh pages of new books and of the Upper Field and of the Lower Field, with their goalposts, and of the tennis courts and of the red and yellow of the maples. And I can see the Skipper, younger then.

"That was well played, Pulham," I can hear him saying. "Show fight, always show fight."

Every autumn I can see the faces of my form. Their names run through my mind, and their nicknames, and their physical peculiarities. It was a good form. Out of it came a banker and a state senator, two doctors and a scientist, a drunkard, and a good many brokers and lawyers. One was killed along the Meuse in the Argonne drive, and one was killed in a motor accident, and one has died of heart failure—five of them been divorced, two of them are dead-broke—on the whole not a bad record. I wish that I were back. I have often said that to myself before I have gone to sleep. I wish that I were back where there was someone like the Skipper to tell me what to do, someone who knew absolutely what was right and what was wrong, someone who had an answer to everything. There was always an answer at school, and a good answer. No matter what the world was like you could still play the game. I wish to God that I were back.

THE GARDENER OF SOULS

by Joseph Auslander

Who is the master teacher? He
Who from despair and fear sets free
The restless, sullen soul of youth
To range the harsh terrain of truth,
And from the blind abyss of folly,
The blackest pits of melancholy
To climb, to fall, to cling, to grope
Up the grim Everest of hope
Until above himself he stands,
A new strength in his bleeding hands,
And knows that by his faith he won
The shining summits of the sun.

Who is the master teacher? He
Who shows that to be truly free
No pain can be too much, no price
In discipline and sacrifice
Too great; that freedom is a pledge,
A promise and a privilege,

A glory earned, a grace to cherish,
Or lightly held, as lightly perish.

He is the teacher who gives vision,
And courage to outface derision;
Who in an angry time can teach
A tolerance in thought and speech
Which stones may strike, but never reach.
He is the plowman who plows deep
The stubborn soil where passions sleep,
Each one for good or ill a seed,
And plucks the nettle and the weed,
Laboring hour upon hour
To bring the best in man to flower,
And finds in labor for the Lord
His recompense and his reward,
Toiling as his great Teacher toils,
Who is the Gardener of Souls.

★ *Those who educate children well are more to be honored than they who produce them; for these only gave them life, those the art of living well.*

ARISTOTLE

★ *Education of youth is not a bow for every man to shoot in that counts himself a teacher; but will require sinews almost equal to those which Homer gave to Ulysses.*

MILTON

CLASSROOM GADFLIES

by N. Bryllion Fagin

THE FIRST INKLING THAT PERMITTING STUDENTS TO ASK QUESTIONS might be dangerous for the teacher came to me one evening when I was entrusted, for the first time, with a course in the modern novel. I was twenty-three years old and most of my students were older, and possibly more widely-read, than I. Yet I wasn't scared. Boldly I stood before them and, with the aid of notes copied from impeccable sources, told them all about the then fashionably acceptible novelists: American, English, French, German, Russian, Scandinavian. . . . They listened to me, and I was intoxicated with my received critical opinions and my gifts of exposition and articulation. I was, apparently, a successful teacher.

Then, at the end of one of my lectures, a man stood up to ask a question. I knew him by name as a contributor of poetry to various little magazines and I was proud that such a personage was one of my students. Since he may still be contributing poetry to little magazines, I shall suppress his real name and call him Mr. Johnson instead. It was this man, for whom I had a great deal of respect— and perhaps a little envy as well—who stood up and asked: "What do you think of George Gissing?"

From *The Educational Forum*. Copyright 1955 by George Banta Publishing Co. Reprinted by permission of the editor.

For a mere second I was stunned. Gissing, at the time, was only a name to me. But I quickly regained the poise and self-confidence which a teacher, I had been told, must have, and plunged: "Why, it is still too early to say anything definite about Gissing. He is a talented young writer who is destined to do great work. All he has done so far indicates brilliant promise."

Mr. Johnson's reaction to my answer made me uneasy. He stood there, in the rear of the room, contemplating me for a full minute, then said quietly, "Thank you," and sat down. He never came again to my class.

That very evening I consulted an encyclopedia and discovered the slip I had made: George Gissing had died in 1903.

Since then I have learned of many other dangers to which a teacher exposes himself by permitting his students to ask questions. He is urged to encourage expression in his classroom. He must not tolerate passive listening: he must stimulate thought, inquiry, "participation." And in almost every class there are a few vocal students who are only too happy to rise and shine. The other day I happened to mention the name of John Galsworthy and a Miss Johnson promptly raised her hand. "Did you know," she asked, "that Galsworthy was a member of the Society for the Prevention of Cruelty to Animals?" I had not known it, and therefore thanked Miss Johnson for adding to my stock of knowledge. But she wasn't satisfied; she proceeded to tell me and the class all the details of Galsworthy's activities in behalf of dumb creatures.

How to turn the Miss Johnsons off without discouraging the Mr. Johnsons is a problem I have not yet been able to solve. I once began a course by announcing that I would welcome all legitimate questions and comment. The result was an icy atmosphere which it took me a month to thaw. No one apparently knew what was legitimate. After a while I found myself blessing the few vocalists who dared to intrude upon my monologue.

Nor are the Mr. Johnsons always innocent poets. Myself when young once took delight in tripping up a professor whose knowledge of modern poetry was somewhat frail. By now I can spot the perverse imps in a class who are ready to capitalize on the imperfections of my memory or scholarship. From my side of the desk or lectern their efforts to flatter their egos at my expense appear to me somewhat less than amusing. I sometimes resort to complimenting them on their mental vigilance.

Neither am I always amused by the congenital debators who somehow appear in most classes and are ready to engage in combat at the drop of a word. Sometimes the word is an opinion which arouses their indignation; sometimes it is my failure to mention one of their literary enthusiasms: T. S. Eliot, Henry James, William Faulkner, Charlie Chaplin or (in one recent case) Mickey Spillane. They glory in appearing impudent. "You are just temperamentally not able to appreciate Truman Capote!" a fiery-eyed crusader informed me publicly. "Perhaps," I admitted affably.

Yet, in honest summary, I find that I—along with all other teachers—owe a debt of gratitude to these bad, mad, perverse, provoking students. They bring color and sound, tension and irritation into a classroom. Everything but dullness. They make me wary of my shortcomings, puncture my complacency, and keep me from sinking into comfortable slothfulness. I sometimes catch a suspicious anticipatory gleam in a bright eye just as I am about to repeat an ancient anecdote or a threadbare joke—and I desist. They make me reread the books on which I lecture, check my old notes, prepare new ones, and curb my stylistic extravagances. And during examinations it is exhilarating to come upon a paper that does not give me back all my own thoughts, many of which, when written down, do not deserve a passing grade.

★ *Several years ago in a nationally read magazine there appeared an illustration of dramatic teaching. The class was one in English composition and the lesson was on the writing of short stories. The teacher (a woman) was standing in front of the class when suddenly into the classroom burst a man who rushed up to the teacher and kissed her. After the kiss, the man left the room and the teacher turned to the class saying, "there is the end of the story; now you write the first part. . . ."*

JAMES T. BLANFORD
in 'The Balance Sheet' quoted by High Points, 1955

BOYDEN OF DEERFIELD

by Lewis Perry

ON A SEPTEMBER MORNING IN 1902, AN INCONSPICUOUS AND almost frail young man who had graduated from Amherst College the previous June walked up to the front door of the old schoolhouse in Deerfield, Massachusetts, which was Deerfield Academy. It was no coincidence that, within, the board of five trustees was holding a meeting to decide whether or not they should close the Academy. Chance no doubt played some part when the trustees finally decided to engage the applicant as the new principal,—for the outcome of almost all such interviews is unpredictable,—but chance has had very little to do with the fact that Frank L. Boyden, the young man from Amherst, has remained as principal now for forty years.

Approval of the choice was not universal. As the neighbors looked out of their windows at this one-hundred-and-twenty-pound youth with glasses,—not at all the type they had hoped for,—the feelings of many were that Deerfield Academy, which had had its ups and downs since its foundation in 1797, was in for another disappointment and had much better close up for good. Little would be added to the ancient luster given it by such a former head as Dr. Edward Hitchcock, who had propounded and proved to an astonished world the theory that the earth is millions of years old.

Always a believer in athletics, although apparently no athlete himself, the newly appointed principal on his first afternoon in office called out the fourteen boys in the school for football practice. They were an oddly assorted group dominated by a big freshman whom we shall call Smith. In a scrimmage Smith was thrown heavily and let go some oaths which constituted a great part of his meager vocabulary. Instantly the diminutive new principal stopped the scrimmage, looked the six-footer in the eye, and said, "Cut that out." "Yes sir," said Smith. This was Frank Boyden's first case of discipline, and no more important case has come up in his forty years of service.

Late that afternoon a townswoman who had seen the principal crossing the road in the morning leaned over her fence to exchange ideas with a neighbor who was working in his garden. "I saw the new principal this morning," she said. "He'll never do."

"You're wrong," chuckled the gardener. "I was at their football practice this afternoon. We've got a man."

On that first day Mr. Boyden called on Captain Ephraim Williams, a patriarch of the village. He found him sitting in a rocking chair before a blazing fire, a shawl on one arm and in his other hand a fan. "I have a shawl and a fan," he said, "because I am not sure whether I am going to have a chill or a fever." But Captain Ephraim Williams, like Sophia Smith and Mary Lyon, thought the education of the Deerfield Valley of supreme importance. These people were willing to scrimp that boys and girls might be educated. Consider Dickinson hired a woman to keep house for him at twenty-five cents a week, and when he discovered that she was saving money on it he married her! In the old cemetery at Deerfield are two tombstones, and on the bottom of one is the following inscription: "These stones were gratuitously erected by Consider Dickinson in memory of his Father and Mother-in-law." But Consider Dickinson and his wife left their fortune to found the Dickinson High School in order that the boys and girls of Deerfield might have an education.

Seldom if ever can the ways and means of education which have proved successful in one country, one school, and, I am almost tempted to say, in one teacher's classes be transplanted to another country, school, or class. In education, certainly, the style is the man. So, to approach the secret of Mr. Boyden's great administration at Deerfield, it is necessary to know something about the town itself.

With its wide streets, spreading elms, old colonial houses, and exciting ancient history, it is, of course, one of the most beautiful and fascinating towns in New England. In the seventeenth century the settlement was several times raided by the Indians, the most serious raid being in 1704, when many captives were carried off to Canada, some never to return. In one of the earlier raids on Deerfield and the neighboring town of Hadley, tradition has it that one of the "regicides" who had condemned King Charles to death reappeared to warn and rally the defenders. With the somewhat later history of Deerfield is connected the name of Eleazar Williams, undoubtedly the great-grandson of the Reverend John Williams, of Deerfield, and somewhat more doubtfully the "Lost Dauphin" of France, as he steadfastly maintained he was until his death in 1858. The "Lost Dauphin" once told George Sheldon, the historian: "When I am on the throne of France, I'll send over a battleship and take all the people of Deerfield to Paris and give them a good time."

Deerfield has always been more a part of the world than some of its small neighbors, and its inhabitants for centuries have been not only readers and lovers of books but, together with scenes and settings in Deerfield, the stuff of which literature and art are made. Somehow the chance remark which a wonderful lady of over eighty made to me this summer seemed to epitomize the spirit of the place better than I can. "In Deerfield," she said with some pride, "we have always danced."

2

Some sixty years ago Polish people began coming to the Valley, to cultivate the tobacco and onion fields. Saving their money and buying up farms, they have become a very substantial part of the population of the region. Even in 1902 they were there in great numbers, and whatever admiration one may feel for cultivated natives of Poland, one cannot help thinking that the granite doorsteps of Yankee farmers were probably more fertile soil for seeds of education than the front yards of immigrant Polish peasants. Nevertheless, Frank Boyden set about spreading the gospel that

every boy and every girl in the neighborhood should have an education, and that they should get their education at Deerfield Academy.
So the new principal hitched up his buggy and began to call on
the neighbors and the people of the surrounding farms. To any
one who knows Frank Boyden, that was a perfectly characteristic
thing to do. He has an interest in people which is genuine, and many
of the staunchest supporters of Deerfield Academy today are the
sons and the daughters of the people whom he called on forty
years ago.

From the first it became apparent that it was the new principal's
ambition to make of Deerfield Academy a community school.
Besides an evident belief in athletics as a kind of scholastic tonic
and, for the town, a social solvent, he soon showed concern for
the social manners of his boys and girls. The four receptions a
year which he arranged may not seem to be an infallible recipe
for social graces, but they pleased the town and Mr. Boyden.
Consequently, they were popular in school. The neighbors brought
in ice cream and cake, and the neighbors have been doing so ever
since. When one goes to the great commencement dinner where at
the present time fifteen or sixteen hundred people sit down, some
part of the dinner, you will find, has been brought in by the
neighbors.

Naturally, when a strange young man comes to town and begins
to secure a foothold, local prejudice and opposition appear, and
that happened here. The political leaders of the town did not like
to have their control questioned. But the good women of Deerfield were staunch allies of the new principal. One morning on
the post-office steps a local politician was heard to mutter as he
stroked his beard, "These women are raising hell around here.
They want to cut off from the check list the names of voters who
have died. Why, if we did that, we shouldn't have enough voters
in Deerfield to send a representative to Boston."

I do not propose to describe the difficulties which Mr. Boyden
encountered. Year after year in town meeting the voters saw the
wisdom of granting the money which he asked for his school, from
1876 to 1924 a combination of the Dickinson High School and
Deerfield Academy. On occasion, however, some few ventured
the opinion that the principal was actually stealing the school from
the town and seeking to make it his own. Eventually the amend-
ment to the State Constitution making it illegal to appropriate

public money for private institutions made it impossible for the town to continue its generous gift, and it established its own high school in South Deerfield. For a time it seemed that Mr. Boyden's work was to end in failure, and that the growing respect and affection which he had inspired in town was to end only in pleasant memories. This deprivation, however, proved to be the greatest single influence in making Deerfield Academy a national scchool. Mr. Boyden's instinct for appraising a situation is close to unerring. On this occasion, as on others, he stood by his guns, refused to make weakening compromises, retained the respect and affection of the town—and, providentially, received financial succor from friends at a distance. Mr. Boyden never speaks of those days of struggle and discouragement, but they were an important element in making him the man he is today.

3

To the old friend no less than to the casual visitor the same teasing question remains unanswered: "What is the secret of Deerfield Academy?" To say "Frank Boyden" is to make no real reply, for the school and the man are inseparable. Mention of his name brings to mind a shy, quick, unobtrusive, short-statured, spectacled man in his early sixties, having no marks of the athlete, no pretensions of the scholar, no assurance of the businessman. His dress is invariably sober, even somber. A more obviously selfless person could hardly exist. Certainly Frank Boyden is no type, yet Deerfield Academy is as clearly the image of its principal as ever was inked impression on a printed page. In the one as in the other you find the same honesty, simplicity, earnestness, and interest—the same lack of ostentation in what they have, and the same welcome for what they seem to think you can bring. This idea may be one of the great secrets of effective education anywhere.

Interest—the quick, real interest in the other person; the human interest that years ago prompted Frank Boyden to hitch up his horse and go call on his neighbors; the interest that inspires quiet questions rather than showy answers—that seems to be the secret of Boyden and of Deerfield. No one can fool schoolboys for long. They are quick to detect any insincerity, any hypocrisy, anything that is not genuine. They are equally quick to respond to sincerity, to real interest, to genuine affection. They know when a school, from the head down, cares. The honorary degree given to Mr. Boyden by Yale a few years ago was given "for his researches into the minds and hearts of youth." And no one knows better than he that it is hearts that should logically come first. "I have never known a teacher," said a former pupil of his, "who has so completely given himself to one object, and that object the development of character."

Mr. Boyden has always kept in close contact with boys. He accepts no boy without first having had a personal interview with him. In the fall, when school starts, he meets new and old boys separately every evening for the first few weeks. By Thanksgiving he has instilled into the hundred or more newcomers so much of the spirit of the school that they are indistinguishable from boys who have been in Deerfield two, three, or four years. Very early Mr. Boyden informs the students that he has few rules and no penalties. By some magic, perhaps that of keeping them busy, he makes them content with the few strict rules that do exist.

Once Mr. Boyden asked a man working in the stable how he managed horses so well. "I manage horses just the way you manage boys," the man replied; "give them a little rope but not too much." I am sure that Mr. Boyden's knowledge of horses and love of horses have helped him in his management of boys. Only this summer, in the midst of an important conference where a college president and heads of schools were in solemn conclave, a high-spirited horse broke his halter in the Deerfield stable and dashed out into the school garden. Mr. Boyden, with no excitement, left us for perhaps five minutes, then quietly returned to his place at the table. I learned afterwards that he had caught and led back into his stall a horse which nobody else in town would have been able to manage. "Work 'em hard, play 'em hard, feed 'em up to the nines, and send 'em to bed so tired that they are asleep before their heads are on the pillow," was the summary of the Deerfield method that he once gave to an old friend of his in the town.

It would seem impossible for any other headmaster to run his school as Mr. Boyden runs his. Imagine having your desk in the midst of a hallway through which all the boys in school pass in the course of a morning. He must have an enormous correspondence, and perhaps he can dictate some letters while sitting at his desk, but I have never seen him do it. There he sits, and boy after boy stops, asks him a question or two, and then passes on. It is Mr. Boyden's method of knowing his boys. I once said to him, "How in the world can you be a schoolmaster with so many interruptions?" "Well," he said, "there are always interruptions in life." Many times, however, I have seen him on a motor trip, dictating letters to his secretary hour after hour. When the task is finished, the secretary takes the train back to Deerfield, with notebook full, to type the letters which Mr. Boyden signs on his return. Many of the rest of us are overborne by our correspondence. He makes correspondence secondary.

The most important element in Mr. Boyden's success with boys and girls is not only his interest in them but his genuine interest in their interests. Love for boys is a great advantage if the boys do not know it. Psychology is a handy gift if other people do not know it. After forty years he still coaches the baseball, football, and basketball teams.

Early in his career at Deerfield, Mr. Boyden took his baseball team to a neighboring town for a game. So busy in making arrangements had he been that he had no time for breakfast that morning. When he got to town where the game was to be played and had attended to numerous necessary details, he discovered that he would have no time for luncheon, either. In the sixteen-inning game which followed, Mr. Boyden distinguished himself both at bat and in the field. On his return in the train that evening Mr. Boyden, for the first time in his life, "passed out" completely. No words of devotion, of course, could have ever begun to express so much. The members of the team, who in some instances had been sent to Deerfield to break up the school, told Mr. Boyden to go home for a week; they said that they would run the school!

One beautiful October afternoon not long ago, when the Deerfield Valley was at its best and the maple trees around the playing fields were bright with autumn, the football team was playing Loomis. Late in the game Deerfield had the ball on the Loomis five-yard line. Looking over at Frank Boyden, who was sitting on the bench surrounded by excited substitutes, just as the ball was put into play, the wife of one of the masters was heard to breathe, as quick tears came into her eyes, "Put it over, oh, put it over. Do it for the Little Fellow." What boys and girls, men and women, parents, towns people, and friends from afar have done and will do "for the Little Fellow" is one of the glories of Deerfield.

Nor is his interest confined to boys. The girls, a comparatively small number, who have been to Deerfield know also of Mr. Boyden's sympathy and understanding. Some years ago there was in school a Polish girl. Disobedient, rebellious, and indifferent to appeals of all sorts, she was one of the very few who had ever seemed untouched by the spirit of the school. After leaving Deerfield she kept books in her father's store. There she was still unhappy and dissatisfied. Somehow Mr. Boyden learned that her ambition was to go to Normal School. Saying nothing to anybody, he went to the school, got a place for her, and then faced the difficult task of persuading her father to release his bookkeeper. Eventually he succeeded. After finishing at the Normal School, this girl taught Vermont Yankees in a school of her own! Later on she confessed to Mr. Boyden the cause of her difficulties in Deerfield. "I thought you were trying to change me from being a Pole," she said.

One day two Polish boys came to the principal and said that they wanted to attend Deerfield Academy. "Why do you want to come?" he asked. Almost in unison the two replied, "So we can sit on the bleachers." He has put a good many Polish boys and girls on the bleachers, and the imagination which he has shown in dealing with this alien element in the community has been a source of great strength for the Academy.

Other examples of this same sympathetic, understanding imagination (which perhaps may still better be called "interest") come to mind. At the end of a very busy day a particularly garrulous mother, with her son, got to Mr. Boyden. The longer the mother talked, the more convinced Mr. Boyden was that the boy should not come to Deerfield. As they were leaving the room, the boy looked at the principal and said, "I do want to come so much." Immediately the half-hour explanation of why his admission would be impossible went by the board. "You shall," said Mr. Boyden.

A few years ago a young fellow with an exceedingly poor preparation for the work applied late in the summer for admission. The principal was obliged to tell the boy and his parents that there was absolutely no place for him. When school started in September, to the surprise of everyone, this boy appeared with the rest. Not having the heart to send him home at once, Mr.

Boyden told him to stay around if he wanted to do so, but that he doubted very much if there would be room. Teachers who had sampled what he had to offer were even more positive. After a week, however, a vacancy occurred, and Mr. Boyden sent word that he might have a term's trial. That night, as he was bidding him good night, the principal asked him how he liked the school. "Pretty well," said the boy, "but I think you ought to have a box in the school where boys could drop their complaints." "I have been here for only an hour," said the son of a United States Congressman, "but I have already discovered seven or eight things which could be improved."

Mr. Boyden has a sense of humor with a New England tang to it. Like a wise schoolmaster, he does not use this humor at the expense of his boys. I imagine that most of his graduates are impressed with other qualities. He has a firm directness in his dealings with his pupils which they understand and admire. I have never heard him "jolly" them or use sarcasm, but the humor is there. No one likes a good story more, though he tells few himself. No one chuckles more over a witty bit of repartee. He is the cause of humor in others, but since 1919 he has been too busy and his job too serious to spend much time in pleasantries.

Every Deerfield boy and every man who knows much about Deerfield has heard the story of Tom Ashley. There is not space here to tell again what I consider to be the best American story of a boy's development and a remarkably clear illustration of Mr. Boyden's philosophy of education. The gist of it is that Tom Ashley came to Deerfield as an inarticulate, underdeveloped, almost hopeless boy. Within four years he was the leading boy in school— a great athlete, a fine scholar at Deerfield and, later, at Amherst; he subsequently died leading his troops in Belleau Wood. The most prized scholarship at Amherst is the one named for Tom Ashley.

But how did Tom Ashley happen to come to Deerfield in the first place? When Mr. Boyden discovered him in the town, this unhappy boy's only asset seemed to be that he was strong for his years. Mr. Boyden asked him to come to the Academy, but Tom grunted a refusal. On the first day of school Mr. Boyden asked Tom's father to come to the village post office with his son just before school was going to start. During the conversation with his father, Mr. Boyden broke off suddenly to say, "There's the bell,

Tom. Would you mind going up to the school and opening the door? Tell Miss Hawkes that I will be there in a few minutes." Tom, glad of something to do, took the keys to the school and did as he was told. Then he waited around for Mr. Boyden. Mr. Boyden was busy all the morning and kept out of Tom's way. When it was time for lunch, he asked Tom to stay. After lunch he said to Tom, "You know about some of these young fellows who are coming from the high school this year. I don't know anything about them. Won't you go out and help them with their football this afternoon?" This was the one thing which Tom would have been willing to do, and from that afternoon he was a bona fide member of Deerfield Academy. I should say that Tom Ashley did more for Deerfield Academy than any other boy who has gone there in these forty years. It was Tom Ashley, according to the principal, who persuaded Mr. Boyden that Deerfield should cease being a local school and should open to boys from all parts of the country.

4

The grade at Deerfield is high. Early in a boy's career his choice of college is decided on, and the work he shall take to attain his own objective. There is, I believe, no school catalogue. The development of the apparent capabilities in each boy is the system and, so far as is feasible, each boy sets his own standard. The result is a belief in the school, on the part of teachers and boys, which I have seldom seen equaled. The relationship between the boy and authority is simple, direct, personal. Mr. Boyden has never been satisfied with giving his boys the best training possible and then sending them to college to sink or swim. If in the first term at college the danger signals are flying, Mr. Boyden has been known to get boys back to Deerfield during the Christmas vacation for a checkup and, if it is deemed necessary, for help.

The faculty at Deerfield is well paid; Mr. Boyden has made a great point of this, and in the advice he gives to younger headmasters (and there is no head of a school whose advice is more sought after) he always says: "The first requisite of a successful school is that the teacher should be well paid." One of the things which strike the visitor at Deerfield is the enthusiasm of the faculty. They need enthusiasm, for the duties they have to perform are varied. There always seem to be three or four teachers around, whose greatest pleasure is to show the school to strangers or to entertain the numerous visitors. In most schools the members of the faculty are rarely seen by the visitor; at Deerfield the teachers seem to be a visible part of the school.

Not long ago, just before commencement, one of the rare instances of fatal illness in school came to a senior in Deerfield. In spite of good doctors and good care the boy was sinking fast. Almost the last request he made was to ask if he could be given his diploma earlier than other members of his class. When Mr. Boyden brought it to the sickroom, the boy looked up, smiled, and said, "Well, I made the grade."

In all this care, concern, and devotion Frank Boyden has been aided by Mrs. Boyden, who since 1905 has been the very heart of the machine. Mrs. Boyden is an unusual scholar in science and in mathematics, a rare teacher, and she has given herself, as Mr. Boyden has done, completely to the school. Ask Deerfield boys about Mrs. Boyden, and you will get answers which deepen your faith in the importance of schools.

I have said very little directly about the religious side of Deerfield. After Mr. Boyden had been in the Academy about a year a sincere but perplexed old lady in the town said, "One of our last principals always carried a Bible in his hand, but the religious interest in the school was very low. I have never seen Mr. Boyden with a Bible, but he seems to have brought here a profound religious faith." Indeed, Mr. Boyden speaks very little about religion. I have heard him quote only one passage from the Bible in his speeches, but I have heard him quote this one a number of times: "Whatsoever things are true, whatsoever things are honorable. . . . whatsoever things are lovely, whatsoever things are of good report; if there be any virtue, and if there be any praise, think on these things." That seems to be the core of his faith. As you sit with him and his boys on a Sunday night before the fireplace, and the School sings hymns and listens to a good speaker who understands the heart of youth, you regain something that the last twenty years have made obscure: a belief in whatsoever things are honorable or of good report.

No account of Mr. Bolden would be complete without mention of this side of him. When a great architect was surveying Deerfield before a new building project, he estimated that some elm trees on the campus would have to be cut down. "No," said Mr. Boyden, "I can't lose my shadows. When boys rush out of the schoolroom in the afternoon into the sunlight they may be noisy and turbulent, but when they reach the shadows of the trees, they become quiet and orderly." I doubt if any other schoolmaster has made such practical use of this bit of psychology.

I well remember the first time I saw Mr. Boyden. It was the last day of the winter term in 1919. It had been a hard winter, with more sickness than usual, and Mrs. Perry had asked me at breakfast what I was going to do that day. "I shall dismiss the school, clear my desk, and then sleep for fourteen hours," I replied. Only the first part of the program was successfully carried out. About eleven o'clock a stranger came into my office, a short, energetic man with what seemed to be particularly large glasses. Of all things, he carried under his arm pictures of school buildings and school boys. Now every head of a school is in the way of seeing a good many pictures of school buildings, and I was not immediately very much interested. But we sat down, and Frank Boyden began to talk about Deerfield. For the first time I heard the story of Tom Ashley. For the first time I realized what a private school could do for a community, though this came by inference, not from what Mr. Boyden told me. For the first time I felt an excitement about this school in the Deerfield Valley. Finally Mr. Boyden said, "I hope I'm not keeping you from your lunch." "Oh, no," I said; "It's not nearly lunch time yet." But when I looked at my watch, I found that it was a quarter to three. The experience that was mine has been duplicated, I imagine, by many other listeners entranced by the magic of Frank Boyden.

★ *If we work upon marble, it will perish; if we work upon brass, time will efface it; if we rear temples, they will crumble into dust; but if we work upon immortal minds, if we imbue them with principles, with the just fear of God and love of our fellow men, we engrave on those tablets something that will brighten to all eternity.*

DANIEL WEBSTER

YE SCHOOLMASTER'S CALENDAR

by Frederick James Moffitt

A compendium of prognostications,
forecasts, warnings and hints for pedagogues.

JANUARY

Mostly, it snows, except in California and Florida, where board members and taxpayers are taking their vacations. Mostly, the school roofs spring leaks, the buildings creak and groan, and the school buses develop pernicious anemia. The janitor loses his cheery smile as the heating plant languishes with a severe case of rickets, and the classrooms are too hot or too cold, depending upon who is talking. Icicles hang from the cornices and the Taxpayers' Association. Chilblains itch the school budget.

The birds of the air grow fewer in number, so the Bird Watchers Society decides that the newest teachers may bear a little watching. The Watchers are joined by other citizens with similar ideas and leisure time, and the community bridge clubs are enlivened thereby. Virtually everybody enjoys the indoor sport but those watched.

Now the hardy pigeons, along with sparrows, grackles and itinerant bookmen, take up their winter quarters at the school. Their raucous songs add to the merriness of midwinter and the pigeons bill and coo. But this is the season when the local merchants have ceased to coo and only bill!

A few students go ice fishing and are promptly dunked, but their loss does not materially lower the scholastic averages. The principal sports of January are basketball. The basketball team wins or loses the championship, either one of which is equally disastrous for the school superintendent.

The executive desk gradually piles up with the debris of midwinter: rejected report cards, an unfinished dissertation, circa 1920, dismembered paper clips, repossessed postage stamps minus the original glue, bills, curriculums and curricula, memos about this-a and that-a, lost mittens and overshoes, and other impedimenta which probably seemed important at the time. They make an effective shelter for hibernation.

In mid-January comes the annual thaw, the rains, the mud, the slosh, the hope of better things ahead. The following week winter returns, and few school superintendents will really believe that these are among the most exciting days of the teaching year.

FEBRUARY

Every day now it snows a little bit more, and the roads alternately freeze and slush so that the school bus can no longer pick up the hill kids, nor can the school get State Aid for its attendance quota. The only reply to the superintendent's applications for that job in California, Florida, Liberia and points south is an overtinted picture post card from his predecessor, who knew when to get out while the getting was good!

The air crackles with static electricity, and the simplest light switch becomes a shocker for the unwary, but that doesn't pay the mounting electric bills which will generate a different kind of electricity when they are presented to the board of education.

Out in the Midwest the basketball season arises in crescendo and gore as sectional championships are piled on sectional championships and the blood flows freely. In the more effete eastern sections the glee clubs are practicing for the Easter Music Festival in order to get a head start on the cunning little cold germs who are likewise marshaling their forces for that selfsame celebration!

The Ski Club boobytraps muddy halls with poles, rubbers, wax and broken kneecaps, while the Homemakers' Club boobytraps the unwary superintendent with cakes, cookies, crumpets and calories.

The month drags a little bit, and the faculty gives thanks for the old emperor who stole a day from February to make a celebration in August. Although now the sap begins to run and the pussy willow swells with buds, many a school superintendent will assert that these are not among the merriest days of the pedagogical year.

MARCH

Spring creeps slowly up from the Southland, and now the border school superintendents are holding outdoor classes in their new campus-type schools and frantically competing with the catfish to try to get a quorum at roll calls. But mostly, March is moody, and so are school folk. Whether it's weather or what, the trouble curve rises sharply, and the taxpayers come out of their winter quarters ready for trouble. Herbivorously speaking, the little grievances which have been frozen up send forth their hardy tendrils, and everybody complains that the cafeteria meals aren't what they used to be and probably never were.

But the air is bracing. The superintendent congratulates himself that the school has escaped the annual epidemic of measles, and the next day he himself comes down with mumps, after having exposed the entire kindergarten. There are some who say that he probably did it on purpose, for they wouldn't put it past him. (Ah there, Mrs. Busty!)

Faculty meetings grow listless, and there are mysterious huddles among the teaching staff. Vague and muttered references are made about stratospheric salary schedules and offers of fine positions in faraway places, but no such offers clutter the desk of the superintendent. Community gossip is to the effect that he will be lucky if he can stay where he is!

Yet there is something in the March wind that buoys up his spirit. Maybe it's the first robin that chirps outside his window, or the little lamb gamboling on the hill, or the bluejays calling from the old maples. More likely, it's because the quarterly examinations are over and the senior class casualties are fewer than he suspected. It looks, too, as if the school building is going to stand up another year, and the school board has decided that a little salary increase might be given to the teachers, if and when.

Whatever it is, it's good, and many a schoolmaster is sure that teaching school is a pretty satisfying job, after all, and that the latter days of March are among the most stimulating in the march of months.

APRIL

The earth turns. The sun enters Aries, and the world wobbles on its axis. So does the school superintendent if there is any wobble left in him after the winter storms. The bees begin to hum softly and sharpen their stingers for busy work in June. The raucous cries of the crows resound as they flock together for their annual gabbles. April is the month of school conventions, confabs and conferences.

It is house cleaning time in the land. The housewife, clearing the attic, finds ancient pictures which she donates to the school, and the Stag at Bay, slightly cracked, is hung in the study hall despite howls of anguish from the art teacher. The superintendent, too, feels the urge to clean house and attacks the debris on his desk with renewed vigor and nostalgic memories. The mildewed stack of petitions for his removal, the letters of protest condemning his actions and person, the photographs of the class of 1910—whatever made him think they should be saved? The tarnished loving cup (now a receptacle for leaky nonleakable fountain pens and broken indestructible pencils) which once proudly signified a school victory in some long forgotten hassle—whyever did he think it made any difference in his community relations?

In the grip of April madness, he consigns the whole business to the wastebasket. It is retrieved later by an alert secretary, who realizes that these mementos will help strengthen his soul in any battles ahead.

Hardly has April Fool's Day passed, with the school board inclined to make merry over renewal of contracts, than Arbor Day, the harbinger of Spring, descends upon the school with belated ice, snow, sleet and hail. The children skip and sing as they gaily plant the memorial arbor tree and contract runny noses. The dendrologists assure the superintendent that trees should be planted in October, but Arbor Day is a pretty thought nevertheless, and the tree can be removed stealthily as soon at it withers.

The superintendent busies himself by cutting down orders for library books to pay the bill for newer and gaudier uniforms for the band. Classes in baton twirling increase in numbers, activity and lack of outer garments, and indeed a school administrator feels a pleasant kinship to the batons as, gyrating, they rise and fall.

There is a great flexing of muscles, not only among the physical education folk, as they arrange playdays and other mass disturbances, but also among parents, taxpayers and pro bono publicos.

But the superintendent, good husbandman that he is, continues quietly to plant and prepare, and there are many who will agree that these are the pleasantest days in a school year.

MAY

There is a healing balm in the air, the days grow longer and the sunsets more lovely. The school administrator settles back, happy in the knowledge that another successful school year is drawing to a close. In increasing numbers the feathered friends return from their winter vacations. The big Breasted Viragos, the Screeching Pee-Wees, the Rubble-Throated Gnat-Strainers and the common American Cackler rebusy themselves in the affairs of their young, while the Pye-Eyed Cuckoos add to the merry community medley of song.

Flowers bloom. In the northland the shadbacks burst in their few days of glory, and throughout the land the lilacs flower briefly and fade. So with the superintendent, who is invited to speak at the district P.T.A. and feted by the Mothers Club, following which, like the lilacs he fades into one more bramble along the wayside.

The schools rush toward the climax of June even though the graduates-to-be—or not to be—develop sudden limps and sprains. In some sections May Day is observed with a Queen of the May (who, by amazing coincidence, is also the daughter of the school board president) chosen amidst acclaim and recrimination. In former times May Day was celebrated with merry dancing, a practice strongly condemned by the Puritans. In many schools now the sophomores hop and the juniors prom in May, but the Puritans still stick around. Some school administrators declare a "skip" day when the young folk are given a vacation as an antidote for Spring Fever; others don't declare but the kids do. Baseball leagues open their season, circuses come to town, and grandmothers die by the dozen. The wise superintendent sits on the popping lid and grins reassuringly because there isn't much else he can do about it.

Truth to tell, he is busy arranging his finances for the summer. All past experience points to a long, dry time and a special personal draught in August unless he can persuade the local bank to carry him as it always has by ancient and honorable tradition. But, despite these minor annoyances, the teachers, scholars and superintendents generally agree that the days of May are surely the most enjoyable of all the merry months of pedagogy.

JUNE

So, this is it! The birds sing, the daisies and buttercups bloom, and Indian paintbrush covers the meadows. But all these kindly evidences of nature's good will are unheeded by the school superintendent, who is caught in the protocol of commencement tickets, who, how many, and you better find them or else!

Final revisions must be made in the Commencement program. The big-name speaker, who accepted the date so assuringly some months ago, is monetarily seduced by a neighboring district; the tuba player is suddenly called up for military service; the director of the school choir is laid low with a strep throat and a mean disposition, and the piccolo player falls in a nearby ditch. The school administrator, bachelor of all musical instruments and master of none, must substitute for the piccolo player if "Pomp and Circumstance" is to be rendered with its accustomed squeals.

The local printer not only misspells the names of graduates but leaves out prominent participants and italicizes those who have failed the final hurdle. Hurriedly, the programs are reprinted with the order of march reversed and the pure Latin of the class motto so mangled that the community's old Harvard graduate will point with alarm for years to come.

Relying upon confident advice from the weatherman, the board of education decrees an outdoor commencement. As usual, it rains, and the spectators flee, but our Master of Ceremonies must stay to the bitter end. Community rumor is thereby vindicated, for there are many who claim that he doesn't know enough to come in and out of the rain, anyway. (Ah there, Mrs. Busty!)

It is over all too soon. Once more the birds sing; again those of the daisies and buttercups that have not been uprooted to supply stage decorations lift their pretty heads. Again, the sun shines, and, as the superintendent thoughtfully packs up the caps and gowns (three missing and no arrangements to finance them) for return to the supply company, he will agree that these June days rank high among the happy days in a pretty good sort of a world after all.

JULY

Summer blooms, and there is a mad rush to get somewhere else, even though it may be much more uncomfortable than here. The propaganda from summer camps works its will on parents and kiddies alike. The young are packed, sandwiched and forwarded in great quantities to parking places where they will learn words and deeds not yet included in school curriculums by the most liberal educational innovators. The uncouth learnings, however, will be blamed on the schools in September.

For a brief space, the school superintendent is left to ponder on his uprisings and down-sittings, particularly the latter, which are in the majority. As he sits in his quiet office, writing reports that will never be read and correcting the examination papers left by fleeing teachers, the only sounds which disturb the executive noddings are the buzzings of the master clock as it finishes its untimely course and the squeakings of the mice as they merrily chew the wainscoting and beget their families without janitorial interference. There are a few phone calls asking for help on crossword puzzles, but aside from such routine the office is as deserted and lonely as any other banged-up battlefield.

The July superintendent is torn with difficult decisions—Shall he flaunt the Taxpayers' Association to go on a few weeks' vacation? Shall he dare let the belated applications for college entrance pile up on his desk, knowing well that he will pay for it later? Or shall he join that naïve and persevering group that actually believes that doctoral degrees can be obtained by attendance at some beautifully indefinite number of summer school sessions? Better, and more productive, to buy himself a butterfly net and chase the elusive lepidoptera on the sunny hillsides.

But July is not really so bad. There is always a little time to read the good books that have gone unread for gosh! these many months, a space to get reacquainted with the family, some happy mornings to work over the educational article that will eventually be rejected by an unsympathetic publisher, and a moment or two to admire the evening sky as the sun sinks below the hills—these are satisfying days offered by no other profession on earth in quite so great a degree.

AUGUST

Now, the wild raspberries ripen in the brambles and, from sad experience, who kens the raspberry more intimately than the school superintendent? Now, the distant hills are a little tired and dusty and so is the tag-end of the vacation period. Parents, children, teachers, school administrators, and a long-suffering populace look forward to the beginning of school when civilization will again take control.

The dog days come, and late summer madness descends upon the community. The Legions assemble for marching contests, the firemen gather for carnivals, and the pitchmen unfold their tents for the county fairs. These gala fracases are not open to the school superintendent except in his ex officio capacity, where he is drafted as judge (the oldest fire engine), conciliator (is bingo harmful to the young?) and provider of reluctant school bands and queens for the cornstalk festival. His ability, wisdom and judgment in these important decisions are violently disputed by all participants, and his critics grow in numbers and vociferocity. He is amazed to discover his most demure little teacher as drum majorette in the gaudiest parade. Truly, he lives in an ivory tower, and there are unplumbed talents in his faculty of which he has not been aware. The summer camps are closing, and the little inmates return loaded with their pet frogs, snakes, newts and poison ivy. The biology teacher may welcome the supply of new specimens, but the remainder of the faculty is not so enthusiastic. Now the crickets and newcomers to the district take up their chorus, and the world is filled with their pipings. These are days of bittersweet with summer almost gone and the plans for the year ahead still only plans on the superintendent's desk.

Now, there are last minute repairs to be made in the buildings, last minute speculations as to whether the school buses will survive another winter, last minute compromises in the amount of cubic space per child, last minute defeats on the age of entrance into kindergarten because Mrs. Busty never heard of the "planned family" campaign, last minute appeals to teachers who have been compromised by neighboring districts.

But there are also last minute hikes and last minute fishing trips, last minute campfires, and last minute farewell parties. For the days of summer are numbered, and the number rapidly diminishes, but these are times of great anticipation and planning for another year.

SEPTEMBER

There is an erroneous assumption among the uninformed laity that the year begins in January. School administrators know better. In all well regulated school districts the year actually begins the first Tuesday after the first Monday after the first unwilling faculty meeting in September. In the slightly pixilated educational calendar, commencement marks the end of the year, while the final equinox is the beginning. The month of harvest is the time of planting!

In the elementary school the youngsters are sorted without too much difficulty and packed for processing, but it is in the upper reaches where real trouble begins. Strange and fearful credentials are presented for evaluation and placement, schedules tangle themselves inextricably, spare rooms evaporate into thin air, and there is shocking shortage of seating space. New teachers wander disconsolately looking for nonexistent classes as the selfsame classes dash madly for out. It seems impossible that a foresighted superintendent could have planned everything so inefficiently. But on the following day, when lost bus drivers have been located, new football candidates have been recruited, and the condemned furniture has been removed from the storeroom for one more try, a great calm and peace descend upon the scene. The year is under way.

There are, of course, minor annoyances for the front office—someone will surely demand an investigation of the price of cafeteria meatballs, the football coach will come under severe criticism after the ill starred game with Murder Hill, the unfortunate absence of the three R's will be linked to communistic tendencies of the janitor, clamor will arise that the books in the school library are subversive, the new guidance director will be accused of making ill tempered remarks about the community, and one or two unblooded teachers, deciding that teaching is not their forte, will depart forthwith.

However, the now renewed superintendent need lose no sleep

over these small happenings. It is September, the month of beginnings, of flaming leaves, when days are warm and clear and pleasant. Indeed the nicest days of the whole school year.

OCTOBER

Now, the Parent-Teacher Association organizes for the year with new officers and plans for action. Unable to draft any chairmen for the Committees on Membership, Finance and Entertainment, the president appoints the superintendent, ex officio and without enthusiasm. As he takes over the triple responsibility, he finds himself involved in new troubles. The Membership Committee presents the least difficulty because he can always put the heat on recalcitrant parents by judicious use of community rivalries, contests and prizes (an ever-bearing cactus plant for Grade 5). The Finance Committee is more demanding, for the cookie fund shows a deficit of 80 cents for which the chairman must account. Some mild finagling with the cafeteria supplies is probably in order. It is with the Entertainment Committee, however, that the superintendent really runs into trouble. Free speakers are likely to be a little too free, and last year's Christmas pageant has already been used up and depleted. In desperation, he double-dates a speaker whom he has obtained for the local service club. Ruefully, he learns that the jokes for service clubbers and P.T.A.ers are not entirely compatible.

Shinbones, shoulder pads, helmets, and broken noses pile up in every corner, and the smell of Dr. Whoosis' Rubbing Compound pervades each nook and cranny of the school, for now the football season enters its most sanguinary phase. Bandaged-headed heroes limp through the corridors, self-appointed quarterbacks plot diagrams on the newly scrubbed walls, and over-age alumni make futile attempts to regain their scholastic eligibility. Letters of condemnation appear in the sports columns of the local newspapers, and the superintendent's own unbrilliant record as a member of the Yale Scrubs of 1915 is exhumed for head shaking analysis. As the Letters to the Editor increase, the school administrator wonders if the current emphasis on the communicative arts is not being a bit overdone. He is in a sad dilemma, for, if the football team clobbers the neighboring district, he loses some fine professional friendships, but, if it fails to clobber, his local supporters grow cold and distant.

Now the hunting season opens, and the ensuing racket is not wholly confined to the local deer or pheasant population. Unfortunately, there is no closed season on school superintendents, and school patrons show marked ability at stalking, sniping and still hunting, while the usual "drives" go forward with unabated enthusiasm. Many a school administrator ponders on the anomaly that the state demands definite qualifications for hunting licenses and keeps careful census on casualties on the deer population, but superintendents are stalked without benefit of license or other credentials. Maybe it is because superintendents can be replaced with less trouble than mooses can.

Now comes the modern style Halloween, and the community is organized for parades, parties and similar psychiatric outlets for youthful spirits. The littlest kiddies show an inventive capacity of which the superintendent should be proud—but he isn't. The janitorial staff presents new demands for salary increase because of extra labors in collecting dedunked doughnuts from unlikely corners.

But October has its compensation—the crisp sparkling air, the honeyed days of Indian Summer, the first unmortgaged paycheck, the success of teachers who didn't seem to have it, the spectacular progress of seniors who yesterday were kindergartners, the power of teaching and of learning, the joy of progress—it is now that these glories come to every school superintendent in gracious abundance.

NOVEMBER

As the days grow shorter, the gathering-in and settling down proceeds apace. The raucous shouts from the football field are muted as the team continues to fall part, and the community agrees that the unfortunate record is due entirely to the superintendent and his fantastic and unrealistic attitudes toward scholarship. There is a vague feeling that there ought to be a change of policy or, better yet, a change of school administrators. But, glory be! Football now yields to basketball, and here we go again!

In the northern climes, storm warnings are erected and storm windows are hoisted to exclude what little sunshine and fresh air may have formerly found their way into the executive office. In the South, the superintendent is busy preparing for the hordes of vacationing migrants who will shortly descend with demands for added room, more sunlight, newer curriculums, and greater prominence in the school play. Suggestions and complaints will gush forth from the vacationers who probably never had it so good before.

Election time draws nigh. Candidates for office plot new ways by which to exploit the little ones and get across their appeals for votes. Glad-handing gentlemen and persuasive ladies, hitherto aloof, express a burning desire to speak at assembly programs, donate small prizes for forensic contests, provide blotters with patriotic mottoes, or just be good friends and let's forget the past. Fortunately, all schools are completely divorced from the political arena (Ah there, Mrs. Busty!) and the astute superintendent can take these joyous manifestations of good will in his normal stride. Years of political finagling in his own professional organizations have kept him in the pink of condition for the less bloody contests among the laity. Nevertheless, he who boasts a Republican wife, a Democratic father-in-law, and a mother who is a past president of the Daughters of Temperance may well feel a smug measure of security denied to less fortunate planners.

Election Day being over, American Education Week becomes the next movable feast where the school head can strike a lusty blow for public relations. Each year this gala affair increases in momentum. Visiting days, school assemblies, radio announcements, canned and uncanned speeches, newspaper releases (fill in your own name, pedigree and condition of the populace), commemorative stamps, posters, booklets, scripts, bumper strips, napkins, parades, window displays, and the kitchen sink—all these aids are available to anyone writing or wiring headquarters. The conglomoration of public relations materials will probably slightly confuse the public, which feels that it has mostly been in favor of education right along.

It is with some relief that the school superintendent looks forward to the Thanksgiving celebration, for although all pretense of study is abandoned in order that misshapen turkeys may have the blackboard space and the Pilgrims may argue with the Indians at too many successive school assemblies, yet there is something indefinable around the place—a feeling of thankfulness, gratitude and appreciation for the opportunity of leading forward the sons and daughters of a people who are free and God-fearing and who are darned well going to stay that way.

DECEMBER

Now come the shortest days in the year, and there are not nearly enough hours to do the things that need doing. All the school is a stage, and the young folk and teachers alike are caught up in an age-old morality play, and you can probably guess who is the biggest ham actor of the lot. Stage properties, costumes, lights and lines must be gathered, and if the formal teaching and learning process languishes temporarily, a tolerant community is not unduly critical at this season of mystery and mistletoe.

The near-by forest preserves are denuded for Christmas trees (court action later), which shed their greenery impartially in the skiddy halls, the cafeteria butter and the innards of the grand piano. Angels, elves and fairies flit uncensored through the corridors in diaphanous and nonfire-resistant garments of visibility which makes the superintendent long for the return of the unspeakable jeans and pedal pushers that have hitherto been the object of many fiery faculty meetings.

The scholastic family increases by leaps and bounds and other unseemly cavortings. All the neighboring academies have closed a few days early and their students descend on the school to pay courtesy calls and to forment envy and discontent. These foreign ranks are swelled by visiting alumni, hoped-for alumni, and alumni-who-never-were. It matters not, thinks the superintendent jovially, our own spring vacation comes early this year, and all visits will be repaid in kind.

The old guard of the faculty, mindful of examination and scholastic standards to be met, makes a heroic effort to hold the line with business as usual. Alas! It's a losing battle as one by one they throw away the books and precious lesson plans.

The climax approaches! The annual charity drive is declared a big success. The newspaper editor prints a letter from a satisfied patron of the schools. The superintendent's annual speech at the Mothers Association is well received, even though he has not revised it for the past several years. At the December meeting of the board of education all the bills are paid without noisome comment.

The Christmas pageant is particularly well done, and no one forgets his lines. As the curtain falls, Tiny Tim (one of Mrs. Busty's offspring, no less) limps forward, front and center, and in the name of the student body wishes Our Hero health and happiness. Believe it or not, the tightfisted, generous, hardboiled, sentimental old coot of a school superintendent feels a thrill go down his spine and a lump in his throat.

Truly, he thinks, the individual days of the school year are filled with trouble and unease and frustration and worry and petty annoyances, but someway and somehow all these days add up to a wonder and a joy which makes the business of teaching school the finest business in all the world.

THE TEACHER FROM MARS

by Eando Binder

THE AFTERNOON ROCKET EXPRESS TRAIN FROM CHICAGO CAME INTO the station, and I stepped off. It was a warm spring day. The little town of Elkhart, Indiana, sprawled lazily under the golden sunshine. I trudged along quiet, tree-shaded streets toward Caslon Preparatory School for Boys.

Before I had gone far, I was discovered by the children playing here and there. With the dogs, they formed a shrill, raucous procession behind me. Some of the dogs growled, as they might at a wild animal. Housewives looked from their windows and gasped.

So the rumors they had heard were true. The new teacher at Caslon was a Martian!

I suppose I am grotesquely alien to human eyes, extremely tall and incredibly thin. In fact, I am seven feet tall, with what have often been described as broomstick arms and spindly legs. On an otherwise scrawny body, only the Martian chest is filled out, in comparison with Earth people. I was dressed in a cotton kimono that dangled from my narrow shoulders to my bony ankles. Chinese style, I understand.

Thus far I am pseudo-human. For the rest, a Martian is alien, from the Earth viewpoint. Two long tentacles from the back of my shoulders hang to my knees, appendages that have not vanished in Martian evolution like the human tail. The top of my skull is bulging and hairless, except for a fringe of silver-white fur above large conch-shaped ears. Two wide-set owlish eyes, a generous nose and a tiny mouth complete my features. All my skin is leathery and tanned a deep mahogany by the sun of our cloudless Martian skies.

Timidly I stopped before the gates of Caslon Prep and looked within the grounds. The spectacles on my large nose were cup-shaped and of tinted glass that cut down the unnatural glare of the brighter, hotter sun. I felt my shoulders drooping wearily from the tug of more than twice the gravity to which I was conditioned.

Luckily, however, I had brought leg-braces. Concealed by my long robe, they were ingenious devices of light metal, bracing the legs against strain. They had been expensive—no less than forty *dhupecs*—but they were worth even that much.

Gripping my cane and duffel-bag, I prepared to step into the sanctuary of the school grounds. It looked so green and inviting in there, like a canalside park. It would be a relief to escape from those Earth children. They had taken to tossing pebbles at me, and some of the canines had snapped at my heels. Of course I didn't blame them, nor must I resent the unwelcome stares I had felt all around me, from adult Earthlings. After all, I was an alien.

I stepped forward, between the gates. At least here, in the school that had hired me to teach, I would be accepted in a more friendly fashion. . . .

Ssss!

The hiss of a thousand snakes filled the air. I reacted violently, dropping my bag and clamping my two hands around my upraised cane. For a moment I was back on Mars, surrounded by a nest of killer-snakes from the vast deserts. I must beat them off with my cane!

But wait. This was Earth, where snakes were a minor class of creature, and mainly harmless. I relaxed, then, panting. The horrible, icy fear drained away. Perhaps you human beings can never quite know the paralyzing dread we have of snakes.

Then I heard a new sound, one that cheered me somewhat.

A group of about fifty laughing boys trooped into view, from where they had been hidden behind the stone wall circling Caslon's campus. They had made the hissing sound, as a boyish prank. How foolish of me to let go of my nerves, I thought wryly.

I smiled at the group in greeting, for these were the boys I would teach.

"I am Professor Mun Zeerohs, your new teacher," I introduced myself in what, compared with the human tone, is a reedy voice. "The Sun shine upon you. Or, in your Earthly greeting, I am happy to meet you."

Grins answered me. And then murmurs arose.

"It talks, fellows."

"Up from the canals!"

"Is that thing alive?"

One of the boys stepped forward. He was about sixteen, with blue eyes that were mocking.

"I'm Tom Blaine, senior classman. Tell me, sir, is it true that Mars is inhabited?"

It was rather a cruel reception, though merely another prank. I waved my two tentacles in distress for a moment, hardly knowing what to do or say next.

"Boys! Gentlemen!"

A grown man with gray hair came hurrying up from one of the buildings. The boys parted to let him through. He extended a hand to me, introducing himself.

"Robert Graham, Dean of Caslon. You're Professor Mun Zeerohs, of course." He turned, facing the group reprovingly. "This is your new instructor, gentlemen. He will teach Interplanetary History and the Martian language."

A groan went up. I knew why, of course. The Martian tongue has two case endings to every one in Latin.

"Now, gentlemen, this is for your own good," Dean Graham continued sternly. "Remember your manners. I'm sure you'll like our new professor—"

"I'm sure we won't!" It was Tom Blaine again. Behind him an air of hostility replaced the less worrisome mockery. "We've never had a Martian teacher before, and we don't want one!"

"Don't want one?" The dean was more aghast than I.

"My father says Martians are cowards," Tom Blaine continued loudly. "He ought to know. He's in the Space Patrol. He says that in the War, the Martians captured Earthmen and cut them to pieces slowly. First their hands, then—"

"Nonsense!" Dean Graham snapped. "Besides, the War is over.

Martians are in the Space Patrol, too. Now, no more argument. Go to your dormitory. Professor Zeerohs will begin conducting class tomorrow morning. Oscar, take the professor's bag to his quarters."

Oscar, the school's menial robot, obediently stalked forward and picked up the bag. Somehow, I felt almost a warm tide of friendship for the robot. In his mechanical, rudimentary reflex mind, it was all the same to him—Martian or Earthman. He made no discrimination against me, as these human boys did.

As Oscar turned, Tom Blaine stood as though to block the way. Having his orders, the robot brushed past him. A metal elbow accidentally jabbed the boy in the ribs. Deciding against grabbing the bag away from steel fingers, Tom Blaine picked up a stone and flung it clanging against the robot's metal body. Another dent was added to the many I could see over Oscar's shiny form.

The rebellion was over—for the time being.

I realized that the boys were still hostile as I followed the dean to his rooms. My shoulders seemed to droop a little more.

"Don't mind them," the dean was saying apologetically. "They're usually outspoken at that age. They've never had a Martian teacher before, you see."

"Why have you engaged one for the first time?" I asked.

Graham answered half patronizingly, half respectfully.

"Many other schools have tried Martian teachers, and found them highly satisfactory." He didn't think it necessary to add, "And cheaper."

I sighed. Times had been hard on Mars lately, with so many dust storms raging up and down the canal regions, withering the crops. This post on Earth, though at a meager salary, was better than utter poverty. I was old and could live cheaply. Quite a few Martians had been drifting to Earth, since the War. By nature, we are docile, industrious, intelligent, and make dependable teachers, engineers, chemists, artists.

"They always haze the new teachers," Dean Graham said, smiling uneasily. "Your first class is at nine o'clock tomorrow morning. Interplanetary History."

Freshened after a night's sleep, I entered the class room with enthusiasm for my new job. A hundred cold, unfriendly eyes watched me with terrifying intensity.

"Good morning," I greeted as warmly as I could.

"Good morning, Professor *Zero!*" a chorus bellowed back, startling me.

So the hazing campaign was still on. No, I wouldn't correct them. After all, even the Martian children I had taught had invariably tagged me with that name.

I glanced around the room, approving its high windows and controlled sunlight. My eyes came to rest on the blackboard behind me. A chalk drawing occupied its space. It depicted, with some skill, a Martian crouching behind an Earthman. Both were members of the Space Patrol and apparently were battling some space desperado. It was young Tom Blaine's work, no doubt. His father claimed all Martians to be cowards and weaklings.

My leathery face showed little of my feelings as I erased the humiliating sketch. Ignoring the snickers behind me, I grasped two pieces of chalk in both tentacles, writing with one and listing dates with the other.

1955—First space flight
1978—Earthmen claim all planets
1992—Pioneer-wave to Mars
2011—Rebellion and war
2019—Mars wins freedom
2040—Earth-Mars relations friendly today

"Interplanetary History," I began my lecture, "centers about these dates and events. Not till Nineteen fifty-five were Earth people assured that intelligent beings had built the mysterious canals of Mars. Nor were we Martians positive till then that the so-called Winking Lights of your cities at night denoted the handiwork of thinking creatures. The exploring Earthmen of the last century found only the Martians equal to them in intelligence. Earth has its great cities, and Mars has it great canal-system, built ten thousand Martian years ago. Civilization began on Mars fifty centuries previous to that, before the first glimmering of it on Earth—"

"See, fellows?" Tom Blaine interrupted loudly. "I told you all they like to do is rub that in." He became mockingly polite. "Please, sir, may I ask why you brilliant Martians had to wait for Earthmen to open up space travel?"

I was shocked, but managed to answer patiently.

"We ran out of metal deposits for building, keeping our canals in repair. Our history has been a constant struggle against the danger of extinction. In fact, when Earth pioneers migrated in Nineteen ninety-two, it was just in time to patch up the canals and stave off a tremendous famine for Mars."

"And that was the appreciation Earth got," the boy charged bitterly. "Rebellion!"

"You forget that the Earth pioneers on Mars started the rebellion against taxation, and fought side by side with us—"

"They were traitors," he stated bluntly.

I hurdled the point, and continued the lecture.

"Mars won its independence after a nine-year struggle—"

Again I was interrupted.

"Not *won*. Earth *granted* independence, though it could have won easily."

"At any rate," I resumed quietly, "Earth and Mars today, in Twenty-forty, are amicable, and have forgotten that episode."

"We haven't forgotten!" Tom Blaine cried angrily. "Every true Earthman despises Martians."

He sat down amidst a murmur of defiant approval from the others. I knew my tentacles hung limply. How aggressive and intolerant Earth people were! It accounted for their domination of the Solar System. A vigorous, pushing race, they sneered at the Martian ideals of peaceful culture. Their pirates, legal and otherwise, still roamed the spaceways for loot.

Young Tom Blaine was representative of the race. He was determined to make things so miserable here for me that I would quit. He was the leader of the upper-class boys. Strange, that Earthpeople always follow one who is not wise, but merely compelling. There would have to be a test of authority, I told myself with a sinking heart.

"I am the teacher," I reminded him. "You are the pupil, Mr. Blaine."

"Oh, yes, sir," he retorted in false humility. "But you'd better teach history right, Professor Nothing, or not at all!"

I hastily switched to the Martian language.

"The Martian language as is well known, is today the official language of science and trade," I went on guardedly. "Through long usage, the tongue has become perfected. Official Earth English is comparatively cumbersome. For instance, the series of words meaning exaggerated size—big, large, great, huge, enormous, mighty, cyclopean, gargantuan. Is 'big' more than 'large,' or less? You cannot tell. In Martian, there is one root, with a definite progression of size suffixes."

I wrote on the blackboard:

bol, bola, boli, bolo, bolu—bolas, bolis, bolos, bolus—bolasa, bolisi, boloso, bolusu

"Martian is a scientific language, you see."

"Bragging again," sneered a voice.

An eraser sailed toward me just as I turned from the board. It struck full in my face in a cloud of chalk-dust. As if at a signal, a barrage of erasers flew at me. They had been sneaked previously from the boards around the classroom. I stood helplessly, desperately warding off the missiles with my tentacles. The boys were yelling and hooting, excited by the sport.

The pandemonium abruptly stopped as Oscar stumped into the room. His mechanical eyes took in the scene without emotion. One belated eraser flew toward him. His steel arm reflexively raised, caught it, then hurled it back with stunning force. To a robot, anything that came toward it must be returned, unless otherwise commanded. Tom Blaine yelped as the eraser bounced off his forehead.

"Dean Graham," said Oscar like a phonograph, "wants to know if everything is going along smoothly."

I could see the boys hold their breaths. Oscar went the rounds daily, asking that routine question in all the classes. If this disturbance were reported, the boys would lose an afternoon of freedom.

"Everything is well," I murmured, though for a moment I was sadly tempted to take revenge. "You may go, Oscar."

With a click of internal relays, the robot left impassively. He had seen or heard nothing, without being otherwise commanded.

"Afraid to report it, eh?" Tom Blaine jeered. "I told you Martians are yellow!"

It was more than gravity now that made my shoulders sag. I dreaded the days that must follow.

Even outside the classroom, I was hounded. I can use only that word. Tom Blaine thought of the diabolical trick of deliberately spilling a glass of water before my eyes.

"Don't—don't!" I instinctively groaned, clutching at the glass.

"What's the matter, Professor?" he asked blandly. "This is nothing but water."

"It's sacrilege—"

I stopped there. They wouldn't understand. How horrible to see water spill to the ground in utter waste! For ten thousand years, on Mars, that precious fluid has been the object of our greatest ingenuity. It hurt to see it wantonly flung away, as they might flinch if blood were shed uselessly before them.

As I stumbled away from their laughter, I heard Tom Blaine confide to his cohorts:

"I got the idea last night, looking in his room. He was playing with a bowl of water. Running it through his fingers, like a miser. I've got another idea, fellows. Follow me to the kitchen."

I wasn't aware till half through the solitary evening meal in my rooms that the food tasted odd. It was salty! The boys had stolen into the kitchen and salted my special saltless foods. My stomach revolted against the alien condiment. Mars' seas, from which our life originated long ago, held no sodium chloride, only magnesium chloride, with which all Martian food is "salted."

I went to bed, groaning with a severe headache and upset stomach from an outraged metabolism. Worse, it rained that night. I tried to shut my ears to that pattering sound. Millions of gallons of water were going to waste, while millions of Martians on my home world were painfully hoarding water for their thirsty crops.

The pains eased before morning. What torment would Tom Blaine and his relentless pack think of next? The answer came when I found my spectacles missing. My eyes were almost blinded that day, more from glare than senile failing of vision. They watered and blinked in light that was fifty per cent stronger than on more remote Mars.

"Lower the blinds, Oscar," I ordered the robot when he appeared as usual.

"But, Professor," Tom Blaine protested, jumping up as though waiting for the moment, "think of our eyes. We can't read our lessons in the dark."

"Never mind, Oscar," I said wearily.

The robot stood for a moment, relays clashing at the reversed orders. When he finally left, he seemed to shrug at the strange doings of his masters, Earthmen and Martians alike.

"Have you any idea where my glasses are, Mr. Blaine?" I asked in direct appeal. I tried not to sound timid.

"No, of course not," he retorted virtuously.

I nodded to myself and reached for the lower left-hand drawer of my desk, then changed my mind.

"Will you all help me look for them?" I pleaded.

They ransacked the desk with deliberate brutality.

"Why, here they are, Professor!"

Tom held them up from the lower left-hand drawer in mock triumph. I put them on with trembling hands.

"How careless of me to leave them here yesterday." I smiled. "One must have a sense of humor about these things. Now we will decline the verb *krun*, to move."

I went on as though nothing had happened, but my whole head ached from hours of straining my eyes against the cruel glare.

That night, utterly exhausted, I went to bed only to find my anti-gravity unit jammed, obviously by human hands. One of my few pleasures was the ability to sink into restful slumber in the low-gravity field, after suffering the tug of Earth gravity at my vitals all day. Earthmen on Jupiter know how agonizing it becomes.

I passed a sleepless night, panting and aching under what grew to be the pressure of a mountain. How could I go on against such heartlessness? Tom Blaine and his friends were ruthlessly determined to drive out their despised Martian teacher. If I complained to Dean Graham, it would be an admission of cowardice. I didn't want to betray my race. But I was miserably aware that I had not a single friend in the academy.

Oscar appeared in the morning, with a message from Dean Graham. The mechanical servant waited patiently to be told to go. When I swayed a little, he caught me. His reflexes had been patterned not to let things fall.

"Thank you, Oscar." I found my hand on the robot's shiny hard shoulder. It was comfortingly firm. "You're my only friend, Oscar. At least, you're not my enemy. But what am I saying? You're only a machine. You may go, Oscar."

The message read:

Today and tomorrow are examination days. Use the enclosed forms. At three o'clock today, all classes will be excused to the Television Auditorium.

The examinations were routine. Despite my unrested body and mind, I felt an uplift of spirit. My class would do well. I had managed, even against hostility, to impart a sound understanding of Interplanetary History and the Martian lauguage.

I looked almost proudly over the bowed, laboring heads. Suddenly I stiffened.

"Mr. Henderson," I said gently, "I wouldn't try that if I were you."

The boy flushed, hastily crammed into his pockets the notes he had been copying from. Then he gaped up in amazement. Tom Blaine, at the desk beside him, also looked up startled. The question was plain in his eyes. How could I know that Henderson was cheating, when even Tom, sitting next to him hadn't suspected?

"You forget," I explained hesitantly, "that Maritans use telepathy at will."

Tom Blaine stared, his mouth hanging open. Then he jumped up.

"Are we going to stand for that? Spying on us, even in our minds—" He gasped at a sudden thought. "You knew all the time about the glasses. You didn't expose me." He flushed, but in anger rather than embarrassment. "You made a fool of me!"

One must have a sense of humor about those things," I said lamely.

The rest of the examination period passed in bristling silence. More than ever, now, they were hostile to me. More than ever would they show their antagonism. How could I ever hope to win them, if patience was taken for cowardice, understanding for malice, and telepathy for deliberate spying?

Why had I ever left Mars, to come to this alien, heartbreaking world?

At three o'clock, examinations were over for that day. The class filed to the Television Auditorium.

A giant screen in the darkened room displayed a drama on Venus, then news-flashes from around the system. An asteroid, scene of the latest radium rush. Ganymede, with its talking plant show. Titan's periodic meteor shower from the rings of Saturn. A cold, dark scene on Pluto, where a great telescope was being built for interstellar observations. Finally Mars, and a file of Earthmen and Martians climbing into a sleek Space Patrol ship.

"The Patrol ship *Greyhound*," informed the announcer, "is being dispatched after pirates. Captain Henry Blaine is determined to blast them, or not come back."

"My father," Tom Blaine said proudly to his classmates.

"My son," I murmured, leaning forward to watch the last of the Martians vanish within.

When the armed ship leaped into space, the television broadcast was over.

There were no more classes that day. I dragged across the campus toward the haven of my rooms, for I needed rest and quiet.

A shriek tore from my throat the instant I saw it. A horrible, wriggling snake lay in my path! It was only a small, harmless garden snake, my reason told me. But a million years of instinct yelled danger, death! I stumbled and fell, trying to run against gravity that froze my muscles. I shrank from the squirming horror as it stopped and defiantly darted out its forked tongue.

The outside world burst into my consciousness with a thunderclap of laughter. Tom Blaine was holding up the wriggling snake. Once the first shock was over, I managed to keep my nerves in check.

"It's only a garter snake," he mocked. "Sorry it frightened you."

But what would they say if a hungry, clawing tiger suddenly appeared before them? How would they feel? I left without a word, painfully compelling my trembling limbs to move.

I was beaten. That thought hammered within my skull.

They had broken my spirit. I came to that conclusion after staring up at a red star that winked soberly and seemed to nod in pity. There was my true home. I longed to go back to its canals and deserts. Harsh they might be, but not so harsh as the unfeeling inhabitants of this incredibly rich planet.

I went to my rooms and started to pack.

Angry voices swiftly approached my door. The boys burst in, led by Tom Blaine.

"Murderer!" Tom yelled. "A man was strangled in town two hours ago, by a rope—or a tentacle! You looked murder at us this afternoon. Why did you kill him? Just general hate for the human race?"

How fantastic it sounded, yet they weren't mere boys, now. They were a blood-lusting mob. All their hate and misunderstanding for me had come to a head. I knew it was no use even to remonstrate.

"Look, fellows! He was packing up to sneak away. He's the killer, all right. Are you going to confess, Professor Zeerohs, or do we have to make you confess!"

It was useless to resist their burly savagery and strong Earth muscles. They held me and ripped away the light metal braces supporting my legs. Then I was forced outside and prodded along. They made me walk up and down, back of the dormitory, in the light of sub-atomic torches.

It became sheer torture within an hour. Without the braces, my weak muscles sagged under my weight. Earth's gravity more than doubled the normal strain.

"Confess!" Tom snapped fiercely. "Then we'll take you to the police."

I shook my head, as I had each time Tom demanded my confession. My one hopeless comfort was the prayer of an earthly prophet, who begged the First Cause to forgive his children, for they knew not what they did.

For another hour, the terrible march kept up. I became a single mass of aching flesh. My bones seemed to be cracking and crumbling under the weight of the Universe. My mental anguish was still sharper, for the tide of hate beat against me like a surf.

Where was Dean Graham? Then I remembered that he had gone to visit his relatives that evening. There was no one to help me, no one to stop these half-grown men who saw their chance to get rid of me. Only the winking red eye of Mars looked down in compassion for the suffering of a humble son.

"Oscar's coming!" warned a voice.

Ponderously the robot approached, the night-light in his forehead shining. He made the rounds every night, like a mechanical watchman. As he eyed the halted procession, his patterned reflexes were obviously striving to figure out what its meaning could be.

"Boys will go to the dormitory," his microphonic voice boomed. "Against regulations to be out after ten o'clock."

"Oscar, you may go," barked Tom Blaine.

The robot didn't budge. His selectors were set to obey only the voices of teachers and officials.

"Oscar—" I began with a wild cry.

A boy clamped his hand over my mouth. The last of my strength oozed from me, and I slumped to the ground. Though

I was not unconscious, I knew my will would soon be insufficient to make me resist. The boys looked frightened.

"Maybe we've gone too far," one said nervously.

"He deserves it," shrilled Tom uneasily. "He's a cowardly murderer!"

"Tom!" Pete Miller came running up, from the direction of the town. "Just heard the news—the police caught the killer—a maniac with a rope." He recoiled in alarm when he saw my sprawled form. "What did you do, fellows? He's innocent, and he really isn't such a bad old guy."

The boys glanced at one another with guilty eyes. Fervently I blessed young Miller for that statement.

"Don't be sentimental," Tom Blaine said much too loudly. "Martians are cowards. My father says so. I'm glad we did this, anyway. It'll drive him away for sure. We'd better beat it now."

The group melted away, leaving me on the ground. Oscar stalked forward and picked me up. Any fallen person must be helped up, according to his patterned mind. But his steel arms felt softer than Tom Blaine's heartless accusation.

The class gasped almost in chorus the next morning, when their Martian professor entered quietly, as though nothing had happened the night before.

"Examinations will continue," I announced.

It was small wonder that they looked surprised. First, that I had appeared at all, weak and spent by the night's cruel ordeal. Second, that I had not given up and left. Third, that I hadn't reported the episode to Dean Graham. The punishment would have been severe.

Only I knew I was back because it would be cowardly to leave. Mentally and physically I was sick, but not beaten. Besides, I had heard young Miller insist that I was not such a bad old guy, after all. It was like a well of cool water in a hot desert.

Examinations began. Oscar entered, handed me a spacegram and clanked out again. Nervously I opened and read the message. My tentacles twitched uncontrollably at the ends, then curled around the chair arms and clung desperately. Everything vanished before my eyes except the hideous shocking words of the spacegram.

My world was ended. Mars or Earth—it made no difference. I could not go on. But existence must continue. I could not let this break me. Grimly I folded the paper and laid it aside.

I looked with misted eyes at their lowered heads. I needed a friend as never before, but hostility and hatred were the only emotions they felt for me as I turned to them one by one. They hated their teacher, though they knew him to be wise, humble, patient, as Martians are by nature.

And I was beginning to hate them. They were forcing me to. Savagely I hoped they would all fail in their examinations.

I switched back to young Miller, who was biting his pencil. Forehead beaded with sweat, he was having a difficult time. Thoughts were racing through his brain.

Wanted so much to pass . . . enter Space Point . . . join the Space Patrol some day . . . Not enough time to study . . . job in spare time after school hours . . . help parents . . . In what year did the first explorer step on Neptune's moon? Why, Nineteen-seventy-six! Funny how that came all of a sudden . . . Now what was the root for "planet," in Martian? Why, *jad*, of course! It isn't so hard after all . . .

Wish that old Martian wouldn't stare at me as if he's reading my mind . . . How many moons has Jupiter? Always get it mixed up with Saturn. Eighteen, six found by space ships! Funny, I'm so sure of myself . . . I'll lick this exam yet . . . Dad's going to be proud of me when I'm wearing that uniform. . . .

I turned my eyes away from Miller's happy face. A deserving boy, he would be a credit to the Space Patrol. Others had their troubles, not just I.

Abruptly there was an interruption. Oscar came clanking in.

"Dean Graham wishes all classes to file out on the campus, for a special event," he boomed.

The boys whispered in curiosity and left the classroom at my unsteady order. The campus was filled with the entire school faculty and enrollment. My group of senior classmen was allowed to stand directly in front of the bandstand. I felt weak and in need of support, but there was no one to give it to me.

Dean Graham raised a hand. "A member of the Space Patrol is here," he spoke, "having come from Space Point by rocket-strato for an important announcement. Major Dawson."

A tall, uniformed man, wearing the blue of the Space Patrol, stepped forward, acknowledging the assembly's unrestrained cheer with a solemn nod. The Patrol is honored throughout the System for its gallant service to civilization.

"Many of you boys," he said, "hope to enter Space Point some day, and join the Service. This bulletin, received an hour ago, will do honor to someone here."

He held up the paper and read aloud.

"Captain Henry Blaine, in command of Patrol ship *Greyhound*, yesterday was wounded in the daring rout of pirates off the Earth-Mars run."

All eyes turned to Tom Blaine, who was proud of the ceremony in honor of his father. The official held up a radium-coated medal— the Cross of Space, for extraordinary service to the forces of law and order in the Solar System. Dean Graham whispered in his ear. He nodded, stepping down from the rostrum and advancing.

My gasp of surprise was deeper than those of the others as he brushed past Tom Blaine. Stopping before me, he pinned the glowing medal on my chest. Then he grasped my hand.

"I think you'll be proud to wear that all your life!" He turned, reading further from his bulletin. "Captain Blaine's life was saved by a youthful Martian recruit, who leaped in front of him and took the full blast that wounded the Earthman. His name was—"

I found myself watching Tom Blaine. He didn't have to hear the name. He was staring at the spacegram he had stolen from my desk, but hadn't had a chance to read till now. He had sensed my momentary agitation over it, and had hoped perhaps to use it against me. It read:

WE DEEPLY REGRET TO INFORM YOU OF THE DEATH OF YOUR SON, KOL ZEEROHS, IN HEROIC SERVICE FOR THE SPACE PATROL.

—THE HIGH COMMAND,
                              SPACE PATROL.

But now my weakness overwhelmed me. I was aware only of someone at my side, supporting me, as my knees threatened to buckle. It must have been Oscar.

No—it was a human being!

"Every one of us here," Tom Blaine said, tightening his grip around me, "is your son now—if that will help a little. You're staying of course, Professor. You couldn't leave now if you tried."

We smiled at each other, and my thin hand was nearly crushed in his young, strong grasp. Yes, the teacher from Mars would stay.